MW01625138

Man vs. "boy":

Are you a Man or a "boy?" Outward appearances can be a window into a person's heart and character, but don't be fooled. Outward appearances do not always reveal the true substance and character of a Man. You may be a male, but this does not mean you are a Man. Thank God our hearts will always give us the true answer. Deep inside we know who we are, and we know who we are not.

If you struggle with a clear answer, here are a few traits that will help you determine whether you are a Man or "boy?" You may find it helpful to ask others about the Man or "boy?" question. You will be surprised to find how much others can assist in determining whether you are a Man or "boy?"

The Man vs. "boy" List:

"boy"	MAN
1. Blames others for problems	1. Takes responsibility for problems
2. Cowers in confrontation	2. Stands up to confrontation
3. Pouts	3. Accepts consequences gracefully
4. Runs from responsibility	4. Looks for ways to take responsibility
5. Protects himself first	5. Protects others first
6. Worms his way into position	6. Walks in God-given authority
7. Argues	7. Settles/Discusses viewpoints
8. Resents Men	8. Encourages Men
9. Envious of others success	9. Shares/Celebrates success of others
10. Mothers/Coddles other "boys"	10. Fathers other Men
11. Hides true thoughts	11. Honest & forthright in relationships
12. Manipulates perceptions	12. Seeks Truth
13. Wimpy in spirit	13. Filled with Spirit
14. Follows controlling female	14. Leads strong women
15. Insecure in self-identity	15. Secure in self-identity
16. Pornography & sexual problems	16. Stable & healthy in relationships
17. Emotionally weak	17. Emotionally strong
18. Panics in crisis	18. Strong & stable in crisis

"boy"	MAN
19. Tolerates evil	19. Attacks & rebukes evil
20. Cheats	20. Plays by the rules
21. Desires power without earning it	21. Obeys limits of his own authority
22. Harbors prejudice	22. Loves and honors all people
23. Self medicates/Indulges himself	23. Abstains/Self controlled
24. Demands he's right	24. Admits he is wrong, after seeing it
25. Defensive & easily offended	25. Relational & takes the hit
26. Walks in fear	26. Walks in faith/Overcomes fear
27. Refuses to grow up	27. Has chosen to be a Man
28. Plays the "poor old guy"	28. Will not allow anyone to pity him
29. Won't distinguish Men from "boys"	29. Knows he's a Man, and who is a "boy"
30. Puts off dealing with problems	30. Deals with problems
31. Follows matriarchal leadership	31. Follows Patriarchal leadership
32. Ignores creditors	32. Deals with creditors
33. Quits/Gives up after "trying"	33. Never gives up/Plans for victory
34. Avoids advice from others	34. Receives/Promotes advice from others
35. Strives to have things his way	35. Strives to have things right
36. Complains about circumstances	36. Makes the best of situations
37. Long term anger at Mom & Dad	37. Resolves family relational problems
38. Gives Keys of authority away	38. Retains Keys of authority
39. Angry if Manhood challenged	39. Stronger when Manhood challenged
40. Thinks homosexuality is a choice	40. Knows homosexuality is dysfunction
41. Pushes/Rushes into decisions	41. Leads/Thinks before he acts
42. Desires females to rescue him	42. Allows women to help him
43. Controls and abuses family	43. Protects & nurtures family
44. Waits to resolve conflict	44. Restores relationships immediately
45. Tells lies	45. Speaks the Truth
46. Pacifies his enemies	46. Declares war against enemies
47. Says he's sorry frequently	47. Asks for forgiveness when appropriate
48. Resents being told what to do	48. Secure with requests or orders
49. Refuses to forgive/Holds grudges	49. Forgives
50. Loves flattery	50. Will not tolerate flattery
51. Happy to remain a "boy"	51. Desires all "boys" to be Men
52. Is bothered by list of "boy" traits	52. Is empowered by list of Man traits

KEN VENTURA

VENTURA PUBLISHING

Ventura Publishing books may be purchased for educational, business, or sales promotional use. For information, please write: Special Markets Department, Ventura Publishing, P.O. Box 6687, Santa Barbara, CA 93160.

Design and layout by Clark Langon/Cross Promotions - www.crosspromoter.net
In association with Doug Rietz/Art of Marketing - www.artofmarketing.com

Library of Congress Cataloging-in-Publication Data is available upon request.

ISBN 978-0-9826668-0-7

Foreword: by David Conn

In light of the remarkable confluence of critical issues facing mankind, which are unprecedented in number and nature, "Man vs. boy" is one of the two or three most important books for a spiritually thirsty and hungry public during the opening decade of this millennium.

The message is powerful because it is personal in nature. The author's words and phrases leap to your heart and will not turn loose until, by way of personal courage, we begin to see our own intimate history of humiliations, the guilt, and even the more graceful moments that are like quiet calls. For God indeed waits with loving patience for the golden times when we are signaled or even jolted by a surge of blessed messages such as we see in this book.

"Man vs. boy" offers a bonus of insights. Although the message is personal and heart-moving, there is the added certainty that we will gain deeper understanding into causes of world, national, family, or other interpersonal friction. It results from our naturally applying the author's Man vs. "boy" list of criteria to every hurt, struggle and unanswered question in our past or future. "Man vs. boy" forces a realization that most human tensions stem from a vast segment of world and family leadership comprised of "boys" rather than Men. This book makes us see that throughout the world something is terribly lacking! With an extravagance of cultural diversity and relativism, we see little or no powerful effort to remedy the matter. Not, that is, until now!

Ken Ventura's strengths and principles are long aligned with Truth, and he is sure of his purpose. The book is unwavering. It shows society how to energize a value that has become almost dormant. The theme is a Godly production of Men that will bring women the "Covering" of love, protection and respect that they purely deserve.

But why so bold and, as some might mistakenly think, audacious? I believe Ken's approach is the way it needs to be. It is his essence, a spiritual conviction. Remarkably, it is not just his spiritual conviction, it has an affinity with God's Holy Word put forth in the Bible. And that is what makes this book so honest and compelling.

Because of its Truth, "Man vs. boy" is infectious. By way of you it will affect others. I mean to say that if you're a boyfriend it will affect your girlfriend; if you're a girlfriend it will affect your boyfriend; if you're a wife it will affect your husband; if you're a husband it will affect your wife; and if you're a parent it will affect your children. It is, as the Bible says, "quick and powerful, sharper than any two-edged sword, able to pierce even to the dividing asunder of bone and marrow, soul and spirit, and is a discerner of the thoughts and intents of the heart."

But there is even a more important issue than the "bonus insights" I mentioned earlier: This book is a primer. It brings guidelines by which women can better discern the "boy" in the Man or the "Man" in the "boy" as the case may be. Because Ken Ventura's criteria are obviously sound, even inarguable, we see how a Man or a woman becomes better equipped to discern the Man or the "boy" and to differentiate one from the other.

This book tells of growth, maturity, and the attainment of a responsible life. The author brings us compelling personal stories from the lives of several Men in which we learn events and discoveries that contributed to their growth as they gained a blessed courage and became Men. In other cases, enlightened women learn to become "Covered" (made whole and much stronger). Experience how women become new creations and forgiving people who are now able to survive earlier abuse and the anger engendered by it.

"Man vs. boy" is electric. It zings us. It is multifaceted, and it is a comprehensive delivery of the ways and wonders of how society's critical need is fulfilled. The world needs Men. I know of no one who understands this near to the degree that Ken does. You can identify with this book, because it was written by a Man who has experienced these truths since childhood.

Toss political correctness to a wastebasket. Ride the mind of a Man who believes in the Way, the Truth and the Life; for he spotted a major weakness whereby "boys" give their "Keys" away and then go years without understanding how to retrieve them. Learn that every male can become a Man and hold his Keys intact for the critical tasks ahead.

Read the book boldly. You can trust it.

David Conn — January 2010
Author – "The Cult That Died" & "Lednorf's Dilemma"

Stand up like a Man!
For I will demand it of you, and
you will answer to me.
God[1]

1 Job 38:3, The Bible

KEN VENTURA

To My Best Friend

Table of Contents

Introduction 21

The Great Mandate!

America's Greatest Untapped Natural Resource!

Chapter 1: From "boy" to Man 33

Called to Overcome

How a "boy" Becomes a Man

Ken

Should I Follow Joe Into Battle?

When Manhood Fails to Happen, Everyone Suffers

Who Can Stand Before Envy & Jealousy?

You Can't Give What You Don't Have

Father Issues

Bob

Diagnosing the Man

Obtaining Manhood

Chapter 2: Overcoming and Obtaining Manhood 71

Why is Man vs. "boy" So Important?

Obtaining Your "Man Diploma"

The Bar Mitzvah

The Band of Brothers

The American Dream

Facts Vs. Truth

Sorry Vs. Forgiveness

Chiropractic Adjustment

Defeating Fear

Brian

Chapter 3: Your Keys 93

Men Who Behave Like "boys"... and Lose
What are a Man's Keys?
A Man's Heart: The Relational Tool
Overcoming Depression
Diagnosing With The Victory Scale
Mike, One Man's Total Victory
Capturing Your Keys
Diagnosing Your Keys
Repentance
Taking Your Keys Back
Keys of Power
Recovering All The Keys

Chapter 4: Your Gates 121

Rebuilding Your Gates
Identifying the Open Gates
Identifying Emotional Enemies
Your Spiritual Enemies Want Your Keys
Declaring War
John
Closing the Gates
John's Victory
Needs Vs. Neediness
Destroying Mr. Cruelty
Overcoming Rejection
John's Testimony – Walking in Victory

Chapter 5: The 5 Callings 167

Understanding the 5 Callings
The 5 Callings of the Corporation
Knowing Your Calling – What Motivates You
What's Your Calling?
Why Understanding the Callings is Important
Walking In The Wrong Calling
Judging Other Callings
God's Corporation: Ephesians 4:11
Modern Day Indulgences
Many Are Called, But Few Chosen

Chapter 6: For Women: The Covering 205

PART I: Sarah
Act I – The Father's Covering
The Covering From Conception
The **"uncovered"** Woman
Forgiveness
Act II – The Husband's Covering
Sarah's Personal Testimony

PART II: Kathy, Your Father Loves You
Kathy's Covering
Understanding Her Covering
Kathy Forgives Her Dad
The Power Of a Loving Father Figure

PART III: Overcoming Abuse
Maria
Does She Feel Beautiful?
Pam's Knight in Shining Armor:

Chapter 7: Walk Like a Man! 291

The Patriarchal Man
Making your Life a Fortress
Scott
Getting My House In Order
Prayer For Sarah and Setting Boundaries
Enforcing Your Boundaries
Relational Circles
The "No Codependency" Clause

Chapter 8: Behold The Man!.. 335

The Perfect Man
Jesus in History
A Governor Beholds The Man
The Original Band of Brothers
Zechariah Beholds The Man
Isaiah Beholds The Man
Our Role Model and Hero
The Real Man, Jesus
The Glorified Man
Reflecting Our Role Model
Today's Battlefield
He Will Build It, and He Will Come
Jesus and His Father
Men Called to Love

Famous Quotes From Men: 374

Vince Lombardi
Abraham Lincoln
Winston Churchill
Theodore Roosevelt
Ronald Reagan

Dedication:

This book is dedicated to building up and encouraging one of God's greatest creations, people. My prayer for all Men and women who dare to succeed is that the insights on the following pages take you to the next level in your journey of overcoming the challenges in life. When all the scores are in and the last page of your life is written, your life will be a testimony for the fighting spirit of mankind and the overcoming Spirit of God.

Men, this book was written for you. Keep "Man vs. boy" as a reference to help you navigate amidst life's challenges. This book will train you on how to become a Man, how to walk as a Man in your Mandate, how to recapture your Keys of authority, how to close the Gates of your life where your enemies have gained access, how to identify the Covering, and how to walk in your Calling as the Patriarch God intended you to be. In short, this book is dedicated to training you how to win as a Man!

Women, it is all about Chapter 6! Chapter 6 represents 25% of this book and is dedicated to women who have been abused and mistreated by irresponsible "boys." This chapter is designed to equip women to better discern the difference between Men and "boys," and to help them choose relationships that strengthen their identity by attracting loving Men. Women can overcome the epidemic problem of having been hurt and deceived by "boys" who have blamed them for their failures and problems. Not only is there hope for all women, but as women grasp the principle of the Covering, those long time wounds of their hearts will heal and their strength and femininity will flourish.

The words you are about to read will impart principles learned by very successful Men and women who honor our most reliable and trusted source, the Bible. For it is God our Father who is the true author of Men, and learning of Him will help you better understand your Great Mandate and Calling as you walk as the Man you are meant to be. Man was created in the very image of his Creator to take dominion over life's challenges and circumstances within his sphere of influence. It is time for all Men to fully capture their original Mandate. Are you ready?

"And God said, Let us make Man in our image, after our likeness: and let them have dominion ..."

Moses – Genesis

Acknowledgments

The stories and insight shared in this book could not have been portrayed without the help of some very loving and giving people who were willing to share so selflessly some of the deep and intimate parts of their hearts and lives. For this I am deeply thankful. Of course, their names have been changed for confidentiality and some stories have been consolidated for ease of reading. These are their stories, and I hope and pray their courage and perseverance will motivate and inspire millions of people to stand up and take back what has been lost or stolen.

In the pages following, I have taken the liberty of using the proper name for the word "Man" to show the difference between an adult male who is a "man" simply by virtue of his gender, and a real Man who exudes the characteristics of integrity and responsibility. The use of the proper name Man in no way implies deity or special treatment. The use of the title Man merely implies a male is walking in the God-ordained authority given to him as he journeys through life in victory. I have taken this same liberty for the terms Mandate, Manhood, Keys, Gates, Calling, Covering, Truth and Patriarch. Using the proper name for each of these terms implies a Godly authority attached to their definition.

Throughout this book, I have also used the term "boy" to signify an adult male who has not chosen to be a Man. The term "boy" does not refer to a pre-adolescent boy who possesses a heart of adventure and playfulness. These traits are normal, good and important building blocks that are built into every Man.

I issue a special warning and a promise to all who dare to read through the pages of this book with a forthright openness and honesty: ***You will never be the same.*** As you enter into the lives and challenges of the people who have been bold enough to share the Truth about overcoming in their lives, you will be challenged to rethink your own life, and make new decisions forever changing the way you relate with God, your family, and your loved ones.

Introduction

The Great Mandate!

It is encouraging to know every Man was once a "boy." Every Man has at one time displayed many of the characteristics listed in the "boy" category of the Man vs. "boy" list. A real Man will seek in his heart to be free of all "boyish" traits. The good news to all males is we are all called into a Great Mandate. This Great Mandate prescribes we start out as "boys," then we grow into Men and overcome the world's challenges set before us.

Every culture on earth agrees with this process, because it is a natural and God-given ordination. A male who remains a "boy" into adulthood is abandoning his God-given Mandate, and he has settled to remain a "boy." A male who strives to become a Man will continue to press into his Calling until he becomes the full Man that God has called him to be.

I have a friend named Mark who is an incredible outdoorsman. He is a rugged survival trainer who is not afraid of much. He is considered a Man's Man. Mark recently read the list of traits showing the difference between a "boy" and a Man. After looking at the list for a while, he said to me, "Sharks I can handle. Lions are no problem for me. I am not afraid of bears, wolves, poisonous snakes or critters of any kind. But how do I conquer this little 'boy' inside of me who keeps making me look like a fool? This little 'boy' is frightening to me. He is stronger than any animal I have encountered in the wild." I told Mark that he asked a great question, and a question that will be clearly answered throughout this book.

It is very simple: Men conquer the "boy" within. Men fight to protect truth and the innocent, whereas "boys" blame, cower, and run. But again, don't be fooled. Fighting doesn't mean merely fighting outwardly against someone or something in the physical sense. A real Man will fight in his life by facing relationships head on, and he will take responsibility for the overall well being of those around him. This means he will not cower either emotionally or spiritually when challenged, and he will not blame anyone for anything, ***ever***.

Read the Man vs. "boy" list again if you must. The list supports the point that all males are not necessarily Men. Do any of the points on the list strike a chord in your heart? In short, the Man vs. "boy" list reinforces the ideology that a true Man will take responsibility for all of his God-given duties and problems, and the building and nurturing of healthy relationships with the loved ones in his life is his highest priority.

America's Greatest Untapped Natural Resource!

America's greatest untapped natural resource is not our oil, gas or coal; it is our Men. Adult males who are walking as "boys" represent a vast and untapped potential asset for our country. Millions of struggling males in America could transform from liabilities to assets for their families and their country literally overnight, if only they are given the proper training and Truth about their Mandate. Masculinity in males may be dormant, but know well that masculinity dwells in all males and is a force to be reckoned with. Let us tap into our greatest natural resource, and let us build Men!

America has become feminized and metro-sexualized because males have not successfully passed Manhood to their sons. Parents have coddled and pandered to their children to the point where the current generation of males don't know how to be masculine, and they believe the lie that they need to be feminine in order to love and nurture. Nothing could be further from the truth. Men like George Washington, Winston Churchill, Ronald Reagan and Martin Luther King have clearly shown us Men can and must be strong and masculine leaders to properly love and protect their families, as well as our national heritage.

The truth is the feminization of America is destroying our country. It is rapidly leading this nation further into the secular progressivism that is driving us down the road to bankruptcy and destruction. Many who will be reading this book are Generation X males (born 1965 – 1985) or even Generation Y males (born after 1986). Statistics show 40% of the Gen X fathers in our country are fatherless, and they were not trained to become Men due to a huge shortage of healthy and masculine role models. These untrained males are now adult "boys," and they are going to put the final nails in the coffin of America if we do not rise up and retrain them now.

An even higher percentage of Gen Y fathers (the Net Generation) are fatherless because our country has continued to accelerate on a downward spiral with respect to traditional morality and family values. Many of these adult "boys" have grown up and are now fathers themselves, and most are truly at a loss regarding how to be a Man and how to raise their children properly. The Gen Y males certainly are not looking to the flailing Gen X males for masculine role models with confidence. The presence of Men in this generation is few and far to be seen. The decline of the Man will continue to propagate if something is not done. We must stop this epidemic if we are to save the family structure and America! Males must be trained to be Men, and the time is now.

"Freedom is never more than one generation away from extinction. We didn't pass it to our children in the bloodstream. It must be fought for, protected, and handed on for them to do the same, or one day we will spend our sunset years telling our children and our children's children what it was once like in the United States where Men were free."
Ronald Reagan – 40th President of the United States

Restoring Our Nation:

We all know "boys" who have fathered children. Inside their hearts, many of these fathers are ashamed because they have unanswered and pressing questions regarding their Manhood. They do not know where to go, or who is able to pass on to them the legacy of being a successful Man and father. Many do not see there is a problem until it is too late. Some of the common questions for today's fathers are:

- "How do I learn to raise my boys to become Men, when I was not taught or raised by a Man?"
- "How do I raise my little girls to become secure and self confident women who are Covered with proper love and protection, when I have never seen what this looks like?"

If you know one of these fathers, or if you are one of these fathers, you are fortunate. There is hope! This book can be your ticket from desperation into freedom. There are many males who desperately desire with all of their hearts to overcome every obstacle thrown before them, but they do not know how to win. Their marriages are broken, they are suffering financially, their dreams are shattered, and many of their children are lost to seductions of modern society. Businesses are destroyed and lives are enslaved to a series of chains and the bondage of shame, debt and condemnation, all because somehow the secrets to success that made America great are lost in translation from one generation to another.

Furthering the problem, family connections and ties in America are rapidly disintegrating. More and more, family members split up and go their own way with minimal connection and communication with one another. The elderly have become "throw-away" people. They are put into nursing homes where they are sentenced to only commune with other elderly people and strangers. Precious relationships are lost, and the younger generations do not reap the blessings of wisdom and experience from their elders.

Many of these elderly are military veterans who represent some of the most mature and seasoned Men living today. These Men have overcome the fear of death on the shores of Omaha, the mountains of Iwo Jima, the lands of Korea, Viet Nam, Iraq, Afghanistan, and in many other battles over the past 70 years where liberty was challenged. These Men are a treasure of courage and character, but they are slowly disappearing. Fewer and fewer trained Men are around to take responsibility for passing Manhood to the younger generation, and it is creating a huge void for the American family.

In generations past, the promotion of competition and character to males in our schools was the primary factor in developing healthy Men. Competition and character were encouraged in sports, academics, military, community involvement, family structures and in our overall patriotic world view. As our culture became feminized, competition and character were put on the back shelf as footnotes. From the time that legislators and judges began banning the Bible from public classrooms, competition was subtly labeled as "unfair," and character no longer was taught as a primary emphasis.

Due to America's educational institution's disdain for the masculine world view, our schools have lost our nation's core teachings of the importance of family and freedom, and we now teach secular humanism based on selfishness and entitlements. Equality has become our nation's mantra, but in our zeal we have gone past equality into "sameness." Many schools are teaching that males and females are the same, even though science, psychology and theology prove otherwise.

The emotional and physical make-up of males and females are entirely different. There is a glory in woman, and there is a glory in Man, but when the genders are blurred they both lose their glory. Sports, academics, community involvement and family structures have become a target for promoting neutered males and masculine females in the name of "equality" and "fairness." As genders have become blurred, so have our moral boundaries. The final result being: we have an abundance of powerless and castrated males ("boys") followed by a country full of unhappy, overworked and tired females.

In the name of "fairness," we have done our children a huge disservice. We have coddled and pampered our children's untrained wants and desires to the point where homes have become child centered and child ruled. Then we wonder why kids are running over us and why they are not succeeding in life the way God intended. We have to look at the cold and hard fact that we have taught and encouraged their poor behaviors. The fruit of our actions is undisciplined children who have skewed morality and poor character.

How do you ruin a male child and create an adult "boy?" You spoil and overindulge him. You abstain from disciplining him and you give him whatever he wants, whenever he wants it. You reward him for his disobedience. When he lies to you, give him candy. When he is selfish and demanding, you give him a new toy. When he is lazy and does not do his chores, you give him special treatment and reward him because he feels he is "entitled" to all of these things.

Does this sound grimly familiar to the socialistic world view that we have tolerated in this nation? It is abusive to rear children in such a manner. An entitlement mentality has crept into American culture, and a plague of irresponsible "boys" is the consequence. The end result of this type of upbringing is a male child who remains a "boy" indefinitely. The "Peter Pan" syndrome develops and he becomes the eternal child.

We are headed to becoming a welfare state. We have overindulged our kids to the point where they are the most obese and spoiled children in the world. It is no wonder they grow up and expect entitlements. We have trained them to be self-focused and over-indulgent. Why should they work hard and earn their way? Doesn't family and government owe them food, shelter, healthcare, money and happiness? Can't they just fill out a form and demand their rights and receive all the benefits? Can't males just remain "boys" forever?

We will lose our Republic in the next generation if we do not stand up now. Abraham Lincoln said, **"The philosophy of the classroom today is the philosophy of the government tomorrow."** We must teach our children to rule and govern themselves in the manner that our forefathers envisioned. Instead of teaching our children to be self-governed, in many cases we allow a socialistic school system to work against our core values as a nation. While we are busy worrying about money and working to keep roofs over our heads, the entitlement mentality of our education institutions is seducing the hearts and minds of our children.

These "New Age Un-progressives" are attempting to brainwash and indoctrinate our children with the final solution of socialism in the public arena. I prefer the term "Un-progressive" and Un-social," because they are neither progressive nor social. They oppress freedom and they destroy the culture and family structure at every level of society. Their hijacking of the label "progressivism" and "socialism" is an example of their deceptive tactics. They do not promote social progress. They promote control and blame. Of course, they have repackaged it to look pretty as they steal precious life and freedoms from our children.

New Age Un-progressive ideology attempts to capitalize on immature people's unrealistic and selfish desires. In a child's mind, everyone should get what they want when they want it, without doing the work. They want the trophy, but they do not want to practice. They want the cookies, but they do not want to eat their vegetables. Competition has become a bad word, when winning is supposed to be the reward of achievement. Happiness has become our expected right, when our founding fathers clearly wrote in the constitution that "pursuit" of happiness is our actual God-given right.

Our nation does not have the right to bear the title as the best and strongest nation in the world without earning it. We do have the right to strive for that title and obtain it through Godly principles. Our constitution's founding principles of freedom, self-government and liberty demand that we obtain this status based on our willingness to fight for righteousness, and our ability to achieve through good character. Success and freedom are definitely not free - or easy.

Every mature Man knows that in the real world you have to earn your way. In the real world the ultimate joy is personally overcoming great challenges. In the real world lions eat Bambi, and the fearful quail that fly away too soon get killed. In the real world there is an entirely different job description between male and female; equal in importance, equal in necessity, but completely different in description. In the real world a "boy" is expected to become a Man. In the real world Manhood is earned through obedience to God.

Many males desire to restore the Republic without restoring the Man. It will not happen. Restore the Men, and the Republic will be restored. The American Republic has been great because of its strong Men, not because a person voted Republican or Democrat. Remember, the Republican Party did not come on the national scene until Abraham Lincoln became President in 1860. The strength and power of America was brought forth by responsible God-fearing Men who were committed to their personal convictions first and to political platforms second.

Many males today would be happy if everyone voted for their particular political party, as if that would fix this nation. An emasculated Republican is just as nauseating and powerless as an emasculated Democrat or Independent. We can consistently vote our party and still neglect our wives and children. We can vote party line and still act like immature, irresponsible "boys," but the nation will continue to spiral down into insignificance.

Americans are concerned that terrorism is the greatest threat to America in the 21st century. Islamic terrorism is indeed one of the greatest threats against our freedom; however, there is an additional threat we must first consider that is growing right in our very midst. The real internal threat to America is called "boys." Irresponsible "boys" are relational terrorists who are sabotaging the American family. "boys" are eating away at our strength by terrorizing and abusing millions of women and children because they are not doing their job as Men. This is all happening on our watch, and we the people have sat by and allowed it. We must face the truth. Our nation is not protecting our children.

The behaviors listed on the "boy" category of the Man vs. "boy" list clearly describe a direct and intentional assault on the family structure, and the hearts and well-being of our women and children are its casualties. In America, the casualties are high. The divorce rate for marriages has surpassed 60%, and statistics also reveal that half of the children have no available father figure in the home. The statistics read like a casualty report from a lost, bloody battle.

Compounding the problem, it has become politically and socially incorrect to call a "boy" a "boy." Courage and tough love have become old fashioned. Showing honor for the values that our forefathers established is frowned upon. Few males have had the courage to stand up and deal with their Manhood. Males no longer want to have their masculinity challenged, because it is no longer considered valuable. Masculinity that displays protective love has wrongly been labeled as harsh, unloving, controlling and intolerant.

When did love, honor, patriotism and courage become politically incorrect and passé? When did the golden rule of "treat others as you would like to be treated" and "if a Man will not work, he shall not eat" become forgotten and outdated principles?

Today in America, the war is between ideologies. The war is about Man vs. "boy." Man vs. "boy is the Normandy and Iwo Jima of the day. This war is won or lost in the hearts and minds of the Men as they stand up and master the points given on the Man vs. "boy" list. The Man vs. "boy" battle is the bloodbath that every male must walk through and overcome. The Man vs. "boy" war truly separates the Men from the "boys."

When we fought World War II from 1941 to 1945, everyone knew a loss of the war would possibly mean an end to American freedoms and our Democratic Republic. A loss could mean that a brutal form of socialism would be imposed on America and the world. Those left alive would have been required to speak German, and they would be forced to swallow and embrace the tyrannical ideologies of Nazism.

Today's war is far more subtle, but the stakes are just as high. Over the last 50 years, destructive ideologies have permeated our nation like a deadly virus. Today's enemies are just as evil and clever as those we fought against in WWII. The new weapons are socialism and modern New Age Un-progressivism, and the neutering of males is the foundation of their doctrine. Un-progressives are pushing to create a nation of "boys" who are castrated and cowardly. Our enemies know that the true power of America is in its Men, and they have covertly declared war against the Man. The enemies of freedom know that if you destroy the Men, the women and children are finished. This is why we must fight this battle at the core of these ideologies.

In World War II, not until America was brutally attacked by the Japanese at Pearl Harbor did most Americans wake up and fight. After the attack, one of Japan's leading Admirals, Naval Marshal General Isoroku Yamamoto was quoted as saying, "I fear that all we have done is awaken a sleeping giant, and fill him with a terrible resolve." The Admiral was correct. When America finally awoke to the truth that we needed to stand up and fight, no force could stand in her way.

True to form, most "boys" do not wake up and see the cultural and social battle until they have suffered great loss. This loss usually comes in the form of loss of freedom, loss of property, loss of employment or loss of marriages and children. A time of loss has come upon our country once again. The American male has suffered great financial and relational loss, and it is time for the great sleeping giant to awaken once again. It is time for American Men to stand up and fulfill their Great Mandate.

Every major problem we suffer in America can be attributed to the foundational void of real Men. Our destroyed marriages are the result of untrained Men. Our fatherless children are the result of a lack of Men. Our economic and social problems are the consequence of a shortage of Men. Therefore, to fix our problems we must rebuild our Men! Men of character wrote the Constitution and the Bill of Rights, and it is Men of character who will save and protect the virtues and legacy of our great land. A "boy" does not see the true value of the self-governing principles portrayed in the Constitution, because a "boy's" world view is based in selfishness. A "boy" just wants to get his way without earning it. To our shame, America is full of "boys."

A Revolution of Character:

Men in America are crying out for a revolution of character. After a full generation of poor training and teaching, the American male is left emotionally and spiritually crippled. If you are discouraged, defeated and have lost the hope and inspiration for victory, may you be touched by the heart of God. May you be revived to a life of joy and understanding through the principles written in this book. May the winds of wisdom reveal to your heart that every Man is designed and ordained to overcome the "boy" within.

The Apostle Paul of Tarsus gave clear instructions when he encouraged us to take off the "boyish" nature working against our Great Mandate, and simply put on the new Man we are called to be. Paul also made it very clear that God gives all Keys of authority to us for the building up and edification of our loved ones. If we attempt to use authority for selfish desires or to control others, we will bring hurt, shame, destruction and loss into our families, and we will pay a devastating price beyond our comprehension.

"Man vs. boy" will show you that putting on your new Man can be as easy as changing into a new set of clothing. Once your Manhood is established, you can then use your Keys of authority to fulfill the Great Mandate prepared for you. The training and principles outlined in this book will ensure you march forward to build your lives and your families with an eternal victory. Your victory will influence and contribute to your local community, and in turn it will bring you the joy and peace of God that passes all understanding. It simply is a choice.

Choose this day whom you are going to serve. Are you going to serve your selfishness and be a "boy," or are you going to serve self-sacrifice and be a Man? It is our job as males to become Men who walk in righteousness and authority. It is our duty to be Men who display a loving and responsible character to those around us. All of us can receive our destiny to become Men who will not blame others for our failures, and become Men who walk in love as we fulfill our Great Mandate.

Abraham Lincoln was correct when he said, "A nation divided will not long stand!" There is a battle raging between Man and "boy," and the outcome has not been decided. So who is going to win? Is it going to be the Man, or is it going to be the "boy?" For each one of us only time and providence will tell.

Men, today I put before you this question. Are we going to allow a group of self-consumed and irresponsible "boys" to hijack our nation like terrorists? Are we going to sit down on the job and allow immature "boys" to take away our liberty, our land, our rights, our families and our Judeo-Christian heritage? I challenge you to do the work and become the Man you were meant to be.

I believe Men will win this final battle for America. Men in this country can and will stand up and become the Men they are called to be, just as they have in generations past. We must become Men who will not allow the deadly virus of "boyishness" to spread through the ranks and over our land like a plague. We must build Men who will leave behind the entitlement mentality and fight for the Truth and freedoms outlined in our Constitution. The "boy" virus must be stopped, and "boys" must be dethroned in this country. Once again, the values of our forefathers will be honored in America.

We the people are America's greatest natural resource. Can you hear the voices of our fallen soldier's blood crying from the ground for Men to stand up? Can you hear the voices of our forefathers such as George Washington and Abraham Lincoln crying out for a full on offensive charge against the cultural and ideological viruses that have infected this great land? I challenge and encourage all males to grow up and leave behind the "boy" in them who tends to be selfish, timid, inconsiderate and irresponsible. May each of us be resolved to extinguish the "boy" in us who loses in the daily battle of overcoming life's challenges, and prepare a Patriarchal legacy of victory for our families and our children. It's not too late.

For those of you who are searching for a greater understanding of your purpose in life as a Man; for those of you who know God can and will fulfill all of your heartfelt needs and desires, but you are just plain stuck; for those of you who know God has deposited deep within you something very special just waiting to be released, this book is for you.

Well, the truth is, there are simple answers, they just are not easy ones.

Ronald Reagan – 40th President of the United States

1

From "boy" to MAN

Called to Overcome:

Victory is everything to a Man. Men are designed and destined to overcome. Men are created in God's image to rule, to reign, to subdue and to take dominion in their lives. Our time living on this earth is on the job training for our eternal purpose to rule and reign in the authority God has given.

The first enemy a Man must defeat is his own pride and selfishness. This is the ultimate eternal victory, the victory over the fallen nature of mankind. This is victory over death, and this is your victory, if you choose to receive it. This is a victory God has already won for you, but the "boy" residing within you will not receive it. It is a Man who makes the choice to receive the overcoming power to obtain victory, and it is a Man who will give credit where credit is due. A Man will overcome all odds, and then give the credit to his real Father, his loving Creator.

"It is the duty of all Nations to acknowledge the providence of Almighty God, to obey his will, to be grateful for his benefits, and humbly to implore his protection and favors."
George Washington – First President of the United States

If a male is not overcoming and obtaining the victory he is called to obtain, he is already dying. This death is usually not a physical death, and this death comes in many forms. It may be the death of hope or the death of our dreams. It may be the death of a business or the death of our prosperity. It may be the death of a marriage or the death of our relationships with children and loved ones. Ultimately, our lack of victory is even the death of our emotions, our conscience and finally our sensitivity to God.

When a male fails to enter his right of passage into Manhood, he will experience a brutal death in many forms. As a "boy," he will experience loss, frustration, anger, depression and even suicidal thoughts that lead him to sabotage his life. "boys" have no power. Everyone near a "boy" will suffer the fall-out of his failures, and women and children will experience the greatest casualties. This is not only true for "boys," this is also a brutal reality for untrained Men. There are many males who have passed into Manhood, but who are failing miserably because they have not been trained how to succeed and overcome as Men.

Are you sick and tired of losing in life? Is part of your masculinity dormant? Are you done with seeing other males around you go down in defeat, because they have been poorly trained as Men? Are you ready to get serious with your life? Are you ready to toughen up, and take on your enemies once and for all, and win? We must become Men to fully overcome the challenges of life, because the alternative to fulfilling our Mandate is a long and emotionally painful death.

The good news is our real Father in heaven can and will impart to us, in a very short time, every tool necessary to absolutely destroy death in all forms. No weapon formed against a Man will prosper, if he will simply learn to use the tools and principles God has made so readily available to him. So what are the tools and what are the principles? Read on.

The goal of this book is to encourage both Men and "boys" to get up and grab hold of the most important challenge ever put before mankind. Our challenge is to become Men and walk in our God ordained Mandates and Callings. Our challenge is to become the best we can be for our wives, our children and for our God.

In addition to becoming a Man, it is crucial to recognize that becoming a Man is only the beginning of our journey. We must learn to walk as Men with our Keys of authority in hand and be living examples for our loved ones. If you are a Man who is simply untrained on how to overcome in your life, then this book will impart to you how to retrieve back all the Keys of authority you have given away over the years, as well as those given away by your fathers and forefathers.

In the pages following, there is insight and testimonies from many Men who have overcome in their personal and public lives. May these stories assist you in your Mandate to rebuild the foundations of destroyed lives and to repair the damages caused by generations past as you go forward and win in life.

"If you can accept losing, you can't win."
Vince Lombardi – Championship Football Coach

How a "boy" Becomes a Man:

Every male has a God-given right to pass into Manhood, and just like any right it must be pursued and enforced. There are many ways Manhood is obtained, and there is always a similar formula for this most important and momentous event. Sometimes the training for Manhood takes years to achieve, and sometimes it appears to happen overnight. We all have different life experiences and circumstances; therefore, opportunity and necessity play a different role for each one of us.

Manhood always involves the process of mentorship and impartation from another Man. It always will include the willingness and desire of a "boy" to make the jump in his heart from "boy" to Man and receive this timeless impartation. It may be a father, an uncle or even a grandfather who takes on this role. It may be a coach or a close family friend who will usher in a Man's right of passage. It may even be a boss or a teacher reaching into your life and making the difference. Since Manhood is imparted, only a Man can impart it.

It is a father's primary duty to impart Manhood to his son. He must encourage and solidify the Manhood of his son. If he has failed to do so, he has failed his son miserably. A female can never impart Manhood. She can only promote Manhood. Neither can a "boy" impart Manhood. Once again, you cannot give what you do not have. Men make Men, period.

Ken:

Looking back, I can clearly see when I personally received the impartation of Manhood. I was only 11 years old, but this momentous event left a lifelong impression on my heart. It all happened during football season.

YFL was the Youth Tackle Football League in the Santa Barbara area in the 1970's. I could not wait to sign up to play football. I was always athletic, and football was definitely my favorite sport. For months my anticipation grew as the time approached closer for football season to begin. Daily, I would dream of the glory of scoring touchdowns and of "taking guys out," just like the Men I admired in the NFL.

Finally, in the heat of summer, football began. Those of you who played football know all about boot camp. Boot camp occurs in the first few weeks of football where a good coach will take a rag-tag bunch of out of shape "boys," and attempt to turn them into a machine of Men. After two days of grueling punishments, which in my mind had nothing to do with the glory of football, I was at home moping around before practice trying to think of how I could get out of going into the next scheduled trial of punishments.

I remember the intense hot 100 + degree August weather awaiting me, and the loud mouthed coaches who felt like the enemy of my soul screaming at me to give my 110% effort. Of course, struggling next to me were my sweaty and complaining comrades, whom I could only guess in their pain, cared about as much for my troubles as I cared for theirs.

"I didn't sign up for this!" I thought as I recalled the endless running, calisthenics and crab walks I was about to endure. Even to this day, I remember what time the next practice was supposed to start, 4:30 p.m. Every muscle in my body ached with pain as I pondered this crisis "I somehow got locked into." Everything in my "boyish" soul wanted out. To my shame, I even thought of quitting. As the clock ticked towards the dreaded 4:30 p.m., I knew my time was coming.

Since I was still a "boy" inside, I had my retreat plans all figured out. I decided when the time to go to practice came, I would merely say to my Dad, "I'm injured" or "I don't feel well" or "they cancelled practice, so I don't have to go." Well, I guess my plans weren't really figured out, because I couldn't even decide which lie to go with.

Can you believe it? I had become a coward, a liar and a betrayer all in one "boyish" retreat. This was a far cry from spiking a football down before a huge stadium of screaming fans all honoring my name. I'm sure you can easily see the cowardice and the lying, but the betrayal was in potentially abandoning my teammates. To make matters worse, my step-mom, who unfortunately just loved football, would make sure to remind me of football practice every single hour, adding to the intense gravity of my desperate situation.

The time came when my Dad was ready to drive me to football practice. My Dad was a Man. He had his challenges in life just like every Man. Raised with strong role models, and after being trained in the 82nd airborne as a paratrooper, serving as a fireman, a paramedic, and building homes as a General Contractor for many years, my father had picked up what it meant to be a Man.

As a former New York State Jr. Golden Gloves boxing competitor, my Dad was trained not to cower or to be intimidated. He was the kind of Man you would not dare challenge carelessly, and he was also the kind of Man you loved enough to not want to challenge. To this day, I am thankful for him.

So D-Day arrived for me. With my heart trembling, I went for it. In a wormy kind of way, I squeaked out to my Dad how I really did not want to go to practice. I did not lie to him about being injured, because the power of being in the presence of real authority makes you think twice about doing such things. The response I got from my Dad touched me on a level piercing my heart and soul.

My Dad stared at me with a look so intense and so God-like that I remember it to this day. Calmly and strongly he said, "You need to go to practice. Those other guys are counting on you." The air was serious and still as my heart pondered the ultimate challenge for every "boy," the challenge to put away my selfishness and my childishness, and receive The Great Mandate.

Outwardly, this was an everyday non-eventful conversation between a Man and his son. But inwardly, my Dad was asking me on a level deep within my heart to grab hold of being a Man, and I knew it. He did not demand I go to practice. A demand from him would have been an order from a Man to a "boy." If he had demanded it, I would have gone to practice and stayed a "boy." He presented me with the opportunity to receive what he had received, Manhood.

I immediately felt the potential shame of choosing to stay home. It was more than I could bear. I had never even once thought about my teammates before my Dad mentioned it. I was actually much more inclined to suffer pain and do the right thing for the sake of my teammates than myself, once I considered the whole picture. This is very important, because it is essential to know males are driven by a deep down need to stand and protect those around them.

And there I was, sitting in a car with a Man whom I loved and respected, who was challenging me to become a Man. Under this direct training and given the right understanding, my choice was easy. On my own volition with strength and conviction in my heart, I eagerly said, "Let's go." I could hear myself speak, and my voice sounded different. It sounded older, stronger, and more confident.

Immediately, it was as if the sky had opened. All the shame, the fear and the cowering I was feeling throughout the day gave way to a great sense of authority and achievement. I experienced a freedom very similar to when I outwardly accepted the Lord in my life when I was younger, except this had an additional element to it. For the first time in my life I felt like a Man. And it felt right! I remember feeling amazed I could go from wallowing in the very bottom of the sewer to standing at the very pinnacle of life, in just a moment of time, merely by making the right choice.

I could see my Dad was subtly proud as he put the car in gear. His approval welled deep over into my soul and spirit, and I was filled with his strength. As we drove in a peaceful silence to football practice, my mind started to think differently. I watched my Dad drive and thought I would soon be able to drive myself to practice. I had never even thought of driving a car before that day.

As I got out of the car and grabbed my football pads and helmet, my Dad put his hand on my shoulder and said, "Ken, I am proud of you. Have a great practice. Now show these guys how to hit!" I felt 10 feet tall as I approached my teammates on the field. It was as if the glory of God had settled on my shoulders, and nothing was going to stop me. I felt like a giant!

Looking back, I can see my whole world view had just changed. At 11 years of age, I went from the mentality of expecting people to take responsibility for me, to a mentality of taking responsibility for myself and for my teammates. The journey of being a Man had begun.

My decision to receive Manhood led me to become a leader for the team that year. Over the many years of football, I played on teams that set records that may even hold to this day. I can look back and see now the reason why I was a leader of my peers. I made the decision to become a Man inside regarding football and sports, and I believe my teammates sensed I had received something that made me a safe and right leader to follow. My teammates were not only following me, they were following my Manhood.

That year in football, I learned Men and "boys" alike are willing to follow the strength and authority of a Man. I became a player who would hold the line with a "Never say die!" attitude. Many times I reassured my teammates by saying, "We can do it! We can beat these guys!" And most of the time we did win. More importantly, we could leave the field with our heads held high, because we had given our all on the field, and we had won in our hearts.

I received Manhood from my father. The impartation had happened, and without even knowing it, I was leading my friends into Manhood. It was simple, painless and nearly invisible to the untrained eye. But it was real. Manhood is real, and I greatly thank my Dad for doing his job.

In those days, my Dad was a busy entrepreneurial Man. There were a thousand other things that could have occupied his day other than taking his son to practice. I think of what the outcome would have been if my Dad had not been there to father me. What if I would have quit football, because no one was there at that moment in time to show me how to be a Man? How many opportunities to impact our children's lives do we allow to pass by, because we refuse to take the time to do our job and be a Dad?

Should I Follow Joe Into Battle?

In the years following throughout high school and college, I began to notice there were many males around me who were still "boys," and these "boys" were hurting people. In family settings, sports competitions and even work environments, I found when people follow "boys" it usually leads to defeat and loss for everyone on the team. Men would get the job done, "boys" would not.

It became commonplace to see a "boy" abandon his buddies with cowardice in times of trouble, leaving them to be clobbered. Usually my gut feelings on identifying a "boy" would prove to be true. I could see "boys" wanted to lead, protect and have success as Men, but they lacked the kind of impartation I had received from my Dad when I was only 11 years old. Frequently, "boys" end up harming the people they are trying to lead. It is a sad, cold and hard Truth; "boys" will repeatedly suffer loss and defeat in their lives until they become Men.

As "boys," we all have done some pretty foolish things growing up. My friend Joe seemed to set the bar for "boyish" behavior. Joe was a close friend of mine in 8th grade. We used to run around the school grounds together during lunchtime throwing balls and causing havoc with any person crossing our path. Although both of our fathers were strong Men, we were still very good at acting like "boys." As the old saying goes, "Boys will be boys!" It is good to remember that receiving Manhood is an event, but walking as a Man on a daily basis is a challenging journey. At the young age of twelve, many "boys" are simply not ready or willing to fully grow up.

Our antics would usually amplify when we would encounter girls, especially pretty girls. Being avid snow skiers, Joe and I loved to jump over anything and demonstrate our ski moves. Many times when girls were sitting on the grass eating lunch, out of the blue we would run full speed and jump over these unsuspecting girls, doing some kind of trick ski maneuver over them. We called one specific jump, "the pitch out." We were known for them.

Since we were "in" with the popular crowd, hopeful young females would look forward to any attention from popular "boys," even if this meant getting frightened and slightly humiliated by athletes showing off their grace and skill as they soared inches over their heads.

One beautiful sunny day during lunchtime, we were parading around campus looking for excitement. We saw this sweet girl named Carrie eating on the grass with a few friends a little away from the main lunch crowd. Joe had always liked Carrie, but Carrie seemed to be a little above the rest of us. She was reserved, well mannered, and she was slightly royal in her qualities compared to the average 8th grade student. Carrie was definitely out of Joe's league.

All of a sudden, Joe said to me, "I am going to finally meet Carrie! Watch this! Come on. Let's do a pitch-out over her." Something in my gut told me not to follow Joe as he bolted off. I watched as Joe took off in a full run like an antelope across the plains. Joe was arguably the fastest male in the school. When he ran, you felt like you were watching nature's finest in motion. He looked brilliant as he was galloping towards her like a Man on a mission. But on this day, Joe was not a Man on a mission. He was a fool on an errand.

As Joe approached Carrie at full speed, I noticed he was running a little faster than normal. Carrie's back was toward us; therefore, she was unaware of the "exciting" event about to happen to her as she gently nibbled on her sandwich. When Joe launched off the ground to fly over Carrie, he looked like a long jumper coming off the block. Unfortunately, for both Joe and Carrie, he faulted. He jumped about a foot too late.

As he rose up towards Carrie, he completed his usual "pitch-out" looking like a pro skier soaring through the skies. And then it happened. Both of Joe's feet slammed right into Carrie's head, making a sickening thud I can still hear and feel to this day. Glory had turned to tragedy.

Carrie immediately began to cry furiously, while her friends used words against Joe rarely even said in the boy's locker room.

Joe's pale, white skin turned apple red as he sheepishly squeaked out, "I'm sorry," about 20 times in a row. After five very long minutes of crying and sobbing, Carrie's tears began to subside. She then demanded that Joe leave her sight at once with sharp words cutting him right to the bone.

I remember feeling embarrassed to even be associated with Joe when he moved my way to leave the scene of the crime. As he followed about 10 feet behind me, I heard him jokingly say, "Do you think I still have a chance with her?" I shook my head in disbelief and kept walking as I waved for him to follow me. I couldn't even look at Joe, but I must admit that I really appreciated Joe's ability to laugh at himself when he did something foolish. I kept thinking to myself, "I am so glad I did not follow Joe on this mission." My heart went out to that poor, sweet girl named Carrie.

Would you follow Joe into battle? On that day the answer was definitely "NO!" To Joe's credit, on other days he was a good leader to follow. This further bears witness to the Truth that becoming a Man is both a one time event as well as a process of growing up. Therefore, in every situation we experience in life, we need to evaluate and decide whether the leader we choose to follow is leading as a Man or a "boy."

The best way I could identify and answer the Man or "boy" question was to ask myself, "Would I follow this person into battle?" If the answer was "Yes," I knew the male in question was a Man. If the answer was "No," I knew the impartation of Manhood had somehow failed to be passed on to this person, and he was still a "boy." The reason I would not follow a "boy" into battle is a "boy" does not have what it takes to lead and protect those around him. And I am not talking about training here; I am talking about the substance of Manhood.

In other words, I knew a "boy" would lead the team and me right off a cliff, because the substance of Manhood is just not in a "boy." In the case of Joe, at this time in his young life, following him meant he could lead me into humiliation as an accessory to the crime of injuring some unsuspecting female. Joe's folly was symbolic of what many males are experiencing in their lives today. Instead of impressing Carrie, Joe literally kicked her right in the head.

How many of us have injured the women in our lives while we are off trying to impress the world in some "boyish" show? Many males try hard to impress the girl they love. But due to their lack of training and "boyish" demeanor, they end up slamming their loved ones in some way thereby causing damage to the relationship.

The consequence of Joe's action was immediate and destructive. The odds of Joe ever having a chance with Carrie had become slim to none. The damage was done. Carrie never gave Joe the time of day after that episode. Fortunately, Joe was raised in a household in the presence of an awesome father who was there to impart Manhood. Eventually, Joe decided to fully grow up, and Manhood settled upon him gracefully as he became a great husband and father.

When Manhood Fails to Happen, Everyone Suffers:

What does a "boy" do when this important transformation to Manhood does not occur? What does a "boy" do when he is neither taught nor challenged to become a Man? Who is going to be the bearer of bad news to an adult male who is a 35, 45 or 55 year old "boy," and has missed the primary duty of his Mandate?

Since a "boy" has missed his Mandate, everyone around him is paying the very high price of picking up the slack for his irresponsibility. Most of us know what I am talking about, and most of us have paid the high price for being in a family or friend relationship with a male who is a "boy," because they live all around us. Taking care of a "boy" is a disconcerting and miserable experience at best.

It is no better for the "boy." An adult "boy" has to deal with a huge secret nobody seems to want to talk about. He experiences shame, disrespect and failures on a profound level because he always feels inferior, insecure and jealous of Men who appear to have it together. Many times a "boy" will try to act masculine and manlike, but it's fraudulent and everyone around knows it. When a "boy" tries to pretend he is a Man, it's like he's dressing up in a uniform not belonging to him, tap dancing around and giving military orders with the authority of an eight year old. It just does not work.

No one can take a "boy" seriously, because he just doesn't have it. Ultimately, a "boy" will develop deep frustration and anger due to his lack of authority, because nobody will give him the following or respect he desires. This will usually lead him to be controlling and abusive in order to feel like he actually has some power. His "boyish" behavior only magnifies the problem, because he has now engaged in a personal campaign to sabotage his life. Eventually, a "boy's" controlling antics causes the very people he wants respect from to further disrespect him.

How can a "boy" win after he has compounded his problems from years of running from his Mandate and a lifetime of letting people down? The answer of course is: ***a "boy" must become a Man, and he must become a Man today.*** He must also overcome the envy and jealousy against those Men who were fortunate enough to have fathers who imparted Manhood to their sons. It is the Men who were properly fathered that can impart the Manhood that "boys" desperately yearn for.

Who Can Stand Before Envy or Jealousy?

Generally, "boys" will outwardly honor and display a healthy respect for true authority, but under their façade, they are frustrated about their own lack of being a Man. They are actually in awe of Men, because real Men have something they desire to possess, and "boys" are desperate to know how to acquire it.

When a male is young, obtaining Manhood is a healthy and natural desire, because it leads him to strive to become like the Men who are his role models. As a male gets older, the respect he has for Men will subtly turn into envy, if he does not transform into a Man. This will create relational problems with all of his relationships, because his heart is well aware he has still not become a Man.

It is quite unfortunate when a male stays a "boy" well into his 20's, 30's, and 40's and beyond, because eventually his insecurities and fears will turn into envy, jealousy and even resentment against every male who walks as a Man. A "boy" will avoid developing close relationships with real Men. Deep down he wants what a Man has, but not knowing how to get it can be incredibly frustrating and painful for him. He fears being found out, and his insecurities and fears greatly hinder his ability to build healthy relationships with any person around him. His marriage will be compromised and distant, his relationship with his children will be confusing and destructive, and his Mandate will be thwarted.

King Solomon was very familiar with the antics of a "boy." He called them "fools," and his book of Proverbs is full of descriptions of the behaviors of a fool. Solomon understood that jealousy and envy were the calling cards of a "boy." He wrote in Proverbs **"Wrath is cruel, and anger is outrageous: but who is able to stand before envy?"**[1]

One of the Bible's wisest earthly Men is saying it is very tough to stand before someone who is angry with you, but envy is said to be worse than both wrath and anger. Wrath and anger will eventually dissipate away like the passing of a bad storm. But a "boy" who envies is forever putting forth curses against the person he envies. A "boy's" jealous heart will continually send out thoughts and "prayers" of defeat and demise against those of whom he is jealous. A "boy" cannot stand someone having the Manhood he so deeply desires to possess, because this is a constant reminder of the deficit in his soul and his failure as a male.

This is so contrary to how God has called us to be. We are called to pray for and encourage our fellow teammates. Point 8. on the Man vs. "boy" list suggests: "boys" resent Men, and a Man will encourage Men. As Men, we need to work with true authority, not against it.

For all of the times we were envious or jealous of one another, we must realize the damage we have done and repent for our selfish behaviors. Our fear of growing up has caused many of us to work against the very Men in our lives who are there to strengthen us. It is eye-opening to think many of us have shunned and excluded the chosen Men that God has installed in our lives. These Men are there to assist us in building our character, but we sometimes miss the opportunity for impartation because of our jealousy. Every "boy" must accept the Truth that Men make Men. It is time to learn a more excellent way.

You Can't Give What You Don't Have:

When I was young, friends of mine had fathers who were still "boys" throughout their upbringing. I remember those same fathers nagging my friends, or debating with them about how or why they should act. Having no recognizable authority, they would try to manipulate their sons into

---

1 Proverbs 27:4, KJV

pretending to be Men. These fathers just could not give to their sons what they themselves did not have.

In addition, there was no inward respect given by the sons to their fathers in these instances. Deep inside, a son knows if his father is weak and castrated. Sons who have weak fathers feel a shame within themselves nagging at their soul. They are embarrassed to compare their fathers with other fathers, or they will exaggerate their father's exploits and manly abilities in an attempt to handicap their deficiencies. What a sad story it is when a son feels he must pretend his father is a Man, when he clearly knows he is not.

So let us not pretend anymore. Let us look at ourselves, and let us examine the areas of relationship with our fathers and the significant male figures hindering our walk as Men. To face the shame of failing as a Man, and to admit we have failed to achieve our Great Mandate, is one of the most courageous and giving acts we can do as Men.

"If you are losing in life, you are surely behaving like a 'boy.'"

Father Issues:

Do you have father issues? The number one reason a "boy" fails to enter into Manhood is he holds on to anger, bitterness and resentment against his father. How could I have received Manhood from my father when I was 11 years old, if I were bitter and angry with him on the day in the car before football practice? I loved my Dad; therefore, I freely received from him.

Such is not the case with many males walking around today. Many males have been neglected, abused, abandoned, lied to, manipulated and controlled by the very father who has a Mandate to encourage and fashion the armor of his son. This is tragic and crippling for a son, because these abuses make it very difficult for a son to receive from his father. It becomes even more tragic when a father is still a "boy." Even if the son does forgive his father, how can he obtain Manhood from a male who does not possess it?

The good news is there is hope, if you are trained how to overcome these challenges. Even though the injuries and wounds fathers inflict on their sons are very tragic and crippling, there are answers and total victory for all males if they choose to overcome and conquer. The answer is in "forgiveness" and "understanding." When forgiveness and understanding work together in the heart of a Man, he becomes unstoppable. Thus, you have the purpose for this book, to make Men unstoppable in their quest to fulfill their Mandate.

Has your Dad dropped the ball in some way that leads you to harbor feelings of resentment, anger or disapproval towards him? If you are like most males today, you have unresolved father issues. The purpose of this book is to give you tools to break free from the bondage of the lies you are holding on to.

The best way to conquer lies in your life is to first acknowledge there indeed is a problem. Then you must overcome through understanding the dynamics of the problem, and finally you must apply forgiveness principles. Of course, this is not a new concept to anyone, because both secular and religious teachings include forgiveness as part of the answer. But are you bold enough and Man enough to once and for all close the door of pity and hurt? Can you take responsibility for your own Mandate by understanding and forgiving your Dad, as well as the other significant males in your life who have failed you?

Believing lies about why people have hurt or abandoned you is the number one cause for remaining a "boy." Lies we believe about our fathers are the most devastating. This is why understanding Truth about the dynamics of your relationships is so important. Most males have a deep longing to walk fully as Men, but they believe lies about their circumstances and about their relationship with their fathers. This leads them to justify their "boyish" behaviors, and it keeps them in the bondage of "boyhood."

If you are willing to look at your life and correct the lies you believe regarding who you really are and why people have let you down, you are well on your way to totally overcoming and eradicating the "boy" in you. Resolve the breaches between your father and yourself, and let God's principle of understanding and forgiveness work in your life. You will then be on your way to victory as a Man.

I cannot overstate the importance of forgiving your father for anything done to you by him in the past. This doesn't mean you have to force yourself to forget about abuses, and it does not mean you are giving your Dad a pass on his responsibilities. Believe me when I say, God our true Father will ensure all Men are accountable for their own actions, both good and bad. I have never seen a "boy" get away with anything when all is said and done.

Forgiveness is simply the cancellation of the debt or the offense done to you. The act of forgiveness is not forgetting about the debt. It is remembering the debt and the offense without the pain and bad feelings associated with it. This is why understanding is so important. When you understand why people do the things they do, it becomes much easier to set them free in your heart. How often have we been upset with someone because we did not understand the whole picture? Many times, when we do find out the whole Truth, we are then able to let the offense go.

The whole point in becoming a Man is based on having faith that walking as a Man is the right thing to do, and God our Father will reward those Men who diligently seek to overcome. Simply put, if you do not forgive your father and allow God to heal your heart in the areas you have been wounded, your walk as a "Man" will be severely compromised, and your full right of passage into Manhood will be on hold. Your father in some way may have already imparted Manhood to you, but there may be critical steps of forgiveness you need to take to ensure you are walking totally as a Man.

God has created you in His image, and He has proven throughout history He desires to impart to you His loving, forgiving and Fatherly nature. So I encourage you to identify any offenses perpetrated against you by your father or significant males in your life, and put the offenses on the altar of forgiveness for your sake and for the sake of your family.

There is a Man named Bob who did just this. In the true life story following, Bob faced the fears holding him back for decades, as he overcame the challenges of forgiving his father and the stumbling blocks of jealousy.

"The harder you work, the harder it is to surrender."
Vince Lombardi

Bob:

Bob was 49 years old when he came to me for help. He was married with four children in their teens. I was sitting at a covered patio table in front of my property at the time I first saw him drive up the driveway. As he walked up the pathway towards my house, it was painfully obvious that here was a potentially dignified Man who had loss and failure written all over his demeanor.

As I arose to shake his hand, I could see right through his defeated eyes. Here was a soul crying out in despair for help. Like many males living throughout America today, Bob was struggling with his Manhood. The relationship losses had mounted up to the point where he was willing to pour out his heart to an almost total stranger in the hope there was an answer to life's most pressing questions.

Bob sat down next to me at an outdoor table nervously attempting to engage in small talk. After the formalities were observed, he soon revealed to me that for over 30 years he was absolutely consumed by pornography, and it was destroying both his marriage and his family. Bob was also suffering greatly from the financial lack he was experiencing by working as a salesman, and he was incredibly discouraged about life in general.

The interesting thing about Bob was his high intellect, and that he carried himself with an outward dignity. Bob was a self-professing Christian, and he was also highly trained as a theologian. He attended excellent Christian seminaries, and through the years he enrolled in many classes and seminars specifically to deal with his problems regarding lust and pornography, to no avail.

Bob was one of the millions of males who are responsible for violating Point 16. on the Man vs. "boy" list. "boys" have pornography and sexual problems, and Men are stable and healthy in relationships. For decades he had failed to become a Man, thus leading him into a life of abusing and even molesting women both emotionally and physically. Before I go on with Bob's story, I would like to give a definition for "molest," because this term is widely misunderstood in today's society.

To "molest," is to make indecent sexual advances towards someone. A person is being molested if they are subjected to unwanted or improper sexual activity from another person. This means any improper touch of a sexual nature is a form of molestation. This includes everything from mild inappropriate touch all the way to extreme rape. It is all about boundaries. If you are entering someone's physical space indecently or inappropriately with a sexual intent of any kind, you are intentionally molesting that person.

Even verbal sexual comments intended to promote sexual advances are a form of emotional molestation, because they violate the heart and spirit of a person. Just stop for a minute and think about what I am saying here. Really think about it. Have you ever improperly subjected a female with even the slightest bit of sexual connotation for the purpose of potentially breaking sexual boundaries? If you have, you've just entered into a form of molestation. It is a larger than life epidemic Men must overcome. The repercussions of molestation are present not only in our country, but all over the world.

Throughout his life, Bob had grown accustomed to breaking the sexual boundaries of girls and women in very subtle ways. His preoccupation with sex and pornography led to inappropriate thoughts and physical violations against females. He could barely go out in public without thinking sexual thoughts about the females coming across his path. For years he battled in a war of bondage between the knowledge it was wrong to fantasize about sex in this manner and his desire to fulfill his lusts.

Eventually, Bob found himself on the dark streets of bad neighborhoods combing the streets for hookers. To his disgrace and the disgrace of all males, he partook of the ultimate molestation by paying money to an "uncovered" and emotionally injured female for sex. Living as a "boy" led him straight into adultery. Before he knew it, he was quickly falling off a very tall cliff into a valley of divorce, shame and failure.

The devastation falling upon his family after the exposure to these episodes was beyond belief. The most prolific writer could never portray the pain and grief a woman experiences when her husband or father betrays her so. Bob's failure to become a Man had dropped a bomb of despair and agony on his wife and children, and there was no hope in sight.

There were periods of six months to a year where he had "white knuckled" his sexual and lust problems by abstaining from acting out, (from further molesting and abusing females and behaving as a "boy") but this in no way was victory. The torment and the misery he was experiencing and in turn imparting to others around him became so incredibly strenuous on his wife and children, divorce and absolute separation seemed to be the only solution.

Diagnosing the Man:

After decades of dealing with "boys" who were losing in life, this case was actually not difficult to diagnose; however, it was not my diagnosis that was important, it was Bob's. Bob needed to see the truth before he could pull out of the hole he created. As he started to share the deeper issues of his life, I began to get to know him on a level few had dared to travel before. Bob was good at talking about his failures and past indiscretions. He somberly reiterated a well-rehearsed soliloquy of the many past offenses he committed over his lifetime.

Actually, Bob was a little "too good" at it. His story and explanations were almost impenetrable as he played the poor old guy to perfection. I felt there was a subtle pride and arrogance coming from him, even though he was talking about his failures. Finally, I asked Bob the one question that usually unravels all the knotted justifications of a "boy" who is afraid to reveal the Truth about his fears.

I asked Bob, "Do you feel like a Man? I don't mean a temporary feeling you feel at this specific moment of time, but an overall assessment of your feelings about yourself over the past several years."

Bob thought for a moment as the years of tension and fear appeared to overcome his countenance. He did not answer the question at first, and he looked very ashamed and exposed as he nervously tried to find a place to put his hands.

I then asked him on a scale of 1 to 10, how much he actually felt like a "Man" or a "boy." I explained the numbers 5 - 10 designated that he felt like a Man to different degrees, and the numbers 0 – 4 designated he felt like a "boy" to different degrees. This is what I call the "Victory Scale." Remember, 5 or above means Man, and 4 or below means "boy."

I thought to myself that Bob felt like a "boy," and an immature one at that. At the time, I definitely would not have followed Bob into battle. If I were to give a number on the Victory Scale, it would be no higher than a 2 ½.

Bob looked up at me intensely, and then he said, "If I have to be honest with you, I have never felt like a Man. I am 49 years old, and for all of my adult life I have always felt like a "boy" in Man's clothes. I feel like I am between a 2 and a 3."

I looked at him in amazement as he gave me the exact number my heart was saying. I do not know why I was amazed, because I have seen this same confirmation hundreds and hundreds of times before. When a person's heart speaks, everyone around can hear it, if we only will take the time to listen.

I then said to Bob, "Do you want to become a Man today?" He looked at me with bewilderment as he considered this concept that perplexed him for most of his adult life. I could tell by his eyes he was remembering the incredible loss and devastation he had experienced in his life, as well as the grief he had perpetrated upon others.

He then replied, "What do you mean? How can this happen today? How can I become a Man just like that?"

I then asked for permission to speak into his life. I explained to Bob why asking for permission to speak into a person's life is so very important. A true Man will never take advantage of another person by overstepping boundaries. Just because I had some insight into an area in which Bob was unfamiliar, this did not give me the right to speak into his life without honoring him as a Man and respecting his boundaries. (Chapter 7 of this book further explains the importance and significance of having good boundaries.)

We must always seek permission when we intend to speak into a person's life. My job was to give Bob the tools, guidance and insight at his request that someone else had mercifully given to me. Bob had some very serious boundary issues, specifically in his relationships with women. As a new friend, it was my job to diligently respect his boundaries in a show of my respect for him, and to give him a taste of how he should respect the boundaries of others.

Bob replied in a calm and direct voice that he greatly desired I share anything and everything that could help him overcome this great challenge literally decimating his life.

With permission and authority in hand, I decided to ask him the second question that causes "boys" to tremble in fear. I asked him about his father. I asked him if his father was a Man. He said he felt like his father was a Man; however, his father had never given him the approval he desired. Bob's father was a farm-bred salt of the earth type of guy who was very rough around the edges. He told me his Dad had a tough time sharing his emotions, and the only approval he remembered was when he or his brothers did well in sports.

Both of Bob's older brothers were all-American athletes and were a tough act to follow. Bob was fairly good in sports, but he was no all-American by his own account. And by his Dad's account, Bob was unaccepted and a great disappointment. As Bob recounted stories about his father and his childhood, I could clearly hear the sad little boy who never received the approval of his father. Bob was stuck in the injuries of childhood, and I knew it was the time to be brutally honest.

I told Bob how Manhood is something imparted and then received from a Man to a "boy," and it normally happens in a young male's early teen years. I explained about the Jewish tradition of Bar Mitzvah, and he told me he was very familiar with the tradition because he was trained as an Old Testament theologian. Bob revealed to me he had justified his "boyish" behaviors in his mind for decades. He thought that since he was a Christian, he automatically was a Man, even though his heart never bore witness to his Manhood.

I began to explain to Bob how many males have attempted to embrace the principles of Christianity in an attempt to fulfill their deep longing to become a Man? And in doing so, they sometimes fail to fulfill the very first Mandate a Christian is called to overcome. They fail to become a Man. This in turn causes them to miss the Man who Jesus is, as well as a true relationship with their true Father in heaven.

Such was the case with Bob. I began to show Bob that his frustrated relationship with his father had affected his relationship with God and every relationship in his life. As the principles flowed out of me, I could see Bob was tracking every word, because they told the story of his life. And his was a life of shame, despair and disappointment.

I shared with Bob that a Man knows whether he is a Man, or whether he is a "boy." A Man will not question whether he is a "boy" or not, because deep in his heart he knows he has received Manhood. There is no debate. He is who he is.

I then I asked him another question. "What happened? Why did you fail to become a Man? Was there any event you recall representing what may have gone wrong?"

Bob went into deep thought. We sat there across the table from one another for what seemed like five minutes before he responded. It felt like he was attempting to open huge and rusty iron doors as he desperately grasped for a key that would open his future. "There was a time..." he said, and at that moment I knew he was going to become a Man on that day.

Bob explained, "There was a time when I was eleven years old. It was Saturday and I woke up early. I wanted to do something nice for my family, and for months I was learning how to cook breakfast from other family members. I decided to make breakfast and surprise the whole family. Well it came out fantastic! The whole family seemed impressed. Everything was delicious, and it all turned out great.

"Then it happened. As we were all eating, my Dad looked up at me. I expected him to give me a compliment for the meal and the presentation I had prepared. I had hoped for some kind of affirmation, or some words showing his approval of me. He then said 'Someday you're gonna make somebody a good wife.' There it was. I was devastated. Those words seemed to have become part of me."

I looked at Bob intently, who was now showing tears. I said to him, "Bob, there is your answer. For nearly forty years you have believed a lie. Those words did indeed become part of you. You have somehow received the lie you are not a Man, and you can never be a Man. Your Dad basically called you a girl, and you received it. All it takes is one critical foundational lie we believe, to set our whole course of life in the wrong direction. You actually believe you don't have what it takes to be a Man."

I looked Bob right in the eyes and asked him, "Are you a Man, or are you a woman?"

Bob just nodded his head, as he seemed to appreciate the direction I was leading him. I went on to say, "Bob, sometimes you just have to start at the beginning of your life and reassess things. When a child is born, there is one question everyone wants to know. Is the child a boy, or is the child a girl? This is a profound universal question that must be answered, and fortunately our anatomy gives us away. After the gender is determined, the course of the child's history is set in stone. Boys are to become Men, and girls are to become women. God and genetics have determined a Truth that cannot be plausibly denied.

"Anyone or anything denying the God ordained gender of a child is subconsciously or consciously working to destroy the child. Whether your father intended it or not, he was used by the enemy to plant a seed of doubt about your masculinity. To add to the injury, the timing could not have been worse. I was the same age of eleven when I received Manhood. This is a time when a young boy is desperately searching to obtain respect and Manhood from his father. In your case, it was thwarted by poor relationship skills and miscommunication between you and your father. You have carried this lie with you until this day, and it has kept you in a state of doubt about your Mandate and your identity as a Man.

"I can tell by your tone of voice that you also have become bitter against your Dad and are harboring an unforgiving heart. This has not only prevented you from growing up, but it has also prevented you from receiving the gift of Manhood your Dad was supposed to impart to you. Does this all make sense to you, Bob?"

Bob leaned back in his chair nodding his head in agreement looking at me in a state of wonder. He then pensively said to me, "Yes, you are correct. I have never really thought this event had such an impact on me, but it is obvious it has. After this happened to me when I was eleven years old, I set up some kind of barrier between my Dad and me. All through high school I did everything I could to obtain his approval, even though

I was angry with him. There always was an underlying animosity with him, because I knew nothing I did would ever make him happy with me.

"I hate to even think about it, because it brings up memories of how much I feared what my Dad thought of me. It got to the point I did not even want to know what he thought, because I knew I would be severely disappointed and rejected by his responses. This caused a huge separation between my father and me, and I ended up just blaming him for all my problems. Even though I was always seeking his approval, there was always a deep down, underlying anger I felt against him for not accepting me."

My heart went out to Bob as I could literally feel the pain of his childhood. I was grieved by what I was hearing. I rarely experienced these same problems with my Dad, because I usually felt an unconditional love from him even when he was disapproving of my actions. Over the years, the relationship deficiencies Bob was experiencing with his Dad had become commonplace to me, because I have sat across the table with many Men who grew up with a similar story. I knew in my heart it was time for Bob to get through the huge barrier keeping him from moving into Manhood for all of these years.

I then explained to Bob, "I can clearly see why you did not receive becoming a Man. You could not receive Manhood from your father because you were bitter and angry against him. You cannot receive from someone whom you are angry with. It just doesn't happen. And guess what? You are not allowed to blame your Dad for not becoming a Man, unless of course you want to remain a 'boy' forever.

"Bob, you have been neglecting the primary duty of your Mandate since you were eleven. It appears that for all of these years you have not been trained correctly. You haven't been Man enough to look at your pain straight in the eye, and grab hold of what God has for you once and for all. It is time to grow up, don't you agree?"

Bob looked up at me with a sad remorse and nodded.

I then said, "You are 49 years old, how much longer can you hold on to this unforgiving attitude? How much longer are you going to continue to injure your family by walking as a 'boy' who has lost his way? Isn't it time to forgive your Dad?"

Bob had a bewildered look on his face as he shook his head in frustration. He said defensively, "I have forgiven my Dad for many things, but I have never thought to forgive him for anything regarding how I was made to feel like a 'boy.'"

I then explained to Bob, "God loves us enough not to push us into Step #2 before we accomplish Step #1. Step #1 for all 'boys' is to become a Man, and this means we must forgive others and take responsibility for all of the problems and deficiencies in our relationships. Step #2 is to live the rest of our lives walking as loving and responsible Men. If we miss Step #1, we're history.

"Bob, forgiveness is not forgetting about the bad experiences you suffered at the hands of your father or other people in your life. Forgiveness allows you to remember the offenses without feeling the intense emotionally pain associated with them. Forgiveness really will set you free from the 'boyish' prison cell you have locked yourself into.

"If you cannot say with confidence you have achieved the accomplishment of becoming a Man, your life will have some serious problems. Your life will look like the 'boy' category from the Man vs. "boy" list. Actually, this is exactly what your life looks like right now. Your relationships, your job, and your desires are all handicapped because you are attempting to do a job without having the authority, the tools, or the blessing to do it. God works and leads through Men, not 'boys.'"

I then told him, "You have to take responsibility for your own life and move past your own weaknesses and the weaknesses of your father. Do you see if you do not become a Man you will never overcome pornography or your tendency to plug your emotional umbilical cord into 'uncovered' women? (See Chapter 6 for an explanation about the "uncovered" woman.) Do you see if you do not become a Man, you will continue to lose everything dear to you; your family, your children and your legacy? Males are made to be Men, and they are made to overcome life's challenges. We are made to be filled with God's approval, not the approval of mankind.

"If you are not filled up with being the Man you were called to be, you will have to fill up with something else. That something else for you has been pornography and inappropriately seeking the approval from 'uncovered' women and wanna-be Men. We have to be the Men we are created to be. We have a choice to either become Men, or to experience a lifetime of death.

"Right here is where the game is either won or lost. A Man's heart is where the choices are made causing him to overcome or not. But first you have to see the battlefield and the direction God has chosen for you. Like a sailboat on a windy day, a Man has to see which direction the winds of God are blowing him, and allow those winds to take him to his destiny. You can win in life, if you can find the Man you are called to be."

Bob lowered his head and looked at the ground as if he was trying to find something. He then lifted up his head and said, "I have let everyone down my entire life. I do not know who I am called to be."

I immediately replied, "Bob, you are called to be a Man. Inside each and every Man is a Mandate and a Calling unique to that Man. This is something you are born with. Your Calling is yours and yours alone. Only you can do the job you are called to do with your family. Your Calling cannot be taught to you and it cannot be learned. It is a gift from God. If you allow your Calling and your Mandate to come forth out of your heart, you will fulfill your destiny and be the Man you were created to be.

"Life has a way of putting people through a lot of punishment. Over time, the world sometimes can steal the knowledge of your Calling away from you without you even realizing it. This is what has happened to you. You have almost totally forgotten about who you are and who you are called to be. I am going to remind you of your Mandate and who you are."

Bob looked at me deeply and said, "I do not have anything left. I have lost it all."

I said, "Bob, you have lost nothing. You are alive and well and your Calling is yours for the taking. Your Calling and your Mandate are gifts no person or devil can ever take away from you permanently. You have allowed the guilt and shame of your sexual sins to persuade you to make poor life decisions. The power of your sin will be broken when you finally decide to be a Man and allow God to take away your guilt and shame. All you have to do is live your life from this day forward allowing God to fill up the depths of your heart, and you will overcome every challenge put before you.

"It is time for you to allow your heart, not your mind, to lead your life. Your mind is one of your heart's greatest assets, but if you continue to allow your mind alone to lead you, it is over for you. This has not been working for you, has it?"

Bob stared into my eyes intently as he breathed out a long, low sigh.

I said, "You cannot force your life to go the direction you think you want it to go anymore. It is time for you to let God take hold of the reigns of your spirit, and allow your heart and your conscience to make your choices. Can you see it? Do you see it is time to die to the selfish 'boy' in you and become a Man?"

Bob crossed his arms and slowly turned his head to the side. He then said, "You do not understand what I am going through. It has been so difficult for me."

I stared right into Bob's solemn and defeated eyes and said, "I do not need to understand. Life is supposed to be difficult. Difficulties are what separate the Men from the 'boys.' This is the only way we have the opportunity to overcome. Anyone can overcome when there are no challenges or difficulties. Every male on this entire planet has a burden he is carrying that nobody is going to fully understand. Your challenges are between you and God Almighty.

"It is not my job to understand and overcome your problems. It is your job. If I solve your problems for you, I become your savior. I am not qualified to be your savior. I will help you see it, but I am not going to get your victories for you. You have been carrying your burdens long enough. It is time to lay them down and become a Man. It is time for you to stop hiding under the cover of the people who have hurt you. It is time for you to choose."

Bob responded back saying, "I can't. I do not know what to do."

I replied, "Yes, you can. And you will. Your wife and your children are depending on you. You must. You must live the life you were meant to live. You must live the life given to you when you were brought into this world. God has been with you from the very beginning. He knew you before you were even born, and He promised He would never leave you or forsake you. Right now He is asking you to receive your Manhood, your Calling, and the life He has prepared for you. Are you ready to start living?"

I could hear and feel a soft breeze blow through leaves of the trees and over our faces as Bob slowly relaxed his shoulders. A long period of silence came upon us both, as I looked at my dear brother battle in the valley of decision. It was as if his entire life was replaying in his head from the time he was a child. God was indeed speaking to this Man's heart, and I was astounded at what I was seeing.

Slowly, Bob began to nod his head softly as if responding to a still, small voice deep down in his heart. He looked at me gently with eyes of agreement. With a calm desperation in his voice, he asked, "What do I do?"

Obtaining Manhood:

Yes, Bob asked a big question, "What do I do?" Thank God there is a simple answer to that question. Thank God there is absolute order in the Universe. All we have to do is honor a few basic principles and everything will come into order.

I then said to him, "Bob, it is so simple. Do you trust me?"

He said he did. I said to him, "It is time for you to get right before God and take care of business; the business of becoming a Man once and for all. It is time to fully forgive your father."

Bob looked down at his hands, and then he put them tightly to his face as he slowly shook his head back and forth. I could sense my own heart beating fast in my chest as I awaited his next move. As he pondered the course of action for his life, I recalled back in my own life when I sat with my Dad in the car so many years before deciding if I was going to go to football practice as a Man. Bob was in the valley of decision, and I could feel his soul warring against itself.

After a few minutes of what seemed like an eternity, Bob looked up at me. He then said, "Okay, I am ready. I know deep down I have needed to do this for a long time. I need to let go of the past. I need to become a Man."

I looked steadfast into Bob's eyes and said, "Do you think you can revisit the scene of the crime in the kitchen with your Dad when you were a young boy of 11."

Bob replied, "Yes, of course, if you think it would help."

I said, "Bob, what do you think God was feeling and thinking when you were so hurt and shamed by your Dad that day? I think it is time to get real with God - your real Father." He looked at me like a deer in the headlights as he grasped for strength to continue talking. It was obvious that Bob had never considered God's heart regarding his relationship with his Dad and how he was shamed in the kitchen.

I said, "Bob, the Lord was there with you and aware of every single detail of that dreadful day. Think of how you would have felt if you saw your Dad treat one of ***your*** sons like he treated you.

Bob quickly responded saying, "I would have been very upset! An adolescent boy is very impressionable concerning his father. I needed my Dad's love and approval in some way, and he openly rejected me in front of my whole family. Even now, when I think of what he said, I can feel my whole body shaking inside."

I replied, "I think I understand, but I know that God understands perfectly. If you go a little further and find out God's whole heart on the matter, I am sure something fantastic will occur in your life. What else is the Lord saying to your heart about your Dad?"

Bob closed his eyes as he gently dropped his head slightly down. I could tell that he was praying. For the first time in his adult life he was boldly going where he never had gone before. He was revisiting the scene where his Manhood was thwarted, and his Father God was going there with him.

After several minutes, he looked up with tears in his eyes. His voice began to break as he softly stated, "I judged my Dad. God is showing me that He was there, and His heart was broken over what transpired. I feel God is saying that there is nothing more He wants than to see father and son reconciled and loving one another. I am seeing my Dad in a whole new light. I remember even as an adult, my Grandfather would discredit my Dad by saying things to him that were demeaning and disrespectful. My Grandfather had done the same thing to my Dad throughout his life. I had always seen my Dad as the abuser. Now, I see that he was also abused and neglected by his father."

I added, "Are you seeing how believing this lie has robbed you of your true identity, your Manhood and your life?"

Bob replied, "Yes! I have been behaving like a little hurt 'boy.' And it was totally unnecessary, because it was all a lie. My Dad had no idea what he was doing. I feel like we both were duped."

I said, "Well, you both were duped, as well as your Grandfather and who knows how many generations before him, but the game is not over. Let us go into prayer and ask God to repair the damage that occurred between you and your Dad? You have the opportunity to take responsibility for this whole relational mess that was created by you and your forefathers, and ***you*** can be the one to break the chain and establish a new legacy for your family. Your mistakes, your pains and your tribulations can be used for good to start a new life for your wife and children. It is never too late to make things right. You may be thinking that you are already 49 and too old to become a Man and win in life, but your life may not even be halfway over. Today is your day to start living!"

Bob nodded his head boldly and said, "Yes, let's do it. I am sick and tired of believing lies and losing."

The relief of tension was overwhelming as we bowed our heads in prayer, and Bob began to truly repent and finally deal with the issues regarding his father that he had run from for so long. The presence of God Almighty seemed to envelope this precious Man as he told the Lord he truly forgave his Dad for saying such foolish statements throughout his life, and for not displaying the loving insight he needed as a young boy. Bob then forgave his Dad for failing to teach and impart Manhood to him as a father, and for not teaching him about his sexuality or how to conquer lust and pornography.

It was as if we both could literally see the chains of bondage release from Bob's life. Bob could see for the first time in his life he had done the same things to his own young "boys" without even knowing it. Since Bob had not become a Man himself, how could he possibly impart Manhood to his teenage sons? He repented for the same mistakes his father had made, and he then forgave himself for holding onto his childish behaviors for so long.

In addition to this, Bob began to acknowledge all the times he had judged and avoided real Men, because he was jealous and fearful they would cause him more grief. He clearly and deliberately laid out his heart and asked God to give him his Manhood.

Instinctively, Bob knew there is no one better than our true Father in Heaven to pass on the gift of Manhood to His son. Our Lord Jesus was the only perfect Man who ever walked the earth, and even Jesus received the blessing of approval from His Father in Heaven. As it is written in the Book of Matthew, when Jesus formally received the Holy Spirit in baptism and took on the yoke of His calling on earth, the text reveals that out of the clouds came His Father's voice saying, **"This is my beloved Son, in whom I am well pleased."**[2]

What an incredible affirmation it is to have your Father in Heaven speak His approval over you. The good news is this approval is reserved in Heaven for every Man asking for it. It is reserved for every Man who will seek the Lord, knock on the doors of Heaven, and request it.

I then said to Bob "Do you recognize I am a Man?" He responded with a yes, and I put my hand on his shoulders and prayed; ***"Lord, this day I give to this Man what you have so freely given to me. I stand in proxy for his father who is not able to be here at this time. On this day, he is ordained as a full-fledged Man made in your image. May all the blessings and benefits of his Calling rest upon him for all the days of his life. Restore unto him the years that have been eaten away, and lead him into what it fully means to walk as a Man in the image of your perfect Son."***

With that prayer, it was as if the heavens opened for this Man named Bob. Throughout his entire life, his heart was waiting for a Man, any Man, to recognize and declare his Manhood. On this day, it finally happened, and there was no turning back. Bob was now Bar Mitzvahed.

I looked directly into Bob's eyes and said, "I believe God is saying that you are now a Man, and with you He is very pleased." The presence in the atmosphere around us became peaceful and alive. I looked up and noticed how magnificent the sun's rays looked piercing through the oak trees. As tears flowed down Bob's joyful face, I was in awe of the wisdom and simplicity of God's timeless ways.

For thousands of years, males have been receiving Manhood from the Men in their lives through all kinds of different ceremonies, rituals and public events. This was a simple talk between two guys sitting on the patio on a beautiful Saturday morning, but for Bob and me, it was better

---

2 Matthew 3:17, KJV

than a scene from a dramatic movie. Bob had finally received the long awaited victory of his Manhood.

I looked at him again and said, "Are you a Man?"

He responded with authority and excitement I can recall to this day. He said, "Yes, I am a Man! I have received it! You are right, Ken. This is real. All of my life I knew something was missing, and it was so easy to do. God has taken away all of the guilt, shame and condemnation I have battled for most of my life."

With absolute conviction, Bob began talking about how he was going to go home to lead his family as a Man, diploma in hand. Thirty-eight years of hell and defeat from the lie he received at age 11 had ended. The peace of God settled on us both, as we took in this momentous occasion toasting lemonade, arms held high. Bob had achieved his first major victory, but to be sure there were more to come.

"When I was a boy, I spake as a boy, I understood as a boy, I thought as a boy: but when I became a Man, I put away boyish things."[3]
Paul of Tarsus - First Letter to the people of Corinth

Making Things Right:

Bob had just received Manhood in his heart, but I still had to be straight with him. The forgiveness he gave to his father was the key unlocking the prison doors, but I knew the work had only begun. Bob still had to walk out of the prison. I then told Bob if he really wanted to live a life of joy and freedom, he was going to have to face the fact he had done a lot of damage to the females in his life.

I said to him, "Bob, do you realize every time you have included a female in your sins of pornography and sexual indiscretions, you have caused further emotional and spiritual pain and injury to come upon the females in your life?"

3 1 Corinthians 13:11, KJV (boy substituted for child)

Bob looked down at the ground and contemplated what I was saying. He sat there speechless as he began to see the gravity of his sins against women. I could sense he wanted to make excuses for his actions, but he knew instinctively I was not in the mood to listen to any blaming or whining.

The air became tense as I continued to say, "Bob, males naturally seek a connection with the femininity of women. This is the way God made us. God took out of Adam a part of him, a rib, and then He beautifully fashioned a woman. There is always going to be a deep longing for a male to connect with that part missing within him. It is a normal Manly desire to connect with God's feminine creation through healthy relationships with women.

"When the foundation of a relationship is loving and right between a Man and a woman, the woman will respond by blossoming into all her glory. She will radiate the love of God as she pours back blessings into the Man she loves. And this will be the Man who passionately loves and nurtures her.

"In today's promiscuous world, males are forever tempted to fulfill their God-given desire to be complete with a female through sexual gratification only. There is no true relationship being built, and the loving interaction between a Man and woman is not promoted. This is a perversion and misrepresentation of the beauty of a bridegroom uniting with his bride.

"If you are truly able to bond and relate properly with your wife as a Man, your God-given needs will be met. You will feel satisfied with your connection with femininity, because the longing in your heart will be fulfilled. This is another reason why it was so important for you to become a Man today. As a 'boy,' you will never be able to connect with your wife in a way that will fulfill either you or her. As of today, you have the foundation to rebuild the bridges that have been destroyed between you and your wife and daughters.

"Forgiving your Dad is just the precursor to really doing your job as a Man. You must now restore your relationships with the females in your life. Now you have to make things right by asking forgiveness from the people you have hurt. First we forgive others, and then we ask forgiveness from those we have harmed. This is the process we undergo in our walk to freedom as a Man."

Bob nodded his head in agreement as the shame of his actions began to further permeate his countenance. He said, "Okay, I'm hearing you. Tell me more."

I then said, "If you do not recognize the magnitude and the severity of your actions, you are going to have a tough time obtaining the forgiveness your heart so yearns for. It is not until we place the crimes of forgiveness on the altar and admit fully to them, that we can receive mercy from the judge. Do you really realize the consequences of abusing and molesting God's children in any form? You have some serious work to do if you are truly repentant about breaking the physical and emotional boundaries of so many women."

Bob looked at me with fear in his eyes and said, "I know pornography and my indiscretions have hurt my wife and my little girls, but I do not know what to do."

I replied, "I'm sorry, I am not going for that. I believe in your heart you know exactly what you need to do. It is time to get up, wipe off the dirt, and knock off the 'boyish' mentality. You were Bar Mitzvahed and received Manhood today. This means you cannot keep your 'boyish' ways any longer. It is time for you to get trained and start walking as a Man. A Man does not say, 'I don't know what to do.' You are 49 years old for the love of God. A Man will find the Truth. A Man will do what his gut is telling him to do.

"Do you realize, every time you have opened the doors to lust and pornography, you have exposed your wife and little girls to the hoards of hell? You are the leader of your home! Do you want your little girls to end up on the Internet, or in a night club seducing 'boys' to give their Manhood away? You will surely reap what you sow. This is one of the laws of life that no Man can escape, whether he believes in God or not. What is your gut telling you to do? And none of your religious garbage is going to fly here. It is time to get real with your wife and your daughters, because you have maliciously hurt them by behaving like a lustful little 'boy.' What are you going to do?"

I could see Bob had never been challenged like this before in the reserved and friendly Men's church meetings he was so used to attending for the past three decades. His eyes were as big as plates. I did not know if he was thinking of running away, or hitting me. In my heart, I knew I had to be tough with him, but I still had to make sure he knew I really was his ally.

I then said to him, "Bob, I am going to be your friend always. I am speaking with you this way to wake you up. Do you feel I am for you or against you?"

He responded by saying, "I know you are for me; however, I am not used to being challenged like this. But this is okay. For the first time in my life, I need to hear the hard Truth. The people I am around usually do not give it to me straight."

I responded by saying, "Bob, this is one of your problems. You have set up your world by surrounding yourself with people who are afraid to be honest with you. I have to give it to you straight. This behavior is what most 'boys' do. A Man will surround himself with other Men who are not afraid to tell him the truth. I can tell that most of your friends feel sorry for you. They are probably afraid that if they are really honest with you, it will hurt you and cause the friendship to be jeopardized. Is this working for you? Do you want to have your friends afraid to tell you what is really on their minds?

"As a Man, you are no longer allowed to have anyone feel sorry for you. This is what 'boys' do. A 'boy' loves to have people feel sorry for him. A Man cannot stand for someone to feel sorry for him. You have been spiraling down the drain of depression for how many years now? I think it is time to get over yourself, and start living like a Man. It is a tough pill to swallow, but it is easier than the life you have been living. Remember, working for God can be tough. But working for the devil is even tougher, because there is zero victory and zero mercy. What is your heart telling you should be done regarding your wife and little girls?"

Bob looked at me intently with eyes of fire. He said to me, "Honestly Ken, until today I have never been so clear about how bad I have hurt them. I have been focusing more on my failures than I have on the pain and grief I have caused my family. I have been so selfish. I need to ask all of them to forgive me for a lifetime of neglecting them and for my selfish behaviors."

As the last few words came out of Bob's mouth, his voice began to crack and tears started to flow down his cheeks. This time they were not tears of joy, they were tears of honest remorse.

I knew this was going to be one of the best days of his life. I looked right into Bob's eyes and told him it was time to put his sins before God. I said to him, "Bob, I am very proud of you! You are doing it. You're standing up." I shared with him a few additional things as he gently poured out his heart to the heavens.

He then prayed, ***"Oh God, forgive me for hurting my little girls. Forgive me for not taking care of my daughters and my wife. I have been so blind. Please forgive me for the neglect, the pride, the abuse and for any molestation I have committed against any females throughout my life. Have mercy on me. I ask you to somehow turn the curses I have brought upon my family and myself into blessings. I am done with myself. Please help me! I will serve you from this day forward. Amen."***

After hearing Bob pour out his heart to God regarding his mistreatment of the women in his life, it appeared our work was almost done for the day. We sat in silence for quite a while. It felt as if an unseen surgery was occurring in the depth of his being while we gazed up through the spreading oak trees. As I have seen hundreds of times before, Bob had received and understood the miracle of Manhood, and he had taken the first step in the long road to restoration and victory in his life. He declared war over his selfish behaviors, and he dedicated the rest of his life to serving his family. Not bad for a day's work. Bob had really done his job.

As we parted that afternoon, I could see years of bondage and depression had given way to encouragement and hope. I found myself watching Bob walk back down the driveway towards his car a changed Man. It was awe-inspiring. He even had a slight jump in his step. Defeat and failure had been destroyed, and they had disappeared from his countenance. I couldn't help wonder what was in store for him in the days to come, as Bob was about to face down all of the fears challenging him throughout his life.

"We are never defeated unless we give up on God."
Ronald Reagan– 40th President of the United States

Walking It Out:

It is interesting to note what happened following this important day when Bob received his Manhood. Bob did go home and ask his wife and children to forgive him for a lifetime of neglect and abuse. Of course, his family was slow to believe his words; but over time, Bob's actions proved he had indeed changed. They could not deny something great had happened.

Gradually, Bob rebuilt the trust damaged in times past by his selfish actions. Over the following years, he experienced absolute victory over pornography, even though temptations were continually knocking at the doors of his heart. Many times he felt the urges to delve into Internet pornography, but the defeated thoughts of giving away his Manhood and hurting his wife and children were much stronger than the allure of temptations.

Here is the nugget to remember. ***Manhood is power!*** When Bob walked as a "boy," he knew he did not have either the strength or the authority to win. "boys," by definition, simply do not have what it takes to succeed. As a Man, he knew he had absolute authority to overcome the destructive thoughts caused by guilt and every temptation.

Bob actually did enter into pornography again one evening when he was working late at his computer. The immature and "boyish" demeanor he felt come upon him was very upsetting, because it made Bob feel like a "boy" again. In the days following, he became even stronger in overcoming the temptations of lust. Bob learned to immediately shut down the damaging attacks from the enemy of his soul by using the principles outlined in Chapters 3 and 4 of this book.

It was amazing how his wife and children perceived the change in Bob from "boy" to Man. Bob began to impart Manhood into his two young Men, and he began to provide an emotional security to his wife and his daughters he had failed to provide in the past. Both of his sons had already developed similar lust problems in their teens, and his daughters at a young age were already behaving in a promiscuous manner. Thankfully, Bob's victory quickly became their victory. His new strength as a Man was truly making an impact.

What a contrast to the days when he walked as a "boy." Bob recalled what it was like after falling into the temptations of pornography when he was a "boy." He would sulk and blame himself for weeks and months at a time with no victory in sight. This exposed his family to a life of loss, discouragement and oppression. To make matters worse, he would then blame his wife and his children for not assisting him or being behind him the way "The Bible" says they should.

What a miserable existence his family was delivered from. Bob's family was being asked by him to give honor and respect to a rebellious "boy," who was masquerading as the head of the family. Thank God Bob became a Man. After seeing his horrific errors, Bob asked every member of his family to forgive him for abusing them with wrongly applied biblical verses and his "boyish" manipulations. Due to the changes Bob made, he soon began to feel the respect and love from his wife that he had so long strived for. Not a day goes by where everyone is not thankful in their hearts for the great victory taking place in Bob's household.

Of course, he has a lot of work to do. Just because he made the choice to receive Manhood, this did not mean everything became perfect overnight. Men can take either the blame or credit for what they impart to their children. Bob decided he would rather receive the credit for getting it right. Bob had spent the first 49 years of his life walking as a "boy." It will take several years and maybe decades for all the repercussions of his bad choices to be healed.

Even now, Bob is still hard at work rebuilding trust with his wife, and he is honoring his family by walking in his newfound authority. The good news is, Bob is winning! Today, Bob has hope as well as the tools to win, because he has chosen to become a Man. He is learning how to use his Keys of authority, which will be discussed in depth in Chapter 3 of this book. Good going Bob!

"As long as you're breathing, it's never too late to become a Man."

2

Overcoming and Obtaining Manhood

"To him that overcomes will I grant to sit with Me in My throne, even as I also overcame, and am set down with My Father in his throne."[1]
Jesus of Nazareth

Why is Man vs. "boy" So Important?

Speaking in front of a large group of people as I was delivering the "Man vs. boy" message, I was compelled to ask the following: "By a show of hands, how many males in this auditorium feel like they are losing in life's battles and challenges? I am not talking about having a bad hair day or getting a flat tire. I am asking if you feel overall that your life has been

1 Revelation 3:21, KJV

a loss. Are you losing in life? Do you feel like you have not been getting the victory for years, and because of this, you are very discouraged and hopeless? If this is you, be honest with yourself and please raise your hand."

I looked across the platform into the seats to see over half the males in the audience slowly raising their hands with a solemn guilt pasted across their faces. Something was happening in the room that was on the borderline of frightening. Most of us know there is a huge problem with the status of the 21st century male, but seeing so many males publicly admit they felt that their life was a failure was an overwhelming and sad experience.

To compound the drama of this delicate moment, I recall the dumbfounded looks from those Men sitting next to them who had no idea so many males were struggling right in their very midst. The whole episode rolled out before me appearing as a pathetic army not knowing which way to face as we gathered for our first roll call. With shame in my heart, I thought, "God, this is your people? This is your army? What have we allowed ourselves to become?"

My heart sank as the gravity of the scene played out in a moment of silence, and I knew I must challenge and encourage these Men.

I then said, "Is this acceptable? Again, is this acceptable to us? Please, look around. Is it okay that we sit next to our friends and families month after month and fail to see or acknowledge that the failures and losses of our loved ones are scattered across the battlefield?

"Our United States military trains our soldiers that no Man is to be left behind in battle. Did not Jesus say that He would leave 99 of his sheep in the fold, to go save the one sheep that is lost in the wilderness? Here are our brothers, and they need us! They are hurting and they are dying, and behind every one of these brothers are women and children who are also hurting, because there is not an available Man to lead them."

I went on to say, "The Bible is clear. Pure religion before God and the Father is this; to visit the fatherless and widows in their affliction, and to keep ourselves clean from the evil of this world. And we call ourselves religious? We call ourselves clean? Look around at the fatherless. We are the fatherless! Our children are the fatherless, because many of us have not been taught how to be a loving and protecting father. Our wives are the widows, because many of us have never stepped up to the task at hand of making the choice to be a Man by taking care of them like God takes care of us.

"We have fallen away from our first Callings, because we are too self consumed and busy to notice or care that right next to us are many hurting people. Family breakdowns, financial problems, addictions, pornography and neglect to our God-given relationships and duties have permeated our army. How can we watch each other's backs, when we are losing so badly in our personal lives? If one of us is suffering, we all suffer. Men! It is time to take a stand!"

I knew in my heart right then and there it was time to declare war. It was time for the "boy" in us to die, and for the Man in us to stand up and live. The Man vs. "boy" war was on, and oh what a battle this would be. I knew we needed additional tools to help us obtain the victory. It was time to write a book, and no punches could be withheld. Men must be trained, and they must be trained today to fight like never before.

The Man vs. "boy" List:

After more than 20 years of troubleshooting various companies, corporations, ministries and the personal lives of many Men, I have chosen the Man vs. "boy" list as my favorite tool for determining the maturity of a male. Like being born into this world or being born-again, obtaining Manhood is something that either has happened or it has not. The Man vs. "boy" list is like a mirror letting you know areas of your life needing attention.

The Man vs. "boy" list was derived from the many Biblical references in the Old Testament (Hebrew Bible) and the New Testament defining what it is to be a Man with character. Since the Bible is God's written covenant of redemption for Men, it probably is no surprise the Bible uses the word "Man" over 2500 times. The Bible has much to say about being a Man.

Webster's dictionary defines Manhood as "The state of being a Man, and having masculine character and qualities such as virility, courage and resolution." Is this what you see when you look in the mirror? Do you see virility, courage and resolution?

Different dictionaries may have slightly different definitions for Manhood; however, most definitions use the phrase "State of being a Man." The state of "Being a Man" is something so tangible and noticeable, most people can attest to whether a male is either a Man or a "boy." There is an unseen diploma issued when a "boy" has become a Man. Do you have this diploma? Do the males around you have this diploma? You may want to look at the Man vs. "boy" list again to test yourself.

In addition to this diploma, there are special Keys of authority given to Men that are specifically his to use throughout his lifetime as he overcomes the challenges of life. When a male fails to receive his Mandated diploma and the Keys of authority given with this diploma, he has sentenced himself to a life of defeat, discouragement and bewilderment. However, when a male receives this diploma of Manhood and learns to acknowledge and utilize the Keys of authority ordained for him, everybody wins and the Man will journey through life overcoming all challenges thrown at him as he fulfills his true Mandate.

Obtaining Your "Man Diploma":

A diploma is a specific written proclamation designating an achievement in a specific field of study. Behind each diploma are months and even years of learning, studying, obedience and impartation. It is both a process and an event. This process is crucial; however, the diploma is crucial as well. Both are generally needed for success in a field of expertise.

When individuals complete the requirements for high school, college or any type of schooling, they are usually given a diploma. When an Attorney passes the State Bar exam, he is given the credentials and the license to practice law. When a Contractor passes a State test for a Contractors license, he is given the legal right and a license to operate as a Contractor. He either has a diploma or a license for a certain achievement, or he does not.

The same goes for Manhood. You are either a Man, or you are not. Once you have become a Man, you still have the choice to walk as a Man or to behave like a "boy." Just as an Attorney can choose to quit his practice and not use his credentials as an attorney any longer, any

Man can choose to walk as a "boy." There is no gray area. Manhood and "boyishness" do not mix.

This becomes even more evident when you consider the Man vs. "boy" list. The difference in behavior between a Man and a "boy" is as noticeable as the difference between night and day. As mentioned before, most people usually agree on whether a certain male is either a Man or a "boy," it literally feels like the person has received a "Man Diploma." As Bob found out in the previous story, Manhood is very real. The Jewish culture has always recognized and understood this truth about Manhood. Therefore, let us next look at the Jewish tradition of Bar Mitzvah.

"I will insist the Hebrews have [contributed] more to civilize men than any other nation. If I was an atheist and believed in blind eternal fate, I should still believe that fate had ordained the Jews to be the most essential instrument for civilizing the nations … They are the most glorious nation that ever inhabited this Earth. The Romans and their empire were but a bubble in comparison to the Jews. They have given religion to three-quarters of the globe and have influenced the affairs of mankind more and more happily than any other nation, ancient or modern."

John Adams - 2nd President of the United States

The Bar Mitzvah:

In Jewish tradition, when a young "boy" reaches the age of 13 he is given a ceremony called a "Bar Mitzvah." This ceremony is a social event in Judaism marking the coming of age of a young male into the Jewish community by acknowledging his Manhood. As a newly initiated adult Man, he is now responsible to fulfill all of his moral and cultural duties before God.

In Hebrew, Bar Mitzvah is translated as "son of the commandments." This implies the Bar Mitzvah or "son of the commandments" must now obey, fulfill and honor all of the 613 commandments given in the Torah as written by Moses. The Torah is the first 5 books of the Hebrew Bible (Old Testament).

The Bar Mitzvah is the acknowledgment by society that the young male is no longer a "boy." He formally receives Manhood for the rest of his life, and he is expected to act as a Man from that day forward. The solidification of his Manhood is both instantaneous and permanent. The Bar Mitzvah ceremony is the milestone affirming a young Man's identity as a Man of God who is responsible for the proactive disciplines of the Torah (The Law). The Torah is a written expression of God's heart. Chapter 3 of this book will tie in the importance of our hearts.

Before the Bar Mitzvah, all the actions and behaviors of the "boy" are the responsibility of his father. If the "boy" lies or steals, his father takes responsibility and pays. Historically, if the "boy" hurt or even killed someone or something, the father took responsibility and paid for all damages.

After the ceremony of the Bar Mitzvah, the young Man must take full responsibility for every action in his life. He must now pay for all his mistakes. As a Man, he is fully responsible for the legal, moral, emotional and spiritual implications and repercussions of all his actions. If he chooses to display any of the behaviors in the "boy" category previously listed, there will be social, cultural and even legal repercussions. On the same note, if he exhibits the responsible and loving characteristics of a Man, there is incredible respect, love and honor reserved for him by his family and their culture.

It is important to note, many times a Jewish young Man in history would live at home with his father to the age of 30. His father's role moves from a teacher who lovingly disciplines to a coach who lovingly encourages. Living in a learning environment with his father in no way is a statement he is still a "boy." This is actually a highly effective training system where the father will spend many years teaching and training the young Man how to walk as a Man and properly utilize his Keys of authority.

This process acknowledges there are two phases to getting victory as a Man. The first phase is receiving Manhood through an impartation from one Man to another via the Bar Mitzvah. The second phase is the timely discipleship of a son as he learns how to walk and win as a Man. This reemphasizes the point you must first become a Man before you are able to win as a Man. If you are wondering where the Jewish people learned such effective and prosperous training principles for their young Men, they are all found and taught abundantly in the Hebrew Bible (Old Testament).

Historically, Men in every culture have embraced the initiation of males into Manhood in some form. The right of passage of Men is a timeless and poignant principle written on the heart of every male. It is a Man's greatest responsibility in life to share his faith, passion and Manhood with his son.

Manhood is to be built upon and solidified by the father and son relationship, and it is to be founded upon the loving blessings imparted. Sadly, Men in America have made a significant departure from the principles of Manhood. We must embrace the principles of the Bar Mitzvah once again if we are to save the American family structure. Men must be equipped and trained to go into battle in strength and victory.

Every male must know he has a right to pass into Manhood. He must publicly declare with confidence in the presence of other Men he is a bona fide Man of God. His public declaration of Manhood becomes an eternal diploma engraved in his soul. This diploma becomes a tangible marker giving him confidence, strength and boldness in his times of need. He will always know he is an affirmed and blessed Man of God, because loving and sincere Men have taken the time to ensure his right of passage into Manhood.

If your upbringing did not include the principles of acknowledging and encouraging your right of passage into Manhood, it is not too late for you. In the chapters following, you will journey with other males as they return back and pick up the Manhood left behind in childhood. Just as in the case of Bob in Chapter 1, you too can capture back everything lost. If you are a Man who has already received Manhood and are familiar with your right of passage, read on and learn how regular unassuming Men achieve the fullness of victory.

The Band of Brothers!

Shakespeare's "Henry V"

William Shakespeare wrote plays during a time in England when the Bible and the principles of walking as a true and distinguished "gentleman" were permeating the British Isles. He was the Man who coined the term Band of Brothers as he described what was the true nature and conduct of what it meant to be a "gentleman" of England. Look at his words of encouragement for Men to rise up as a Band of Brothers at a time when the nation needed the Men to stand and fight.

"We few, we happy few, we band of brothers;
For he to-day that sheds his blood with me
Shall be my brother; be he ne'er so vile,
This day shall gentle his condition;
And gentlemen in England now-a-bed
Shall think themselves accurs'd they were not here,
And hold their Manhoods cheap whiles any speaks
That fought with us upon Saint Crispin's day."
St. Crispin's Day Speech
Shakespeare's HENRY V - C. 1599

Interpretation on St. Crispin's Day Speech:

We may be few but we are happy, because we have become a Band of Brothers and companions in a worthy cause. He who gives his all today and sheds his blood with me shall be my brother. Even if you were a vile human being with no reputation or title, you are now my respected brother if you are here to fight with me this day. And this day you will become knighted as a true gentleman of England. The so-called knights of England who are not here to fight with me are home in bed even as we speak.

These so called "gentlemen" who are sleeping in their beds, and who have failed to show up for this fight, are going to curse themselves for not partaking in today's battle. If anyone of us who fights today speaks about this battle fought on St. Crispin's Day, these so called gentlemen will know they have missed it, and they will hold their Manhood as cheap because they have failed to show up and to fight. These so called gentlemen are not Men. These gentlemen should have chosen to fight with us in honor, but instead they have chosen to sleep away the day and sacrifice their Manhood.

The American Dream:

America was founded by a Band of Brothers who proved themselves gentlemen as they fought for the causes of Truth and freedom. Shakespeare's St. Crispin's Day call to arms is quite appropriate for the 21st century male. It has become obvious America today is inundated with "boys" who do not have their Man Diplomas. Using the phraseology of Jewish culture, many American males have not been Bar Mitzvahed. Using the ranch/contractor mentality I grew up with, many American males just do not have their balls.

America has become a nation full of mama's boys and metro-sexuals. We have developed a neutered Peter Pan pseudo-maleness that is incapable of imparting true Manhood. Even when American "boys" come into their Manhood, they are so untrained in utilizing their Keys of authority, that they display many of the characteristics of the "boy" from the Man vs. "boy" list. Do you remember when the worst thing you could call a male was a sissy, a coward or a chicken? The feminization of the males in our culture has hurt and dismantled the family structure that made America a leader in the world, and it has diminished the prosperity Americans experience in the marketplace.

Since the beginning of our nation, from the pilgrims to the founding fathers, we were a nation of Men. The great pioneers of the past pledged even unto death to preserve our great society of prosperity and freedom we enjoy. Our desire for self-sufficiency, our taming of America's tough lands and our core belief in God demanded it. We have become the strongest and most influential nation in history, because we were founded by Men who held their ground, and expounded the great principles of freedom, self-government and the pursuit of happiness and property[2].

At this solemn hour, we too must pledge ourselves afresh to the next generation and pass on to them this great gift of a nation that is strong, prosperous and free. America began as a nation of Men. Let us continue to be a nation of Men.

In America over the last century, there has been a systematic and continual disappearance of the process of leading "boys" into Manhood. Why do we not see in today's males the same strength, faith, resolution and courage that were found so prevalently in the Men returning from World War II. The honorable character seen from that era has lead many to consider those Men as "The Greatest Generation?" Men like these are hard to find nowadays. We can therefore see why America has been on a downward spiral, circling the drain of failure. The lack of Men has lead to a lack of authority and power.

This failure is compounded as even more and more "boys" are missing this process as they wander through life. They remain "boys" well into their 20's, 30's, 40' and even 50's, and often have very little masculine authority to give or impart to their sons. You cannot give what you do not have. To our shame, in America there are fewer Men around to teach and bestow this important and critical impartation of becoming a Man, and we have become weak. Never in recorded world history do we find such a shortage of Men and fathers.

The key to the future of the United States of America is in the hands of the Men who decide to follow the God of our forefathers. Turning our nation around will require a great vision, a great plan, a great commitment and great Men. True greatness is found in a consistency of vision and persistence. It is time to be great Men and commit ourselves to a new vision with purpose.

Today I am placing before you a worthy cause and a renewed pledge of allegiance to be Men and one of the Band of Brothers, so our nation can fulfill its destiny as a shining light upon a hill. This cause will take all of the resolve we can find, all of the energy we can deliver and all of the commitment we can promise.

---

2 Property – Many Founding State Constitutions include property as a basic right

Once and for all, we can unite this nation under a Judeo-Christian banner and a common idea whose time has come, with a power that cannot be subdued. It can begin with you. Our first order of business is to become the Men we are destined to be, for Men are the foundational building blocks of our nation. If this message resonates in your heart, enlist with thousands of other Men into the "Man vs. boy" Band of Brothers by visiting or website at www.Manvsboy.com. Together, we will make the difference.

"Anyone can give up, it's the easiest thing in the world to do. But hold it together when everyone would understand if you fell apart, that's true strength."
John Calvin Coolidge - 30th President of the United States

Facts Vs. Truth:

If we are serious about overcoming as Men, it is imperative we understand the difference between facts and Truth. I will make this short and sweet for you. Men follow the Truth, and "boys" follow selfishly selected facts. Facts represent data. Truth is the God breathed interpretation of the data. Let us use Abraham Lincoln as an example. I will give you some facts about his life.

Abraham Lincoln Facts:

1816	His family was forced to be homeless.
1831	Failed in business.
1832	Ran for state legislature - lost. Rejected from law school.
1833	Borrowed money for a business and went bankrupt again.
1835	Engaged to be married, fiancé died and broke his heart.
1836	Had total nervous breakdown - bedridden for six months.
1838	Sought to become speaker of state legislature - defeated.

1840	Sought to become elector - defeated.
1843	Ran for Congress - lost.
1848	Ran for re-election to Congress - lost.
1849	Sought the job of land officer in his home state - rejected.
1854	Ran for Senate of the United States - lost.
1856	Vice-Presidential nomination and received under 100 votes.
1858	Ran for U.S. Senate again - again he lost.

What would your deduction be about this Man regarding his success in life? If you simply followed only the data given, you would probably miss the Truth and deduce honest Abe was a loser. However, the Truth is much different. Abraham Lincoln left a mark on our lands forever giving him position as a victor. Lincoln is a picture of character, persistence and integrity. It is a good thing Lincoln did not read this list of facts and believe them as Truth. We would have lost a great leader.

If you want to learn about somebody who didn't quit, here is your Man. He was born into poverty and he faced defeat throughout his life. He lost eight elections, twice failed in business and suffered a nervous breakdown. He could have quit numerous times, but he chose to be a Man. Lincoln was a champion because he never gave up. Ultimately, in 1860, he became one of the greatest presidents in the history of our country. This is the Truth.

Today's media companies are masters of using facts to get people to believe what they want them to believe. When only negative facts and data are presented, people usually come up with a negative conclusion. On the other hand, if a media company desires for you to have a positive view of someone or something, they will only present positive data.

The problem with both of these examples is they have nothing to do with the Truth. Truth is determined in your heart as it is revealed by the author of Truth, God. As you read through this book and make decisions about where you are in life, remember not to deceive yourself with data leading you away from the Truth, for it is the Truth that makes you free.

Sorry Vs. Forgiveness:

A few years back, I was asked to help in restoring the relationship between a father and son. The son's name was Adam. He was 19 years old at the time. His father's name was Jeff. Jeff was a successful businessman who loved his son dearly. Adam had been working for his father for many years and had developed excellent computer skills. He had performed work for me as well, and he always proved to be both a proficient and responsible worker. But there was a big problem. Adam's lack of forgiveness towards his father was keeping him under his Dad's control, and it was sentencing him to living his life as a "boy."

One day, I noticed Adam was acting differently during work. I asked him if there was something wrong. The floodgates just opened up as he began to tell me his Dad had developed a pornography problem over the past few years. He confided with me that he had repeatedly discovered massive amounts of illicit websites on his Dad's computer, and he was heartbroken about it. His father was his idol, and his father was considered a respected member of his community.

Adam went on to say he had mentioned the sites to his Dad, and his Dad said in cavalier fashion he was "sorry." He implied most of the time he was going on the sites for research purposes for his work. Many times, Adam's father asked him to remove the embarrassing evidence off the history of his computer.

This secret was crippling Adam, and he had never shared it with anyone. His loss of respect and bitterness against his Dad had kept him from receiving Manhood. Eventually, Adam moved out of the house and set some major boundaries with his Dad, but there was no reconciliation in their relationship.

All three of us met to see if they could start the healing process in the relationship. Father and son sat across the table from one another painfully pretending they were comfortable. The gap between them appeared insurmountable. The son was distant and on guard, because he decided he was not going to allow his father to hurt him anymore. His father, though he had and a strong and commanding personality, played the victim. He kept saying Adam was overreacting, and there was no reason for their relationship to be so distant.

After 20 minutes of getting nowhere with both Adam and Jeff restating their views on the matter *ad nausea*, I asked Jeff if he had ever asked for forgiveness for including his son in his indiscretions.

Jeff quickly responded by saying, "I have said, 'I am sorry,' many times!"

I then said to Jeff, "'Sorry' is an emotion or a feeling, forgiveness is a new contract. There is a huge difference."

Jeff denied there was any difference between saying "I am sorry" and "forgive me." He then retorted, "They are the same thing, you're splitting hairs!"

I asked Adam if his father had ever actually asked for forgiveness, and he said, "Absolutely not!" Jeff proceeded to say he was "sorry" to Adam eight different times over the next half an hour. Yes, I counted every time he said, "I am sorry." Each time there was zero reconciliation.

The air was thick and tense with this horrible feeling of discomfort. How awful it is when there is discord between people, especially between father and son. They were at an impasse, and Jeff was not budging on the forgiveness principle.

Finally, with a little force, I got strong with Jeff. I said, "Jeff, if there is no difference between 'I am sorry' and 'forgive me,' then you won't have any problem asking for forgiveness, because you have already said 'I am sorry' numerous times. Jeff looked at me with fearful and nervous eyes. I knew he was cornered by the Truth.

Adam then chimed in and said, "Yes, Dad if they are the same, then you can say 'forgive me' just as easily!"

Jeff looked at his son and paused for what seemed like minutes. He broke the long silence by saying, "Son, will you f- f –f - f." And this is all he could say. He looked at me as if I was a police officer ready to arrest him for breaking and entering, and then he tried again. "Will you f –ff-f –ff." Can you even believe it? This guy could not say, "Forgive me" to his son.

I had always known in my heart there was a big difference in these two humbling acts of repentance, but right before my eyes what I was witnessing was astounding. This father could easily say he was sorry to his son, but he could not say the words "Forgive me."

I then said to Jeff, "Are you getting it Jeff? Forgiveness is God's way of reconciling relationships. Inside your heart, you know this is true. This is why you are struggling with asking for forgiveness. I have a lot to say to you if you can bear to hear it."

Jeff looked at me helplessly. He sat stunned in his seat.

I said, "When we ask for forgiveness, we are signing a new contract to repair the fact there has been a breach in the relationship. This contract says both parties agree to clear the slate of all offenses that have occurred, and they will start out fresh and new in the relationship. This is great news for you if you can grasp what I am telling you. You have the opportunity here to take advantage of one of God's greatest gifts to us, forgiveness.

"The relational principle of forgiveness leads us directly to the cross Jesus endured for the purpose of bringing us back into a relationship with our Father in heaven. We can forgive one another because God our Father in heaven has granted us forgiveness through His Son. Saying, 'Please forgive me' is totally different from saying, 'I am sorry.' 'I am sorry' may be a nice gesture to mend someone's hurt feelings by letting them know you feel sorrow, but it does little to nothing to repair the spiritual offense that occurred.

"'Sorry' is really a poor and weak attempt at repairing trust. When we say we are sorry, most of the time we are only trying to appease or placate the person we offended. 'Sorry' is the 'boys' way of trying to slide by without really getting the job done. When you ask for forgiveness, you are actually taking the first step in rebuilding trust by establishing a new covenant with the person you have offended."

Jeff looked at me again like a deer in the headlights with his mouth stuck half open. I motioned to his son and asked him again, "For the love of God, please ask your son for forgiveness for the pain you have put him through these past years, so you can begin to rebuild your relationship with him."

I could see something was sinking in as Jeff began to slowly nod his head. He then looked at his son and said, "Please forgive..." and before he got out the word "me," he began to weep like a child.

This was not an ordinary cry. This cry came from the depths of his heart. I could tell God was doing a deep work in this Man who had finally humbled himself before his son. I knew instinctively Jeff was severely abused by his father as a child, and later Jeff shared all the details of a life filled with insecurity and a longing for the love of his father.

The beautiful thing that occurred was that immediately after Jeff asked his son for forgiveness, the heavens seemed to open. All of the strife and the uncomfortable feeling of heaviness just vanished away as the peaceful presence of God fell over our table like a warm blanket. If I ever had any doubt there was a difference between saying, "sorry" or in asking for forgiveness, it is gone forever now. Sorry is for "boys." Forgiveness is for Men.

I will never forget the peace I saw in Adam as he said to his father, "Yes, Dad, I forgive you. And please forgive me for not standing up sooner and being honest with you about what I was going through."

As I watched the interaction take place, I noticed that Adam was a Man. This was the first time he had ever fully addressed his Dad Man to Man, and by doing so he overcame the controlling pecking order that had developed in their relationship. It was so clear; Men forgive. To become a Man, we must forgive, and we must ask for forgiveness for our failures. I was so proud of Adam.

I left the meeting in awe of God and his principle of forgiveness. The relationship between Adam and Jeff did not become perfect overnight. Time is always a critical factor in building back trust and closeness after they have been lost. Over the following months, Adam and Jeff continued to work on their relationship. The important point is the principle of forgiveness allowed Adam and Jeff to rebuild on a new and solid foundation.

As each one of us moves forward to achieve our goals, remember the principle of forgiveness is one of our strongest and most powerful tools for fully obtaining our Manhood and for restoring the relationships we have neglected. Forgiveness is the door we must pass through to obtain our Keys of authority, and forgiveness is the cornerstone of our character for the Man we are called to be. I suggest you get used to saying, "Forgive me" to God and to your loved ones, because every imperfect Man will need to use this powerful tool often, if he desires to fulfill his Great Mandate.

Chiropractic Adjustment:

As someone who has spent a great deal of time on ranches and building homes, I have had my share of back issues. There have been times I have been taken totally out of commission because of a very small misalignment of my spine. I would go for years as strong as an ox, but after just one wrong twist or movement something would go out of alignment.

There have been a few times I found myself almost totally incapacitated. One time, I could only lie down and look up at the ceiling for nearly two days. I could barely get dressed to even go visit the chiropractor. Thank God I have a chiropractor that is excellent at what he does. After a few adjustments by my doctor and some very heartfelt prayer by me, to my astonishment, I walked out of the office feeling like a different person. It still took a few days to get back to normal, but the adjustments made by him took me from being totally incapacitated to actually functioning fairly normal.

This reminds me of how most males are walking around as they attempt to overcome the challenges put before them as Men. The process of becoming a Man and walking with your Keys in hand is no different than the chiropractic adjustments I would receive from time to time. Once the vertebras were put in order, everything else would then strengthen in my physical body.

And so it is with Men. In general, after we find God, we are not broken. We simply need alignments. I used to go for months with back problems and just hope it would work itself out. Maybe it would, or maybe it would not. But now I choose to deal with life straight on and take care of business immediately. Why do we walk around in pain and loss if we don't have to, especially since it is so easy to make the proper adjustments? The answer is, through both ignorance and lack of training, we have failed to defeat public enemy number one, fear.

Defeating Fear:

As we saw in the stories about Bob and Adam, forgiveness is the key to unlocking a males Manhood. After we are determined to be a Man, then the real battle begins. This is the battle against fear.

Deep inside, every male knows when he has missed it, and he knows he is allowing fear to conquer him. Men can usually recognize when there is a huge hole in the core of his being where fear is chewing him up. All the more reason for males to reassess their lives and make sure they get it right.

The solution to the Man vs. "boy" question is every male must declare war against fear, and he must defeat fear. Every male desires the courage of a lion. Courage, by most Men's definition, is overcoming and defeating fear. Every Man must dedicate his heart and soul to destroying the enemy of fear, so he can move forward to achieve his Great Mandate. Fear cannot be tolerated. In every sense of the word, fear must be challenged, beaten down, conquered and destroyed.

Fear can come in many different forms. It may be fear of loss, fear of consequences, fear of what others think or even fear of failing. In my football story, my fear of failure and my fear of experiencing intense physical pain at practice brought out my "boyish" behaviors. Fear is the one common denominator bringing "boys" to the place where they are compelled to lie and be irresponsible cowards. Thus, it is imperative we overcome fear, because fear is a building block for our selfish "boyish" behaviors.

The good news is: overcoming fear through life's challenges is what makes life exciting and fulfilling. We all love movies like "Rudy," "Hoosiers," "Rocky" or "Remember the Titans," because these movies play on the timeless theme about "boys" who overcome fear and the challenges of life. In all great movies there is a common theme where males are challenged to the core of their hearts by fear. This challenge calls for us to make a choice. We can play the "poor old guy" and cower to fear, or we can choose this day the victory by following after the Man who resides deep within each of us.

Here is a simple tool to conquer fear. It is called Truth. Fear is an imposter that can only lie to you. Fear says in your mind, "I am going to lose! I am no good! Bad things are going to happen to me!" The Truth says, "I can overcome any problem thrown at me. I can do it! After I conquer this problem, there is a huge promotion waiting for me." Anyone can turn the tables on fear immediately. ***You must*** only make the choice to believe this simple Truth.

Every problem comes with the opportunity to overcome and reap the rewards. When a Man learns that behind every challenge, every problem and every crisis there is a promotion and additional Keys of authority awaiting him, fear is done. When fear is exposed as the weak liar it is, we are embarrassed to admit we have given power to something so fraudulent and powerless.

Fear is nothing but smoke and mirrors presented by your enemies. Fear may feel real, but it has no power at all when we expose it for what it is and thereby remove our Keys of authority (our power) from it. Fear is a liar and an imposter. The sooner we defeat fear and expose it as a liar and an imposter, the sooner we conquer and destroy it. Next is the story of Brian. He is an example of a Man who declared war on fear and won the battle at hand.

***"For God has not given us a spirit of fear; but of power, and of love, and of a sound mind."*[3]**
The Apostle Paul – Letter to Timothy

Brian:

Brian and I were on the airplane heading for Dallas to buy real estate. We were talking about our families and other small talk. Brian is the leader of a national defense institute, an organization fighting the legal battle for the religious rights of families, churches and businesses. As we were talking, he began to tell me about some tensions at his office in regard to how he was getting along with his employees. Brian was very concerned about the situation, and he had lost all peace in his heart concerning the matter.

The conversation became more serious as he turned and said to me, "I need your advice. I keep having rebellious employees who do not respect my authority, and I am fearful of having to go through the pain of finding more new employees. Not long before this trip, I had to fire

3 2 Timothy 1:7, KJV

several employees who were insubordinate and not respectful of me and my authority."

I could see by his countenance he felt very jaded and fearful. As he continued to share the situation, it became apparent to both of us that his thoughts and feelings of fear were manifesting themselves through all of his employees.

Brian continued, "I am fearful the new employees will do the same as the previous employees have done, and cause more grief and strife in the office. I am starting to see just because an employee has a cross around his neck, it does not mean he respects authority or strives to maintain a team spirit."

I looked at Brian intently and said to him, "Brian, please stop!" I could tell he was taken back by my boldness But I gave him a reassuring gesture and continued. I said, "Brian, can I share with you my heart on the matter?"

Brian eagerly nodded and said "Yes, of course."

I then said, "You have lost your Keys, because you believe a lie. The problem with believing lies is they always come with grief and bondage." Brian was all ears, and he urged me to continue.

Since Brian was all ears and urged me to continue, I further said, "You are blaming your employees for something that is clearly your responsibility. Your employees shouldn't respect your authority, if you are not going to take responsibility for everything going on in the office. You are spreading fear all around like a virus. Do you think maybe your fear is pushing your employees to respond in an inappropriate manner?"

Brian backed up in his seat as he contemplated what I had just said to him. I could tell this was a tough blow to him, but I loved him enough to be honest with him. He gently nodded his head and asked me to explain more about this concept of the Keys.

I then shared with Brian a few principles on the Man vs. "boy" list. I specifically told him about how a Man is never allowed to blame anyone for anything, if he desires to have authority and be respected as a Man. I told him plainly, "If a Man blames, he is going to lose some Keys of authority, and it is going to hurt someone."

One of the traits I really like about Brian is his ability to listen intently to what I have to say as he considers my position. This is what makes him one of the best attorneys in the nation. Just when I thought he was about to come back with one of his well-constructed courtroom arguments, he just put his head down in his hands and sighed. He said, "Oh Abba Father! You're right. I am walking in fear, and I have allowed fear to permeate the office."

Right there on the airplane at 30,000 feet, I saw a Man repent before God for acting as a "boy." He said to me, "I just realized God does not want me to be driven by fear. It is unfair to my employees for me to allow fear to control or drive them crazy. I have been operating in a management style that has hurt relationships with my employees, and I have been obsessed with micro-managing at their expense. My fear has translated into micro-management."

Brian then prayed right there on the plane. He said, "Lord, forgive me for walking in fear, and for giving my Keys of authority away, and for allowing it in my office. I am done with you. Fear, I am done with you! Get out of my life, now!"

I was taken aback as I saw this Man next to me experience something extraordinary. He was transforming right before me. At that point, with a little guidance he took his Keys back in force. A calm and even heavenly countenance came over Brian. He next told me he felt relieved and empowered. He saw clearly that the fear and worry was the major problem he was battling, and through his prayer he knew fear was defeated on this day.

Brian then said, "On Monday, I am going to walk in the office with boldness and call an immediate staff meeting." Right on cue, on Monday, Brian did call for the staff meeting. He phoned me excitedly later in the day and said, "I did have the staff meeting. You wouldn't believe the looks on their faces. I brought them all into the conference room and said, 'I am sorry. I need to ask each and every one of you to forgive me, because I have been in sin.'

"The staff then looked at me with jaws dropped, wondering what in the world was happening with me. I then said, 'I have been guilty of the sin of fear. And God has not given us a spirit of fear; He has given us a Spirit of power, love and a sound mind. Yet I have been guilty of fear, and I have allowed fear to affect the way I have treated all of you. Fear will never exist in this office or in my management style from this day forward.

I will not allow it to exist here, and we are going to move forward with the confidence and the promises God has given us.'"

Ever since that moment, Brian's office has been functioning smoothly. Everyone respects one another, and the employees on staff are incredibly dynamic. They all noticeably display a servant's heart. Brian now says, "When fear rises up anywhere around me, I immediately recognize it and stamp it out, because I know how damaging and fatal fear can be! I will never give away my Keys to fear again!" Way to go, Brian! A Man will admit when he is wrong, and he will always strive to make things right.

"It often requires more courage to dare to do right than to fear to do wrong."
Abraham Lincoln – 16th President of the United States

Training Men:

There is a verse that says, **"My people are destroyed for a lack of knowledge."**[4] Most males have never been trained properly on how to recapture their Keys of authority, or to destroy fear in all its forms. When it comes down to becoming a Man and walking as a Man, ignorance is not bliss. Our lack of training is keeping many of us in serious bondage, and it is keeping us from overcoming. There is a secret every male must know if he is to overcome fear. We are given special Keys of authority to conquer fear.

I urge you now to take your stand and keep reading. You can learn today how to annihilate fear and all of its ugly friends by recapturing all of your Keys of authority. Becoming a Man through forgiveness is only Step #1 of your Mandate. Learning to walk with your Keys in hand by overcoming fear is Step #2. This next chapter will explain all about the Keys of authority a Man is given, and how to retrieve them back when lost.

---

4 Hosea 4:6, KJV

3 Your Keys

"It is not the critic who counts. Not the man who points out how the strong Man stumbled or where the doer of deeds could have done better. The credit belongs to the Man who is actually in the arena. Whose face is marred by dust and sweat and blood. Who strives valiantly, who errs and comes up short again and again."

Theodore Roosevelt - 26th President of the United States

Men Who Behave Like "boys" – and Lose!

Okay, so maybe you think you are already a Man. You were Bar Mitzvahed sometime in the past and you know you have your Manhood. Men and women will both follow you into battle, but you know there still is a big problem. You are losing in areas of your life, and at times people are following you right off a cliff. You and your loved ones are getting slaughtered because you are behaving more like a "boy" straight from the Man vs. "boy" list than you are a Man. You are getting slammed because you have lost your Keys!

You may be untrained, or maybe you have been just plain unwilling to change in certain areas of your life. If you are like most Men, your lack of training and lack of knowledge has caused you to become discouraged and a little angry. You may be outwardly going through the motions, but inside, your heart has just shut down.

Either way, the important point here is this; if you are losing on many battlefronts, it's most likely because you have given away your Keys, and you probably do not even realize it yet. Most males today are untrained and afraid to admit their weaknesses. Let me assure you that there is hope. If you are willing to put on your army gear and look at the problem, I can promise you the solution is very simple. You can diagnose the problem and get your Keys back…. Today! Retrieving back your Keys of authority can be your destiny.

What are a Man's Keys?

The term Keys is an easy and identifiable symbol used as a representation for spiritual authority. A Man's Keys are his power. A healthy and secure Man will guard and protect his Keys and keep them in his possession at all times. This is a similar concept to how a Man will guard and protect the keys on his key-chain in the natural world. As legal guardians, our natural keys enable us to utilize our authority and access jurisdictions such as vehicles, homes, offices and mailboxes. Similarly, our spiritual Keys enable us to utilize and access our authority over God-given spiritual jurisdictions.

Every Man has been given Keys of authority allowing him to do his job in the natural and spiritual realms with God's full legal blessing. If you are married, you have Keys to lead in the marriage. If you have children, you have Keys to lead, love, protect and guide your children. If you own a dog, you have the Keys to take care of that dog. Whatever you are responsible for before God, you have been given Keys of authority by God to fulfill your duty to rule and reign in life. Anytime you feel that you have violated your conscience and given a piece of your Manhood away, you most likely have given away a Key.

Men usually give their Keys away because they are looking for love, approval or intimacy from others. When a Man builds his identity and self-worth on the fleshly approval of another person, he gives away his authority, his power and his Keys to that person. Our identity and self-worth are supposed to be based on what God thinks about us, not people. We are first and foremost to look for praise and affirmation from our heavenly Father, because our true self-worth is established by Him. If you have fear of what another person says or thinks of you, or if you change your normal behavior because of their expected response, you are giving this person power over you and you are relinquishing your Keys to him or her.

As an adult, if you feel you have to explain or justify yourself beyond healthy accountability you are under someone's control. Accountability should never demean you or put you in a place of inferiority. If you feel inferior to another person, you have allowed that person to control your behavior. When you are trusting in another person to give you accolades and provisions to meet your emotional and spiritual needs, you are setting up a stronghold of codependency in the relationship. This causes you to give away your Keys, because consciously and/or subconsciously you desire their approval more then the approval of God. This is a form of idolatry, and you will remain emotionally and spiritually enslaved to this person until you break your dependence of their approval.

Just as no soldier would be foolish enough to go into battle without his weapons and his protective uniform, no Man should be so foolish as to enter the battles of life without his Keys. A Man without his Keys of authority intact is like a professional quarterback without possession of the football or the protection of his 300-pound linemen. Nothing good is going to happen and no points will ever be scored, ever. Are you getting it? Your Keys are very important! They are your passport to victory in every area of your life.

Men give away their Keys when they allow someone else to do their job. Men give away their Keys when they violate their own conscience and acquiesce to another person when they know they are to hold their ground. In short, Men give away their Keys when they back down in defeat and cower to the control of another person when they know in their heart they are supposed to personally use the authority God has given them. Men are not to allow other people to make important decisions for them. It will result in a loss of their Keys, and a complete loss of personal God-given power.

How do you know you have lost your Keys? And how will you get your Keys back after you have identified the loss? Good news! It is easy. Listen to your heart, and follow a few basic principles outlined in this chapter.

A Man's Heart: The Relational Tool

God has given you a built-in barometer telling you when you have lost one or more of your Keys in your relationships of your life. This incredible barometer is called your heart. When a Man compromises the relationships in his life, his heart will quickly and perfectly reveal to him the relational loss by causing him to feel down or depressed. It is that simple. Your heart, also known as your spirit, is given to you to build and maintain healthy relationships.

This is what separates Men from animals, and truly testifies you are made in God's Image. All Men have the fantastic ability to restore relationships and walk in God ordained authority using their hearts as barometers. Your heart and your emotions are tools for you to use to fulfill your Mandate. When you are down, fearful, depressed, or when you are feeling defeated on any level, you are temporarily losing in your Mandate. This means there is a problem somewhere regarding a certain relationship. If the feelings of defeat, fear or depression are ongoing, you have probably lost your Keys of authority in one of your relationships, and it is time to get your Keys back.

Statistics show that most males battle continual depression or periodic feelings of being down throughout their entire life. Many Men immediately get angry and fearful when they feel depression overcoming them. This is because most males have not been trained to recapture their Keys after they have given them away and/or allowed them to be stolen. The word "depressed" implies you are getting "pressed" by someone or something that is weighing heavy on your soul and spirit. Untrained males will remain down and depressed for long periods of time, because they do not know how to take charge of their emotions and use their emotions as a tool to win.

In actuality, feelings and emotions of depression and fear are a blessing, if you know why they are there. When a male experiences depression, his emotions are supposed to be the tool making him aware he needs to address any relationship problem head on. His heart is telling him on a deep level he is missing it in some area of his life, and there is action needing to be performed right away.

When we are losing, we must immediately fight against the attack challenging us and proactively retrieve our Keys of authority back. Once again, our emotions are God-given tools to help us know when we are losing in a relationship. When a Man is properly trained, he will use his heart to lead and guide himself into standing up and getting the victory. Are you getting it?

Overcoming Depression:

Depression and fear can actually be easily overcome if you are properly trained. Depression is a feeling in your heart telling you that you are getting pummeled. Fear is a feeling in your heart warning you that you are going to get pummeled some more if you do not get up and fight. It is no different than when your physical body gives you pain to warn you that you are in harm's way.

Any doctor will tell you the principles behind pain are both helpful and necessary in getting better. One of the timeless questions from a doctor is "Where does it hurt?" A doctor uses the presence of pain to assist him in diagnosing a physical problem for the purpose of getting the victory for our physical health. A doctor will become seriously concerned for his patient if he learns his patient no longer has the ability to sense pain. This probably means the patient has taken a turn for the worse.

Pain is a God-given tool strategically sending signals by letting our bodies experience a physical stress or malfunction of some kind. Just as pain is a physical alarm warning you there is something wrong in the body, depression is a relationship alarm signaling something is wrong in your spirit. Depression and fear are the emotional pains we feel assisting us to get the victory in our lives regarding our relationships, if we are trained how to manage our feelings correctly.

"***Where*** does your body hurt?" is the timeless physical question asked by doctors. "***Why*** does your heart hurt?" is the timeless emotional question our emotions are asking us. God has given us the incredible emotional gift of our heart and our feelings so we can ask the "***Why***" question regarding what has happened in our relationships that need to be conquered or adjusted. Once a Man realizes what a powerful and essential tool his heart is in overcoming relational challenges, he becomes mighty in walking as the leader he is called to be.

When our heart indicates we are feeling the pains of uncertainty and depression, there is a three fold reaction that generally occurs which we must be aware of in order to obtain victory in relationships. First, there is spiritual heaviness brought on by the conflict that is occurring in the spiritual realm caused from interaction with people and tormenting spirits. Secondly, there is the mental attack that occurs within our thought life attempting to lead us to a point where we mentally sabotage our situation with thoughts of defeat and surrender. Thirdly, there is an actual chemical release within the various internal systems of our body causing us to feel unbalanced and fearful, because we have entered a state of "fight or flight."

We have a choice at this point to conquer depression and fear, or medicate ourselves to the point where we cannot feel the influences of depression on our heart, mind, and physical bodies. It is sad when we medicate our heart and mask the feelings of depression, rather than diagnose the problem and obtain emotional breakthroughs in our relationships. Alcohol, drugs and unrestrained sex are cheap substitutes for the relational and emotional victories in store for a Man. Many Men will walk in ignorance for decades simply because they have not been trained in some very basic principles regarding how their hearts are a tool for victory.

The answer to why you are depressed and fearful is... ***"I am depressed and fearful because I am losing, and I have made poor choices!"*** What will you lose when depression is allowed to have its way with you? You will lose your Keys of authority You will probably lose them because you are untrained, and you did not rise up to the challenge of conquering your enemies. When Men win in life, they are not depressed or fearful. Your Mandate requires you hold on to and utilize your Keys of authority. If you lose your Keys and desire to fulfill your Mandate as a Man, you must retrieve them back at all costs.

Depression (Losing) feels like such a big deal when you're going through it. Depression feels overwhelming because it creates the delusion there is no end in sight. Have you ever seen a storm that did not end? The storms coming against your personal life will always recede and lead to peace when you follow a few basic principles. If you are trained, the voices of depression will be exposed as liars and your victory will be just a moment away. I will say it again, because every Man needs to really understand this concept. ***Our emotions and feelings are our God-given relational tools to overcome adversity and depression, in order to restore our relationships for the purpose of fulfilling our Mandate.*** A trained Man will never follow his emotions blindly; however, a trained Man will include his emotions in every decision making process.

Deep down, every Man desires to strive to achieve excellence. Every Man was created to demand victory in his life, and every Man is given the authority and the ability to win each and every battle against fear and depression. If you have allowed fear and depression to worm its ugliness into your untrained soul, I urge you to rise up and say no to them today.

I suggest you figure out where the relationships are damaged in your life, and reconcile them immediately by utilizing the healing acts of repentance and forgiveness. This in turn entitles you to sternly take possession of your Keys of authority again by telling depression and fear to leave your life and return back to hell where they belong.

Losing your Keys can have no place in your Mandate. By understanding how to use your heart as a tool in overcoming the challenges of depression, you have learned another important principle helping to bring about a quick and long-lasting victory.

Diagnosing With the Victory Scale:

Do you feel you need a step-by-step walk through on how to conquer fear, depression and loss in your life? No problem. Our next step is to evaluate how you are really doing in life. How happy do you actually feel concerning the deep levels of your heart? How well are you really getting the victory? It is crucial you listen to what your heart is saying, so be honest with yourself and hear the words of one of our great American Presidents.

"Don't be afraid to see what you see."

Ronald Reagan – 40th President of the United States

Have you ever truly diagnosed the victory you are getting in different areas of your life? Remember reading about Bob when he was asked whether he felt like a "Man or boy?" He was given the "Victory Scale" to determine where he felt he was on a 1 –10 scale. Remember, the numbers "1" – "4" were given for "No Victory," and numbers "5" - "10" were given for "Victory." A good way to look at your life is to think of it as the score at halftime when a team is regrouping for the second half. Also remember, it is not over until it is over. You still have the rest of the game to play.

So how does the score look? How content are you regarding the victories in your life? If you are playing football and you are up by one point at the first half with the score being 21 - 20, you would be about 5 on the Victory Scale. If you were down by four touchdowns at halftime, this would be put on the Victory Scale at about a 2. The important point here is to be honest about where you are. If you are lying to yourself and saying you are winning in life when you're really not, victory is not going to happen.

Let's consider the Man vs. "boy" war again. Are you walking more like a Man? Or, are you walking more like a "boy?" If you're like most Men brought up in the America of today, "Man vs. boy" is very convicting. So let your heart give you an honest number of where you are on the Victory Scale. No matter what the number is, I challenge you to continue reading and allow your Victory Number to increase as you learn from these incredible testimonies by other Men.

"You and I have a rendezvous with destiny. We will preserve for our children this, the last best hope of man on earth, or we will sentence them to take the first step into a thousand years of darkness. If we fail, at least let our children and our children's children say of us we justified our brief moment here. We did all that could be done."

Ronald Reagan – 40th President of the United States

Mike - One Man's Total Victory:

Has your heart given you your Victory Scale number? A friend of mine named Mike learned this same process, and here is his story. I met Mike 15 years ago through mutual friends at a family get-together. Over the years Mike had owned and operated a local retail company, until more recently, he started an investment company with partners. At the time I sat down with Mike, he was 46 years old. He had been married for 25 years with four children ranging from 17 to 22 years of age.

Mike and I crossed paths throughout many years as the children we raised grew up together attending the same schools and playing on the same sports teams. Mike was aware of my consulting firm for Men in business, but we had never discussed our personal lives with one another. There came a time when I was in need of his administrative services; therefore, I invited him to meet me at a coffee shop to discuss business and to get to know him better.

As Mike walked in, immediately I could sense something was very wrong. He was dressed professionally in a suit and tie and looked very together in his outward appearance, but I was stunned at his downtrodden demeanor. His face looked very fearful and haggard. In my heart, I didn't see the suit or the nice tie. The look on his face reminded me of the opening scene in "Saving Private Ryan" when a grizzled, severely injured and fatigued soldier staggered up the battlefield covered in mud and blood carrying one of his own blown off arms. Mike was another male losing the Man vs. "boy" war.

I can still see him shaking my hand and sitting down looking dazed and disengaged. The scenes from Normandy kept filling my mind. I felt in my heart as if he had taken massive shrapnel wounds covering his body from a direct mortar hit from being in the open line of fire. I shook off the thought and attempted to act normal in front of my friend. Then, as he sat right in front of me, it started again. I could not help picturing him with his helmet half blown up looking like Head-wound Harry from SNL.

I thought to myself, "I have to get this guy into an emotional triage hospital immediately or he isn't going to make it through the day." Of course this is not why I had come to the meeting. A week or two before this meeting, I had asked Mike to assist me on a business plan as a consultant, because I knew he had a real gift in preparing professional presentations.

There I was... pondering whether I was going to ignore the fact this Man was getting totally beat down in life. Although I had known Mike for 15 years as an acquaintance friend, I really did not know him personally as a close friend. This was our first business meeting, and I could see he was clearly losing in life. Initially, I had no intention of talking with Mike about the Man vs. "boy" war. I kept saying to myself, "What do I do now?"

Sitting across the table was this good-natured Man who was getting seriously pummeled in life. Emotionally, it was apparent that Mike was injured. How could I talk about some everyday business transaction with him in such a condition? No good soldier can just sit by and watch a fellow soldier of the Band of Brothers suffer in such misery, so I decided to be direct. It was obvious that Mike needed desperately to talk to someone.

"How are you doing?" I asked in a pleasant voice. Mike first began to share some factual information in his life, and some of the general problems he had been experiencing over the past few years. I noticed immediately Mike is very sensitive to others, and he is very, very smart. The more he talked, the more I liked him. He just opened up. I learned more in the first 20 minutes about Mike and his family than I had known in the previous years as an acquaintance.

My heart was pierced and convicted by the words of a Man who obviously loved his family and who loved God dearly. And yes, Mike was a Man. I would follow this Man into battle on one of his good days, but this was not one of them. On this day, it was very clear Mike was losing. And I could tell by his lack of command he was quite familiar with being a "boy."

As the testimony of his life was laid out before me, I could hear his heart crying to me from deep down within saying, "I am getting annihilated, can you help?" Mike had heard my counseling helped a few mutual friends. Eventually, he said, "Ken, if you know anything that will help, I sure would appreciate your assistance."

As soon as I perceived Mike was in a place to receive a little insight, I stopped Mike in his tracks by asking him the dreaded question, "Are you winning in life, Mike? On a scale of 1 to 10, how well are you winning? Of course, I thoroughly explained the Victory Scale to him."

I knew I couldn't let him go another day without him knowing about some of the incredible principles I had learned over the years. These principles have saved so many others, and myself, from so much loss.

Mike then responded he felt like a "7" or a "7 ½."

I said to Mike, "Are you sure? My heart is telling me you are losing, and any number above '5' is a number that represents winning. What is really the Truth?"

Mike sat back in his chair. He then dropped his head sheepishly, and said in a reserved voice, "Ken, I have to be honest with you. I am getting killed. I do not know what to do or where to turn."

I looked at Mike intensely, and said to him, "Mike, you are a Man. I can see this. But if you are depressed and losing in life, you must be making poor decisions and behaving like a 'boy' in some very critical areas." I then shared with Mike about Man vs. "boy". As he listened to the differences between a "boy" and a Man, I started to see the strong Man deep inside Mike rise up. Understandably, he was extremely apprehensive about the thought he might be considered a "boy" by anyone; however, the more I explained the concept, the more receptive he became to the idea a Man can walk as a "boy" merely by making the wrong choices in life.

I then said, "It looks like you have been losing in areas of your life, because you have not been trained how to walk as a Man and keep your Keys of authority intact. You have given away your Keys, and you do not even know what you have given away.

"The question you have to ask yourself is this, who has your Keys? And remember, if you do not have them, this means somebody else does. They have to be somewhere. Authority is never just left on a shelf. Someone always wants authority, if it is available for the taking."

I could see I was speaking directly to his heart and soul, as the revelation of what I had just asked him began to permeate his spirit. Mike loved the symbolism of the Keys as a tangible representation of a Man's authority. As he reflected on the history of his life, I could see the light was coming on.

Mike then began to get very real. He said to me, "I am constantly gripped by the fear of failing in everything I do. I struggle with the fear I will never be successful with my family, my business or anything in life.

I feel in my heart I am not winning in my life on any level. I am definitely no higher than a "4" on your Victory Scale, and I am seriously depressed."

I then gave him some very good news. I said, "Mike, do you want to win today?"

He answered with a stern and resounding "Yes."

I then shared with him about getting a chiropractic adjustment regarding his spiritual life, and how it is a simple thing to get your life back in order. I then said, "As a matter of fact, if you hang in there and learn the basics of a few principles God has taught me over the years, by the time you get home you will have much of this straightened out."

Mike looked at me with amazement and expectation as a glimmer of hope began to appear in his eyes. Hope is so important. After 20 plus years of losing as a Christian, Mike was desperate for hope. He had done so much seemingly right. He was honoring the Ten Commandments, as he knew them. He had worked 12-hour days for decades. He had doted on his wife and children while attempting to bring them up in a church with much prayer and Bible reading.

Mike was even a leader in the Men's group at his church, where he spent much of his time organizing Men to attend major Promise Keepers events. He still was getting hammered in his life, and he didn't know who or what was to blame for his losses. Financially, his businesses were always behind. He had entered into multiple partnerships, all ending in relational strain. Overall, he had little faith things were going to get better. After all, he had been doing what he had thought was right for 20 years, and the results were dismal and depressing. Mike considered himself a Christian Man, but he felt lost and bewildered regarding the promises of God.

"If the foundations be destroyed, what can the righteous do?"[1]
King David, Book of Psalms

---

1 Psalms 11:3, KJV

Capturing Your Keys!

"It is so simple," I said to Mike. "As you are walking through your life, you are not obtaining victory because you have given away your Keys. It is a Man's Keys that give him the power to win. When a Man does not have his Keys of authority in hand, he is like a little puppy walking around with his tails between his legs. His failure to retain his Keys has turned him back into a 'boy.' Everyone can spot a 'boy' from a mile away. People feel they can walk all over a 'boy,' because there is no real threat he will rise up and defend what is rightfully his. Is this what you are feeling is going on with you?"

Mike was hanging on to my every word. He said, "Yes, I think I know what you mean, but I need to understand more about these Keys. I have attended many Men's training seminars, and I have never heard of the term 'Keys' used to symbolize authority like this."

I explained to Mike, "Jesus Christ used the symbolic word 'Keys' for authority when He was explaining to Peter how the gates of hell would not prevail against His church."

"Jesus said, **'I will give you the Keys of the kingdom of heaven: and whatsoever you shall bind on earth shall be bound in heaven.'**[2] This means Men are given Keys of authority for the purpose of building holy and victorious lives for a greater cause. The cause is advancing God's family and his kingdom into righteousness. By utilizing our authority on earth, God is promising He will back up our actions with His strength, His insight, and His presence directly from His throne in heaven.

"This is incredible when you really consider it. There is no stopping our victory when we realize what a great opportunity we have here. Our perfect example, Jesus of Nazareth, taught us the word 'Keys' represent the God-given authority He gives to us as believers in order to conquer the gates of hell in our personal lives. Jesus then went on to actually use His Keys by overcoming death and fear in all its forms.

"This is why getting Bar Mitzvahed is so important. When a 'boy' decides to become a Man, he then receives the Mandate to utilize his Keys of authority to become successful as a Man. Every Man knows deep down he has been given those Keys. And every Man knows when he has given away those Keys, if he is honest and bold enough to look at it."

---

2 Matthew 16:19, KJV

Mike looked at me in absolute agreement. He was speechless for a time, as the gravity of what I was saying began to sink in.

I then asked Mike, "The real question here is: ***Who has your Keys?"*** This is truly the question of the ages. I explained to Mike we give away our Keys when we allow someone else to do our job. We give away our Keys when we violate our own conscience and acquiesce to someone when we know we are to hold our ground. In short, we give away our Keys when we "wuss out" and cower to the control of another person, although in our heart we know we are supposed to personally use the authority God has given us.

I said to Mike, "God never loses a battle or a war, ever! I suggest you look at the way He utilizes His authority and get on His side, because working against Him by giving away your Keys does not appear to be working for you."

Mike wasn't saying too much outwardly, but I could hear him saying inwardly, "Ouch! This Man vs. 'boy' thing is a sore spot for me."

Diagnosing Your Keys:

Mike just sat there gently shaking his head back and forth. It was as if a lifetime of pain and deception was laid out on the table and shown to him for what it really was; a pile of weak lies about who he was, and what he was called to do as a Man. I couldn't tell if he was devastated or excited by this new insight about walking as a Man and acknowledging his Keys. Mike appeared dumbfounded as he looked up from the table slowly catching my eye.

He then exclaimed, "Okay, Okay! All my Keys are gone! I trust what you are saying. Now what do I do?"

I gently laughed at the irony of it all. I could hear his heart saying, "This is all fine and dandy. Now I know ***why*** I am getting slaughtered, but what the heck do I do now?"

I smiled back at Mike and said, "Have no fear soldier. It is time for you to kick the tar out of your enemies for the first time in your life. Are you ready?" I then began to share the nuts and bolts of how millions of Men have overcome in life.

I methodically explained to Mike that after we give our Keys away, they become the possession of the person or people we have given them to. And once again I asked Mike the question of the hour. I said, "Who has your Keys? Whom have you acquiesced to regarding your God-given authority? Someone has your Keys, because you obviously by your own admission do not have them. It is clear you are not getting the victory. Either somebody has taken them, or you have given them away somewhere along the line. What has happened?" I left the question out there hanging in the still air for a moment.

I could see Mike was feeling quite uncomfortable looking at his life so closely for the first time in this manner. Surprisingly, after only a moment's hesitation, Mike looked at me directly with a steadfast stare and said, "I know who has them. I know where they are. I gave a handful of my Keys to my Dad. I have given the bulk of them to my wife. I have given some to my kids, and I have given Keys to my business partners. Now that I think about it, I have an adult 'boy' relative who has been pick pocketing me of my Keys routinely for years. Every time I am around him, he has his hand in my pocket taking my Keys. Frankly, I am sick of it."

Well, I must admit this wasn't the first time I had ever heard a Man tell me he has given away his Keys to his Dad, his wife or to other family members, and it most assuredly won't be the last. The speed Mike picked up on the concept of the Keys left me both pleased and astonished at the same time.

I then explained to Mike, "As most of us well know, the giving away of authority has been going on ever since Adam first gave away his Keys to his wife Eve in the Garden of Eden by failing to do his job of protecting her. Of course in doing so, Adam also gave his Keys away to God's number one enemy, Satan. Anytime you violate your conscience and come under the control of another, you are giving your Keys of authority away to that person or being. This single action by Adam has in effect caused an innumerable amount of pain, suffering and devastation to all mankind.

"Mike, this is the same kind of pain and suffering you have been devastated by for years as an untrained Christian Man. Let me encourage you by saying you can immediately recapture your Keys, if you so desire.

I assure you all the despair you are experiencing will be over, if you just do your job and regain your authority."

It is important to note a threefold process was occurring in Mike. First, he reestablished his Manhood by realizing and then declaring he was a Man. Secondly, he received the revelation that all Men are given Keys of authority and the power to succeed in life. This includes understanding that a Man who is not living in victory has definitely given away his Keys. Mike immediately came to the realization he did not have most of his Keys, and he did a speedy diagnosis of where he had lost his Keys, and why he gave them away. Finally, Mike came to the third and most essential step in recapturing those all-important Keys. This is a big one. It is called "repentance."

Repentance:

Mike accepted the Keys concept and he could clearly see he had given away his Keys. He had allowed both loved ones and business partners around him to wrongly take and utilize the Keys of his life. At the time Mike and I were talking together, there was only a verbal version of the Man vs. "boy" list; however, Mike quickly realized how he had been walking as a "boy" by a few examples I shared with him.

The Man vs. "boy" list has become very helpful to many Men, because it helps them understand where they have missed their Mandate. Men are simple. Sometimes Men just need to know what to repent about, and the Man vs. "boy" list is an excellent tool that helps Men see where they have missed it. This in turn allows them to ask for forgiveness in the areas where they have sinned and fallen short. If Men do not realize where they have erred, they will not ask for forgiveness and the relationship will not be restored. The Man vs. "boy" list encourages males to face their fears and take back their Keys.

Mike soon understood this important revelation: ***Every time he had behaved as a "boy," he had given away one or more of his Keys.*** To his deep regret, he had systematically diminished his Manhood over the years. With every "boyish" behavior and selfish action, his Mandate and his Manhood were disintegrating. Mike also began to see how giving away those all-important Keys had seriously damaged and compromised his family on every level. Every member of his family was suffering to some extent from the torments of fear, loss and discouragement, all because Mike was not doing his job.

I then got very serious with Mike. I said to him, "Every time you walk as a 'boy,' you are in effect shirking your responsibility and you are giving your Keys away. There is a very important point here. You need those Keys back in your control in order to get the victory in your life. You do not get new Keys until you take care of the ones you have already been given.

This means you have to go back and retrieve the Keys you have left behind. Our God is a relational God. Every time we behave as 'boys,' we hurt the relationships in our lives, and we give away the Keys that God has entrusted to us. Keys are for relationships. They are not for us to simply have power. ***God cares more about restoring the relationships in our lives than about any other aspect of our victories.*** Once again, our Keys are for establishing and keeping good relationships, and they must be fought for on every level.

"Behind every 'boyish' action there is relational damage done to those we love. Behind every 'boy' who shirks his responsibility, there is a woman, child, or loved one who gets neglected and abused in some way. By going back and retrieving our Keys of authority, we are in fact taking action to rebuild the damaged relationships in our lives. This is God's built-in system for a Man to go back and get it right by restoring his relationships. This concept is really beautiful, once you grasp it."

Mike was obviously captivated by the principles he was hearing, because he was hanging on every word coming out of my mouth. I could see he was an extremely relational person who would make it a point to love others, as he wanted to be loved. Mike's main problem was that he was never taught that giving away Keys is the most unloving thing a Man can do.

Losing our Keys actually castrates us of the actual authority enabling us to protect and nurture our family. Mike's ignorance about his Keys of authority had actually caused him to hurt the very people he had spent his life attempting to serve. He looked across the table almost in total disbelief and said with a chuckle in his voice, "Are you saying I have lost my balls?"

I was glad Mike was lightening up a little as I replied, "You can call it what you like. But Yes, I am saying many Men are walking around castrated of their authority. I use the word Keys because I can't very well be saying the word 'balls' every five seconds in public or on the podium at speaking engagements. Saying "testicular fortitude" is too wordy, so I am going to have to stick with Keys for now because that is the symbolic term used in the Bible."

Mike laughed a little and then turned serious again. He said, "This makes so much sense. I must admit, although I am glad to hear the Truth, it is tough to actually look at the fact I have hurt my family through my ignorance all of these years. It is kind of overwhelming. What do I do now?"

I always enjoy hearing this question, because I know a Man is about to change his life in a spectacular way. I joyfully replied to Mike, "When a Man recaptures his Keys, there is an incredible opportunity for God's healing to come forth to the damaged relationships in his life. There is always mercy and grace as we walk through life in our ignorance, but going back and repenting for the times we have neglected others is the highest form of mercy and grace. God loves us enough to give us the opportunity to restore things. Is there anything more noble or more loving than a Man to go back and make things right? If we desire to be Men, we must go back and repent for our lack of training and our irresponsibility. We then must take back our Keys."

After hearing these principles I was sharing, Mike gladly and willingly repented for the loss of each and every Key he determined was not in his current possession. I suggested he talk to God, and then Mike entered into a simple, honest and heartfelt prayer.

"God, I am putting myself before you. Forgive me for giving away my 'Keys of authority,' and for allowing them to be stolen. Forgive me for giving them to my father, my wife, to family members and to business partners. I realize now my Mandated authority is not to be given away. All of these relationships are my responsibility. Forgive me for blaming these people, because I have clearly given my Keys away through my ignorance, negligence and default. Show me the way to recapture my life back. Amen."

The tone of Mike's prayer was very sobering and personal. I could sense the presence of the Lord I know, and I could see He was working intimately in Mike's heart right in the middle of a busy coffee shop.

Mike's countenance revealed something fantastic was happening. I have seen it hundreds of times, and every time it is truly amazing to watch. Right before my eyes I was seeing a Man go through the timeless process of getting true victory in his life.

As Mike was evaluating the choices he had made in his life, he began to see many of the times he had cowered to his father and his wife in the name of some false Christianity. He had mistakenly believed "turning the other cheek," meant he was supposed to acquiesce to others regarding his Mandated authority. It was clear the fog was lifting off of Mike. I then moved him into the very important next stage of recapturing his long lost Keys.

Taking Your Keys Back!

I said to Mike, "Now that you have repented for not doing your job and for giving your Keys away, the good news is you can take your Keys back right now."

Mike then asked, "Should I ask God to give me back my Keys of authority?"

I responded, "Mike, I appreciate your heart on this. It seems like the right thing to do is to ask God for your Keys back, but regarding repenting to God, you have already done this in your heart. When it comes to retrieving your Keys, it is no different than taking anything back when stolen. You just do it.

"If someone stole your wallet and he was sitting at the next table, you would immediately go up to that person and take it back. This is your duty as a Man. You would not politely ask for your wallet back. You would reach out and take hold of it, because it is yours. You do not have to ask God or anyone else. If it already belongs to you, you know it It has already been given to you by God, and you have a Manly duty to immediately get your 'wallet' back at all costs.

"If you do not get it back, you will have to go through life with no money, no driver license, no bank cards, or without anything else that is in your wallet. You know how difficult it would be to replace all of those items, and to allow someone to keep it for any length of time is unthinkable. The same goes for your Keys of authority. To walk around without them is unthinkable to a trained Man, because he knows he will fail in every aspect of his life without his Keys. Keys must be retained at all cost!

"Let me tell you about Moses and the parting of the Red Sea. Who parted the Red Sea for the Israelites?"

Mike quickly answered, "God parted the Red Sea."

I then replied, "Yes, God did part the Red Sea; however, the Old Testament says Moses cried out for help from God, and God said to him, **'Why are you crying out to me? Tell the Israelites to move on. Raise your staff and stretch out your hand over the sea to divide the water so that the Israelites can go through the sea on dry ground.'**[3]

"In actuality, Moses was already given the staff of authority to part the Red Sea. God had given him the staff of authority to lead the Israelites out of the bondage of Egypt. In the same way, he has given Men the Keys of authority to lead themselves out of the bondage in their lives. Moses made the same mistake you just made in thinking God would to do all the work without your direct involvement. God rebuked Moses by saying **'Why are you crying out to me?'** In a sense, God is saying the same thing to all Men today who are crying to Him about their lost authority.

"God does not need crybabies in His kingdom. I believe God is saying to all of His Men, 'Why are you asking me to get your Keys back for you? I love you enough to give to you all Keys of authority you will ever need throughout your entire life. You mistakenly gave them away. Therefore, you must take them back today.

"I believe God is also saying to Men, ***'How can you walk in any kind of power or victory and expect your commands to be fulfilled, when someone else possesses your Keys of authority?*** Reach out and recapture your Keys now, and hold on to them. Utilize them for the rest of your life, and I will make sure your authority is always honored in the spiritual and heavenly realms because you are my son, and I love you'."

Mike appeared overwhelmed at the boldness of my comments, as his eyebrows seemed to lift over his forehead. I could tell the "boy" was

---

3 Exodus 14:15-16, NIV

getting shaken out of him. He then soberly stated, "I like it! Taking back the Keys I have given away does seem like the Manly thing to do. It seems right. Since you put it that way, I can see it is something I must do. I understand. I need to retrieve my own Keys, because I am the one who gave them away."

Mike sat quietly for a long time with his eyes closed. I then realized that I was sitting across the table from a Man who was about to take some serious ground. In his own words, here is the final step of how he recaptured his Keys.

Mike's Personal Testimony:

"I knew at this moment it was time to pray to God to take back all I had given away. It was time to retrieve my missing Keys. As I was praying to God to assist in restoring my Keys, it helped to picture in my mind physically going and taking them back from where I had left them. I saw myself putting all my Keys back in my pocket with a fervent declaration this is where they will stay. I literally declared out loud, 'I am taking my Keys back from every person I gave them to, and from the spirit of fear I have cowered to for so long. This is where these Keys belong, and I am not giving them up! Nobody is going to reach in and grab them ever again.'

"It was helpful for me, symbolically, in my mind, to actually see myself going up and removing my Keys from somebody's hand or wherever those Keys were located. Whether they have them around their neck or wherever I felt they had them, I took my Keys back. I could literally sense where each person was keeping my Keys. For each person, there seemed to be a symbolic reason for the place my Keys were located.

"As for my Dad, he had them in his upper pocket. My Dad symbolically did something that left a lasting impression on me. When I was around my Dad on days when he knew I was hurting for money, he would pull out this wad of hundreds out of his upper pocket in his shirt and flip through them as if to say, 'You are a "boy," and I have your Keys.' My Dad would lick his fingers and count through his money, and then he would stuff it back into his pocket with a look of absolute power over me on his face.

"This literally was so symbolic of my Keys. My Dad would always keep the money thing over me in a controlling way. By allowing my Dad to control me with money, I let him have a part of me that violated my conscience. I realized my Keys were symbolically in his shirt pocket. Therefore, I took them back, right out of his pocket. I can't tell you how it happened, other than I just saw myself telling him I was taking them back, and then I took them back. I put my Keys in my pocket, and they are there to this day."

Keys of Power!

Mike performed a similar process for all of the relationships where he felt he had compromised his Mandate and given away his Keys to another person. The results were predictably outstanding. For the first time in many years, Mike declared, "I have it! I have the victory! This is incredible! I have been a Christian for over 25 years, and I never even heard of this teaching about my Keys of authority." I looked at this unstoppable Man who was most definitely on his game.

I asked Mike where he was on the Victory Scale and he answered, "I have the Victory, I really feel like a 7."

I could see he did. He left the coffee shop with such a peace and authority that he couldn't help but smile broadly to everyone he passed on his way out. Fear and hopelessness had turned into faith and hope for his future as a Man. The Truth really does make you free, and it can be so simple. God makes it easy. Obviously, my business with Mike waited until another day.

To think just three hours earlier, this awesome Man walked into the coffee shop having very little hope and a heart full of fear, shame, and sadness. Fear had gripped him for years, but on that day fear was exposed and slammed to the ground. Mike tells everyone that from that day forward his life continually became more victorious. Joy and peace have came back into his household in a miraculous way. God's ways are so easy and good.

"For my yoke is easy, and my burden is light."[4]
Jesus of Nazareth

Mike and His Father Unite:

Less than a year later, Mike found himself peacefully sitting in the living room of his father's house talking about life over coffee. Mike had feared his father's opinion for over 40 years, yet there he was sharing all the intimate details of his heart and mind with no reservations. He confidently shared the journey of his life. He particularly shared his victories of the last year, as he trusted in God, and the new principles he learned about being a Man.

At one point in the conversation, Mike calmly told his father he loved him, and he fully forgave him for any breaches in their relationship. He told his father about the unforgiving attitude and bitterness he harbored for so many years in his heart, and how he chose to overcome all the lies and traps of the world by reclaiming his Keys of authority. With eyes of steel and an authority only a Man can explain, he looked at his Dad straight in the eyes and told him lovingly he was never going to give his Keys to him or to anyone else again.

Mike kept looking across the coffee table at his Dad and waited for his response. To his amazement, his father said, "Son, I am very proud of you, and I love you. You are right. You should never give your balls to anyone, including me. Forgive me for not being the father I could have been."

The two Men sat in silence, as the heavens seemed to be rejoicing over one of life's greatest mysteries. God had won again. A father and a son had been reunited. As Mike left his father's home that day, the Men hugged in an embrace healing two lifetimes of damaged emotions. The

4 Matthew 11:30, KJV

pain and sorrow of life had somehow been turned into love and joy for these two Men who never really wanted to hurt each other.

Mike later told me the conversations he now has with his father are profound and united. He said, "It feels like how we will interact in heaven. Now there is a mutual honesty and respect for one another and a love that goes beyond all human understanding."

Their relationship is now between two Men who are not afraid to walk in Truth. Mike has truly conquered the "boy" within him, and he has entered into the grace and the power of God with all the blessings thereof. The amazing restoration that occurred between Mike and his sons is equally moving and powerful. You may read about them in an upcoming book. I am in awe of his life as it unfolds before the world as a well-written screenplay, a screenplay that has only just begun.

"He will turn the hearts of the fathers to their children, and the hearts of the children to their fathers."[5]
The Prophet Malichi

Recovering All The Keys:

Can you see why it is so important for Men to understand the principle of the Keys? By learning about our God-given authority and destroying the lies and our fears, we are actually fulfilling the great commission of our Mandate and restoring our most valuable belongings, our relationships with loved ones.

Jesus of Nazareth reinforced the principles of the Keys and the power thereof when he said, **"I am he that lives, and was dead; behold, I am alive for evermore, Amen; and I have the Keys of hell and death."**[6] He also said, **"All power (Keys) is given unto me in heaven and in earth."** [7] God understands the Keys of authority because He created them.

5 Malichi 4:6, NIV
6 Revelation 1:18, KJV
7 Matthew 28:18, KJV

Remember, God wants you to have authority and power and use it for the good of others.

Every Man is to walk as a microcosm and an example of how God runs the universe. He runs it by a perfect and designed authority He Himself has ordained. When we miss God's teaching about the Keys, we miss the victory and the power He has reserved for us. Jesus went to the cross willingly for the purpose of destroying death and to capture the Keys of authority Adam and mankind had given away. How can we allow His great victory to pass us by?

Jesus truly is the Lord, and He knows how to win. When we go back and recapture our lost Keys, we are glorifying this same process of forgiveness, restoration and authority Jesus displayed for us as He achieved victory over death on the cross. Once again, it really is very simple. God has chosen to give us His Keys freely, and all we have to do is learn of Him and walk as He walked.

Overcoming as a Man is a simple two step process. First you become a Man. Next you acknowledge, recover and keep your Keys of authority by walking as a Man. The first Man Adam clearly behaved as a "boy" when he fell into sin in the Garden of Eden. To make matters worse, he violated Point 2. on the Man vs. "boy" list and blamed both God and his wife for his own irresponsible behavior. This is the second commandment for Men, "Thou shalt not blame." Of Course this comes after the first commandment Adam broke, which is "Thou shalt not behave as a 'boy.'"

Remember Adam's classic "boy" reply? He said, **"The woman you put here with me, she gave me some fruit from the tree, and I ate it."**[8] This is definitely a "boy" comment if I ever heard one. It is hard to tell whom Adam was blaming more. Was he blaming God more for giving him the woman, or was he blaming the woman more for giving him the fruit?

Adding to the transgression, what is the deal with Adam calling her "woman?" This "woman" was his wife! She was the person whom he had become intimate and one with, and she had a name. Her name was Eve. Adam's sin of behaving like a "boy" had immediately caused his marriage relationship with his wife to become distant and weak. There was no closeness evident between them anymore. There was just blame.

---

8 Genesis 3:12, NIV

Adam had even stopped calling her by her first name. Does this look familiar to anyone?

Satan's cowardly and "boyish" influence had obviously entered the heart of mankind, and there it was to stay. Being a Man created in perfection, Adam had already become pretty adept at behaving like a "boy." This goes to show you how fast we become "boys" when we give away our Keys. Adam taught us giving our Keys away is being a "boy."

Ideally, for Adam to walk as a Man, he would have taken responsibility for his actions and restored the loss that occurred. However, his newly fallen nature made it impossible for him to do so, because only God can cleanse sin through forgiveness. Since there was no sacrifice yet, there was no immediate potential for forgiveness and restoration for Adam. Adam therefore was eternally stuck as a "boy" with feelings of great guilt and shame. Adam was in desperate need of a Savior, and this Savior's name is Jesus Christ.

This is exactly how many of us feel before we discover we can indeed recover our Manhood and our Keys through the principles God has given us through His Son. We are looking for a Savior. We are looking to someone or something to make it better and to give us the answers, because we know inside we are getting slammed by the enemy. Thus we must look to the answer given to Adam. Fortunately for Adam, we read in the book of Genesis that he was given a sacrificial blood covering for his spiritual nakedness, and he was told by God that Satan is cursed above every beast of the field. He was also told through his wife's offspring there would come a ***Man*** who would destroy all the evil "boyish" works of Satan.

God knew only a perfect Son of Adam could restore the line of Adam to perfect Manhood. Thus, the remedy of Jesus Christ was foretold to Adam and his wife Eve. At a time appointed, the sinless Son of Adam would one day miraculously be born through a virgin by the seed of the woman. He would crush the head of the serpent (Satan) and regain that which was lost. He would swallow up death and sin - in full victory - and then freely give this victory to any willing person who calls upon the Lord. There are the Keys, right there. Do you see them?

"The first Man Adam was made a living soul: the last Adam (Jesus of Nazareth) was made a quickening spirit."[9]
Paul of Tarsus – Letter to the People of Corinth

Adam was the first Man, and God gave to Adam all of the Keys of authority pertaining to this world as seen in the book of Genesis. Jesus was the only perfect Man since Adam, and he was born of God as a direct descendent from the lineage of Adam. He came to recover all of the Keys lost in the Garden of Eden by overcoming death and sin on the cross, and destroying death by rising from the dead.

Jesus willingly went to the cross and died as a sacrifice for the sins of all mankind. Jesus the Man, the Son of Adam, obtained the legal right to every Key of authority in heaven and earth. This is why Jesus said after He arose from the dead, **"All power (Keys) is given unto me in heaven and in earth. Go ye therefore, and teach all nations, baptizing them in the name of the Father, and of the Son, and of the Holy Ghost."**[10] In a sense, Jesus is saying, "Tell everyone about the Keys! I paid a high price for them!"

This principle of recovering our Keys applies to our salvation in Christ, and it also applies to our personal lives and our family systems. As Men, we have the opportunity to recapture the family Keys lost through the mismanagement of our fathers, our grandfathers, and all the way back to Adam himself. Jesus is the anointed Man who came to show us the way to recapture the personal Keys of authority lost when we compromise our conscience and sin before God.

This is done through the principle of forgiveness. Jesus has already retrieved every Key that exists. All we have to do is become Men, apply God's principles of forgiveness, and then retrieve our Keys by the example and name of Jesus of Nazareth. Thus, every Man can make his life a testimony and an example of the greatest and most loving Man who ever walked the earth.

---

9 1 Corinthians 14:45, KJV
10 Matthew 28:18, KJV

Has your father or your grandfather failed to recapture his Keys of authority, thereby leaving you and your family system in a state of confusion and devastation? The good news is you can go back and restore the damage your forefathers have caused, because Jesus of Nazareth paved the way of victory for you. You can go back and pick up the pieces and the Keys, and you can bring all of your family back into peace, prosperity and victory. This is your Mandate, if you choose to accept it. All you have to do is die - die to your selfishness and your old "boyish" ways.

Both the Old Testament (Hebrew Bible) and the New Testament declare this Mandate as given in Isaiah when he wrote, **"And <u>they</u> shall build the old wastes, <u>they</u> shall raise up the former desolations, and <u>they</u> shall repair the waste cities, the desolations of many generations."**[11] The "they" Isaiah is referring to are you and me. We are those Men, the Band of Brothers, who are called to rebuild the destroyed families left behind by many generations of irresponsible "boys." Therefore, fight the good fight, and remember we are the chosen generation who will never surrender our Keys to our enemy. Take your Keys and the victory. They are yours.

---

11 Isaiah 61:4, KJV

4
Your Gates

Rebuilding Your Gates:

Now let us move onto the next stage of victory. So you're a Man, and your Keys of authority are intact. Let's say you keep a copy of the Man vs. "boy" list close to you in order to ensure you don't slip back into behaving like a "boy." What next? Can a Man get a complete victory with these two very important assets of Manhood and Keys in place? The answer is "Yes," but it does help to be further trained. This chapter is about rebuilding the Gates of your life, and getting trained as a Man.

We have seen in the first 3 chapters that becoming a Man is about overcoming our unforgiving and blaming nature. We have also seen that being a Man with authority is about overcoming our fearful nature. Now we will see that building the foundations and Gates of our lives is about overcoming our selfish nature by learning to love others.

Identifying the Open Gates:

Many Men are being taken out of commission or neutralized because they do not know how to keep their Gates closed. You may be asking, "What exactly do I mean by the term 'Gates.'" Just as the term Keys is used to symbolize the God ordained authority Men are given to overcome and manage their daily lives, the term Gates is used to symbolize the specific emotional and spiritual areas of our lives we are responsible to oversee and protect.

The term Gates is used to describe areas of our lives where we give outside influences access to our minds, hearts, thoughts, emotions or senses. Ideas can enter into our Gates. Attitudes can enter into our Gates. Feelings can enter into our Gates. Music can enter into our Gates. Videos or visuals can enter into our Gates. Most importantly, belief systems can enter into our Gates.

We have the choice to allow either constructive influences into our Gates or to allow destructive influences into our Gates, as we are tempted through our selfish human nature. In other words, Men willingly allow constructive influences to enter their lives; "boys" indulge in allowing destructive influences to enter their lives.

Since every Man is called to overcome and fulfill his Mandate, Men must realize we will have enemies whom are set up against us to stop us from succeeding in our Mandate. These enemies desire to get inside our Gates so they can use us, control us, and eventually destroy us. Our enemies do not care how they get in our Gates, they just want in. Remember, it only takes one Gate to be open for a whole city to be sacked by our enemies.

These enemies are perceived in many different forms. For the sake of making our job simple, I will break our enemies down into two basic categories. We have ***Emotional Enemies,*** and we have ***Spiritual Enemies.*** Emotional Enemies come from within, Spiritual Enemies come from without, and their job is to destroy you.

I will say it to you a different way on a personal note. Your Emotional and Spiritual Enemies are going to do everything in their power and ability to enter through the open Gates of your life to reap havoc upon you and your Mandate. They are like the rebels in the game Risk. If you do not eliminate them immediately, more rebels will appear every time you roll the dice. Unseen enemies will always multiply if given the chance. They are like viruses.

I believe God gives us natural and tangible examples on earth for everything spiritual. The human body's immune system is an excellent example of how we are supposed to protect ourselves emotionally and spiritually from enemies. There is a multitude of germs and viruses floating around in the world looking for a host body to inhabit. Once a germ enters the body, it is the job of your immune system and your white blood cells to attack and kill all unwanted intruders. Any failure of the white blood cells to do their job results in immediate disaster. Unchecked, the viruses or germs will literally take over until the person becomes very sick and dies.

From my college biology classes, I recall seeing first hand under a microscope how our white blood cells will immediately eliminate germs and viruses after entering the body. The germs and viruses have a mission to accomplish. Their mission is to use a host body for the purpose of stealing precious life and multiplying. It is amazing to see how well the white blood cells detect and eliminate intruders with no mercy. Science still cannot fully explain the mystery of how or what drives our white blood cells to hunt down and kill these unwanted guests with such efficiency.

Your Emotional and Spiritual Enemies are just like the germs and viruses attempting to reside in your natural body. They desire to use your body and soul for the purpose of stealing your life and your Keys, so they can live and multiply in this world. It is the duty of every Man to model the job of the white blood cells by identifying and destroying all intruders. How do we identify intruders and destroy them? Read on.

Identifying Emotional Enemies:

Emotional Enemies are the personal traits Men battle internally such as Lust, Anger, Fear, Envy, Pride, Unforgiveness, Lying, Addiction, Depression, Perversity, Deception or Rebellion. They are a host of personal sub-characteristics working against a Man as he strives for victory in life. These Emotional Enemies have one common factor. ***Emotional Enemies are all based on our desire to serve ourselves and to take care of ourselves first. All of our emotional enemies are rooted in selfishness.***

Selfishness is a distortion of our Mandate. Our Mandate requires we take care of ourselves as Men and become emotionally strong and healthy. Our emotional strength and success are for the single purpose of serving, protecting and providing for the loved ones we are called to watch over. When we make ourselves the most important objective, we deceive ourselves and overstep our Mandate.

Identifying our Emotional Enemies is a crucial aspect of closing our Gates. Every Man can list three major emotional battlegrounds he knows are a challenge to him. If you truly desire to win in your life, pick three major categories continually fighting against you from the following list. Most of us deal with all twelve of these issues in some way. For now, just pick the top three and today you can learn how to defeat them in your life.

Emotional Enemies

1. Lust
2. Anger
3. Fear
4. Envy/Jealousy
5. Pride
6. Bitterness/Unforgiving
7. Lying
8. Rejection/Addiction/Bondage
9. Depression/Heaviness
10. Perversity
11. Deception
12. Rebellion

Identifying Primary Emotional Enemies:

1. ______________________________
2. ______________________________
3. ______________________________

"Walk in the Spirit of God, and you shall not fulfill the lust of the flesh."[1]
Paul of Tarsus

1 Galatians 5:16, NKJV

Remember to listen to your heart, your emotional barometer, as you determine your primary Emotional Enemies. Every character challenge we face will fall into one of the twelve general categories listed. For instance, having a drinking or smoking problem will fall under the "Addiction" category. Pornography falls under "Lust." Frustration falls under "Anger." Acting out, laziness and self-medicating will fall under "Rebellion." Worry falls under "Fear," and so on. Identify and remember them well, because every Man needs to identify his enemies.

To destroy your enemies, you first have to identify them. The Bible describes at least 12 main Emotional Enemies attacking people. Of course, all of these enemies are rooted in our selfishness. Have you picked the top three Emotional Enemies hounding you and your family over the years from the list? Again I encourage you to mark them and mark them well, because your Mandate for victory demands you know your Emotional Enemies.

"Be self-controlled and alert. Your enemy the devil prowls around like a roaring lion looking for someone to devour. Resist him, standing firm in the faith, because you know that your brothers throughout the world are undergoing the same kind of sufferings."[2]

The Apostle Peter – First Book of Peter

Identifying Spiritual Enemies:

Spiritual Enemies are the evil unseen powers affecting a Man's life. For those who do not believe we have spiritual enemies, understand this is truly Satan's great masterpiece of deception for the Men living in today's world. I have been assisting Men to overcome and fulfill their Mandate for several decades, and I can honestly say understanding we have Spiritual Enemies is one of the single most important revelations a Man will ever receive. Remember, if our goal is to close our Gates and keep our enemies out, we need to identify exactly who and what our true Spiritual Enemies are.

---

2 1 Peter 5:8, NIV

In the book "Destined to Overcome" by the late Paul E. Billheimer, the author clearly laid out the problem all Men face in achieving their Mandate. He wrote, ***"The fallen condition of mankind, the sin of the human heart alone, does not explain the abnormal psychoses and the universal snarling and fouling of human relations. This constant and fiendish disruption of the human social order is explained only by the mass activity behind the scenes of a vast, well organized host of wicked spirits under the control of their master prince. Any spiritual method or technique which ignores the presence and activity of these occult forces cannot possibly offer an adequate solution for the problems plaguing mankind."*** The conclusion is we must identify Spiritual Enemies, because they are very real and very active.

We Must Identify Our Enemies!

Paul, our well-respected father in the faith, made it clear we do indeed have Spiritual Enemies when he stated, **"Put on the whole armour of God, that you may be able to stand against the wiles of the devil. For we wrestle not against flesh and blood, but against principalities, against powers, against the rulers of the darkness of the world, against spiritual wickedness in high places."**[3] This is so clear. Paul emphatically stated we do not fight against people, but we fight against a network of Spiritual Enemies whose goal is to control and dominate us. And these enemies seek to roam around us like lions looking for ways to devour us.

It is so important we realize our emotional and spiritual make-up as Men are perfectly interrelated. Behind every Emotional Enemy we fight against, there is a Spiritual Enemy who is most likely administering an influence. If you can grab hold and believe this principle, you are in the company of well-known and honored Men who have succeeded in their Mandate before you.

Here are just a few of the names of these great men: Ronald Reagan, Winston Churchill, Martin Luther King Jr., Theodore Roosevelt, Abraham Lincoln, George Washington, Isaac Newton, Billy Graham, Milton Hershey, Vince Lombardi, the Apostles, Noah Webster, Jack Hayford, Peter Marshall, and of course, Jesus of Nazareth. Join along with millions

---

3 Ephesians 6:11-12, KJV

of successful Christian Men who all believe the words written by the Apostle Paul.

Why is it so important for a Man to identify his Spiritual Enemies? Men are made to fight and conquer, and fight we will; however, Men cannot and will not conquer an enemy they do not believe exists. Admission to a problem is the first step to overcoming the problem. When Men fail to identify their true Spiritual Enemies, Men will still fight. The problem is they will usually fight people instead of their actual enemies. This includes their wives, their children, their friends, and themselves. Worst of all, if Men are not fighting their true enemies, they find themselves fighting against God.

"But if it be from God, you will not be able to stop these Men, you will only find yourselves fighting against God."[4]
The Apostle Luke – Book of Acts

4 Acts 5:39, NIV

So, who are our Spiritual Enemies, and what are their names? Ironically, they are spiritual influences of the spiritual personalities leading us to embrace the behaviors on the following list:

Spiritual Enemies

1. Lust
2. Anger
3. Fear
4. Envy/Jealousy
5. Pride
6. Bitterness/Unforgiving
7. Lying
8. Rejection/Addiction/Bondage
9. Depression/Heaviness
10. Perversity
11. Deception
12. Rebellion

Did you notice that your Emotional and Spiritual Enemies have the same names? Your Emotional Enemies are emotional ***traits*** you may have embraced working against your Mandate and your destiny. Your Spiritual Enemies are a host of self-conscious and ***evil spirit personalities*** assigned to hinder, aggravate, pressure and disrupt your Mandate. They do this by tempting you to give into the Emotional Enemies of Lust, Anger, Fear, Envy, Pride, Unforgiveness, Lying, Addiction, Depression, Perversity, Deception and Rebellion. Why do they need to be named? It is because Men need a target to attack.

Your Emotional Enemies come from within. They are the selfish and fleshly desires and behaviors you embrace to gratify yourself. Your Spiritual Enemies come from the outside world, as they are the spiritual personalities who cunningly prey on your ignorance and your openness to feed your selfish and fleshly desires. Why are they concerned with you? What are they after?

Your Spiritual Enemies Want Your Keys!

Make no mistake about it. Your Spiritual Enemies want your Keys of authority, because they desire your power. They are committed to keeping you from utilizing your Keys effectively. Spiritual Enemies are constantly working against you in your fight to obtain and enforce your Keys of authority. Just like Satan in the Garden of Eden, their job is to oppose you and keep you from completing your Mandate. They will use any human or earthly vessel within their power to obtain your Keys. They know your Keys will destroy their kingdom, if you possess them and are trained to use them properly.

Your Spiritual Enemies are terrified by the following words of Jesus of Nazareth: **"Behold, I give unto you power (Keys) to tread on serpents and scorpions, and over all the power of the enemy (Your Spiritual Enemies); and nothing shall by any means hurt you."** [5] Note it is implied you must enforce your authority before you can expect the promise that "nothing shall by any means hurt you." In other words, if you do not utilize your Keys of authority and take ground against your Spiritual Enemies, you will get hurt and you will lose the battle at hand.

Before you proceed, make sure you truthfully identify your assigned enemies and remember their names well. If you are not familiar on how to conquer these enemies absolutely and completely, you are about to find a few missing pieces to the puzzle of your life. To truly win, we need to fight our enemies on both the emotional and the spiritual fronts.

Many Men lose because they only fight on the emotional front and think that is all they can do. They usually do this by abstaining from an unwanted emotional behavior and simply "white knuckle it." This is a defensive posture never scoring you any points offensively. Have you ever seen a baseball, football, basketball or any sports team win without attacking and scoring points against their opponent? To truly win, you need to learn to score against and eliminate the spiritual influences that constantly nag and antagonize your soul in addition to abstaining from boyish behaviors.

Do you recall Bob's story in Chapter 1? Bob "white knuckled" his way through urges to emotionally indulge in lust for over 25 years, only to experience consistent defeat in his life. As soon as he was Bar Mitzvahed

5 Luke 10:19, KJV

and learned the spiritual battle at hand, he immediately rose up and began to slaughter and eliminate his Spiritual Enemies. How did he do this? He did it by retrieving his Keys. He then used his authority to close the Gates of his life and remove his Spiritual Enemies once and for all.

The result was absolute victory and joy in Bob's life. If you only fight defensively, very soon the Spiritual Enemies of our soul will score so many points against you, you will find yourself losing and constantly battling the Emotional Enemy of Depression. If you never score any points offensively, eventually you will just give up. To truly obtain victory, you need to go on the offense and take the enemy completely out, thus making it difficult if not impossible for the enemy to attack you anymore.

"Freedom is never voluntarily given by the oppressor; it must be demanded by the oppressed."
Martin Luther King Jr.

Declaring War!

Here it is! Here is the answer to life's problems. Declare WAR! Many Men have never verbally declared war against their enemies. Most Men will live their lives tolerating the enemies both in them and around them, at the expense of their Mandate and the welfare of their loved ones. There are countless victims who are in bondage to the emotional and spiritual ravages of Lust, Anger, Fear, Depression, or whatever enemy that is attacking them. These males go through life repeating a process of abstaining from wrong behaviors for a while, only to fall prey to their seductions once again. There is no victory, because the Man has probably not identified his Spiritual Enemies, nor has he publicly declared war against them.

A Man will not win unless he declares war, because he has not formally entered into the arena of battle. God loves to declare war. Do you remember what God said to Satan in the Garden of Eden after Satan deceived Adam? **"And the LORD God said unto the serpent (Satan), 'Because thou have done this, thou are cursed above all cattle, and**

above every beast of the field; upon your belly shalt thou go, and dust shalt thou eat all the days of thy life. And I will put enmity between thee and the woman, and between thy seed and her seed (The promised Savior); it shall bruise thy head, and thou shalt bruise his heel."[6] Wow! God is pretty good at declaring war. He not only declared war, but he also threw in a couple of expletives like, "You're cursed," "Eat dust," and "You're going down! My Son is going to take you out by crushing your head!"

Of course it is impossible to declare war and win unless you are a Man who is walking in his God ordained authority. A declaration of war is actually a declaration of Manhood. Declaring war is the act of being a Man. Remember Point 46. on the Man vs. "boy" list. A Man declares war, and a "boy" pacifies his enemies.

I have found many Men have never declared war against their enemies even after the enemies are identified. They believe the lie that ***seeing*** their enemies is all that is needed to conquer them. You hear these "boys" say things like "I am depressed," or "I'm too proud," or "I am addicted to pornography," or "I have a drinking problem," or "I want to quit smoking;" none of which gives them the victory. Knowing and seeing there is an intruder in your house is just the first step in removing him from the premises. Next, you must order him out. If he does not obey, you must take it to the next level. You can get physical and/or call in the authorities that will then enforce your legal rights and demands. Lies, fear, rebellion and a lack of training can keep a "boy" from rising up and overcoming his enemies his entire life, unless he learns to "Man up" and declare war against them once and for all.

It is time for all of us to be Men and conquer our enemies. When a Man declares war, he is actually saying he wills himself to never be a "boy" or behave as a victim again. He is saying he is going to use every resource and every Key of authority in or around him to destroy his enemies. He is making a covenant with his Father God in heaven in a unified effort to destroy the works of the devil in and around him.

This is why the Son of Man conquered death on the cross and retrieved all of the Keys of power and authority for mankind; so we might covenant with our absolute and sovereign King in a team effort to bring the glory of God into our lives, and to conquer our Emotional and Spiritual Enemies in His name.

---

6 Genesis 3:14-15, KJV

Previously in this chapter, you identified your Emotional and Spiritual Enemies. Have you ever formally declared war verbally and outwardly against these enemies using the Keys of authority God has given you? Rise as a Man with your Band of Brothers and declare war on all of your enemies. Follow in the footsteps of the victorious Men in the past who have built our heritage.

Public Declaration of War:

America was founded and built upon the public declaration of war. Every national and social American victory came from a declaration of war against the powers desiring to castrate the rights of people and keep them from walking in their God-given authority. The Declaration of Independence of 1776 was a public declaration of war against the powers of tyranny and control that were fighting against the God-given rights of the English colonists.

President Abraham Lincoln publicly declared war against powers of slavery and the powers working to divide America by fighting the Civil War and by his publication of the Emancipation Proclamation of 1863. Following the attack of Dec. 7, 1941 on the American Pacific fleet in Pearl Harbor, President Franklin D. Roosevelt and all of America publicly declared war upon the evil and controlling powers attempting to overrun America and Europe. He then went on to declare war on fear nationally by stating, ***"The only thing to fear, is fear itself!"***

Martin Luther King Jr. publicly declared war against any power embracing the horrendous social injustices of prejudice by stating, "I have a dream." Ronald Reagan directly and publicly declared war against the controlling powers of Communism by boldly stating to the Soviet Union his contempt for the Berlin Wall declaring, "Mr. Gorbachev, tear down this wall!" Reagan also declared "War on drugs" along with many of the nation's leaders over the past three decades. President George W. Bush publicly declared war against the evils of terrorism after 9-11 by stating, "Either you are with us, or you are with the terrorists!" He then organized a worldwide crusade against those who will dare attempt to destroy the Godly American principles of freedom and democracy.

A Man will get victory in his personal life the same way a Man gets victory in the political or social arena. First comes obtaining the proper authority by becoming a Man. Next, there is a ***"public declaration"*** of war. A public declaration of war will always precede victory if this declaration is ordained and orchestrated by the sovereign God-given principles of Truth. By saying, ***"public declaration,"*** I am referring to an outward verbal or written proclamation which is sent directly to our enemy with force for the purpose of declaring and prophesying victory.

Try this universal declaration of war on for size. ***"In the name of God Almighty, I declare war on Fear! I will destroy you, Fear, every time I see you in me or around me from this day forward!"*** Make this more than a prayer. Make it part of your very being just as all the Band of Brothers have done. If you declare war against your Emotional and Spiritual Enemies as a Man, you will never be the same. Read the words of Winston Churchill as he publicly declared the hand of the Nazis would not defeat Britain:

"We shall not flag or fail. We shall go on to the end. We shall fight in France, we shall fight on the seas and oceans, we shall fight with growing confidence and growing strength in the air. We shall defend our island, whatever the cost may be. We shall fight on the beaches, we shall fight on the landing-grounds, we shall fight in the fields and in the streets, we shall fight in the hills. We shall never surrender!"

Winston Churchill

(House of Commons, 4 June 1940, following the evacuation of British and French armies from Dunkirk as German's swept through France.)

With the help of God and God's America, Britain did become the masters of their own fate and captains of their own souls by fighting off the Nazis when they were outnumbered over 10 to 1. World War II has become an incredible example of how God uses Men like Winston Churchill to walk in authority and declare immediate war upon identified enemies.

Can you imagine General George Patton fighting in World War II as a "boy?" Can you see General Patton finding out the enemy was within striking distance and not immediately declaring a full on attack? Can you imagine Admiral Chester Nimitz hiding and not ordering the American

Pacific Fleet boldly into the Pacific waters to affront the enemies of freedom and democracy after seeing the attack on Pearl Harbor?

Have you ever dealt with a person who has said they were going to quit smoking? Few people who try to quit smoking actually do quit unless they are determined. From experience, the only people I have seen quit smoking did so by publicly declaring war in such a way where it was obvious they had already won. Their attitude was so resolved, no one would have dared tempt or force them to smoke again. Men with the victory are determined not to enter back into their "boyish" behaviors. The victim mentality will never get the victory, but a trained Man who honestly and publicly declares war against his enemies will always get the victory when he is on God's side.

There is a popular verse that says, **"Today is the day of salvation!"**[7] So without further delay, I suggest right now in the name of the God who created us, make an outward and verbal public declaration of war against the primary enemies assigned to harass and bring about your demise. Say, "I declare war on 1……., 2……. & 3……."

"Winning isn't everything, but the will to win is everything."
Vince Lombardi

Now, if you feel you are a "boy," you probably are fearful of identifying and declaring war against your enemies. I strongly suggest today you take hold of your Mandate and obtain your Keys of authority by declaring war! Your God, your family, your friends and your loved ones are all counting on you to rise up and do your job.

Your enemies are easily defeated when you go into battle with your armor on and with your God-given authority in hand; however, going to war presumptuously and unprepared is never a good idea. Many males have been annihilated because they went into battle as "boys." I urge you today to reach down deep into the wells of your heart and bring up the gifts of power and authority God has placed within every Man. One Man who did exactly this was John.

---

7 2 Corinthians 6:2, NLT

John:

I met John through a mutual friend in a business meeting. Right off, I could tell John was a true promoter. John is a fun and bold kind of guy who knows how to get the job done. There he was, sitting at a conference table in all his glory talking up a storm. Although all aspects of his life and his outward appearance were clearly dismantled, John was doing what John does best. John was building relationships. I liked him immediately.

Throughout the meeting, John displayed a special gift of leadership and sensitivity that I admired. John was in his mid thirties and had never been married. John was gracious, friendly and outgoing, and we became friends right away.

During the course of our business that day, John began to share his heart with me. He said he felt deep down he was called to do something very special in his life by helping many people. He also said he felt like he was "missing something," causing him to be stuck in a rut. John told me he was having trouble sleeping, and it was difficult for him to stay clean in both his thought life, as well as in his daily activities. I could see John was a true CEO with a mighty calling on his life, but it was obvious to me that inwardly John was losing horribly.

I knew John was a Man, because he was the kind of guy I would definitely follow into battle. There was protective strength and a character within John where I could easily envision him leading a team of people to victory; however, I could see John was walking without his Keys, and that he had never been trained how to close and lock the Gates of his life.

I gave John my cell number. I told him if he felt good about contacting me I would like him to call, so I could share with him about his Keys of authority and the Gates of his life. These terms were new to him, but I could see by his reaction that they spoke directly to his heart. In his eyes, I could also see he had an extreme hunger to win. This was a Man who did not like to lose. I knew by the way we clicked relationally that a call to my phone was forthcoming, and I was really looking forward to it.

The Phone Call:

The next day, as expected, John called me. John was obviously ready to hear the Truth, because he treated me as a long time trusted friend. We decided to meet and it quickly became apparent that his friendship was very real. It was immediately obvious that he was suffering very badly from a lack of knowledge and victory as a Man. I could sense that he was reaching out to me in desperate hope that I would bring help into his life. I asked him where he stood on the Victory Scale from 1 to 10, and he honestly and accurately revealed to me he was about a "3."

As John poured out his heart to me, I recalled being in the same place at different times in my life. Everything within me empathized with an understanding only fellow soldiers in arms can truly understand. It has become clear to me in life, you cannot really bond with someone until you have both won and lost on the same playing field.

John proceeded in telling me that many of the close relationships in his life were compromised, and he made some very serious moral mistakes over the previous decade. He had recommitted his life to serve God about a year before. But the moral breakdown from an affinity to sex, drugs and rock and roll from years past had taken its toll.

John told me the story of when he was finally arrested for the possession of a small amount of cocaine. He thanked the officer who arrested him, because he knew he was on an uncontrollable path to his own destruction. I could see clearly how God had been working on behalf of this precious Man, a Man who was so grateful when God mercifully stopped him in his tracks from wasting his life.

The Battle:

Although John was on the road to fulfill his Mandate, he was having serious trouble sleeping at night and he was still dabbling with marijuana and alcohol. John was not the kind of Man you had to persuade to fight for what he believed in, but John's Calling and gifts were working against him. His strong leadership style combined with his lack of knowledge and training were leading him to fight against himself and those who were near him.

In his business and personal life, he was often brash and bold to the point where at times he was insensitive to the needs of others around him. John also told me his personal problems were a direct result of not having a trained and loving father close to him throughout his life. He intuitively knew his foundation and identity regarding his Manhood had faltered, because it was founded upon a fatherless home where he had experienced a divorce and a trail of loss and broken relationships.

After hearing John's story, I said to him, "John, the bottom line is this; because you believe lies regarding your Mandate and who you really are, many of your Gates are wide open and your enemies are running in and out of your life at will. You do not know how to shut your Gates. Even if you did, somewhere along the line you have lost the Keys of authority that you need in order to kick your enemies out."

It's funny how saying this same comment over and over to Men has made me feel like a parrot that is constantly repeating himself. "Ah-ah, your Gates are open, your Gates are open! Ah-ah you have lost your Keys!" But the plain fact is this; there is a consistent problem spreading like a virus to the American Man, and I for one am not going to sit back and do nothing while my friends and fellow Band of Brothers are getting destroyed at will.

The Dreaded Question:

Right on queue, I asked him the dreaded question that makes most Men's heart stop when they are desperately losing in their lives. I said, "Who has your Keys? If you do not get your Keys back, there is no sense trying to close the Gates you have opened." I explained that your Gates are the twelve Emotional and Spiritual Enemies we have listed previously, and your Keys are the authority to enforce the closing of those Gates.

If a male does not have his Keys of authority intact, there is no use attempting to overcome Lust, Anger, Fear, Envy, Pride, Bitterness, Lying, Addiction, Depression, Perversity, Deception and Rebellion. Of course, I explained to John every male has Mandated Keys of authority given to him upon being "Bar Mitzvahed."

John had never heard of the terms Keys and Gates used in such a practical way for a Man to obtain victory. He loved the concepts, and it seemed as if he was literally pulling the words right out of me as if they were his life rope to salvation.

I could sense John glowing as the revelation of what he was hearing was sinking in. He knew his father had never given him this most important information. This was the kind of guy who didn't like giving away his Manhood or his Keys to anyone. Ironically, he was also the kind of guy who loved to laugh at himself for being caught acting like such a "boy," especially when he was trying so hard to be a Man. For years, John had attempted to force his way through to victory, to no avail. This was an impossible task, because he had not gone back and retrieved the Keys of authority that would give him the power to overcome.

Have you ever tried to get into a locked car without your keys? Most of the time with today's vehicles, it is just not going to happen. If you do try to break in, you will usually damage the car in some way. Even after you break in, you then say, "Now what?" You still cannot drive the car without the keys. The vehicle is rendered useless until you get your keys back. Whether you lost them, forgot them, or just plain gave them away, you must get your Keys back in order to win and destroy the enemies in your life. For years, John had been the guy who had broken into his own car by breaking the windows, and he was still foolishly sitting there looking for ways to get the car started.

Taking Back The Keys:

After laughing with John for a time at how foolish both of us had been in times past for walking as "boys" and for losing both our natural keys and our spiritual Keys, the laughter took on a serious tone. John began to get down to the business at hand. I explained to John about how the book of Nehemiah in the Old Testament is a model for a Man to rebuild the walls and the Gates in his life.

For those who are unfamiliar with the story, Nehemiah was an Israelite held in captivity in Babylon in the 6th century B.C. He was very concerned for his homeland, Jerusalem, and the welfare of its inhabitants. This prompted him to take the bold action of returning to Jerusalem to rebuild the walls and the gates of the city. Nehemiah knew the city gates and walls needed to be secure in order to protect his friends and loved ones.

The process of rebuilding undertook by Nehemiah is an excellent model for rebuilding the broken down and shattered areas of our own lives today. Nehemiah first inquired of one of his brothers how the city walls and gates were looking. This action was similar to what John was achieving as we met to discuss his problems. John was inquiring of a trusted brother to give him the tough news about how bad the walls and Gates of his life were. After learning of the devastation and the brutal Truth regarding the condition of the city, Nehemiah wept and mourned over the loss of his city's ability to defend itself. He then prayed to God the following prayer:

"I beseech you, O LORD God of heaven, the great and terrible God, that keeps covenant and mercy for them that love him and observe his commandments:

Let your ear now be attentive, and your eyes open, that you may hear the prayer of your servant, which I pray before you now, day and night, for the children of Israel your servants, and confess the sins of the children of Israel, which we have sinned against you: both I and my father's house have sinned.

We have dealt very corruptly against you, and have not kept the commandments, nor the statutes for the judgments, which you commanded your servant Moses.

Remember, I beseech you, the word that you commanded your servant Moses, saying, 'If you transgress, I will scatter you abroad among the nations:

But if you turn to me, and keep my commandments, and do them: though there were of you cast out unto the uttermost part of the heaven, yet will I gather them from there, and will bring them to the place that I have chosen to set my name there.'

Now these are your servants and your people, whom you have redeemed by your great power, and by your strong hand. O LORD, I beseech you, let now your ear be attentive to the prayer of your servant, and to the prayer of your servants, who desire to fear your name: and prosper, I pray you, your servant this day, and grant him mercy in the sight of this Man."[8]

After sharing Nehemiah's prayer with John, I could sense by his silence his heart was deeply touched. God promised Nehemiah and all Men if we turned from our selfish and ungodly ways, He would make

---

8 Nehemiah 1:5-11, NKJV

things right. We talked about how Nehemiah took responsibility not only for his own mistakes, but also the mistakes of his forefathers. We also discussed how Nehemiah's story could be an important model in rebuilding the Gates of his own life.

Nehemiah then wept and cried for forgiveness for allowing the gates to become destroyed. I explained to John how Nehemiah went on to obtain the kings favor, and how he was entrusted with full authority from the king to go back to Jerusalem and personally rebuild the walls and gates of his beloved city. Nehemiah was well trained. He immediately asked his king for "Letters" granting him authority to rebuild the walls and gates of Jerusalem and the king gladly gave him his request. Nehemiah knew he would be a fool to attempt to rebuild Jerusalem without the king's Letters of authority, just as Man is a fool if he attempts to rebuild his life without his personal Keys intact.

Next, accompanied by a trusted few friends, Nehemiah did an intense nightly inspection of the walls and gates as he developed a powerful plan to rebuild. Finally, he presented his Letters of authority to the powers that be, and he challenged his countrymen and Band of Brothers to rise up with him and rebuild the walls in an all out effort to shut out the enemies of Israel once and for all.

Just as Nehemiah had worked with his Band of Brothers to rebuild the walls and gates of his city, John proceeded to closely inspect his Gates and develop a powerful plan to rebuild. Incredibly, history has shown Nehemiah and the people of Israel rebuilt the walls and gates of the city in just 52 days by holding the sword of protection in one hand and their tools of workmanship in the other; thus the reason we chose to have 52 points as seen on the Man vs. "boy" list where Men can rebuild their lives.

John was amazed to see how this model was applicable today, as modern day righteous Men fight together in the business and political world to rebuild the walls and Gates of their families and culture. John's repentance before God had been occurring for months. He already had been reflecting at length on the hurt and destruction occurring in his life. Modeling after Nehemiah, he wept and mourned over the devastation of hurting his loved ones, and he sought God for the answer of how to win in his life. The tone in John's voice was sad, but hopeful. As he recounted his history, John took the next step of faith to rebuild the walls and Gates of his life.

Just as Bob and Mike had done in the previous stories, and just as millions of Men have done in times past as they traveled on their journey to complete their Mandate, John identified where he had given away his Keys. John then repented to God for giving his Keys away, and for allowing himself to be taken out of commission by indulging in the sex, drugs and rock and roll mentality through enticements of his Spiritual Enemies.

John's story of retrieving his Keys makes me laugh when I recall the situation. When I first asked John who or what had taken his Keys, there was a long pause. He identified his Emotional and Spiritual Enemies to me candidly, and he truly repented for his sins and the Sins of his forefathers. When I asked him to name the primary Spiritual Enemy hounding him all his lifetime, he just couldn't give me a straight answer at first. He mentioned a few Spiritual Enemies from the Spiritual Enemy List, but there was one he just could not find on the List, and he did not know what to call it.

Finally, he said to me, "I'm sorry Ken, but I have to call this thing by what I am seeing. The name of the main Spiritual Enemy taking my Keys of authority is 'Jack-A**!' Because this is exactly what I behave like when I let this evil thing into my life. And I see this evil thing has my Keys right there in his front pants pocket."

I told him if this is what he was going to call his Spiritual Enemy, it was fine with me. It probably came under the label of Rebellion, but I am not the one who had to deal with it. This was John's enemy. So here in John's own words is how he took back his Keys.

John said, "I see you 'Jack-A**.' I am taking my Keys back right now and I am destroying you with my battle-axe. I am done with you and your 'Jack-A**' ways! I am no longer going to look and act like a 'Jack-A**!'"

Well, I have seen a lot of Men get their Keys back over the years, but this one is definitely on my "Top 5" list. John went on to declare war against many of his Spiritual Enemies during our talk, as I witnessed the chains of bondage just fall off of him. Time has shown the fruit of this session was excellent. Over the months following, John no longer had a great desire to engage in his old "boyish" behaviors.

The ironic part about this story is it did not end there. When John shared with his buddies about the name he decided to call his number one Spiritual Enemy, his friends all agreed the name "Jack-A**" perfectly described the rebellious behavior and the spiritual influence affecting him. This is a good lesson for us. There is no cookie cutter pattern that applies when it comes to a Man overcoming in his life. A Man needs to listen to his heart and follow his spirit, because he is the one who is ultimately responsible and accountable for his success as a Man.

***"He (The Lord) that sits in the heavens shall laugh…"*[9]**
King David – Book of Psalm

Closing The Gates:

As we discussed the irony in his life, I got the feeling John was so content that he was ready to leave the conversation and just relish in his victory. But I said to him, "Hold on soldier, you have not even begun to look at the Gates of your life yet. This is where you are really getting hammered! Getting your Keys back is just a necessary step, you must now enter the greater battle."

I have coached many teams in sports over many years, and I could see John felt he had made progress and was ready to call it a day. It brought me back to my childhood when my football coaches would run us for hours, and just when we thought we were about to drop dead, they then would tell us practice was just beginning. "That was just the warm-up!" they would yell. There I was, pushing John to do the real work and leave no stone unturned, just as my coaches had pushed me in the past.

John went on to identify the Emotional and Spiritual Enemies in his life. As stated previously, it is a good habit to identify at least three major open Gates where your enemy is beating on you at will. Quickly, and with a little assistance, John identified more than three enemies. We talked about how over the years the primary reason he went into sex, drugs and

---

9 Psalms 2:4, KJV

rock and roll was to medicate him from feeling the constant pummeling from his enemies.

This self-medication also numbed John from feeling or acknowledging the shame he felt from getting his behind kicked on a daily basis. Does this sound familiar to anyone? He identified Lust, Pride, Lying, Deception and Depression as the major strongholds tormenting him, and for the first time in John's life, he uttered the following prayer:

Closing the Gates: *Johns Prayer*

"Lord, I ask you for forgiveness for allowing Lust, Pride, Lying, Deception and Depression to have any access to my life through any personal open Gates. I ask for forgiveness for not publicly declaring war against these enemies and for allowing them to steal from me, my family and from your kingdom. Forgive me for using marijuana, alcohol, sex or any other means as a medication to numb the blows or hide from my enemies rather than rising up in authority and taking my enemies out.

Lord, I am a Man who has joyfully received your Keys of authority, and in your name I declare war against the Lust, the Pride, the Lying, the Deception and the Depression hindering my life. Lord, I know it is your perfect and absolute will that I defeat these Spiritual influences; therefore, with your full and Mandated authority I will never tolerate them again. I send them out of me, out of my house, out of my family, out of my work place, and out from every place I step foot on this planet. I close all Gates where my enemies have entered. I say 'No' directly to these influences now, and I declare them dead in my life! In the name of Jesus of Nazareth, who has all authority, I make this declaration."

When a Man makes such a public declaration of war so heartfelt and real, one can only sit by and watch in amazement. There is really not a lot to say except. "Wow!" I asked John how he felt, and he said he felt like a million bucks. I asked John if he felt like he was going to have any problems sleeping that night. He said, "There is no way! Many times in the past when I had problems sleeping, I would smoke or drink in an attempt to fall asleep. This is not going to happen anymore."

I said to John, "John, the good news is for the rest of your life you are going to pummel God's enemies with absolutely no mercy. For the first half of your life you took the beating. Now it is your turn to destroy the same Spiritual Enemies pummeling you for years. You have the privilege of being used as the hammer that breaks the rock into pieces." John loved it.

Over the following months, John matured in an uncanny way. He now sleeps like a baby, unless there is unfinished business where he failed to address his Gates throughout the day. John's "Declaration of War" was really a declaration of Victory in covenant with God.

By declaring war, John is utilizing his Mandated Keys of authority against his Spiritual Enemies. Through this process, God ensures the power and effectiveness of our covenant prayer is indeed performed. Through this covenant, John is becoming closer to God each day, as he understands God's heart and learns principles on protecting our loved ones from evil. One by one, John has been going back to his close relationships and restoring the damage caused where his lack of knowledge and understanding has compromised the friendship.

The Teacher:

Later that month John took another Key back. After John had a run-in with the law the previous year, he had rededicated his life to God. He then met a Christian teacher named Jerry who became a business partner and a supposed mentor to him. As John began recounting his history with Jerry to me, John realized he had relinquished his Keys of authority to Jerry. This story is worthy of mention, because many Men have found themselves in the same situation after giving their Keys to business partners and bosses.

John recalled he was seduced by his mentor's supposed vast knowledge of the Bible. There was only one problem. Jerry was a "boy." This leads us to a very important principle. Following a "boy" makes you a "boy." The problem in the relationship began early on when John submitted himself to Jerry. When I challenged John on whether his mentor was a Man or "boy," John emphatically said Jerry felt like a "boy," and he exuded very little spiritual authority.

John chuckled as he said, "I felt like I was a little 'boy' learning from another little 'boy.' I hate to admit it, but every time he tried to teach me, I felt like this guy was breastfeeding me. It just did not feel right. I am 37 years old. I'm a little too old to be nursing at the paps!" John's candor was cracking me up. He was taking this "boy" thing a little further than I intended. Somehow through the laughter, we managed to continue to get down to the heart of the matter.

John went on to say, "I would never follow this guy into battle. He is a well meaning and nice guy, but I felt like Jerry would back away or just plain bail in the heat of conflict. Now that I think about it, he was always shying away from confrontation and acting like a 'boy.' I don't know what I was thinking.

"Actually, I do know what I was thinking. I thought Jerry's knowledge in the Scriptures was more important than his character as a Man. I totally bypassed my gut feeling, and I continued to submit to Jerry in a way that violated my conscience, because deep down I knew he did not have it." John went on for quite a while telling me all the reasons he had given his Keys away. John's main point was he thought maybe he could reap something from the relationship by just learning factual information.

I asked John if he felt like a Man while he was trying to justify his poor "boyish" decision making process. John sheepishly grinned a little, and he most definitely did not feel like a Man while explaining why he had given his Keys away. John did not like the feeling of being a "boy" and making excuses.

John realized right then and there how important it is to be a Man. He saw how important it is for a Man to walk with his Keys intact, and to never make excuses. John had allowed a "boy" to occupy a position of authority over his life, and in doing so he had violated his own conscience and gave his Keys away to this "boy." It was not his teacher Jerry's fault John compromised his position as a Man. The teacher of course is responsible for his actions, but it was John who put the teacher on the pedestal and gave his Keys away.

Remember from previous chapters in this book, a Man cannot have his Keys taken from him unless he is controlled or deceived into giving them away. Once they are given away, a Man is not allowed to blame anyone for loss except himself. This is called being a Man. Once a Man realizes he has given his Keys away, it is important for him to know why and how he gave them away. If he feels he has to convince others he was thinking rationally when he lost his Keys, he is quickly slipping into the "boy" list. Justifying ourselves is unnecessary. All of the information that we learn from our mistakes is for our private use. We do not need to explain ourselves to others. It is best to file our past away so we can learn, and never be fooled by similar situations again.

After a heartfelt and joyful repentance, John restored his Keys while forgiving both Jerry and himself for entering into an unhealthy relationship. Later, John saw he had actually treated Jerry in an abusive manner, because deep down he resented the fact he had given his Keys to him wrongly. Seeing these dynamics was the first step in restoring the relationship to a place where both of the Men could build and encourage one another without an improper pecking order taking place.

John decided to call Jerry to make things right. He told me later how Jerry then sent him a powerful book helping him grow and overcome as a Man and leader. John's original belief that Jerry could help him had actually proved to be true. Jerry did have teachings beneficial to John. John was just not supposed to give his Keys away to Jerry.

Over the coming months, their relationship grew stronger because John was Man enough to be honest with Jerry, and he removed the ungodly pecking order established between them. In a way only John can describe, today he will tell you, "No more nursing on the paps for me. I am walking as a Man, and God willing, I am not giving my Keys to anyone ever again!"

"I expect to maintain this contest (The Civil War) until successful, or till I die, or am conquered, or my term expires, or Congress or the country forsakes me..."
Abraham Lincoln, June 28, 1862 Letter to William H. Seward

John's Victory:

John had taken a phenomenal amount of ground in just a few short months. He was walking as a Man and everything in his life was looking up, but Mr. Cruelty was still rearing its ugly head in and around John. John had declared war on many of his Spiritual Enemies with tremendous success. However, there were strongholds left in his life plaguing him ever since he was a small child. The names of these enemy strongholds were Abandonment and Rejection.

It is important to note John did not mention these Spiritual Enemies when he first decided to close his Gates and declare war against the enemies in his life. As you may recall, he first took a stand against Lust, Pride, Lying, Deception and Depression with incredible success. These particular Emotional and Spiritual Enemies were just the outer layers of sin tormenting his soul. After a few months of absolute victory over these enemies, it then became painfully obvious there were deeper issues in John's life stealing his identity, his Keys, and his joy.

Thus enters Mr. Cruelty. It is important to note, Mr. Cruelty's main job is to get people to believe they are worthless and no good. Mr. Cruelty is a Spiritual Enemy who promotes severe Rejection, and Rejection is the father of all of our emotional and spiritual problems. If Rejection can find its way into the heart of a person, all bets are off, because the victim of Rejection is going to get destroyed. Once again, it is simple to understand. God is the author of love and acceptance. Satan is the author of Hatred and Rejection.

We must understand that the job of Rejection is to destroy our ability to accept the love of God and love from other people. If it succeeds, we are slaves. It is time for every Man in the Band of Brothers to choose love, and thereby destroy Rejection and all of its foul friends.

Fortunately, John had put himself in the company of a few good Men and women who understood the wiles of Spiritual Enemies. As the issues of Abandonment and Rejection manifested themselves in his daily life, around him were loving people who were there to back up John in the heat of battle. John's Band of Brothers all had Rejection's number, and the scene was set for a battle of the utmost proportions. For John, it was the final battle for his Manhood.

John was almost two years old when his father left John's Mother and family for supposed greener pastures. Yes, John was one of the many children in America who had been abandoned by the primary male figure in his life. This set the course for his life. At the age of 37, he still carried massive scars and injuries of one of life's greatest tragedies, rejection from a father. Like millions of males today who never experienced the benefit of having a loving Man to raise him, John had developed a warped sense of being a Man, and he left a trail of partially broken relationships behind him.

John's pain showed up in nearly every facet and aspect of his life. Remarkably, John has an incredible natural gift of fathering other Men. This is primarily due to a God-given gift of love for people and sensitivity in relationships; however, his love many times was laced with a dose of condemnation and anger. Throughout the course of his relationships and especially when others would make mistakes, John found it very difficult to display love towards them because control, anger and condemnation would somehow leak in. In other words, Mr. Cruelty was hard at work against John.

Needs Vs. Neediness:

It is paramount to recognize that lingering just under the surface of a person that has been victimized by Rejection, is a desperate need to be accepted and loved. Remember, all people have a healthy need and desire for love and acceptance; but when Rejection gets a hold on a person, an unhealthy insatiable neediness takes over. Neediness is the soul's answer to Rejection.

With John, it showed up in the tone of his voice. It showed up in the questions he would ask even when he knew the answer. It showed up when he would make joking comments about being left out or unloved. Personally, it showed up in his long-term battle with being overweight. John was still deeply hurting inside, and his hurts were hurting others. An undeniable Truth is hurt people will hurt people.

I have a very helpful tool for helping others see how the past abuses and trauma in their lives have affected them. When I see people who have been emotionally hurt, I picture what their hearts look like to help give me a word picture of the damage their heart has endured. I have been around people with all kinds of emotional afflictions perpetrated against their hearts. Somehow, seeing a person's heart is as easy as seeing their smile, or noticing their sad eyes.

Maybe I have a vivid imagination, but it is easy for me to get a picture of what has been done to a person's heart. Some hearts are battered, some hearts are cut as with a knife, some are bruised from neglect, some hearts look like they have gaping holes and some have been absolutely pulverized from the emotional abuse from others. Many of you reading this book may feel like a chainsaw has ripped through your heart mercilessly. It may be tough, but looking at the damage occurring to your heart is the beginning of overcoming your enemies and closing your Gates.

When I pictured John's heart I saw a huge, open and bleeding wound looking like it had been made by a sharp axe. This picture symbolized to me the deep wounds occurring when a severe blow from Rejection is received to the heart during the emotional growth and make-up of a small child. Sharp cuts are usually caused by hurtful words. I could also envision there were many small lacerations appearing like cuts by a small paring knife. These cuts were all around his heart and they symbolized the self-inflicted attacks John had made on himself from self-pity and self-hatred, all compliments of Mr. Cruelty.

It was obvious John has suffered from a huge lack of trust in people around him since he was a child. John eventually revealed that his Mom left him on the doorstep of his father's house with no warning, and she did not return for many years. Yes, in John's eyes he was abandoned and betrayed also by his Mother.

A horrible thing happens when a male grows up in an environment of Rejection. He begins to expect Rejection and the loss accompanying it. I call this, "the fear of future failure in relationships." This was the beginning of the end for John emotionally and spiritually, because Rejection is the master calling card for all of our Spiritual Enemies. Like flies to a sandwich at an outdoor picnic, the flies will come. And they know exactly what they are doing.

These Spiritual Enemies begin to create an evil emotional and spiritual network of feelings and thoughts leading their victim to believe the lie he is unloved and unworthy to be loved. This is why I call this attacker Mr. Cruelty, because it is a cruel spirit who abuses its victims mercilessly to the point where the love of God cannot be received anymore.

When a person believes the lie that they are not lovable and they do not deserve love from others, they put the responsibility to feel loved on the friends and family members close to them.

This is an impossible task, of course, because neediness is an insatiable vortex, and Mr. Cruelty knows it. No amount of outward superficial attention, flattery, or compliments can ever heal a person's heart and remove the lies Mr. Cruelty has caused this person to embrace. As long as Mr. Cruelty is allowed to remain in the mix, the bondage of Rejection and neediness will remain. Before a rejected heart can begin the healing process, Mr. Cruelty must be conquered and eliminated from your life.

A "boy" who suffers from Rejection is like a drug addict who needs another fix. You can tell him he is loved and that you care for him; however, these actions only temporarily give him the feeling he is loved. Mr. Cruelty and other Spiritual Enemies will continue telling him the same old lies over and over in his head with the main lie being, "I am not worthy to be loved."

As these voices constantly bombard their prisoner with cruel propaganda, sooner or later the victim will again come to believe no one really cares for him and he deserves exactly what he is getting. Eventually, he is just going to need another encouraging "hit" from one of his codependent friends and the cycle begins again. During the entire behavior pattern, he has failed to do what is right. He has failed to be a Man and die to himself. He has failed to declare war and overcome his Spiritual Enemies by shutting down Mr. Cruelty.

When we fail to walk as Men and overcome our Spiritual Enemies, we remain "boys." It is a Man's job to die to self, and remove the lies and the Spiritual Enemies out of his life. This is the first order of business in our Mandate. If we do not remove our Spiritual Enemies, we will be unable to hear God clearly or to love our family and friends properly.

"Pray for wisdom instead of patience, it's less painful!"

Sabotage!

When a "boy" expects the relationships in his life to fail him, he actually is sending out thoughts and "prayers" of relational defeat to the people he longs to be close to. In other words, he will commit the sin of sabotage against himself. A rejected "boy" will believe the lie that it is just a matter of time before any new friend will join the long, long ranks of people who have rejected him. He is literally prophesying the future failure of his life.

People will feel very apprehensive about becoming close to a 'boy' with Rejection issues, because they will sense the anger and control emanating from him. It becomes a double edge sword driven by neediness. If you become close to a "boy" who suffers from acute Rejection, you will experience a continual unhealthy sucking of life as he attempts to get you to make him feel loved. If you do not get close to him, you will experience the wrath, condemnation and control coming from his hurt heart as he lashes out in revenge against you for not fulfilling his neediness. This is not a pretty picture either way you look at it.

Victory will never happen for a "boy" who is losing to Rejection, because this is one of the laws of the universe. Whatever you sow, this is what you will also reap. In John's case, Rejection had been successful for nearly destroying every important relationship in his life for decades. John had been sowing defeat, rejection and failure into the relationships from the time he was a child, without even being aware of what was happening. The fruit here was he was reaping bitterness, pain and more of his old nemesis, Mr. Cruelty. Mr. Cruelty is a master at leading a person to sabotage his or her own life.

Destroying Mr. Cruelty:

The fantastic news is John previously had made a promise to God and to himself he would walk as a Man. He did not declare he would ***try*** to walk as a Man. He declared he ***would*** walk as a Man. When a Man makes this declaration, he is ensuring every Emotional and Spiritual Enemy will be defeated in his life one by one as the battles are thrown before him. John was soon to find out God prepares the perfect plan for our perfect victory. At the right place and in the right time, there are battles and confrontations scheduled for every Man. Each battle is the opportunity to take back everything, his Manhood, his Keys, his Callings, his family and all of his relationships.

One of the major battles of John's life occurred when he least expected it. On an ordinary night when John thought he was going to spend the evening with his new friends, who happened to be his roommates, all hell broke loose on him. John became aware he was not included in a dinner celebration that many of these good friends were attending.

After his roommates returned home joyfully and dressed to the hilt, John began to feel all the feelings he was so accustomed to. A sick ulcer feeling overcame him as he felt like he was knocked off his feet by a Mack Truck slamming into his chest, but the real problem didn't come from his horrible feelings. The real problem came from the voices (yes, demons are real) inside his head accompanying his feelings of abandonment and rejection.

John became noticeably hyper aware of how everyone was behaving around him. He just knew he had been abandoned and rejected like so many times before. If he looked hard enough for the clues of his rejection and the betrayal from his supposed friends, he knew he was going to find the hard and clear proof that he had in fact been rejected for no good reason. He was destined to prove that people felt he deserved to be left out and unloved. Does this sound like you or anyone you know? If this does sound familiar, pay close attention to the rest of this story.

Months of trust and good relationship building seemed to fall away in a flash. John began to entertain the idea he had been wronged by his new family of friends, his Band of Brothers. Once again he had gotten the short end of the stick. He was going to make sure this time he would stand up and let everyone know he was hurt, and he had a right to be upset. The stage was set for battle as John walked throughout the house looking for an opening to address his perceived enemies, his roommates and ***former*** Band of Brothers.

This is Satan's master plan. It is called bait and switch. Satan knows males are going to fight. His job is to deceive us into fighting our allies. It is called 'friendly fire' in military terms. But as we all know, "friendly fire" is not so friendly. As John's friends chatted and laughed over the evening's fun in the living room, John stomped and moped up to the group with a question he felt he had to ask. He said, "Was there a reason why I was not invited to go to dinner with you tonight?" Condemnation, hurt feelings and blame dripped off his words as John's friends listened intently.

The mood of the house became tense and quiet as it was stated to John, "No, there was no particular reason why you were not invited to dinner." John's anger further flared up as he stormed back to his room obviously very distressed and bitter about the whole affair. Now he had been lied to. There was a reason, so he thought, for why he was left out.

Mr. Cruelty was hard at work telling him that he was betrayed and done wrong by his friends for no good reason… again. It was just as he suspected. John made one of the classic mistakes of a person suffering from Rejection; he chose not to relate any further with his friends or to confront anyone on the supposed betrayal and rejection he was feeling. Yes, he chose to be a "boy."

Everyone in the room loved John, and usually they would go out of their way to include him. But on this night, it was not appropriate for John to be included, and it had nothing to do with John. John's friends were all aware of the battle he was in, and they knew he needed to spend some alone time to wrestle with his real enemies, Abandonment and Rejection. John's friends were trained well to dodge the bullets of friendly fire from a person operating out of hurt and Rejection. Thus the fun of the night quickly resumed, to the chagrin of John.

John shut the door soundly, making a statement to everyone that he had been done wrong. This had little effect on his roommates. They all had been there a time or two themselves and knew of the dynamics occurring. No one was about to let Mr. Cruelty control the household with petty antics. John plopped down on his bed and thought, "I thought my roommates loved me and were concerned for me. What is going on here? Have I been betrayed **again**?" The real battle of his life was on. This is the age-old battle between the minds and hearts and souls of Men, and at that moment John was losing. His fear of future failure in relationships had visited him again very unexpectedly.

John immediately thought about coping with his feelings in the same manner he used to deal with it when he was a "boy." He thought about medicating himself with sex, drugs and drinking. But this time there was something different about John. He was a Man now. Or at least he purposed in his heart to be a Man.

John suspected these thoughts might be coming from his Spiritual Enemies. He had been taught from the Man vs. "boy" training that God only gives us good suggestions. If it were the voice of God, there would be peace, strength and a sense of love attached to it. These thoughts certainly did not assist him to feel strong or loving. They were actually making him feel weaker. John was learning that not all thoughts are the Truth. That is why it is so important to base our thoughts on the Truth, because lies will always lead us down the wrong path. Remember, thoughts are just thoughts. They are not always based on reality.

It is important to know that your comfort zone is not always healthy. Thinking he deserved to be pitied and consoled felt very comforting to John in a sick sort of way, but could he trust these feelings anymore? Comfort zones may be just the familiarity we feel after being raised in families where boyish behaviors are commonplace and accepted.

Such was the case for John. As John was growing into adulthood, he continually reinforced a bad habit of allowing himself to muddle around in his own self-pity by believing the lies that everyone was going to turn on him and betray him. Eventually his undisciplined thoughts allowed confusion to set in, and John would finally begin to believe the false idea that his friends were indeed betraying and condemning him… again!

So there John was, lying alone in his bed thinking thoughts like, "Moving in with these guys may have been a big mistake. I knew sooner or later they were going to show their true colors and turn on me. I cannot believe they were so insensitive as to totally hide the fact they were going out to dinner without me. They lied to me. I just talked to them an hour before, and they did not even mention they were going out to dinner. They have betrayed my trust, and I don't know if I will ever be able to trust them again. This whole thing about the Keys and being a Man, maybe it is all just a bunch of bull. If they were really Men themselves, they would have been honest with me. What a bunch of hypocrites! Why didn't someone tell me what was going on? Don't they care at all?"

The voices in his head finally ended the whole monologue by saying, "How could anyone really be sure what the Truth is anyway?" But under all of this chatter, there was another voice, still and small. John could barely hear the calm and reassuring voice of the Holy Spirit through the brash voices of his Spiritual Enemies. This voice was responding to John's heart. John's heart was saying, "I am hurting and I am sad… and I need help."

For half the night John suffered through the voices and "questions" of his Spiritual Enemies who were trying to dismantle every good thing that happened to him over the past several months. And these voices were sharp and thorough. They used every supposed fact (not Truth) possible to discredit John's new friends. The war was on, and the arrows were flying through the air looking to do further damage to John's already wounded heart.

John was just at the point of giving up on the matter when something happened. John said, "No, I am not going to quit. I am not going to let this thing beat me again!" John then remembered about his relationship with God. At 2:00 a.m. in the morning John prayed to God he would hear the Truth about this situation. He prayed, "Is it me, God? Am I missing it? What is the Truth?"

After a few moments of silence, an incredible peace came over John. He then began to recall feeling this pain in every close relationship in his life. John remembered kids from elementary school making fun of him because he was poor and ashamed of his clothes. He remembered his schoolmates making fun of his crumby shoes. John remembered being called names and the endless words from classmates showing their disapproval of him.

John saw his Mom leaving him on his father's doorstep alone with no explanation of why. He saw girlfriends leaving him and family members who belittled him. As the sad story of his life unfolded before John, he somehow knew his friends would be there to talk to him in the morning. He thought, "I cannot medicate. I will not go back to my old ways. I have got to get somewhere new with this!" Then John fell asleep.

John woke up the next morning with a degree of clarity even though he didn't fully understand what had happened. He was beginning to realize the old belief system in his head had kept him from hearing the voice of reason and the voice of Truth in his life. As he was pondering the situation, one of John's roommates came to his room to talk to him. His roommate said, "Good morning, John. Would you like to talk about how you are feeling?"

John immediately became very transparent and honest with his roommate. As the words flowed out of his heart, it was as if his heart was quickened and he began to understand the Truth of everything occurring. John said, "I felt betrayed and abandoned again last night, and I know it is me. I have had these feelings and problems my entire life, and I know it all stems from the abandonment I experienced from my Mom and Dad." John decided to be a Man as he addressed his Spiritual Enemies with the greatest weapon of all time, Truth.

John quickly learned his roommates had not lied to him at all. The dinner was an unexpected surprise for the roommates, which was planned by other friends. An important point here is John's friends did not share the event with him, because they knew he would respond poorly to being left out. His roommates could literally feel the handiwork of Mr. Cruelty attempting to do his bidding, and they were aware John was highly sensitive to being left out of anything.

In other words, John's Rejection and Abandonment problems were causing others to set strict boundaries with him and his dysfunctional behaviors. This caused John to feel left out. The roommates were doing what they had to do to be safe and healthy with John, but John perceived it as more undeserved rejection.

That morning, the biggest revelation came when John saw how he allowed bitterness and an unforgiving heart to cloud his most cherished relationships. He learned listening to Mr. Cruelty could easily cause him further rejection and more pain to his heart, if it is not dealt with and removed. John was even lead to the point where he was considering abandoning, rejecting, and even betraying his close circle of friends, whom he affectionately called his Band of Brothers.

Wow! Mr. Cruelty was pushing John to do the very things he was accusing others of doing to him. Remember, our Spiritual Enemies are clever, crafty and evil. On this day Mr. Cruelty lost, because John entered into a relationship of understanding and forgiveness with his roommates. The absolute weapon or mass destruction against Mr. Cruelty is forgiveness. I will say it again and again, "Forgive now, forgive always and forgive everyone… especially yourself."

Throughout the day, John became clear about his Spiritual Enemies, and he began a deliberate and thorough process of forgiving everyone who had rejected him, even himself. The next morning at a Men's prayer meeting, John finally put down the gauntlet and totally closed the Gates to Rejection and Abandonment by forgiving his parents and asking everyone to forgive him for his selfish and controlling behaviors.

As soon as the meeting started, John began talking about his battle and how he was determined to get the victory. Within minutes, John made a loud and public declaration of war against these tormentors causing him so much grief throughout his life, especially Mr. Cruelty. Everyone in the room knew John was rising up as a Man and recapturing back Keys to his Manhood. It was obvious forgiveness was quickly becoming John's mightiest tool for rebuilding the broken relationships in his life.

Frank D. Hammond wrote an introduction to his book "Overcoming Rejection' that absolutely nails it. ***"It is as important inner wounds are healed as it is that physical wounds be healed. If a person receives a cut in his hand he is quick to cleanse it and protect it. Why? He knows there is the possibility of the wound becoming infected, and this would complicate his injury.***

This possibility of complication also applies to an inner wound. When an inner wound is experienced, it must be immediately cleansed by applying forgiveness. Forgiveness is a spiritual antiseptic. When one is wounded by Rejection, he must quickly forgive the offending party otherwise an unclean spirit (a spiritual germ) can gain entrance to the wound and cause a spiritual infection called 'demonization.'

Suppose an inner wound were not cleansed by forgiveness, and the wound now becomes festered by resentment, hatred and anger. What can be done? The answer is in the cross of Jesus Christ. The substitutionary death of Jesus provides forgiveness of sin and deliverance from unclean spirits."

(I requested John put in his own words about his journey to Manhood starting with that day at the Men's meeting. The following is John's actual testimony as he recalls the challenges he faced in life.)

Overcoming Rejection: *John's Personal Reflection*

"If you are going to get anywhere in life, you have to be open to allowing God to work on your heart. It has to be 100% submittal to the Lord to free you from the pain. It will hurt to let him in. But God spoke to my heart that day in the Men's meeting and said, 'It's okay. I am not going to hurt you. One by one I am going to pull these roots out of you, and we are going to walk this out together. Forgive your parents fully, and forgive anyone who has ever condemned you. And ask forgiveness from all the people you have condemned in your life, because you have felt the handiwork of Abandonment and Rejection.'

"I then knew it was time to declare war on every Spiritual Enemy causing me to feel abandoned and rejected. I knew it had to be an outward loud verbal declaration of war. I spoke words of forgiveness and the word 'No' to my enemies. I knew I would never be the same again. The peace I feel now is incredible. I know it is done.

"Of course, learning how to walk in the victory as a Man is a process. I know my victory is complete, because I know what the final outcome is. I know I will be challenged again, but the moment the enemy starts to speak, he is going to be shut down. As a matter of fact, it is just going to be a waste of time for my enemies, because I have my Keys of Manhood to destroy Abandonment and Rejection.

"I say to all, ***'Declare war on Rejection and its lies!'*** Let everyone from the East to the West know you are entering into war. Declaring war against my enemies made all the difference for me. The spiritual and emotional realms operate under certain legal laws, and you best operate under these laws if you desire to win. I can tell you from experience, if you have not declared war against your enemies, you are not going to fight and defeat them."

Get Over Yourself!

"In order to die to my own selfishness and neediness, I had to make a conscious decision to get over myself. First I needed to die to my selfish tendencies by destroying the lie I was justified in feeling sorry for myself. On that day at the prayer meeting when I had a breakthrough, a good friend gave me a quote saying, **'I am crucified with Christ: nevertheless I live; and the life which I now live in the flesh I live by the faith of the Son of God, who loved me, and gave himself for me. I do not frustrate the grace of God: for if righteousness come by the law, then Christ is dead in vain.'**[10]

"This verse helped to shut down the selfishness in me, and it caused me to look at how my neediness was working against God. I was frustrating God and everyone else, because I was still acting like a 'boy' in areas of my life. I was putting my hurts and comfort before others, because I had not dealt with my emotional injuries properly. I now know it was my duty as a Man to look at my injuries once and for all and conquer them. I can now love people without the interference of unhealed wounds affecting my ability to be a loving person.

"Christ was the perfect example of being selfless and loving. He showed us his love by giving his life solely for our benefit at the expense of his own life. How can I love those around me, if I am preoccupied with having them cater to Rejection and Abandonment issues? No one can do this. This is why it is imperative for us to overcome Rejection in our lives and die to our selfish ways.

"Christianity says a lot about dying to our flesh and making a decision to be a servant rather than catering to our own desires. This verse and my friend were saying in practical terms that I just needed to 'Get over myself.' Sometimes it is just a matter of saying, 'Stop being so selfish! Ridding ourselves of selfishness is merely a choice we can make at anytime."

---

10 Galatians 2:20-21, KJV

"And he said unto me, My grace is sufficient for thee; for my strength is made perfect in weakness." [11]
The Apostle Paul – Second Letter to the Corinthians

"Paul is not saying here that we are strong in the Lord when we are weak in character. He is saying that we are strong in the Lord when we are weak in self. Then the power of God may rest upon us. It is a simple Truth we must embrace to be fully joyful. You must get over yourself.

"Daily, I now will die to my own selfishness and make sure I shut my Spiritual Enemies down. I ask everyone to make their own crucifixion happen every day by getting over their selfish behaviors. When I wake up in the morning, I begin by making sure my flesh is crucified by purposing myself not to be selfish. I then make sure my spirit is connected to the Lord by making a daily declaration I will not be selfish. In other words, daily I turn on my GPS. (God's Positioning Spirit).

"I now can look forward to the times people will knowingly reject me or say hurtful things. These are the times I can show the love of God and forgive them, because I know interacting this way is how we invite God to bring about true healing in our lives. These times have become opportunities for me to show the love of God and to destroy both selfishness and my own Spiritual Enemies at the same time.

"By responding in this manner, I can show others a true friend will not allow the hurtful comments to interfere with the love we show for one another. I am experiencing incredible victory because I have decided to get over myself. I can honestly tell you, destroying selfishness with forgiveness has been a disastrous blow to my Spiritual Enemies. This makes me very happy."

---

11 2 Corinthians 13:9, KJV

"Be on the alert. Stand firm in the faith. Act like Men and be strong. Let all that you do be done in love."[12]

The Apostle Paul – First letter to the people of Corinth

John's Testimony Continued – Walking in Victory:

"I can truly say to those who make the commitment to understand the principles taught in this book, and to those who do the actual work of applying these principles, their life will be blessed beyond their comprehension. If you actually make the changes in your heart, you will find the people in your life will treat you very different. The same people you have dealt with for years will relate on a whole new level with you. The conversations and interactions with friends, family, and business associates will be noticeably more relational and real.

"One of the business associates I have a contract with is Mandy. Mandy is a professional administrator who works for a very powerful company operating on a high level of business in my hometown. Every time I dealt with Mandy in the past, I felt she was looking down on me with a total lack of confidence that I would do the job well.

"After applying the principles of walking as a Man for just a few months, I could see a huge change in the way Mandy was treating me. I could feel a greater respect from her and a confidence I was going to really take care of her and the job at hand. She no longer attempts to talk down to me, and she definitely listens to me more. It is like she has new eyes and is seeing me differently. It is great!

"I know there is a special covering over me promoting blessings and favor in all of my relationships. Some of it may be my perspective, because I feel better about myself. I know there is a huge acceptance and blessing coming from others, because I no longer sabotage my relationships by allowing Mr. Cruelty to enter my life. People see me walking as a Man,

---

12 1 Corinthians 16:13, NAS

talking as a Man, learning as a Man and acting as a Man. I sense they really do feel the change in me, and many of them have outright told me so. They know instinctively I now have my Keys of authority intact, my Gates are closed, and I have healthy and distinguishable boundaries in my life.

"I have a close girlfriend who I love dearly and have known for years. She and I have had a long-term friendship relationship and we have had many very deep talks in the past about life's pressing questions. Somehow, the alignment in our relationship had always been a little off. Now that I am walking as a Man, her reaction and respect for me has changed entirely. Our interaction is completely different. Order has come into our relationship, and I know she has a great respect for the new me.

"There is an unspoken understanding I am a Patriarchal Man who is watching over her. Women will naturally respect a Man. I know she can sense I am no longer looking for her to meet my selfish needs. She can literally feel the love and protection I have for her. This is something I have searched for with our relationship since the beginning. Since I no longer act as a 'boy,' my desire to be respected as a Man has become reality.

"I notice when I share with her the principles I have recently learned in regards to how a Man should behave, I get an internal confirmation from her I have never received before. Our friendship has moved to a new level of respect and intimacy. The whole spirit of the relationship is different.

"There is no longer a selfish motive behind my interaction with her. I find myself looking out for her as a father or an older brother instead of as a potential boyfriend trying to get what I want. I can see my relationship with her has stepped up a notch, and I love it. It feels right to be looking after her in a way where I am additional protection for her from 'boys' who are like I used to be.

"It is fantastic to see the transformation in the behavior of others towards me as well. I have a well-respected Pastor friend who began to treat me totally different. There is a handshake and a hug people sometimes give you that feels very surface orientated. Then there is an embrace or a handshake that feels very deep and connecting.

"I can see with my Pastor friend that I have moved into a new level of friendship and intimacy. It is very noticeable as he shakes my hand and greets me that there is a greater trust. I can tell by his actions and comments he feels safer to open up with me, because he can sense I am now safer to be around. He can instinctively tell exactly where I am in my life just by my countenance.

"I have been working on using the Man vs. 'boy' principles in my life for about six months, and I am now prospering in every way. Just a few months ago, I was living in an apartment with other 'boys' where there was no electricity, no food, no money for food and no car. I couldn't sleep at night, and I did not know what to do with myself because my media production and promotion business was failing.

"In the final week before I first learned the principles about my Mandate, I was eating bread every day given to me by a buddy who stood in line for hours just to receive free bread. I was eating off of his bread coupons and peanut butter from his house, and I was praying to God everyday that the hell would end in my life. Just a few short years ago I was making 120K a year working as a loan consultant with no financial problems at all. There I was at the very bottom, not even able to buy a cheap burrito.

"After I made the changes presented in this book, everything changed. Like the joke goes, it was like someone was playing a country western song backwards to describe my life. I got my wife back. I got my truck back, my dog back and I got my job back. It was a little different for me as far as the wife and the dog, but in a few short months I was blessed with a new automobile and my business was being blessed beyond my wildest expectations. The main difference this time is I am prospering as a Man, and I will no longer waste money on 'boyish' desires.

"My friends and family relationships are on the road to restoration, and daily, all of my relationships are getting stronger. My relationships are actually being reconstructed. It is like I performed demolition on the bad areas of my house, and now they are getting rebuilt with new and better additions. It is the same structure and the same shell, but inside it has become clean, updated and new.

"When I find myself sliding back into behaving like a 'boy,' I am quickly able to determine exactly why I am weak and how I can quickly change my approach to remove any 'boyish' behaviors. I am convicted almost immediately when I get off in my thinking. My "boyish" behaviors used to appear to me as the size of a pebble. They now appear to me as big as a bolder the size of a truck.

"Whatever the problem is, whether it is bitterness, selfishness, lust or anger, I see myself in a whole new light. In the past, the 'old me' would just blow off my 'boyish' behavior as no big deal. I would have very little remorse for treating people poorly. Now, even the slightest 'boy' behavior is extremely repulsive to me. I no longer placate people with weak 'I'm sorry' statements, and I actually make it a point to restore relationships immediately with the principle of forgiveness when a relationship goes a little sour.

"Relationally safe people are now attracted to me because they can feel I will protect the relationship when challenges arise. The great part about this is these relationally safe people have become a Band of Brothers around me catching me when I miss something. I am learning to get over myself and truly listen to what my friends have to say without being defensive or controlling. I have learned to follow my gut better, and to use my emotions as a tool rather than see them as a hindrance.

"Even when my friends deliver a message of insight or correction with a little extra edge on it, I am learning to receive the basis of their observation without shooting the messenger for a bad or awkward delivery. In the past, in my pride I criticized the messenger so I would not have to receive the Truth or insight they were delivering.

"I liken this to how sometimes UPS will deliver a package where the packaging is a little banged up, but the contents of the package are still intact and together. It would be foolish to accuse UPS for ruffling up the package. They did their job. The contents arrived safely. If there is something broken by them in the delivery, they will fix it.

"The same goes for a brother who is delivering a message. As long as the message is delivered, it is my job to take what is being brought to me and assess the legitimacy of the message. It is so great to have Men around me who are trained how to assist other Men to grow and mature. My brothers have helped to save me from the grief of hurting other people by my insensitivity.

"In my past, I would go for years acting like a 'boy' and hurting my loved ones without anyone pointing out to me the error of my ways in a way I could understand. It is critical to have the support of other healthy Men who have the courage to be brutally honest as soon as possible. Every day a brother waits to tell me the Truth about a problem I have is another day I go on deceiving myself in believing I do not need to change. It is also another day I hurt my friends and family with my insensitivity. Thank God for my Band of Brothers!

"Today, I can easily identify the voices of my Spiritual Enemies. When I hear things like, 'Why is this happening to me? Why is God putting me through this pain? Why me? I don't understand. What's going to happen next? I am never going to get what I want. I will feel better if I...' I immediately know the enemy is throwing darts at me. I used to think they were my thoughts, and I would just go cry in my beer, or my weed or whatever I chose to medicate with. When I allow these thoughts to keep chirping in my head, I know I am entertaining the evil 'boy' who the devil is trying to turn me into. The solution is simple. I just say 'NO!' 'No' is now one of my favorite words, and as a Man I use it frequently. My next favorite words are 'Leave,' 'Go,' 'Adios,' 'Now,' and 'Ba-Bye.'

"I used to think my needs consisted of having all my personal desires and my emotional needs met by others. Now I know my real needs are met when I simply do my job as a Man by loving and protecting the ones God has Mandated me to take care of. When I expect others to meet my neediness by enticing them to make me feel better, I take on the bondage of selfishness.

"The great thing about overcoming selfishness is I now receive the honor and respect from my friends and family that I have always desired. I can actually see it in the faces of those I love. How sweet it is to be on target in my life. All I have to do is continue to be a Man by holding onto my Keys, closing my Gates, walking in my Calling and being the Patriarch God has called me to be. If you want to fulfill your Mandate, do what I have done. Walk as a Man and receive the authority given to you by God."

John Today:

As John allows God to be his true and loving Father, the new principles he has learned has healed many of the broken and injured places in his own heart. John has truly been transformed into a successful businessman and minister who is excited to share "Man vs. boy" with any person crossing his path. John has turned into a spiritual father himself. He ensures that all of the Men and "boys" near him know about their Keys of authority and the Gates we are responsible to keep for our Mandate. John particularly loves to share how he has overcome Rejection by destroying his Spiritual Enemies with a declaration of war and the Truth.

There is a certain feeling a Man gets when he follows his heart and restores the personal relationships in his life far surpassing the temporary rushes of sex, drugs and rock and roll. Everyone around John can now see a new calmness and strength emitting from him as he walks forth to fulfill his Mandate. Over time I have seen the fragments of John's life getting repaired right in front of me, and it has been very encouraging for all of his friends and family to see him get the victory so decisively. Go John!

"Arm yourselves, and be ye Men of valour, and be in readiness for the conflict; for it is better for us to perish in battle than to look upon the outrage of our nation and our altar."

Winston Churchill

(This call and spur to the faithful servants of Truth and Justice was spoken by Winston Churchill in his first broadcast as Prime Minister to the British people on the BBC as the British were being attacked by the Nazis in World War II - May 19, 1940, London).

5

The 5 Callings

Understanding the 5 Callings:

How are you doing with the information so far? Are you getting it? Can you see how easy it is for a Man to take hold of his life and win? If words like Mandate, Keys and Gates now mean something to you pertaining to your victory and success as a Man, then I would like to shift gears and move into a new area that has absolutely revolutionized the lives of many Men.

This chapter is about determining and understanding the general Calling you were made by God to walk in. If you can catch the importance of this chapter and the principles described herein, you will have acquired another immovable building block in your foundation as you walk forward to fulfill your Mandate.

Remember the purpose of this book. Every chapter imparts a plan for victory in a specific area of a Man's life. Of course there are many different ways to get victory. I am offering revelations and ways of achieving victory that are extremely effective and successful. The ways presented here are not the only ways to win. Men have been learning how to overcome long before I was born, and they will be overcoming long after I am gone. The following principles given here will resonate deep within your heart, especially if you are active in a business, a church or any organization requiring teamwork.

In this chapter, I am making a disclaimer to teachers and theologians who may have a different take on Callings. If the principles presented are different from what you have been taught in the past, I ask you to reexamine your foundations and consider that many times a culture or a society will miss important Truths at the expense of the people.

The principles and ideas presented in this chapter are simple and easy to understand. The goal is to win. I know the information submitted here will be an important building block for the success of each and every Man. I believe it will change the way you look at yourself as well as all Men with whom you come in contact. The understanding I am going to impart can revolutionize your leadership, your business, and best of all, every male relationship in your life. With that said, allow the next statement to sink deep into your conscience. ***From conception, every male is wired in such a way that they can easily be identified as fitting into one of the 5 Callings.***

This does not mean each and every one of us is not absolutely and incredibly unique. Every person has a wonderful and unique design, and all people are called to bring their special gifts into blossom. It is time to create a beautiful symphony to the ears and hearts of God and our fellow Men, as our gifts and Callings are used for the greater good.

It is obvious as no two fingerprints are the same; there are millions of different Men and women who are all special and individual creations. But thank God we can make some generalities helping us to function on a day-to-day basis. If you do not have a problem being thrown into one of the two "Man" or "boy" categories of males, you won't have a problem being thrown into one of the 5 corporate Calling categories.

Jeremiah, the Old Testament prophet, made it quite clear God has a special purpose and plan for each Man even before our earthly parents conceive us. Look at what God told Jeremiah regarding his Calling as a Prophet to the nations.

"Before I formed thee in the belly I knew you; and before you came forth out of the womb I sanctified you, and I ordained you a prophet unto the nations."[1]
The Prophet Jeremiah

This verse from Jeremiah displays the incredible intimacy and love God our Father has for us. It shows how He has formed us, He has sanctified us and He has ordained us even before we were born. How powerful it is when a Man realizes God has indeed bestowed upon Him one of the 5 Callings for His service.

The Callings represent positions necessary in every family, every business and every church system. Any place where teamwork is required and there is a battle on the boards, then understanding and allowing the Callings to function is a must. Let's look at the Corporation to begin with, because it is an excellent example portraying the Callings in a manner with which most Men are familiar.

The 5 Callings of the Corporation:

The Corporation is built upon 5 different vocations or functions which all require 5 different types of Callings. The word "Calling" is very similar to the word "Vocation," which Webster's Dictionary defines as: "a resident call or impulse to perform a certain function." This definition implies our Calling is something inherent from the time of birth. It also implies within this call there is a deeply felt passion to fulfill a specific function in life. This gratifies our soul, fulfills our spirit and accomplishes our Mandate.

This is a very important part of who we are as sovereign Men. In addition, our unique Calling implies there is a specific reason for our individual creation. Our individual creation is both planned and perfect for each one of us. Most importantly, our Calling is a loving gift from our Creator given to each and every Man to do His service.

---

1 Jeremiah 1:5, KJV

"Today we may say aloud before an awe-struck world: We are still masters of our fate. We are still captain of our souls."
Winston Churchill – Prime Minister of Britain

The 5 commonly accepted Corporation vocations and departments are as follows:

Name:	Department:
1) The CEO	Chief Executive, President
2) The Operations Man	Director of Operations, Logistics
3) The Salesman	Sales & Marketing, Public Relations
4) The Manager	Personnel Management
5) The Teacher/Trainer	Training, Research and Development

Which one of the 5 Callings are you called to walk in? Just as in the case of Jeremiah, every male is born into a Calling where he has been gifted to achieve success. Every family system, every business system and every church system will all have these 5 basic categories of functions working within them, whether they acknowledge them or not.

There are special gifts and motivations Men in each of these 5 categories will inherently possess in order to fulfill their corporate position effectively. As you read on, the characteristics and motivations of the 5 categories will be given to assist you in determining a general assessment of how you are personally designed.

Why have corporations continued to follow this basic corporate structure for hundreds of years? It is very simple, because it works. Of course, the gifts required for the 5 main Callings may overlap. Men can operate in multiple categories with some degree of success for a time. Most leaders will agree: to be fully successful in life it is beneficial for all of us to determine specifically which of the 5 Callings we are best suited to function. If you have a problem determining which of the Callings you are naturally built to fulfill, I assure you if you spend the time to really evaluate the information and tools in this chapter, you will have dialed into your Calling.

"Train up a child in the way that he should go (in the way that he is built and "called" to go), and when he is old, he will not depart from it."[2]
King Solomon – Book of Proverbs

Knowing Your Calling – What Motivates You?

After years of troubleshooting and counseling Men, I have found there are 5 different ***motivations*** leading Men in each of the 5 Callings. Every Man will have one of these 5 motivations residing within him yearning to express itself, and this motivation will usually be the main incentive for getting him out of bed in the morning. Your motivation gets you moving!

The deep personal motivations of a Man's heart are built into a Man's make-up, and these motivations will consciously and sub-consciously determine the priorities and direction in his life. It has nothing to do with his mood or what he has been taught. This is the hill a Man will die on if put to the test. This is the core motivation of a Man's heart at a level that goes beyond anything you think or say. This is how God has made you!

The 5 motivations can be summed up as following:

- Building - ***CEO***
- Truth - ***The Operations Man***
- Fun - ***The Salesman***
- People - ***The Manager***
- Facts - ***The Teacher/Trainer***

---

2 Proverbs 22:6, KJV

As you look over these 5 motivations, I would like you to consider these are the motivations God himself has shown us through his Son. These 5 motivations come directly from His nature. Jesus made it very clear His number one concern was for "People." To love His "People," He has given us His "Truth" (His Word) and His "Facts." (His Creation) He has offered the opportunity to partake in "Building" His kingdom. And finally, He has offered to us His "Fun" (Joy) as we fight along side of him to establish His kingdom on earth, by sharing all the gifts and Callings He has given us.

As you read on to determine which of the 5 Callings you are blessed with, please understand you have been given a measure of the very substance of God Himself. God has created you with a Calling containing his nature. Knowing and understanding your Calling will lead you to fulfilling your Mandate. Ultimately, it will lead to knowing your Creator in a deeper way.

In your quest to determine where you stand with these 5 motivations, it may help you to first think about how you relate with the other people in your life. Every Man has within him the ability to administer both mercy and judgment in relationships. Are you a Man generally more inclined to act out of mercy, or are you more inclined to act out of judgment?

Simply put, are you more inclined to let an offense just go without punishment during a reprimand, or are you more inclined to administer punishment during a reprimand? Both of these world views are equally good, depending on when or how they are administered. All healthy parents, teachers, coaches and leaders know there are times when having mercy on someone's bad behavior is the best relational choice.

On the other hand, there are times when administering judgment (disciplinary consequences) on someone's bad behavior is the best relational choice. As discussed in Chapter 3, a Man's heart and reasoning are his primary tools given to him to help determine whether mercy or judgment is the best and most appropriate action.

Some of the Callings will have a propensity to be slightly more of a judgment minded world view, and some of the Callings will lean more to a mercy minded world view. It is generally found that CEO's and Operations Men have a make-up accentuating slightly more of a judgment world view, due to the necessary duties of their Callings. Managers and Teachers generally have a make-up accentuating slightly more of a merciful world view, due to the necessary duties of their Callings.

Remember, all of us are made to have a healthy balance of judgment and mercy according to our Calling. People are usually hard wired a little more to one side of the world view scale with regard to their views on judgment and mercy. Therefore, I am listing the two world views as either "Judgment/Mercy" or "Mercy/Judgment" to label which world views is generally associated with a Man's Calling.

The 5 motivations are as follows:

Calling:	Motivation:	World View
1) The CEO	Building	Judgment/Mercy
2) The Operations Man	Truth	Judgment/Mercy
3) The Salesman	Fun	50/50
4) The Manager	People	Mercy/Judgment
5) The Teacher	Facts	Mercy/Judgment

Men with a Judgment/Mercy type of world view are more likely to have a Calling leaning more to "The CEO" or "The Operations Man." Men with a Mercy/Judgment type of world view are more likely to have a Manager or Teacher Calling. Salesmen are found to have both world views depending on which is more fun to them. Remember, these are generalities solely for the purpose of using a broad brush-stroke to quickly identify a Man's probable Calling.

Asking yourself the question of your Calling is the first step. Most Men have never asked the question, "What is my Calling?" In determining where you fit regarding your calling, you will find it is very helpful to ask those close to you what actually motivates you, and if you have more of a Judgment/Mercy or a Mercy/Judgment Calling. Parents are excellent people from whom to get feedback. Every parent will tell you most characteristics a Man exhibits were displayed even when the Man was a very small child.

It is not crucial for you to make a quick or bold decision on which Calling you were made to walk in. You already are who you are. The important point here is to consider how you are made, so you can use this information to fulfill your Mandate and interact with the other Callings in a team effort surpassing your successes of the past.

So which of the 5 motivations will get you up out of bed in the morning? Be honest with yourself and listen to what your heart is saying to you. God desires you make your Calling and your election sure so you will prosper in your life. Look at how the Apostle Paul looked at how the different Callings are supposed to work and interact together.

"The body is a unit, though it is made up of many parts; and though all its parts are many, they form one body. So it is with Christ. For we were all baptized by one Spirit into one body, whether Jews or Greeks, slave or free, and we were all given the one Spirit to drink. Now the body is not made up of one part but of many.

If the foot should say, "Because I am not a hand, I do not belong to the body," it would not for that reason cease to be part of the body. And if the ear should say, "Because I am not an eye, I do not belong to the body," it would not for that reason cease to be part of the body. If the whole body were an eye, where would the sense of hearing be? If the whole body were an ear, where would the sense of smell be?

But in fact God has arranged the parts in the body, every one of them, just as he wanted them to be. If they were all one part, where would the body be? As it is, there are many parts, but one body. The eye cannot say to the hand, "I don't need you!" And the head cannot say to the feet, "I don't need you!" On the contrary, those parts of the body that seem to be weaker are indispensable, and the parts that we think are less honorable we treat with special honor. And the parts that are unpresentable are treated with special modesty, while our presentable parts need no special treatment.

But God has combined the members of the body and has given greater honor to the parts that lacked it, so that there should be no division in the body, but that its parts should have equal concern for each other. If one part suffers, every part suffers with it; if one part is honored, every part rejoices with it.

Now you are the body of Christ, and each one of you is a part of it. And in the church God has appointed first of all apostles, second prophets, third teachers, then workers of miracles, also those having gifts of healing, those able to help others, those with gifts of administration, and those speaking in different kinds of tongues. Are all apostles? Are all prophets? Are all teachers? Do all work miracles? Do all have gifts of healing? Do all speak in tongues? Do all interpret? But eagerly desire the greater gifts. And now I will show you the most excellent way."[3]

The Apostle Paul – First Letter to the People of Corinth

What's Your Calling?

This drill is no different than going to the first day of practice for any sports team. One of the first questions your Coach and the other players are going to ask you is, "What position are you playing?" It is extremely helpful to understand there are 5 basic positions outlined in both the corporate structure and in every system known to mankind. Just as a basketball team has 5 positions that are all equally important, every group of Men will be made up by an assortment of the 5 Callings. When the 5 Callings are all acknowledged and promoted, the group can accomplish any task.

Every athlete knows no matter how hard an athlete trains, every Man is built emotionally, physically and spiritually to best play a specific position. In football, the mental, physical and emotional make-up of an offensive lineman is very different than the make-up of a defensive back. Men will have the opportunity and even the duty to play different positions at times in their lives, but there is usually one position where a Man fits best.

Thank God Men are resilient enough to play other positions when the need arises. However, the objective here is to have as many Men as possible walking in their Mandated Calling in an effort to achieve maximum success in their lives. Every coach knows he will have the best team possible when all of his players are playing in the position where

3 1 Corinthians 12:12-31, NIV

they are built and trained to perform. So, without further delay, here are some basic characteristics of the 5 different Callings.

The CEO – Building: Judgment/Mercy

A Man with the CEO Calling thinks building a kingdom is the most important thing in life. It does not matter what kind of kingdom he is building. It may be a good kingdom or it may be an evil kingdom. But most assuredly, a CEO will always be building a kingdom, because his passion is totally motivated by his desire to create an empire.

The CEO is a natural leader carrying a built-in authority to command other Men. He is not truly content unless he is leading others. Other Men will usually take orders from him, because they can sense he was born to be a CEO. He usually has spent three to five year periods of his life functioning in all of the other Callings. During a CEO's early lifetime, he will have functioned as an Operations Man, a Salesman, a Manager and a Teacher because these practical learning experiences are stepping stones for bringing him to a place where he can effectively lead as a CEO.

One way you can identify a true CEO is he will have a fairly equal balance of all of the 5 motivations. A healthy CEO will have within him an equal measure of the motivators of Building, Truth, Fun, People and Facts, but he won't die on any of those hills. He will die on the "Build the Kingdom" hill.

If you find yourself a born leader having a fairly equal measure of each of these motivational characteristics, you probably are a CEO. A CEO must have each of the other positional traits in order to impart them to the other Callings as he leads. Once again, the CEO's major purpose in life is to build an organization, a kingdom or an empire on some scale.

When a CEO is on, he looks like George Washington, Winston Churchill or Theodore Roosevelt. When a CEO is off, he will build for the devil's kingdom and he can be very rock headed and very controlling. In the church, CEO's are called "Apostles."

The Operations Man - Truth: Judgment/Mercy

The Operations Man lives, breathes, and eats Truth. He usually has an extra special dose of discernment and insight, and you will many times find him perched upon a lookout point with the best view. He must have wisdom and be quick to make decisions, because he has the responsibility of keeping order and making sure the organizational machine runs smoothly. He will thrive when he works closely with the CEO.

A good analogy of the Operations Man is the person who rides shotgun on a stagecoach. Whereas, the CEO is usually the driver of the stagecoach having the overall responsibility to drive and oversee the whole operation, the Operations Man is the right hand Man riding next to the CEO, backing him at every turn. He is an expert at focusing on attacks and distractions from the enemy, and he has an innate ability to handle any potential mishap hindering the mission at hand. The Operations Man is a great troubleshooter who can spot problems before they happen, and he can usually fix them faster than most people can even understand there is a problem.

In a corporation, the Operations Man and the CEO are a fantastic team. The Operations Man will instinctively watch out for the CEO, and he will be his additional eyes and ears. The Operations Man can spend most of his time focusing on the specific problems and duties the CEO has requested he accomplish. He generally is more perceptive to potential problems than the CEO, but he has a tendency to be single minded and sometimes has a tough time seeing the whole picture. The Operations Man is an excellent support system to the CEO, as they both use their God-given authority to lead a company or system.

The Operations Man comes off as having less compassion or mercy when there is sin or problems in the camp. If you don't deal with problems right away, he will become unhinged like a cornered cougar. When serious troubles occur, the Operations Man will usually be the first to repeatedly let you know of your mistakes with comments like, "Why didn't you listen" or "I told you this was going to happen!"

Do not be offended by The Operations Man when he tells you of the problem. He does not want to be right; he just wants to be heard. Most of the time, the Operations Man is very discerning because this is his most needed gift to do his job. He gets paid to make things right. The

Operations Man can become the person "we love to hate" if we are not careful. However, his position is indispensable, because he is usually the Man who both knows how and is willing to deliver the tough word and tough love when necessary.

When an Operations Man writes a book, it is many times fairly short and he says most of the important things in the first few pages. From then on he will keep repeating himself to drive his point into the ground. Operations Men love giving orders and they are good at it. Most of their orders are less than three words, and they usually sound more like a demand than a request. He will rarely give up on solving a problem, because he feels this would be giving up in defeat. An Operations Man cannot handle losing. Losing is never an option. Losing is absolutely unthinkable for an Operations Man.

When the Operations Man is on, he will be the right hand Man for a Ronald Reagan or a Winston Churchill. When the Operations Man is off he becomes negative, critical, controlling, cynical, and he is just plain no fun. In the church, Operations Men are called "Prophets."

The Salesman - Fun: (50-50) Mercy/Judgment

The Salesman is the life of the party, and he is one of the easiest Callings to identify. He loves to have fun! This is why he is such a great Salesman. He knows the more he sells the more fun he can have. He also knows the more fun he has, the more he will sell. The Salesman is everyone's friend for a day. If you ask him to invite people to a party, he will fill the room. The Salesman is generally not your first choice for a counselor, because hashing over all those problems is kind of depressing for him. He would rather bring in new recruits than fix the ones he already has.

The Salesman loves to start new projects. But once the project starts to lose momentum, he is on to the next party. A company and a business will live or die over whether they have good Salesmen. The Salesman appears disingenuous at times, because he moves on to the next sale. In reality he is just doing his job.

If he gets caught up in the drudges of life, he will often lose his joy. He then becomes a liability to any company or organization. The

Salesman has to stay "up" and in good spirits; therefore, he will naturally make a huge attempt to avoid downers at all cost. Get a few good Salesmen together, and the sparks will fly and the parties will scream. But remember, they will be gone when it is time to clean up the mess, unless you can figure out a way of making the clean-up time extremely fun.

When the Salesman is on, your company will prosper, people will have fun, and the chips will flow. When the Salesman is off, he tends to play too hard, and he may take himself out of commission with too much sex, drugs and rock and roll. When he leaves an organization, his charisma and contriving may take a lot of people with him on his way out. So keep it fun, or you will lose your Salesmen, and then your organization. In the church, Salesmen are called "Evangelists."

The Manager - People: Mercy/Judgment

Managers love people. They have a natural warmth and friendliness that is beyond normal human measure. They generally see the good in people, and managers are not overly concerned with dealing with problems in a confronting manner. Managers are always more concerned about people than they are about the company, the program or the church system. Everyone loves the Manager, because he feels safe and usually he is non-threatening. People know that if you go to a Manager with your problems, he will display understanding and generally he will not condemn you.

Managers usually struggle with tough love and are prime candidates for cons. Addicts and rebellious people often take advantage of a Manager, if he does not have Operations Men and CEOs to watch his back. A Manager will give you the shirt off his back, but when it comes to a fight, he may take a very long time to get going. Once he gets upset about an injustice, the fur will fly. You will usually see untrained Managers allow people to walk on them for years, only to finally rise up in a ball of fury. Managers make the best Santa Clauses, and they are very good listeners because they truly have a special gift of empathy.

When Managers are on, they can bring peace, understanding and healing to a situation. When Managers are off, they are labeled as underachievers and they many times tolerate way too much evil. They make great codependents and will allow the devil to remain in their homes for years in the name of love and mercy. The Bible is correct when it implies the true Managers have the highest Calling, because Managers have this incredible ability and desire to love the sheep. In the church, Managers are called "Pastors."

The Teacher/Trainer - Facts: Mercy/Judgment

Facts are everything to a teacher. He is usually analytical and inquisitive. Information, detail, description and accuracy are very important to a true teacher. Teachers make great accountants and they are excellent at "teaching," of course. When they write a book, it usually is as long, or longer than the Bible.

Teachers love information, and they love the impeccable order of the world. Many teachers have this incredible ability to deliver the facts in a way making one feel awestruck. They love to figure out God's Creation and then share it with others. They are generally a little deeper and more melancholy regarding the arts, politics and social ideals. Teachers are not built for heavy confrontation on a daily basis, and sometimes this avoidance of confrontation appears as cowardice.

Many times Teachers are loyal to institutions to a fault, because they do well in regimented systems. Most of the time, Teachers are introverted and they do not like change. They generally are not accustomed to putting it all out on the line. Often, Teachers have difficulty in entrepreneurial ventures, because they will over analyze the risks. They love books, files, notes, grades, and order. However, if you truly want to make Teachers happy, all you have to do is allow them to teach you and share with you the fantastic information they have learned.

When a Teacher is on, he will discover new ideas and technology incredibly beneficial to a company or organization. When a Teacher is off, he can be a complainer who thinks his facts and knowledge are a substitute for God ordained authority. He may attempt to usurp the job of the CEO and the Operations Man, with very little success. In the church, it is no surprise Teachers are called, "Teachers."

What is your Calling?

So I ask you again, "What is your Calling? Is building a great business, church or organization what fulfills your heart? (CEO) Maybe you're a fix-it person who wants Truth and order to come forth? (Operations) Are you the life of the Party and motivated by excitement and fun? (Salesman) Or maybe you're such a people person that spending quality time loving and helping people is everything to you. (Manager) And finally you may be a facts and information person who desires to teach and share your intellect. (Teacher)

Understanding how you are wired can be one of the most profound and useful tools you have as a Man. More importantly, walking in your Calling will lead you into knowing God and fulfilling your Mandate.

"Give diligence to make your Calling and election sure: for if you do these things, you shall never fall."[4]
The Apostle Peter – Second Letter of Peter

When We Don't Understand the Callings?

I will share my experience as a real estate developer and a General Contractor, because this is where I first learned the practicality and the extreme benefits of understanding the Callings. Growing up in real estate development and in building custom homes in Southern California, I learned very quickly how important it is to have the right person do the right job at the right time.

In building custom homes, there are multiple different trades sub-contracted in order to complete the construction of a house. Have you ever hired a person who was not gifted in what you hired them to do? The devastating results of putting the wrong person on the job can cause problems from frustration, all the way to the failure of the entire project. Can you imagine the repercussions of hiring a plumber to do roofing? Can you see the intelligence of hiring an electrician to do the plumbing work?

Most of the tradesmen have been around construction jobs enough to do many different trades performed on site. But is this smart? It will

4 2 Peter 1:10, KJV

generally cost time, money and loss in performance when you hire an unqualified or wrong person to do a job.

Why Understanding Callings is Important?

When Men are encouraged and placed in positions that match their Callings, everything flows. Deadlines are made, budgets are kept, and projects are completed on time. This is called "Blessings."

The best way we can love and assist our fellow brothers is to know their Callings. Once we understand how our loved ones and friends are designed, we can minister to them on a level meeting their needs more readily. There are many aspects in the framework of a person. If we leave out the core Calling that a Man is built upon, we may totally miss how we are supposed to relate with that Man.

As you walk through life, it is pretty easy to see where Men fail in their businesses and endeavors. All we have to do is consider their Callings. Remember, it is a very loving thing to spend time and consider the Callings of our friends. It allows us to assist them on a new and higher level of friendship, because we will be promoting their God-given destinies. Understanding and promoting the Callings of the Men around you is one of the most helpful encouragements you can give to them.

Have you considered what Callings your best friends have? Have you surrounded yourself with the 5 Callings? Can you imagine how much stronger and more productive your life will be, if you made it a point to surround yourself with many different Men who all had a basic understanding of their Callings? This would be even more profound if you made it a point to build and encourage these Men in their particular Callings.

It may be time to do a Calling inventory. Take some time and think about the Men you consider the support system in your life. If you do not have a few of each Calling somewhere near you for support, you are missing out on the additional strength and assistance potentially there for you. With this in mind, you may have some additional work to do by inviting and promoting new Men into your life.

When young David from the Bible went into battle against the monstrous Goliath, he carried five smooth stones into battle with him as the weapons of his warfare. Any one of these stones could have taken Goliath out, and indeed one of them did. David proved this as he hurled a stone right into the head of his adversary, killing him. Let these five smooth stones be examples of the five Callings you have brought into battle with you in the form of trained Men and brothers who surround you for support. Commit yourself to being one of these smooth stones for the Men near you. They desperately need you, and they need your trained assistance.

I will say it again, because this is so important. There are Men around you who need you, and your Calling! Are you "Called" as a Manager? Men need the special loving and relational skills that have been deposited in you. Are you an Operations Man? You are called to deal with problems and the sin that so often gets a piece of your friends and family. Maybe you are a Salesman who is sitting on the couch playing video games. It is time to put away your childish ways and sell the Truth of Manhood.

Our friends and family need us to walk in our Callings to assist them and to bring life, prosperity and joy into their lives. Each one of us has a Calling waiting to come forth and bless our loved ones. Let us do our job and awaken the Callings that have been denied or neglected. Our Mandate demands that we become Men and have our Keys and our Gates in order. It also includes walking successfully in our Callings.

I was in church one day and there were about 30 Men in the congregation. I was standing next to a Minister friend of mine and I asked him, "How many ministry leaders with a Calling on their lives do you think are in this room?" I really thought he was going to give me a number like 10 or 12. He looked around, and then he thought for a moment and said, "I don't think there are any leaders with Callings in this room."

My stomach dropped. Here was a fifty-year-old veteran Minister who had totally missed it in regards to understanding the 5 Callings for Men. Like many ministers today, he thought the Callings were only for those who are full time paid Ministers "called" to preach from a pulpit.

The Bible is clear when it states, **"For the gifts and Calling of God are without repentance."**[5] This means whether we make a choice to serve God or not, the Callings of God are given to us at birth. They are a free and inherent gift in our foundational make-up, and God will not take them back. I felt compelled to tell my friend, "Look closely, there

5 Romans 11:29, KJV

is a whole room full of leaders with 'Callings.' If you can just recognize and build these mighty Men in their 'Callings,' there is no limit to the success you and your church can experience." Every single Man is called to lead in his life in one of the 5 Callings in some capacity. I saw CEO's, Operations Men, Salesmen, Managers and Teachers all around me who have never been told they have been gifted to lead in their God-given Callings.

I don't believe it is overly important to God which outward label we walk in, as long as we fulfill our Calling. We were created to express God's nature through our Calling and overcome in life as we fulfill our Mandate. This means we have to overcome in the business community, the political town square and in the social arenas of church, community service and the arts.

Wherever there are people, you will find the 5 Callings working for both good and evil. A Manager who fulfills his Mandate by counseling and pastoring in a business or corporate setting is no less important than a Man who has the title "Pastor" who is counseling and pastoring a church. A Man who is a born CEO may be no less important or blessed by God, whether he builds God's kingdom through developing a large business, or through a successful corporation. Both can be dedicated to serving others.

Look at Milton Hershey who created and founded Hershey chocolate. As a CEO, he developed a town and a corporate empire dedicated to serving others and developing, building and encouraging Men. Even today, the orphanages and schools he created are testimonies of how God can use a Man to function as a CEO (Apostle) in the business world.

Ronald Reagan defined what it means to walk as a CEO in his public and political life. He ultimately became the President of the United States bringing Communism of the Soviet Union to its knees. George Washington Carver and Isaac Newton are examples of Teachers who were given scientific ideas changing the world for good. I cannot overstate how important it is for us to encourage and support our fellow Men in their Callings.

No Man is ever dismissed or disqualified from walking in his Calling. The Callings are given to us as gifts from God from the time of conception. A Man will either use his Calling for good, or he will use his

Calling for evil. I have seen first hand when a Man acknowledges and receives the Calling given to him, his effectiveness in overcoming in life and in fulfilling his Mandate will increase dramatically and immediately.

Walking in the Wrong Calling:

I have seen Men work in positions for decades where they were not gifted with a Calling fitting with their particular job. You may recall Bob from Chapter 2. Bob worked in sales for over 10 years barely scratching out a living. Bob was a Teacher, not a Salesman. When Bob would go on sales calls, he had all the information on how good his product was, and the statistics of how it would benefit the client; however, he had very little gifting for sales. His limited ability to bring the excitement and the energy needed to make commanding sales made his life as a salesman a miserable experience.

Finally, I was able to share with Bob that his life would probably flow much better if he picked an occupation more in line with his Calling as a Teacher. Within one year, he changed jobs and everything came in line for him. Bob was so much happier as he shared the things he was doing in his new teaching job. It was as if the floodgates of heaven were filling up his life, because he was doing what he was called to do and God was blessing him.

Bill Loses His Grandmother:

Bill is a worker at a manufacturing plant. He recently suffered a death in his family. Bill's work output dropped to a very low production level because he was emotionally distraught over the loss of his grandmother. This concerned the Operations Man because Bill's low output was endangering the company's bottom line.

If we allow the Operations Man to deal directly with Bill, there is a probable chance the Operations Man might threaten Bill to get his productivity up or he would be fired. This would potentially be harmful to Bill's emotional well-being, as it is already a hard week considering his Grandmother's passing.

The Operation Man has a Judgment/Mercy world view leading him to deal with Bill for not putting out the effort. It may seem harsh, but the Operations Man is simply doing what he does best. His job is to get production back in order. It is not in his nature to be overly tuned into the emotional well being of Bill, since he is gifted at keeping the whole machine of the company productive. Besides, the Operations Man may never be quite sure whether Bill is faking his grief over his Grandmother or not. He may go so far as to accuse Bill of milking the situation. The Operations Man knows if the production does not meet certain quotas, the company may suffer and everyone loses, even Bill.

If we have the Personnel Manager deal directly with Bill, we will no doubt eliminate the chance of a relational breach or offense from occurring. The Manager is of course a people person who is driven by his love of people and he has a Mercy/Judgment world view. After finding out Bill has just lost a loved one, the trained Manager would probably give Bill some time off and have someone else take over Bill's job until he recovers. Production then goes back up and everyone is happy. Bill feels loved, the Manager feels appreciated and the Operations Man can sleep at night.

Now, on the same note, you do not want the Manager to do the Operation Man's job. The Manager is not overly concerned with Truth, production and least of all judgment. As soon as he tries to do the Operation Man's job, he most likely will not enforce the iron fist when necessary and crack the whip of productivity when the crew gets lazy.

Many times the Manager will be so concerned about the emotions of the people, that he will neglect the production of the company. In accordance with a "Manager's" nature, a normal crew will see his weakness and take advantage of his leniency whenever possible. The end of this scenario is the slow death of the company's productivity and nobody wins.

The big question many Men have is, "Can we teach the Operations Man to be more merciful or can we teach the Manager to be more judgment minded?" The answer of course is "Yes." You can teach an Operations Man to be more mercy minded. You can teach a Manager who has a built-in love for people to be more judgment minded and to express tough love every now and then. But you better have about 50 years to do it, because you will be going against nature itself to try to get a Man to change the way he has been created.

My point here is these Men are fashioned from conception in Callings that need to express particular motivations and world views. We do not need to force them into changing. Training Men to be balanced is a given, but if we ignore the fact that Men are created to have different Callings, we will be going against the tide, and we will be in for a long and disappointing battle. It is so much easier just to put a Man in the job he was created to do, and lct him do it.

Judging Other Callings:

Every Man I have ever met has judged another Man for not being like him. If you want to be set free right now, I have a mission for you. Ask forgiveness from God for judging other Men for not being like you. Managers judge Operations Men for being too hard. Operations Men judge Managers for being too soft.

Salesmen judge everyone for being too serious and for not having fun. CEO's judge everyone for not taking on the world like they do. Teachers judge everyone for not knowing what they know, and for not researching the facts the way they have. We have sinned terribly before our Maker, and it is time to get it right.

He made us different for a purpose! It is okay for a Pastor not to have the same Judgmental fervor as a Prophet. It is okay for a Teacher to go on and on about factual things important to him, because in some way and at some time we will do better to have that information. ***Let God have his way with Men, and let us not be a stumbling block to ourselves or to Men who have been given one of the 5 Callings.***

Several decades ago, I was given a book written by Larry Burkett about handling finances from a Christian perspective. In certain areas, I knew financially there was something amiss with me. I thought it was a good book, but somehow I judged Larry about the way he delivered the information. It was so subtle it didn't seem like a big deal, but due to my poor attitude towards Larry, I never really embraced the principles of the book.

About 10 years later, I was still battling with finances and I again became aware something was still amiss with me. I then was introduced to Crown Ministries, an intensive 12-week discipleship program teaching the Biblical principles of handling money. I learned so much in the course, I thanked God for the information. I also made the comment in the class that it would have been better if I had obtained the teaching years before, saving me a lot of financial anguish.

Right then and there I felt convicted in my heart. I did get the teaching 10 years before, but I had rejected it subtly, because of some ridiculous minor delivery point. I then came to find out Crown Ministries was a spin off from Larry Burkett's teachings. Larry actually passed on the information from his ministry to Crown Ministries. It was very humbling to realize I had taken a Man's God-given Calling and stamped it out. In doing so, I had also stamped out the very avenue God had ordained to bring me this great teaching.

As Men, we need to understand when we quench the Calling God has deposited into one of his sons, we are actually quenching God. This was a very sobering realization I will never forget. I prayed the following prayer:

"Father in heaven, I acknowledge the gifts and the 'Callings' of God are from you and they are holy in your sight. I have sinned by not realizing their importance and by not honoring these 'Callings' in the Men around me. Forgive me Lord for quenching your Spirit by not allowing you to work through Men with 'Callings' as Apostles, Prophets, Evangelists, Pastors or Teachers. We are made in your image and these 'Callings' are a representation of you. I declare that I invite the fullness of your body 'Callings' to work in me and through me for the rest of my life."

"Teach me to understand and learn of your 'Callings' so we all can edify and encourage one another into victory and unity. Forgive me for the times I have ignored or misused my Calling. May I come to know the fullness of my Calling on earth, and may many people benefit from my relationships with them. I dedicate my gifts and my Calling to you, and from this day forward I will allow you to use my Calling to glorify you and prosper your kingdom. In the name of Jesus of Nazareth I pray. Amen"

A Blessing For Pastors!

To all the Men of God who have been given the title "Pastor" by the church system or denomination with which they are affiliated, I would like to take the opportunity to thank you and bless you for leading Men into victory. In this chapter, I have discussed the overall function and make-up of the 5 Callings so evident in my life over the past decades, and I have shown you how the Word of God and common sense ties these Callings together. This information is published to assist the local Pastor and not to work against him.

Please see I am not suggesting we stop calling the leader of a church "Pastor," just because he may have the gifts and motivations making him better suited to be referred to as one of the other Callings. The local Pastor many times has enough problems to deal with, and he does not need people knocking him down or telling him he should change his title.

Most local Pastors are attempting to build up the lives of the families they are charged with caring for, and most local Pastors are handicapped by only having a few good Men and a host of immature "boys" to help them. As Shakespeare has written, "A rose by any other name would smell as sweet." When a person dedicates their life to shepherding and caring for people, the name we call the person is not overly important. The act of loving and leading people is important.

Throughout the world, the title of Pastor seems quite appropriate for any Man with any Calling dedicated to protecting and leading people before God in a church. The title we give a Man is not as important as honoring his Calling and who God made that Man to be. In Paul's letter to his son in the faith Timothy, Paul clearly asks us to give double honor to elders who rule well, and who labor in the word and doctrine.

The title of Pastor in the church sense is just a title, and it should not be confused with the Calling of "Pastor." Men with the title of "Pastor" in the church system may actually be "Apostles," "Prophets," "Evangelists," "Pastors" or "Teachers," and you will find their motivations and world views will stem from their particular Calling. Failing to understand that our local Pastors may have any one of the 5 corporate Callings has caused many hurtful judgments and unreasonable expectations against them. Our ignorance of the 5 corporate Callings has damaged relationships in the church and hurt the body of Christ.

Both before and after his death and resurrection, Jesus did not make a big deal regarding the titles his followers used, and neither should we. He did make a big deal out of loving and working together as a body and honoring the different Callings and gifts used to edify his people.

When you hire a plumber to fix your pipes, you are really not honoring the title of "Plumber." You are actually honoring the person and his ability and gifting to fix the plumbing. The title of "Plumber" is not important, but his expertise and ability is irreplaceable. The same principle applies with the 5 Callings. It is not the titles we honor, it is the irreplaceable gifts and relational abilities to build and protect the church that we must honor in each and every Man.

The following passage written by the Apostle Paul gives us a clear picture of the 5 Callings.

God's Corporation: Ephesians 4:11-16

"And He gave some, Apostles; and some, Prophets; and some, Evangelists; and some, Pastors and Teachers; For the perfecting of the saints, for the work of the ministry, for the edifying of the body of Christ:

Till we all come in the unity of the faith, and of the knowledge of the Son of God, unto a perfect Man, unto the measure of the stature of the fullness of Christ: That we henceforth be no more children ("boys"), tossed to and fro, and carried about with every wind of doctrine, by the sleight of men, and cunning craftiness, whereby they lie in wait to deceive;

But speaking the Truth in love, may grow up into him in all things, which is the head, even Christ: From whom the whole body fitly joined together and compacted by that which every joint supplies, according to the effectual working in the measure of every part, makes increase of the body unto the edifying of itself in love."[6]

The Apostle Paul – Letter to the Followers in Ephesia

---

6 Ephesians 4:11-16, KJV

In Paul's letter to the Ephesians, he wrote about the 5 Callings giving us a good understanding of what the 5-fold corporate church is supposed to achieve and why. This passage envisions the pure and beautiful symphony created when the 5 Callings are working together in unity to build, protect, edify and encourage the corporate church "in love."

It may be helpful to read the passage in Ephesians 4 again just to make sure you are seeing the brilliance of how we are supposed to work together and love one another in the corporate body of believers. The purpose of this chapter is to acknowledge the 5 different Callings given to Men, and to promote Men to walk in unity and build our local churches, communities and businesses in fulfillment of our great Mandate. When this occurs, it is truly a blessing to Pastors and all Men who seek to love people.

"A house divided against itself cannot stand."
Abraham Lincoln – 16th President of the United States

Modern Day Indulgences:

In the text following, we are going to troubleshoot one of the major problems continuing to contaminate and castrate many local church systems. Once again, in no way do I desire to criticize or indict the very Men of God (The local Pastors) we all have been called to encourage and edify. So please hear my heart for building up the corporate body and use this insight to build up a church that will not be torn down again.

The church of the 21st century has committed a grievous sin against the Lord and the body of Christians by not promoting the fullness of the Lord's Callings to minister from the pulpit or in the town square. In many church and business systems, we have misunderstood the teachings Jesus of Nazareth gave us regarding how Men are ordained to administer their Callings. Remember, Jesus of Nazareth was the only Man who perfectly walked in the fullness of the 5 corporate Callings. As the author and creator of these Callings, He is our example of how to perform them.

"God does not anoint "boys," God only anoints Men. The act of being a Man is both inspired and empowered by God."

Since the time Jesus of Nazareth took His place at the right hand of the Father, the fullness of God's Callings are to be brought forth through the 5-fold corporate body of Men as we see in the Apostle Paul's letter to the Ephesians. God has ordained Men to be anointed with His Spirit. He has ordained His Spirit to minister to His people through His people. The main difference now is we are to do it corporately as a TEAM. This is why he created each and every Man with a specific Calling inherent within him.

It is God who ordains the Callings, not mankind. God would never allow fallen mankind to decide our Callings, because mankind's sinful nature has a tendency to control and use Men for its own purposes. It is the job of Men to recognize and acknowledge what God has already placed within a Man. We are called of God, and this Calling is confirmed by Men. As we acknowledge the gifts and Callings inherent within the Men around us, we can work with each other through relationships in a TEAM effort to fulfill our Mandates. Truly no Man is made to be an island, and no Man is to be a stumbling block in the success of other Men.

Allowing one person to be the responsible party for all of the 5 Callings within the corporate church is a "boyish" interpretation of the Scriptures, and a grievous misuse of the Word of God. When one male becomes the sole source of ministry in a congregation, the other males sitting dormant in the pews become spiritually emasculated.

Everything we have ever learned from sports and business success in has shown us a TEAM effort is absolutely necessary for victory. We all know there are many different positions in a TEAM effort, but to disqualify, nullify, disparage or exclude any TEAM member's participation is selfish, irresponsible and suicidal for the TEAM as a whole.

Paul showed us what the TEAM is supposed to look like when he described and explained thoroughly the Callings and the purpose of the corporate body in Ephesians 4. He specifically said that in the church the Men will walk in the Callings of Apostle, Prophet, Evangelist, Pastor and Teacher. When the 5 Callings are acknowledged, appreciated and united under one banner before the Lord, there is absolutely no stopping these Men from achieving success. This is true in war, in sports, in business, in politics, in families and in any effort involving a corporate group of people.

"Individual commitment to a group effort,
that is what makes a TEAM work."
Vince Lombardi

As we read earlier in this chapter, the good news is every male has one of these Callings placed within him at the time he is created. God is the one who ordains these Callings. Men are simply to recognize an ordination has taken place, and they are to honor it. It is very similar to the Bar Mitzvah. Every male is called to be "Bar Mitzvahed." The Men in our lives are supposed to promote the ordinations of God. Our fathers and brothers are there to teach, acknowledge and recognize what God has already predetermined.

Remember what God told Jeremiah? **"Before I formed you in the belly I knew you; and before you came forth out of the womb I sanctified you, and I ordained you a prophet unto the nations."**[7] It is very clear it is God who creates and designs us, and He is the one who predetermines our Callings.

When we allow another person, even a Pastor, to run the whole show in our spiritual lives, we are behaving like "boys" by forfeiting our God-given authority. Every Man is responsible to build up people in the kingdom of God. Many males have given their Mandated Keys of authority to a so-called Pastor in exchange for a ticket to irresponsibility.

---

7 Jeremiah 1:5, NKJV

By giving their spiritual responsibilities away, they become "boys" who are dependent on the spiritual input of their Pastor.

These "boys" must continue to rely on their Pastor to do a job impossible for one male or one Calling to do. Remember, it takes all 5 of the corporate Callings to achieve the job at hand of building the church. To add to the confusion, many males have not evaluated whether the Calling of their local Pastor fits their personal needs.

Many males are paying money to the local church and subtly entering into a system categorized as nothing less than "Modern Day Indulgences." Males in the church today have often bought their way out of the responsibility of walking in their Mandated Calling. These males have failed to participate in building the kingdom of God. Unfortunately, their behavior has become an accepted norm in Christianity.

Many of us have been paying the local Pastor in the church to be ***all*** for us. We expect him to do our jobs in exchange for a "get out of ministry free" card. This card allows us to exclude utilizing our God-given Mandate and Callings in the building of God's kingdom and His church.

When the opportunity and the obligation to preach to our loved ones and our fellow workers comes along, many of us just flash the "get out of ministry free" card and point them to a "Man of God" who can help them. Heaven forbid we become Men of God ourselves and sow the Spirit of God into the lives of our friends and families. Many males have believed the lie that they are not "Called" as ministers in one of the 5 corporate Callings. Therefore, they pay their tithe to a church system, and then they expect their Pastor and church to carry their Mandated responsibility.

We have in a sense made a silent agreement with our so-called "Pastors." We promise to "tithe" money to them, if they will do the work for us and make us feel better. We think we have a good deal going, because all we have to do is sit there in the pew and be a receptive "boy" at one service a week. Sadly, many of the Pastors are happy with this arrangement, and they tolerate this silent agreement as long as the money flows.

This inhibits healthy and equal relationship building between the males in the church, and it allows for the wealthy or influential members to remain stagnant in the church. The ironic thing about this arrangement is the church desperately needs the expertise and business wisdom of the successful businessmen and leaders who sit silently in the pews. The same principles leading to success in righteous businesses are the same principles contributing to building healthy church systems.

A huge problem has arisen in churches, because most businessmen do not respect the innumerable inexperienced "boys" preaching from the pulpits. How can businessmen be expected to take counsel from a "boy" who has not earned his stripes in the world and who has no discernible authority. A successful businessman can spot a Man from far away, and he generally can feel the presence of God-given authority by a handshake. The gap between businessmen and Pastors increases even further when the Pastor fails to recognize the God-given Callings of the businessmen.

The result of not recognizing the God-given Callings in these successful businessmen is that it leads them to feel inferior as Christians, and they become emasculated regarding spiritual matters in the church. Men do not like to feel inferior or emasculated. They will choose not to participate in church activities when these dynamics occur. The problem becomes further magnified if the businessman begins to stray back into worldly behavior out of boredom or a lack of feeling useful in the church. Many of us have watched "Pastors" and Para-church leaders who have allowed influential "boys" to behave in ways they never would tolerate from those less influential members, because they were fearful of losing financial support.

This is the price of indulgences, and it is founded upon believing the lie that we do not have a Calling. We play the indulgence game by entering into the "Pastor only" system by giving our Priestly Keys of authority to our Pastors. In return, we are free from developing our own personal relationship with God, and we are free from the responsibility of pulling our family and friends out of the fire. In short, we are free to be "boys."

Many Men in the church have compromised their Callings to the detriment of themselves and at the expense of the people they are called to protect and build up. We have handicapped our males instead of loving them and teaching them to walk as the ministers and Men they are called to be. Instead of teaching Men to worship in holiness before the Lord, many of our churches have become music and entertainment centers that cater to the whims of a "feel good" generation.

We have failed to share with them the hard Truth about how they are walking as "boys," and we have watched them hide from their responsibilities year after year. Ultimately, if a "boy's" behavior gets too embarrassing for the church or the Pastor to publicly endure, these "undesirables" are sometimes thrown to the wolves and disgraced for not walking the walk. All of us Men are responsible for this unhealthy "Pastor only" system we have created.

How on earth are we going to reach the world for Christ with this type of establishment, where the 5-fold corporate ministry structure is seldom functioning to capacity? Are we to expect just a few chosen Pastors and Preachers to win over the world? The best we can hope for from the "Pastor only" system is a collage of big churches with pews full of immature "boys." Of course, these "boys" are willing to attend church regularly, but they have little power in their lives to actually obtain personal victories or to change their local communities.

Why do "boys" lack the power to change the world for Christ? It is because we have given our Manhood away piece by piece, and we do not know how to get it back. We have missed the Truth that every male has a Calling in the church, and our power comes from the Keys of authority God gives us in our relationship with him as we walk as Men.

I'll say it again; it's all about the Keys. No Keys, no power. Have you been wondering why you feel powerless, and your prayers are not being answered? The "Pastor only" system has castrated the church by failing to teach males how to recapture their God-given Keys as Men.

Recently, we have had major American leaders openly and publicly repent for taking part in this dysfunctional "Pastor only" system. The repercussions of our errors have really begun to show. Instead of building strong and powerful churches full of mature Men who are sure of their Mandate and their Callings, we have built massive "boy" care centers that are failing to do the job Jesus entrusted to us.

What has happened to the corporate body of believers where each Man willingly and lovingly participates as a leader in his particular Calling? Where are the churches that have so many leaders evident in the congregation that it is hard to tell which one of them is the head local Pastor? Look back in American history during the revolutionary war. There were so many Men of God leading our nation, that today, historians have written thousands of books identifying their great accomplishments. Our founding fathers knew about the principles and the Mandate in Ephesians 4.

Today it is nothing less than a form of idolatry when we make one person our source of ministry, no matter how gifted the person may be. We must take a stand right now and see the error of our ways, because the repercussion of caretaking "boys" is mounting up. Males must be initiated into Manhood, taught the fullness of their Mandate, educated regarding their Keys and Gates, and trained to walk in the 5 Callings. Are we up to the task at hand?

Thank God, with His help, this is changing. Men are standing up in this nation. Because of the hardships and tribulations that males are beginning to experience, Men are rising up and learning of their Callings and their Mandates. This book is dedicated to teaching males how to become Men, to capture their Keys, to close the Gates to sin and to walk in our Callings as Patriarchs. The Band of Brothers is on the move again.

"boys" In the Church:

Our role model, Jesus of Nazareth, is committed to building his elite Band of Brothers. In these exciting but perilous times, becoming a Man and destroying the "boy" in us has reached a new level of importance. The price of playing poker has gone up. Not only is the family suffering unprecedented attacks, but in the last few decades even supposed Christian movements have seduced millions of people away from the much needed message of building up Men.

I am going to give it to you straight. When "boys" head up a movement or a system of any kind, the system becomes ***matriarchal.*** The result of "boys" attempting to lead is a travesty. Their lack of authority and testicular fortitude creates a dynamic where women and children are encouraged to place themselves in compromising and vulnerable positions. In other words, when "boys" refuse to take on their Mandated responsibilities, they are covertly pushing women and children into taking on their responsibilities for them.

Matriarchal movements are not of God, and they are very harmful to the body. Matriarchal males have abandoned their Keys of authority out of fear, and would rather usurp someone else's authority (steal someone's Keys) than do the work of managing their own authority. (Retrieve and utilize their own Keys).

Men who are walking with their Keys of authority intact will quickly identify these harmful movements, because they know they are led by "boys" with a matriarchal world view, and they will see there is always a misinterpretation of the 5-fold Callings. "boys" will usually repel any Godly or Mandated authority structure, because it is a threat to their own lack of maturity and Manhood. A "boy" will tend to push covertly rather than lead. Many times a "boy" will also follow in the steps of King Ahab, the Biblical role model for being a "boy," and allow overbearing and strong women to push for him.

In matriarchal systems, the 5-fold Callings will be totally turned on its head. Teachers will be functioning as Apostles. Evangelists will be functioning as Pastors. Pastors will be seen functioning as Prophets. The 5-fold corporate church may be encouraged, but no one seems to be functioning in the right place at the right time. There will be ministerial confusion pertaining to the church body, creating a system categorized as the "Crazy mix."

Truth, lies and control are bundled together in such a way leaving you feeling your mind has just been corkscrewed. The Bible is preached; however, your heart just cannot get over the feeling something is very wrong somewhere. The males and females running these systems generally have significant cracks in their emotional foundations, and their families and homes are never in a Godly order.

In a matriarchal system, God's 5 corporate Callings quickly turn into the devil's 5-fold corporation. Callings can be used for evil in the same way they are used for good. Instead of Apostles, Prophets, Evangelists, Pastors and Teachers functioning in love and unity, the devil's 5-fold corporation consists of Controllers, Critics, Contrivers, Codependents and Complainers operating in deception and destruction. If you think working for God is painful and tough, try working in the devil's 5-fold machine. It will grind you up and spit you out with absolutely no mercy whatsoever, and the whole time the machine will be thinking it is doing God and you a service.

This machine is lead by false spiritual voices whose primary motive is to take away what God has in store for His sons and daughters. These voices do this by keeping people in a continuous state of childish desires, so they will never know how spiritually blind and desolate they have become. In particular, as long as the males are kept in a state of infancy, they are satisfied being fed milk every week. The fullness of the Spirit of God is continuously replaced with some new form of excitement or toy that gratifies their selfish and proud nature. God's true treasure, His people, suffers neglect as they fail to know their true purpose and the power of God.

Matriarchal movements are actually a test for God's people, and they are always unhealthy and unbalanced. Some movements are noted as having an overzealous longing for the physical manifestations of God's outward signs and wonders, and there is usually a great toleration for sin and "boyish" behaviors. On the other end of the spectrum, matriarchal systems can be controlling and legalistic to the point where they totally deny miracles or supernatural acts of God exist. If you look at the males who support matriarchal movements, you will see a common denominator. They are generally insecure and controlling "boys" who struggle with an abnormal amount of sexual dysfunctions and/or father relationship issues, both in the present and in their past. (Point 16. on the Man vs. "boy" list.)

Fortunately, our true Father God will always do us the service of allowing complete exposure to these matriarchal systems plaguing the churches and the cultures we live in. A true Patriarch will rarely follow these "boys" into battle, because a Patriarch will not follow a "boy." True Men with a Patriarchal world view can immediately spot the lack of authority, power and fruit in most aspects of these movements. A Patriarch will stand on the saying; **"You shall know them by their fruits."**[8]

When the harmful movement is exposed, healthy and trained Men who have their homes and lives in order have the opportunity to rise up and take their position as leaders and rebuild the damaged areas of the body. This is why it is so important for us to be trained as healthy Men. There are many hurting people out there who have been seduced and injured by these supposed moves of God. They are in need of our help.

There is such a famine for God's true authority and power, many people have compromised their consciences and allowed themselves to

8 Matthew 7:16, NKJV

be seduced by outward performance and demonstrative physical healings greatly resembling those performed in New Age religions. What is more important to God? Healing our physical body or healing the "boy" in us who is selfish and who won't admit he is wrong.

Even to this day, as matriarchal movements are being totally dismantled through Truth and exposure of sin, many "boys" still defend their sin and idolatry with a victim mentality and defensiveness. Of course, God can and will heal our physical bodies. But isn't the real battle today about the fight to overcome our selfishness, our "boyish" behaviors and the sin that can so easily beset us? Raising a male off of his deathbed is only a small victory if he goes on to abuse his friends, his family and his Mandate by still behaving as a "boy." The eternal victory is overcoming one's sinful and "boyish" nature and walking as a servant leader to those around us whom we are called to serve. Witnessing a "boy" turn into a Man is seeing a Man raised from the dead.

Look at where we are in the world today. We live in a time where Men have given away their Keys of authority in massive proportions; so much so, even some ministers in the church are ready to embrace same gender marriages and "boy" leaders who are ministering defeat rather than victory. This in turn has caused our nation to be on the brink of appointing and electing "boys" to lead the free world. God help us! May every Man within the sound of my voice stand up and say "No!" It is not too late for us to rise up in our culture both socially and politically and take back the ground we have lost.

As I write this, the world economy is in disarray and there is no end in sight for those who walk in fear. The only way for the right authorities to rule is for the irresponsible authorities to be removed. This is exactly what is happening at this time throughout America. Do you want a quick test to see if a male is a potential leader and a Patriarch? Where does he stand on protecting the innocent women and children? Is he for or against abortion? Does he defend the abused?

Home foreclosures continue to be at an all time high and many Americans are absolutely gripped with fear of what tomorrow may bring. There is a purging occurring in America where the true Patriarchs have the opportunity to overcome this fear, and become the leaders people will follow into the future. We live in a time where we need leaders who are strong and skilled protectors of family and friends. Are you one of those leaders? Are you a member of the Band of Brothers, who is not afraid to put it all on the line for your loved ones? If so, follow the perfect Man and walk in your true Calling, as you take the ground put before you.

Many Are Called, But Few Chosen:[9]

Do you have a servant's heart? Jesus made it quite clear He came not to be served by Men, but to serve Men. To follow the perfect Man, it is necessary to die to our selfish desires, and receive the Calling imparted deep within us. This is why Jesus said, **"So the last shall be first, and the first last: for many are called, but few chosen."[10]** The Greek word for "Called" in this verse is based in the same root word as the word "Calling" in Chapter 4 of Paul's Letter to the Ephesians. As you may recall, the Webster's dictionary definition for Calling is "a resident call or impulse to perform a certain function."

People have used this verse to say that God only chooses a few select Men to walk in the 5 corporate Callings. As explained throughout the Chapter, this belief system is a lie deeply hurting many people. It has castrated the 5 Callings, and kept them from flourishing in many church systems and businesses. Every male is called, but called to do what? That is for you to decide.

As you read the parables Jesus is referring to in context, you will easily see every individual male has a clear choice to fulfill his Mandate and thereby be "chosen" by God. The implied meaning of the verse is, ***"Many are called by God to walk in their Mandate, but few have received and accepted this Calling."***

Can you imagine sitting your son down and saying to him, "I am sorry son, you are just not 'called' to walk in any one of the 5 corporate leadership 'Callings' in your life. Since you are not a leader in any way, in either the church or in the corporate structure, you must totally depend on other Men who are 'Called' as leaders to care take of you and spoon-feed you spiritually. You are destined to be a second-class citizen, and you must be content to sit in your pew and watch Christianity as it is performed on stage at the local pulpit. And since you are not a leader, you cannot own your own business and you are sentenced to a lifetime of

---

9 Matthew 22:14, KJV
10 Matthew 7:16, KJV

working for others who are more equipped than you." This sounds like a ridiculous statement, but this is exactly what much of the church has subtly been saying to its males in the congregations for centuries.

It takes faith in God and the wisdom of His principles to understand and receive the 5 Callings given to mankind. This understanding leads us to know every Man is chosen and invited to participate in God's plan here on earth. Faith does not replace wisdom. Faith fulfills wisdom. This is why it is so important to read the words of the Bible.

Just as the law and the prophets of the Old Testament have given us wisdom, the New Testament is clear about Jesus of Nazareth being the fulfillment of the law; and through faith He is the revelation of the prophets and embodiment of the 5 Callings. Our faith in Him fulfills where our wisdom falls short.

The Bible is clear. All of us are invited to walk as sons, as kings and as priests before God. No Man is destined to sit on the sidelines. Every Man must become the son, the king and the priest he is called to be. If we humble ourselves and receive the Lord's invitation to be in his elite Band of Brothers, we have the opportunity to fulfill the Great Mandate of protecting and healing our loved ones.

Let us not get caught up in the pride of our Callings. We are first to receive our adoption as sons of the Most High God, then we are to walk as Kings and Priests in a manner serving God and His people as we function in the 5 corporate Callings. Our Callings are additional gifts and tools for us to expound the glory of God on earth. Let us walk in the hope of our Calling, in unity of the Spirit and in the bond of peace, so all of our loved ones will be blessed. Remember Peter's words to all Men:

***"Let every Man abide in the same Calling wherein he was called"*[11]**
The Apostle Paul – First Letter To The People Of Corinth

If you have never truly prayed for the Pastors, the church and the 5-fold Callings, pray this prayer for our strength and unity.

---

11 1 Cor. 7:20, KJV

Prayer For the Church:

Lord in heaven, you are the leader of the church and you are holy and perfect in all your ways. Forgive me and forgive all Men for ignoring and disqualifying your Callings in our families, our businesses, our communities and our churches. I pray you bless, train and set free all Men who have participated in unhealthy religious and business systems promoting a false hierarchy of authority.

I pray the church through your guidance is strengthened and encouraged in the knowledge of your ways. In the years to come may all Men become pillars of strength to build and promote the corporate design you have given to us in Ephesians 4. I pray in my life and for my church that Apostles, Prophets, Evangelists, Pastors and Teachers arise up before you in the blessings and direction of your Holy Spirit, for the building of your church that your name be glorified. Help all of us to discover and walk in the fullness of our Callings. Amen.

"I will build My church; and the gates of hell shall not prevail against it."[12]
Jesus of Nazareth – The Book of John

12 Matthew 16:18, KJV

6

For Women: The Covering

This by far is the most challenging chapter in this book. The primary reason for the challenge is clearly demonstrated by The Man vs. "boy" list. Women have been so emotionally and spiritually damaged from males who are walking as "boys," even the mention of words like, "Patriarchal," "Submit," "Obey," "Authority" or "Covering" are discouraging and even threatening for many women. If this is you, be comforted by the incredible stories you are about to read. This book is dedicated to the women and children who have been abused and mistreated by irresponsible males who are walking as "boys."

I have fantastic news for women. There is a solution for your pain. It is called the Covering. You do not have to be a victim of your circumstances. You do not have to live unhappily with the damage caused by the "boys" in your life. This chapter will show you how to overcome the epidemic problem of having been hurt and deceived by "boys" who have blamed you for their failures and problems. Not only is there hope for you, but if you grasp the principle of the Covering, those long time wounds of your heart will heal and your strength and femininity as a woman will flourish.

Every female must learn the Covering is very real, and it is God's gift ***for*** women. The Covering will never work against women. Like the covering from a warm blanket on a cold day, God has made a special provision of love and protection for every female as she journeys through life. As a female receives the love and protection by way of her Covering, she will find that her fears will turn to joy and she will develop hope to build fulfilling relationships in her life.

A Covered woman is a happy and content woman. When a female realizes she has an esteemed and royal identity that includes a precious Covering, her self-worth and security go off the charts. I know this is a big promise to believe for those who have been hurt by "boys," especially when the promise is coming from a Man. But the promise is true.

I have seen many women's lives turn around for good overnight simply because they learned the Truth of their Covering. Overcoming long-term discouragement comes from realizing the Truth about your situation. With the belief of every lie comes emotional and spiritual bondage. Therefore, I ask all women to receive the principle of her Covering with open arms and a soft heart, and there will be no stopping your joy from overflowing like rivers of living water. This is what has happened in the lives of so many women who now know the Truth. One such woman is Sarah.

"Blessed are you who weep now, for you shall laugh."[1]
Jesus of Nazareth

PART I: Sarah

Sarah was raised in a middle class family with many brothers and sisters. For years I watched her grow up from a distance as she struggled to find who God created her to be. Sarah was the classic overachiever. Her lack of personal esteem translated into her attempt to work her way into acceptance and security. By the time she was in high school, she nearly ran the family home consisting of seven brothers and sisters.

1 Matthew 5:4, NAS

It was the classic Cinderella story, as she cooked most of the family meals and kept the home in order by cleaning constantly. As you can guess by now, Sarah's father was engaged in the age-old battle of overcoming his habits of behaving like a "boy." He provided a home and income for his family; however, his lack of relational skills and his failure to impart love into Sarah was taking a huge toll on her.

Throughout high school, Sarah was constantly being told she was too thin and sickly. Of course, this was primarily due to the intense emotional stress bottled up within her from the lack of love and protection she was experiencing. To add to Sarah's grief, she was tortured over why she did not have her monthly period like her sisters and friends after going through puberty. Sarah sought for the answers to overcome her intense emotional pain, but no person around her had the maturity to impart understanding or solutions. Ultimately, most of the counsel she received from friends and family alike seemed to put the blame on Sarah as they guised their counsel in distorted religious principles.

Her greatest pain came from the inferences and accusations from her father that something was wrong with her both emotionally and spiritually. He even went so far as to blame Sarah for bringing on her health problems because of her own rebellion. As a teenager, Mr. Cruelty began to have his way with Sarah as she entered the emotional hell that comes when life's most important relational questions remain unanswered. Her heart slowly began to die.

To escape from the family dynamics, she began taking long runs in the countryside where she could be free of the many voices telling her she was unloved and unworthy of acceptance. As she slowly lost any hope for her heart to be made whole and for her tears to be wiped away, her ability to bond with or trust the people around her was disintegrating.

In Sarah's attempt to avoid healthy relational intimacy, she developed an elaborate scheme of retreat by hiding in the endless tasks of housekeeping and people pleasing. Her final escape came when she latched on to a nice young "boy" who offered her potential friendship and acceptance. She was married at the age of 19 to Scott. Scott was only one year older than Sarah, and he spent his entire life fighting and losing to the same religious system holding Sarah's family in bondage for decades. You will read more about Scott in Chapter 7.

Act I – The Father's Covering:

For years, Sarah's marriage to Scott never lived up to her expectations. Instead of escaping the bondage attached to her family, Scott added to the complexity of her life by becoming an additional component to the whole dysfunctional system. To compound the problem, her father still exercised a great degree of control over her emotionally and relationally even after she married Scott. Sarah's father was also Pastor to both Scott and her. Scott had given his Keys away to the religious machine they both were born into long before, thus any chance of finding a hope for victory seemed beyond all reach for Sarah.

Finally, after seven years of disillusionment and disappointment, I met with Sarah and Scott to talk about their marriage. Sarah walked in looking both bewildered and afraid. Scott had been working with me about walking as a Man for over a year, and he was growing by leaps and bounds. He was gently bringing into the marriage his newfound Manhood, and this was the first time Sarah seemed ready to meet with me. Immediately when I saw her, I knew she was ready to look at some of the deeper issues in her life.

I said to Sarah, "How are you doing?"

Sarah looked at me nervously as if I was already hitting a sore spot. She replied by saying, "Fine." Sarah then paused for a moment and added, "Maybe not so good."

For quite some time we talked about how she was feeling, and I shared with her how happy I was to see Scott and her make an effort to strengthen their marriage. She started to see I was not a threat to her, and that I truly was for her. As she began to feel at ease and warm up to me, I said to her, "Sarah, I have some things I would like to share with you regarding your relationship with your father and the principle of the Covering."

She quietly said, "Okay."

I then said, "It might take a little time for me to share this with you, but I know the information could change your life. I believe you have never been told why you have felt so alone and so unloved in your life. Is this true?"

Sarah responded in a very soft and calm manner as she said, "I have always felt like there was something wrong with me. I am so fearful... of everything. I do not know what to do." I could see her eyes were starting to show tears.

I asked Sarah if her father was there for her, and if she felt like her father loved her.

She replied, "My relationship with my Dad was never the way I wanted it to be. My Dad was always kind of cold. I never felt my Dad offered a warm attitude. I always wanted him to say to me, 'Come and talk to me. Let us work things out and share how we both feel.' But it never happened. I always wanted a Dad who would relate with me and be concerned for me. When I went to him with my health issues, I never felt nurtured. It was as if he did not even hear me. My Dad always made me feel that... I am not worthy of being loved."

As she finished the sentence her voice began to crack and tears began to pour out of her eyes. I was surprised at how fast she got down to her true feelings, so I asked her to continue. I could hear her heart crying out for help under the solemn tone of her voice. This lovely young girl desperately wanted to be healed inside.

Totally broken and crying, she went on to say, "My husband loves me. I know this in my mind, but I cannot seem to feel it in my heart. I feel like I am nothing. I don't know what is wrong with me."

Scott and I sat at the table in the silence of the moment praying in our hearts God would truly bring comfort and healing to this precious woman who was pouring out her feelings. I then said to her, "Sarah, it really is going to be okay. What you are feeling is perfectly normal considering the lack of training and the family dynamics you came from. You will see when you truly understand the Covering principle, your whole life will come into order and peace will pour into your heart. Are you ready for your life to be radically changed for the better?"

Sarah looked both comforted and perplexed at the same time. She wanted to believe everything could be okay, but was that really possible? I could see her heart saying, "Are you kidding me? Do you mean there is even a remote possibility my life could turn out even somewhat meaningful, with a happy ending? Are you talking about ***my*** life?"

I said, "Sarah, your life is so meaningful! There is a great purpose for you to go through all of this pain. You are going to see you have been taught a few lies. These lies have been embedded so deep within your heart and soul, they are messing with every thought you have about who you are and what you are called to do in life. Listen carefully, and I will share with you the path out of this hell you have been in. And it will happen today, if you are willing to look at it and remove the lies out of your life once and for all. Are you ready to be free?"

I could see Sarah was becoming hopeful. The tears were shutting down, and it felt as if she was in shock from hearing things might be okay. Her eyes were as big as saucers as she waited for my next words.

"Your Daddy loves you, Sarah. Inside he really does love you. Can you believe this?"

Sarah was taken off guard, and she began to ponder the question. She paused for a moment and then replied, "My Dad does not love me. He has never been there for me, and he has blamed me for all of my problems my entire life."

I then said, "Sarah, I can really see why you feel this way, but hear me out. Just because your Dad has done a poor job of allowing his love for you to actually get to you, this does not mean he does not love you. He loves you very much. I know this is true, and deep down you know it is true as well. You know there have been times when his love for you has squeaked through."

Sarah slowly nodded her head in agreement as she said, "Yes, there have been times I have felt a little love and concern from him." Her voice was sincere, yet sad. She looked intently at me and said, "But if my Dad really loved me, wouldn't I feel he loved me? Wouldn't he care enough to see how hurt I have been?" Her words seem to pierce the air with the question of the ages.

Like millions of women throughout the world, Sarah was asking, "Why doesn't my Daddy love me?" Once again, I could sense the warm blanket of God I have come so accustomed to, begin to fall on Sarah. It was the perfect setting for the introduction of the perfect answer. For every woman, the answer is found in the principle of the Covering.

The Covering From Conception:

I began by saying, "From the very moment you were conceived, there was an unseen Covering of love and protection from God placed within the heart of your father. This Covering is a blessing and a sign of God's desire to nurture and protect you. The strength and the power derived from this Covering cannot be used to hurt you in any way.

"Control, neglect and abuse of any kind do not come from either God or the Covering. The power to nurture and protect with this Covering can only be utilized when your father has willed in his heart to love you. The love displays itself in two ways. First it provides protection for you. Next it provides nurturing for you. Protection must come first. How can you be nurtured if you are being pummeled? Women must be protected first. This is why I call it the Covering, because it is there to cover you with protection and then nurturing.

"It reminds me of when a Dad tucks his daughter in at bedtime by covering her with a warm blanket. There is an unseen protection and nurturing imparted from a father to a daughter bringing an emotional stability and health to her. This is a timeless act occurring in families all over the world, and it occurs because there is a blessing God truly has imparted to all fathers.

"This Covering can be seen in a healthy father and daughter relationship as the daughter grows up, and it will exist for the life of the relationship. When a young female receives nurturing and protection from her father in a healthy and forthright way, she will exude a sense of being covered by the blessings of God, and her heart will be whole and at peace.

"Mothers receive a similar type of impartation when a child is conceived. It is not uncommon for a mother to know the exact instant a child is conceived within her. A mother may detect the physical change occurring in her body, but she also may be detecting God has imparted a special blessing of love, nurturing and protection within her for her new child. This blessing lasts a lifetime, and it can be drawn upon by the mother whenever she needs it.

"How's your relationship with your mom, Sarah?"

Sarah shook her head and frowned. She then said, "We are not very close. My Mom is in her own world."

I nodded my head and said, "I'm very sorry to hear that, but I can only imagine that your Mom is suffering similar neglect from your Dad. Your relationship with your Mom is very important, but for now I am going to stay focused on your Dad. As you learn about the Covering and how it relates solely with your Dad, you will be able to understand your relationship problems with your Mom very clearly.

"When a mother fails to display loving and motherly behaviors towards her daughter, it is not because the love and nurturing was not imparted to her for her child. It is because the mother has not chosen or is unable to draw from the well of love God has so graciously gifted to her. This usually occurs when she was raised by a male who is a 'boy.' And then, adding to her problems, she in turn marries a 'boy.' In other words, your Mom was not trained to be Covered, and she probably doesn't have the slightest idea how to go about it."

Sarah sat still, as she nodded in agreement. Her solemn eyes looked hungry for more and she blurted out, "I can assure you, she has no idea. And neither do I! Please go on."

I said, "You can literally see when a woman is Covered, because the deep down fears, hurts and worries will not dominate her countenance and her demeanor. Of course, everyone experiences a degree of fear and worry, but there is a difference between a person experiencing a temporary fear or worry and a person who has a constant underlying tormenting fear of life's happenings. Sarah, do you have this kind of fear? Do you have a constant fear tormenting you?"

Sarah was totally blown away at what she was hearing. In a strong voice she said, "That is exactly it! I have been gripped by fear my whole life. My biggest fear has been of what people think of me. I feel like I am constantly waiting for something bad to happen. This causes me to try to live my life in such a way where I am always trying to please everyone around me to avoid disaster from happening. Most of the time, I am gripped with fear. If this is what you mean by the term 'uncovered,' this is definitely me! I feel 'uncovered' and… very exposed."

I replied, "Yes, Sarah. This is exactly what I am talking about. When a female is gripped by this kind of fear, it is a sign she is spiritually 'uncovered.' Her lack of faith and confidence in the protective and nurturing ability of her father causes her to doubt anyone can or will love and protect her. The lack of confidence she feels translates into a world view that destroys her trust in God, and it invites fear and doubt into her life. This world view is very common in America today, because there are so many males behaving as 'boys' and neglecting the primary duty of their Mandate.

"An 'uncovered' woman will feel like there is no stability around her, and there is usually an overall fear of what is going to happen next in her life. This fear comes from knowing deep down there is something missing. She knows in her heart her father (or husband) is not there for her, and he is not meeting her needs.

"This in turn causes her to seriously doubt God, herself and her Dad's love. She will question whether God has really deposited the blessings of the Covering within her father, and she will see herself as unworthy to be loved. Her heart then becomes damaged from the lack of care provided, and her trust for both her father and God is destroyed. Finally she will get to the point where she will not trust any Man, and she will have to create her own form of protection by controlling her environment in any way possible."

"There is no fear in love; but perfect love casts out fear: because fear has torment. He that fears is not made perfect in love." [2]
The Apostle John – First Letter of John

The "uncovered" Woman:

"This means Satan has done his job. He has successfully disrupted the love and the protection (The Covering) to the extent an 'uncovered' woman has totally rejected the Truth God has indeed placed love and protection within her father. Satan's master plan is to destroy the strategic relationships in a woman's life by enticing her to believe the lie she does not need Men.

"This lie usually is brought into her marriage, and she will experience the same problem trusting her husband and all other Men who are in a

2 1 John 4:18, NKJV

position to take care of her. She thinks she is now forced to cope with life alone. She has been set up for the slaughter. And here comes a host of dysfunctional behaviors all intending to do one thing; to falsely make her feel like she is nurtured and protected (Covered)."

Sarah blurted out, "Oh God, that is me! That is me!"

I went on to say, "Yes! An 'uncovered' woman will do anything to make herself believe she is actually in control of her life, but she really is not. She is being absolutely controlled by the lies of God's enemy. She may withdraw. She may become a micro-manager. She may become extremely outgoing or promiscuous. She may be a militant controller. She may take on a victim mentality and become a doormat to other controllers. She may develop food issues. She may outwardly become a man-hater. She may even go so far as to totally reject her identity as a female and turn to lesbianism. No matter what the dysfunction is, deep inside there is a seven year old little girl waiting for her Daddy to show her he loves her.

"All of these dysfunctional behaviors are an attempt to control her environment so she will feel safe. It is all about feeling 'safe.' But here is the real Truth. A woman will feel truly safe only when she trusts in her Covering. You may be thinking you can never trust a male, because they have let you down so badly. God is not a fool. He is not going to give you anything bad. All gifts from God are good, and the Covering he has given you is the best gift. Trusting in your Covering does not mean you have to trust in a Man. If this were true, no woman could trust in their Covering because all males, and females for that matter, are imperfect and all of us will fall short in life.

"You are really called to trust in the Truth that God loves you so much he has provided the blessing of the Covering within your father. It is the father's job to allow the love and protection of the Covering to actually pass through to his daughter. When a father is successful at this, he is actually a living example of the nature of God, and his daughter will grow up healthy and vibrant. When a father fails at building this trust, it is truly a tragedy; however, his daughter can still overcome. She is then asked to receive the Truth, and trust that her true Father in heaven will meet her needs another way. Hopefully, for the sake of healing, it is helpful if her needs are met through the help of a Man close to her in her life.

Sarah contemplated even answering me, as she cautiously glanced at Scott. She turned to me staring right into my eyes and anxiously said,

"Oh my God, that's me! I have almost every one of those dysfunctional behaviors you are describing. I had no idea that my relationship with my father had so much to do with my behaviors. Tell me more, please."

"Okay Sarah," I said. "Trust is the key word here. One of our highest purposes on earth is to learn to trust in the God who created us. We all have the opportunity to learn to trust God loves us. Specifically, for you as a woman, you are asked to believe He will truly cover you either through your father or another Man. Of course, this trust is damaged when fathers let their daughters down.

"The more a female is abused, neglected or ignored by her father, the greater chance her hurts will become infected to the point where she will never trust a Man or God. After the trust in her father is destroyed, she is sentenced to a lifetime of striving to control her environment in an attempt to experience a sense of security and safety. Unfortunately for her, the security and the safety never will arrive, because her controlling behavior is working against her.

"Control is the perfect word to use here, because she must now be controlling if she is going to continue in the charade she is truly Covered and believe that everything is okay. But everything is not okay. Until she discovers the Truth about the gift of the Covering and begins to develop trust in God, she will remain 'uncovered.' In order to feel safe and Covered, she then has a full time job of manipulating her life in such a way as to keep from having to count on any Man for her security. Are you tracking with me so far, Sarah?"

Sarah nodded sharply, and surprisingly she became very open and candid. She said, "Yes, absolutely. I have a tremendous problem trusting any Man. And I know about wanting to control, because I have had a huge problem with eating disorders for most of my adult life. I have been both obsessed and neurotic with food and scales, and I know it has been my futile attempt to control something in my life.

"The ironic thing is this, I am in bondage to the control that food has over me. Instead of me controlling food, food is controlling me. I count calories, I weigh myself constantly, and I am continually making bargains with myself on what I can and cannot eat. It has been terrible. I feel trapped in my own ugly body!

"No matter how hard I try, this voice in my head is constantly telling me I do not look right, and I deserve punishment. Sometimes I just want to die, and starving myself somehow fulfills some kind of sick desire in me. Many times I have to actually feel major hunger pains before I can eat even a few morsels of food. I have several friends who have the same problem. Are you telling me my food control problems are stemmed from my trust issues with my father?"

I said to Sarah, "Yes. Millions of women are suffering from this same problem. Nearly every time you find a woman with an eating disorder, you will find an 'uncovered' woman with a father and/or a husband who is behaving as a 'boy.' You will find an insensitive and irresponsible male who has failed to show his daughter or wife the strength and beauty of being nurtured and protected (Covered).

"I have seen it hundreds of times before. Sometimes fathers are simply just taken out of commission by overworking. Sometimes life's circumstances get the best of a father's time or maybe an untimely death removed him from his daughter. But the stories are usually similar. The lack of a loving father leads to an 'uncovered' daughter, and eating disorders are one of the many consequences that occur."

"This is where Satan makes his move. An 'uncovered' woman will then begin to hear those very familiar voices of condemnation and fear. Thinking the voices are actually her own conscience, she will then begin to act out her fears by setting up a complex system of rules and guidelines doing nothing to actually help her become Covered. I call the voice speaking to you 'Mr. Cruelty,' because it is one of the cruelest spirits I have ever come in contact with.

"Remember, this unloving and cruel spirit is the brutal consequence of when a father has failed to impart protection and nurturing in his daughter. Because her father has not protected her spiritually, Mr. Cruelty has direct access to his daughter. And it is all rooted in one simple lie. The lie saying, 'My Daddy does not love me.' Believing this lie is a calling card for Mr. Cruelty, self hatred, and a whole host of their ugly friends.

"This will open the doors for many cruel spirits of bondage to enter her heart and mind and whisper lies to her day and night. These lies will cause her to hate herself and even to abuse herself on a daily basis. This self-hatred can lead her to demeaning and criticizing herself, starving herself, cutting herself, or hurting herself intentionally by any means possible. They are based on the lie she is worthless, unloved and she deserves to be punished.

"Many times food will become the number one tool for punishment. It is so simple. If you feel unworthy of love, it only makes sense you would think you deserve to be abused and punished. This explains a whole host of self-afflicting behaviors women have participated in, especially promiscuity. It is no coincidence a woman who is 'uncovered' spiritually will outwardly look for approval through lustful attire and promiscuous behavior, and she will allow herself to be 'uncovered' in a physical sense."

Sarah said, "You are exactly right. I actually look forward to feeling pain, because somehow deep inside I feel I deserve to be punished."

I said, "Yes. Many people will counsel these desperate girls with what they feel is common sense good eating habits. This is practically useless in overcoming the problem. The problem is the woman's heart has developed a world view she is unloved and she deserves bad things. No amount of rational common sense training about nutrition and food is ever going to help her overcome the problem, unless the root of the problem is addressed.

"Sadly and ironically, an 'uncovered' woman who develops eating disorders is ***starved*** of love and protection. Subconsciously, her cry for help is acted out as she starves her body physically so someone might see how hurt, 'uncovered,' and starved for love she really is. It is quite common for her to inappropriately dress in highly suggestive clothing in her attempt to broadcast she is 'uncovered.' This of course only leads to attracting and ensnaring more 'boys' into her dysfunctional web, and it compounds the bondage of her problem.

"Many may see her eating problems, but few understand the dynamics of how to lead her back to her Covering. Giving her outward nutritional and behavioral counseling and advice feels like another abusive slap in the face to her, because she knows deep down the core problem is not being addressed. Her heart still has a huge hole in it. This is a tragedy of tragedies. Many well meaning people try to help a female with eating disorders, but they end up hurting her due to their lack of training and ignorance about the Covering. Does this hit home with you Sarah?"

Sarah was overwhelmed as she looked at her husband in disbelief. She said, "Everyone has always tried to tell me how to eat, and it always feels like they are attacking me. I cannot believe this."

I said, "Yes, Sarah. They were trying to cure the symptoms without solving the problem. They may have meant well, but everyone knows being insensitive out of good intentions will not give you any extra credit in this life, or in the life to come."

"Sarah, thank God there is an easy solution. Yes, it is actually easy. It may be a lot of work, but it is easy work if you approach it with the right knowledge and perspective. An 'uncovered' woman must reconcile her relationship with her father and allow the love of God to restore her heart. As she receives the protection and love from God and the healthy Men she invites into her life, she will gradually rebuild the foundations of her fearful and damaged heart. If she does not go through this process, she will be sentenced to a life of controlling her environment in an attempt to feel 'secure' and 'in charge' in order to quash the tremendous fear she feels."

Sarah replied, "Ken, I see it. I was controlling my food and starving myself as a cry for help. I have always known in my heart I wanted attention, but I never saw how important my relationship with my father was in all of this. People were always trying to help me or teach me about how I should eat, and it was just a waste of time. It did nothing to help me with the core problem of not trusting in the love and the Covering of my father."

I went on to say to Sarah, "It is so good you are seeing this. We are slowly unraveling the lies keeping 'uncovered' women in bondage for centuries. And you are no longer going to be one of those 'uncovered' women. The cold and hard Truth is that 'uncovered' women will develop layers of supposed protective measures thereby shutting out the most important relationships in their lives.

"To make the situation worse, all of these dysfunctions and controlling behaviors 'uncovered' women manufacture make it harder for them to be helped by truly loving and trustworthy Men. A healthy and authoritative Man is a threat to an 'uncovered' woman's sense of security, because her trust muscle has been damaged by the males who were supposed to take care of her. She will have an inordinate attraction to 'boys' who do not walk in authority, because 'boys' will readily defer their Mandated authority to an 'uncovered' woman. Real Men literally scare the hell out of 'uncovered' women."

Sarah appeared a little entertained and scared at the same time as I said the last statement. She backed up in her seat and looked at me coolly with a slight smile on her face. She then said, "I have seen this. I have definitely seen this. Tell me more."

The "uncovered" Woman & "boy" Connection:

I went on to say, "Since 'boys' are pushovers and will easily acquiesce their Keys of authority to anyone who demands it, an 'uncovered' woman will be drawn to a relationship with 'boys' even though she has no respect for them. This is because an 'uncovered' woman must be in charge of the relationship in order to satisfy her desperate longing to feel secure and safe.

"Unfortunately, for the 'uncovered' woman, her need to feel safe far outweighs her need to be compatibly matched. There will be a subconscious connection between an 'uncovered' woman and a 'boy' defying all reason. In other words, they both will feel they just click, even though everyone around them is shaking their heads in disbelief over how or why they are together.

"This makes sense, because an 'uncovered' female has the same problem as a male who is a 'boy.' Both of them have suffered neglect and abuse from the primary male in their lives, and this male is usually their father. ***An 'uncovered' woman will usually marry the most available 'boy,' at the most vulnerable time in her life.*** This is a tragedy, because it keeps both of them from finding the true love that God intended for them. Through a lifetime of fear, an 'uncovered' female is in bondage to the plan of God's enemy, and she never will reach her full God-given potential until she rises up in an understanding of the dynamics of her God-given Covering.

"Since an 'uncovered' woman and a 'boy' have very similar problems, emotionally and spiritually there is an unspoken camaraderie between them. This is because they are both casualties of war. Both will generally continue to have frustrated relationships with their fathers or significant males in their lives, and both will never truly know who they are created to be until they overcome the damages caused by the abuses which have been perpetrated against them by the males in their lives.

"Women are made by God to plug into healthy Men through relationships. An 'uncovered' woman must also plug into a male; however, she will do it in a dysfunctional manner. It is as if she has this insatiable umbilical cord flailing around looking for some unsuspecting 'boy' to plug into. As soon as the relationship appears to go sour with the 'boy' in her life, she will detect there is a potential disconnect of her umbilical cord. Like Eve frantically looking for fig leaves in the Garden of Eden to cover herself, she then will desperately search for a new male to plug into to satiate her needs. Of course, it will be a 'boy,' because no real self respecting Man will be fool enough to allow her to plug into him in the rare event she was attracted to him.

"An 'uncovered' woman resembles a heroin addict looking for a fix as she nervously throws out multiple nets in her attempt to reattach to a 'boy.' When she succeeds, the whole process begins again. In the end, the 'uncovered' woman is left feeling desperate, alone, discouraged and hopeless. Of course, by entering into multiple relationships with 'boys,' an 'uncovered' woman will only reinforce her lack of trust and respect for the male gender. By definition, a 'boy' can never fulfill the role of a Man. Sarah, do you still want to remain 'uncovered?' Does this sound like the kind of life you have been having?"

Sarah was calm, yet speechless. Scott reached over and took her hand to see how she was doing. Sarah did not even respond to his advance. Once again she looked at me, gently nodding her head for me to continue.

I continued on by saying, "Let me tell you more about the 'uncovered' woman. The more clearly you see her, the more you will desire to be Covered."

Understanding the "uncovered" Woman:

"Most 'uncovered' women fail to see the dynamics of how their fathers have failed as Men; therefore, they do not forgive properly. This is truly a tragedy, because forgiveness allows God to provide His impenetrable Covering over your heart. There is only one way to truly overcome in relationships in this world. We overcome through forgiveness and honest communication. But before we forgive an offense, we must see the offense. You cannot be pardoned if you have not been charged and convicted.

"For an 'uncovered' woman, the problem is further magnified because it is her father's love she truly longs for. It is difficult for an 'uncovered' woman to diagnose, evaluate or judge her father's past behaviors, because it feels like she is working against getting her needs met by her father in the future. Deep inside she's thinking, 'Since my father is so unloving and insensitive, I will never get my needs met by him.' Nevertheless, it really is the Truth that makes you free. A relational inventory check on your father is exactly what is needed.

"Instead of properly understanding the situation and removing the anger and the bitterness against their fathers, 'uncovered' women become masters of taking out their anger on the unfortunate souls who attempt to be close with them. Mothers, husbands, siblings and children are the first to get the displacement of their wrath, until finally she will come against co-workers and friends.

"Occasionally, she will even lash out at the holy grail of all relationships, her father. Since there is no understanding about the dynamics of the Covering, this only increases the loneliness, frustration, and the deep sadness inside her, and it drives her further from accepting the gift of her Covering. An 'uncovered' woman is then stuck on a ride to nowhere, with no hope in sight. It is so simple; all she needs is nurturing and protection. But how does she get it?"

I looked at Sarah and saw her staring right through me. Her mouth was half open as if she was about to say something, but nothing came out. I could see her heart rising up with a resolve going beyond all explanation. I could also see for the first time in Sarah's life, she was actually experiencing a little righteous anger regarding the real reasons she was "uncovered." To help her direct her anger, I told her who the real enemy is. Sarah, I know you believe there is a God, but do you believe Satan and his demons exist?"

Sarah seemed captivated by what I was saying as she looked at me intently. She said, "Yes, I know evil and the devil are very real. I feel like I grew up with him in my house!"

I then told her, "I am very glad you see it this way, because this is one of the first keys of Truth you need in order to unlock the door to your freedom. Satan does not want you Covered. As a matter of fact, he will do everything in his power to cause you to reject your Covering. Satan and his demonic friends are ultimately the ones responsible for all of your pain and suffering.

"Satan desires to cover you with his fear, his neglect and his control. Remember he is the great deceiver. He poses as a friendly voice offering protection and covering while pretending to be good. But he offers a false covering leading you to stray away from getting the healing you need, and from discovering the Truth about the blessing of your true Covering.

"If God's enemy can get you to believe God has not deposited love and protection within your father or your husband, he will be successful in keeping you from having trust and faith in any Man in your life. This includes your Father in heaven, God himself. And in your case he has succeeded, until today. Can you agree with me that today it is over?"

Sarah nodded her head in agreement and said in a strong and steady voice, "I would like it to be over. What do I do?"

I was so glad Sarah asked what to do, because to this question I knew the answer, and I knew I was about to see a miracle. I then said to her, "Sarah, just listen to the Truth and let it permeate deep down into your heart. You are going to kick fear out of your life today. Usually, all Satan has to do is infect a father with seeds of abuse and neglect towards his daughter, and it is done. A daughter's bitterness and her lack of trust and forgiveness towards her father will lead her into a life of hell and dysfunction.

"Without even realizing it, she will be working for God's enemy. Sarah, you have been working for God's enemy without even knowing it. If you are operating in fear and control, this means you are aiding and abetting Satan even if you do not intend to."

The expression on Sarah's face was both clear and piercing as she nodded her head in agreement. She said, "You are right. Even though I do not want to hurt anyone, I know my controlling behavior hurts others."

I then said, "Sarah, don't worry. The important question is this. Are you willing to make the changes needed so you can win in life? If you are, please take in what I have for you."

Sarah shook her head in agreement and motioned for me to continue.

"Sarah," I said, "understanding where your father dropped the ball is where you must begin. As I said before, if you do not identify the abuse you have suffered through, you cannot properly forgive the person who allowed or caused the abuse. Let me be clear here, abuse and neglect can come in many forms. It can merely be a father who is just not paying attention because he is preoccupied with life's challenges. It can be a father who does not know how to nurture, or a father who is not there emotionally, spiritually, or physically.

"If you were left in a position where any unsafe male had access to you, you were actually abused or neglected by your father. It is your father's job to protect you. Basically, abuse and neglect occur anytime a father does not participate or engage with his family in a responsible manner.

"In other words, if your Dad is behaving as a 'boy,' he is actually abusing and neglecting you, and he is missing his Mandate. If you look closely at the Man vs. "boy" list, you will see every point on the list shows that behaving as a 'boy' brings destruction to relationships. For you, this means the love and protection God has imparted within your father will not be imparted to you, because he is acting like a 'boy.'

"It was not transferred because ignorance, fear and lack of training kept him from loving and protecting you. Have you known other girls who have seemingly abusive or unloving fathers? Does not every one of them experience the same problem with trusting and accepting their Covering? Look at your three sisters. Do you see how your father has wounded the trust in the hearts of every one of them?"

Sarah immediately responded by saying, "Absolutely! Every one of my sisters is seriously struggling with both my Dad and God in different ways. And they all have taken their problems into their marriages. None of them have very happy marriages. They all battle with fear, and none of them trust Men in their lives, especially our father."

I went on to tell Sarah, "I would like you to see your father actually is not the main abuser here. God's enemy, Satan, is roaming about to destroy you and your faith in God's Covering. Yes, your father is an accessory to the crime, but he is also a victim of Satan's cruelty. Remember this, Sarah: Satan does not want you to figure out that God has deposited this incredible gift within your Dad at the time you were conceived. He does not want anyone to know about the blessing of the Covering that your Dad can access. This provides you with the love and protection you long for. Are you getting it?"

Sarah replied boldly, "I am getting it!"

I then said, "There is a false teaching going around the church that attempts to make the pastor of the church a woman's Covering solely because he has the title of pastor. How many times have we all heard women say, 'My pastor is my Covering?' This may sound all well and good on first inspection, but underneath this teaching is the subtle work of Satan. The unbiblical teaching that the pastor is automatically a women's Covering has caused untold pain, dismay and discouragement for women. Remember, God ways are simple, and He always works through families first.

"The Mandate and Keys of protection and nurturing I have been referring to are given to the father for his daughter at conception. These Keys are the blessing and anointing given by God to a Man in order for him to fulfill the impartation of love to his daughter. If a pastor or any other male usurps the Mandated father's position by attempting to be the responsible caretaker of a woman who is outside of his family, he will fail miserably because he does not possess the Keys or blessings necessary to accomplish this job. How can a male complete a task without the blessings of God?

"It is a full-time job for a Man to take care of even one family, let alone two, three, four or ten families. There is such an epidemic of 'boys' in churches that this accepted false teaching continues to wear out most pastors. By definition, 'boys' default on their responsibilities to women; therefore, they are more than happy to allow anyone else to try to do their job for them. This scenario has caused many pastors to attempt to be the Mandated Covering over dozens if not hundreds of 'uncovered' women without the ordained authority. No wonder pastors are so beat up! They are attempting to do a job that is impossible, because they were not given the Keys of blessing and authority to take care of all these 'uncovered' women. This honor is reserved solely for the father or the father figure whom is Mandated by God.

"Sarah, this is particularly important for you because your father is a pastor. Not only is he a 'boy' who is shirking his responsibility with you, he took on the lie that it was his job to take care of all the other 'uncovered' women in his congregation. Talk about an exercise in futility. How can anyone expect your father to take care of other women without having the Mandate to do so? Especially, when he has failed in taking care of his own family where he has been given this Mandate.

"This whole dysfunctional religious system was created by 'boys,' and it resembles a dog chasing its tail. Most of the women in your father's church feel desperate, alone and 'uncovered,' because most of the males in his congregation are 'boys.' It is obvious they are 'boys' because real Men would never follow a male who does not take care of his own wife and daughters.

"Not only is your Dad modeling how to be a 'boy' to the males in his congregation, but the shortage of real Men and the lack of training for Men has further exasperated the 'uncovered' women problem. These women are looking for Men to take care of them, and they only receive neglect and empty promises in return for their hopes. And who also gets further neglected? You do. Your mother and your sisters get further neglected as well, because your father is giving himself to others at your expense, and he is doing it in the name of God. Rather than attempting to be the Covering for women in his church, he would have served better by demanding that the males in his congregation stand up as Men and do their job of taking care of their women. Sarah, you have suffered because your father is a 'boy,' and he is untrained about the true things of God. This must have brought you additional feelings of guilt, abandonment and resentment towards your father and God."

I could see by her solemn eyes that Sarah was undone. Her voice trembled as she exclaimed, "Ken, you are so right! My Dad has spent most of my life supposedly attending to the needs of others in the name of God. All the while he has neglected spending time and attention on me. At times, I have been so angry at God. Then I feel guilty for being selfish about wanting to be closer to my father and for wanting to have him all to myself."

"Sarah," I said, "You have not been selfish. Satan wants you to feel like you are too selfish, because believing you do not deserve your father's love will keep you down. If 'boys' can convince women that they don't deserve to be treated well, then they justify themselves to be excused from doing their job. You were made by God to desire to be Covered by your father and to have his complete love and support. God put in you the desire to be protected, nurtured and loved by your father and your husband. You can be free by simply understanding that your Dad believes a horrible lie.

"Sacrificing his children daily for the sake of his job is not the will of God. God calls us to self-sacrifice, not to child-sacrifice. It is not God's will to neglect our daughters, our wives or our families, ever! If you recall, Abraham put his son Isaac on the altar of sacrifice only once, and even this was an act of love and obedience that was stopped by God. It is clear that Abraham spent all of his days loving, protecting and doting over Isaac. He knew that Isaac was the special child of promise.

"God is so practical. You also are God's special child of promise. He chooses to work through the Men in each family to display His loving nature towards women. Look at the biblical traditions of the Old Testament. If the father is taken away, the oldest available Man is then responsible to protect and nurture the women in the family. This tradition eliminates the chance for improper emotional and physical yoking, because people are not naturally inclined to be sexually attracted to family members. Marriages and families have been destroyed because males have not understood the Covering, and they have ignored the principle of 'Families First;' only to be seduced away by their own pride into the webs of battered and lonely 'uncovered' women. How many pastors like your father have committed emotional, spiritual and physical adultery as a result of attempting to improperly 'cover' an 'uncovered' woman?"

Sarah responded, "I am really getting the picture of what has happened with my Dad, Ken. I am so glad I am hearing this. Most of the women in my Dad's church have no clue about what you are saying. It feels like they have given their husbands a free pass. They expect my Dad to meet all of their needs with little expectations from their own husbands. I do not want to be caught in the web anymore. I need to know how to deal with my Dad and understand the Covering. How do I get over the sadness I feel? How can I be free from resentment and bitterness? What can I do?"

I then said to Sarah, "All you need to do is understand the Truth, and the Truth will set you free. As you now know, this resident Key of love and protection will remain dormant in a father until he understands and draws on it by allowing it to pour through him into you, his daughter. The love you have yearned for is actually in your father waiting to come out. He just does not know how to fully use this Key, because your father is behaving as a 'boy.'

"Your father is untrained, rebellious, and he has not chosen to fully become a Man and he doesn't grasp the difference between Men and "boys." This is his crime. He is a 'boy.' Therefore, the love, nurturing and protection for you have stayed relatively dormant within him for all of these years. Does this make sense to you?"

Sarah gently nodded and said, "Yes, for the first time in my life, this all makes perfect sense."

I then said to Sarah, "The worst part of this is that fear, insecurity and the physical problems you have experienced are actually a result of your Dad not doing his job. I can guarantee if your Dad had allowed God's love to pour out of him into you, his daughter, you would not be having serious problems with fear and insecurity today.

"Your physical conditions including not having your period and the eating disorders came from the incredible stress, fear and hurt you experienced. If you did not experience the stress, fear and hurt, your sicknesses probably would never have come upon you. The reason he blamed you for your problems is you remind him by your mere existence that he is failing as a father and as a Man. Therefore, even the sight of you became a confrontation with his personal deficiencies.

"Nevertheless, it is really true. Deep down your Daddy loves you. It is probably better to say, 'Your Daddy has love for you in him.' This is because God's nurturing and protection for you was gifted to him at your conception. It is a spiritual present I cannot prove is there, but in faith I know it is there. Any father who is truly honest with himself knows it is within him as well. Are you following me, Sarah?"

Sarah replied, "If this is true, everything is going to be different!"

"It is true, and things are going to be different. The reason your father has not shown you the love of your Covering very well has nothing to do with you. He has an additional problem along with his failure to impart love into his daughters. Your father has not decided to grow up and become a Man. This has affected everything in his life. Your father has to live with the fact he is losing on every front in his life, because he has not decided to fully walk as a Man by taking full responsibility for all the Keys he has been given.

"Your father's marriage with your Mother and his relationships with every family member are suffering because he has not decided to become the Man that God designed him to be. You must see his behavior has nothing to do with you; it is all ***his*** dysfunction and ***his*** misunderstanding. Can you see this? Can you see his rejection of you has nothing to do with you? It is ***all*** him. You must see that 'boys' are by definition irresponsible, and 'boys' blame. This is what 'boys' do."

Sarah still seemed to be looking right through me with eyes of steel. She then said, "I feel like I have never been able to love or to say, 'I love you' to anyone. Why is this? Why can't I love? Is there something wrong with me?"

I replied, "Sarah, there is nothing wrong with you. After all you have been through, what do you think is going on? Do you think it might have something to do with the fact 99.9% of the males in your childhood have hurt you by not taking care of you?"

Sarah looked up and thought for a moment. She then said, "It is not 99.9%, it is 100%. I have never been able to trust anyone, and trust is love, isn't it? I guess I can't love the Men in my life today, because deep down I do not trust them. I feel Men have always let me down ever since I was a little girl."

Scott and I were in awe of what we were seeing. It was as if a light had just gone on inside Sarah.

I could see the Truth was setting in further as a glimpse of radiance began to appear on Sarah's face. I could also sense the chains of bondage in her life were being lifted off her with every word she heard and said. Amazed at what I was seeing, I went on to say, "Sarah, your lack of trust in your Covering has directly affected your ability to receive love from God. Now that your husband has learned to impart this love to you, you are not allowing it in. Your first Covering has let you down tremendously. You have been so hurt by the most important male in your life, your Dad, you are subconsciously closing off the solution to your emptiness.

"For the first six years of your marriage, your husband has been untrained on how to love and protect you with the Covering, because no one ever taught him how to be a Man. Now that he has learned how to love and protect you better, you are not allowing the love and protection to come through to you because you have developed a root of bitterness. You have an unforgiving heart against the Covering God has provided for you. Your lack of trust in your Dad has carried over into your marriage with Scott. Do you remember your Dad walking you down the aisle and giving you away to Scott?"

Sarah nodded again and said, "Yes, I remember everything about my wedding."

I went on, "At the point you both said 'I do' and the minister declared you were 'husband and wife,' there was a new Covering placed within Scott just like the one placed within your Dad. Your Father's Covering was released and placed within Scott. This is why it was so important for your father to give Scott the blessing for your marriage. He formally displayed this when he walked you down the aisle to 'give you away,' and this reinforces the covenant made between you and Scott. He gave away the Covering allowing for Scott to impart the special love, nurturing and protection for you that no one else on this planet can provide. No one else has this Covering for you, because you are only married to Scott.

"Even Dr. Laura encourages couples not to 'shack up' because it circumvents commitment. If there is no covenant, there is no Covering given to the Man, and without the blessing of the Covering, it is impossible for a woman to trust that the male in her life will love and protect her properly. How can she trust him? Because of his failure to do things properly and legally, he has already shown her he is not worthy to be trusted.

"To make matters worse, her 'boyfriend' will not be able to provide for her what she really needs, because he has not been imparted the Covering. God will never deposit the Covering in a Man until he has covenanted to remain with his wife until death do they part. This is symbolic of the nature of God. When God makes a covenant and offers His Covering, His promise is forever, and it shall never be broken.

"When a Man and a woman marry, God provides this special blessing because they are entering a covenant for a lifetime. I believe your Dad knew Scott could take care of you better than he could, and he knew Scott was the kind of Man who would eventually 'get it.' And he was right! Scott did 'get it.' He is a Man, and everyone around knows it.

In a way, giving you away to Scott was a very loving thing for him to do in the long run, even if it did not appear that way at the time.

"Sarah, it is time to get your life in order. You do not have to go through life fearful and 'uncovered' anymore. Just because your Dad has faltered in doing his job, it does not mean you have a right to hold it against God and everyone else. This includes your husband. You must let it go. You are rejecting the Covering your husband was given by God, because you are hurt and damaged from your father's irresponsibility of behaving as a 'boy.' It is time to let it go. Don't you agree?"

"Forgiveness allows God to provide His impenetrable Covering over your heart."

Forgiveness:

Sarah looked stunned. It was as if she had just been told a dead relative really wasn't dead at all, and the relative was now here to see her.

I then said to her, "Can you forgive your father for being a 'boy?' Can you forgive both your father and your husband for not being trained as Men?"

Sarah's face looked slightly relieved as she gently nodded her head in agreement. After all Sarah had been through over the years, forgiving her father for being a "boy" seemed to be about the easiest request she had received in a while, especially if it promised an end to a life of fear and unrest.

I went on to say, "Sarah, you are so very special. Your husband loves you so much. He has spent the last year becoming a Man for himself and then for you. He knows God has a very special purpose for your life. You have endured a life of pain and neglect.

"I can tell you, all of the abuse and trauma you have endured over the years have brought you the keys to unlock your destiny. As you use these keys, you will discover your purpose and your identity as a daughter of God. These are keys of freedom placed in your hands forever, and for the rest of your life they can be used to open the doors of bondage for other 'uncovered' women whom you will encounter in the future. No one can take these keys away from you, ever.

"You are a daughter of the King. This means you are a Princess, and a Queen. Just because your father has not fully recognized who he is, and who you are, you do not have to be in the dark as well. It is time to come out of the shadows and blossom as a woman. You must never allow yourself to be taken out of commission again by the lie you are not worthy to be loved. God has paid a very high price by sending His Son to die on the cross, thereby allowing you to have your identity as a loved daughter of the King. You are divinely cherished, and nobody except God is allowed to decide your value as a woman, a daughter, or a wife.

"You are the object of God's heart. Your value is not what you do or what you have done. The abuses you have suffered have colored your identity to the point where you have felt worthless. And this belief has leaked into every aspect of your life. This belief is a lie. God has already decided your worth, and your worth is so high He has given His all to show His love for you.

"To assist you with this love, God has imparted this love within your father and your husband for your well-being. This is called your Covering. It is unfortunate your Dad did not truly understand his true role as your father. You have not seen much proof of this love and protection from him, but I know you have seen it from your husband. Do you see what God has given you? Your husband is a gift only God can give."

Upon hearing this, Sarah began to cry almost uncontrollably. In absolute and total honesty she cried out, "I know God loves me, because He has given me my husband Scott." She held her husband's hand with both of her hands desperately.

Again, I said to her, "Can you forgive your father for being a 'boy?' Can you see your Dad really does love you? All you have to do is give it to God, and He will take away all of the lies, the misconceptions and the pain, as far as the East is from the West. He promised he would do this."

Sarah then said in a broken and victorious voice, "Lord, I forgive my Dad. You are right. I know my Dad loves me." She then held her face in her hands and whispered very quietly and calmly, "Daddy, I forgive you."

Sarah paused for a moment, as the presence of God seemed to radiate around her at the table. She lowered her tearful face into her cupped hands again and said, "Forgive me God… for missing it so badly. I do know I'm loved by my father. Oh God, please take all the pain away." Sarah's soft and trembling words echoed into the heavens as everything stood still.

I then led Sarah in a prayer where she said, "Lord, I do love you. Forgive me for listening to this unloving and cruel spirit of Death haunting me my entire life. I send all Self-hatred, Rejection and Control out of my life. Food no longer will have any power over me. In Jesus' name I am done with it. I am never going to allow Cruelty or Self-hatred to impart lies into me, ever again! I now invite the love of God, the love of the Holy Spirit into my life. Lord, show me your Covering."

The atmosphere around us was electric. It felt like the special effects from a Spielberg movie as one could literally feel the hoards of hell departing off and away from Sarah. Scott and I looked at Sarah in amazement as she communed with God as if He was right there at the table.

Sarah then let out a deep breath releasing a lifetime of anxiety as her shoulders relaxed back into position. Seeing the gravity of this event, Scott surrounded her with his arms and looked at her very closely saying, "I love you, Sarah. Right now as I look at you, you are the most beautiful woman I have ever seen. I am so proud of you. God loves you very much, and things are going to be different from now on." Indeed Sarah did have a glow in her face transcending any beauty ever manufactured by man.

Both Scott and I could see an incredible peace and tranquility envelop his wife. We parted that day with a huge sense of victory, and Sarah was on the road to recovery. She literally glowed with life as she departed looking like a new woman. On that special day, Sarah forgave her father for not being there for her, and for not teaching her to experience the blessing of her Covering; however, the best was yet to come. She was about to see her Covering was alive and well, and there was love and protection in her husband waiting for her reception.

Act II – The Husband's Covering:

About three weeks later, I happened to bump into Sarah and Scott at a friend's home. The friend was a Pastor who invited the couple over for fellowship. Someone actually needed prayer, and ironically, that someone was me. Scott and the Pastor prayed over me for blessings in all the areas of my life. I was truly thankful to have friends that were concerned for me and the situations occurring around me.

One thing led to another, and pretty soon the Pastor was praying for several people. Sarah was silent for close to an hour. She was sitting on the couch next to me, unnoticed as the group was encouraging one another to overcome life's challenges.

Right out of the blue, Sarah dropped to her knees on the floor in front of the couch. Weeping, she spoke out with a voice that pierced the heavens saying, "Lord, please forgive me for not trusting you. I am so sorry for not believing you love me. Please forgive me for not thinking I deserve to be loved. I know you love me, Lord."

The whole room was astounded at the boldness of the timid young woman who rarely spoke up in such a setting. There was a holy hush blanketing the room as everyone looked at this dear girl pouring out her heart to God. In Sarah's own words, here is her experience.

Sarah's Personal Testimony:

"The security I felt in the room that night was overwhelming. I felt so safe. For years I was spiritually engaged to the Lord, but I never felt married to the Lord. I knew I had to speak to God or I would just come apart. I cried out to God the words my heart was speaking, and I knew for the very first time I was trusting in Him.

"Throughout my growing-up years, I desperately wanted to trust the Lord. I wanted to do what God wanted me to do, but I now know I was unable to trust God, because of the fractured relationship I had with my own father. I found it very difficult to trust my Dad, because most of the time he did not prove himself to be trustworthy. He appeared outwardly to follow God throughout his life, but deep down I knew there was something missing in his actual relationship with God.

"As I was crying out to God that evening, someone shared with me the verse from Jeremiah which said, **'Before I formed you in the belly I knew you; and before you came forth out of the womb I sanctified you, and I ordained you a prophet unto the nations.'** [3] When I heard

3 Jeremiah 1:5, NKJV

this verse, it was like an arrow of confirmation shot right into my heart. I immediately knew God really did love me, and he always has loved me. It caused me to know I was His daughter, and we have always been connected. For the first time in my life, I really felt totally loved. It was overwhelming.

"After a half hour of basking in the peace I was feeling, the Pastor's wife asked my husband to stand up and hold his arms out for me. She then said, 'In this Man is your Covering. Walk into the arms of your husband and receive God's love.' I got up and walked into the arms of my husband and held as tight as I could. I did not want to let go, ever.

"I could actually feel God's total and unconditional love coming straight in me through my husband Scott. For nearly 20 minutes, I cried and cried in the arms of my husband. The waves of peace flowing through my soul has stayed with me ever since. I kept saying under my breath between sobs, 'Lord, thank you for Covering me. Thank you for Covering me.' I could feel it was true. I was Covered. It was a very new and freeing experience I will never forget or let go of, not ever.

"I had forgiven my Dad a few weeks earlier, because for the first time I saw he really did love me, but he was unable to impart the love due to his own insecurities. This was huge for me, because it set me free from feeling I was worthless. I had pity on my father, because he was losing to the same lies I was losing to. We both had no idea how badly we were being deceived by evil. This understanding helped me to truly forgive him and open my heart to my Father in heaven. I can see so clearly now forgiving my Dad actually opened up the doors of heaven for me to receive God's love.

"As far back as I can remember, I never felt unconditional love from my father. I worked so hard to be approved and accepted, but it was never enough. The more I worked, the more my feelings of worthlessness built up. I felt I had done everything I could to earn his love, because I did not feel worthy of love just for who I was.

"Of course, for short periods of time, I would get small accolades of how good I was at cooking or cleaning, but this quickly turned into the same old feelings of wanting to die, or thinking I deserved to die. I doubted myself so much. I spent my days trying not to do bad things. I did not want to give my Dad any more reasons not to love me.

"I remember when I was only six years old, my Dad asked me to sit on his knees. He may have meant well, but when he felt how heavy I was on his knees, he called me, 'Two Ton Tilley.' I was devastated inside. I thought my Daddy did not love me, because I was overweight and I did not look good to him. I was only six years old, and inside I felt rejected and alone.

"My Dad never picked up on how much his insensitivity hurt me. I can see now, there was a cruel demonic spirit just waiting to latch onto me as soon as my Dad made the mistake of making an insensitive comment. I now call this spirit 'Mr. Cruelty,' because it has promoted so much cruelty against me in my life. My Dad was a 'boy,' and he was not aware he was not protecting me from the bondage of this hateful spirit.

"As I look back, I can see that I began to hate myself and the way I looked, all because of what my Dad said. This spirit lied to me for 20 years by replaying my Dad's word in my head. I was convinced it was me speaking, but now I know it was not me speaking. For years, I made the mistake of listening to the wrong voices. Before that day when I was six years old, I was totally oblivious to how I looked. After I came to believe my Daddy did not love me, my whole life was set on a path of food disorders and people pleasing.

"This was my attempt to win my Dad's approval through how I looked or what I did. All of my actions were compliments of Mr. Cruelty. It was not until after I learned of the Covering that I began to be healed of these very unhealthy behaviors. I truly forgave my Dad for not being sensitive to me and for not imparting the love and the protection of the Covering upon my life.

"I understood it was Mr. Cruelty tormenting me; therefore, I declared war on Mr. Cruelty. And guess what? The voices stopped, and the torment left immediately. I had allowed the lies of Satan to keep me from hearing the Truth that I am worthy of love.

"Never again will I be fooled by Satan's lies. Mr. Cruelty is such an unloving spirit. Anytime I see the likes of him anywhere around me, I go on the warpath and demand he leave in the name of God almighty. The knowledge my Daddy loves me was definitely the answer. From the first moment I understood the Truth about my Covering, I declared war on this unloving and cruel spirit, and now food no longer is a major issue in my life. I have broken the power food had on me. It is amazing!

"A few weeks later, on the day when I finally got down on my knees before God and reconnected with Him, I truly knew it did not matter how I performed or what I did to win God's approval. I knew He loved me unconditionally as a daughter and even as a Princess. What a relief! I knew I was safe and everything was going to be okay. This was the first time in my life I can honestly say without any doubt whatsoever, that whatever I do, God loves me completely and fully. To this day I have not doubted, even for a second, the love my heavenly Father has for me, and I am so happy inside.

Sarah Today:

"I now have love and joy to give to others, and it is a love I only dreamed of having in the past. I would like to say to all Men that my husband fought for me by simply acting as a Man. He has loved me faithfully all of these years, and I finally believe it. If you are married to a woman who has unknowingly rejected her Covering, it can be overcome.

"A wife desires to see the love of God through a Man. The years of resentment and bitterness will never melt away until she looks God in the face, and makes a decision of whether she is going to accept His love, His Covering, or not. My husband was gentle and kind to me. And even when my husband outwardly appeared to be against me, I knew deep down he was for me.

"Right now, I am totally Covered because I joyfully receive God's protection and nurturing. After 20 years of feeling fearful and afraid, I have hope for tomorrow. I feel like I can say anything to my husband and he is going to help me. If I am off my game, I know he is going to help me to see more clearly and to be a better person. I feel secure, protected, more cared for, and more loved than I have ever been in my life. My husband has my interest first, above his. Even this morning, I was not feeling well. Scott was so attentive to help me by just being there. He offered to pray for me, to get me food, to do whatever was necessary to help me through the day.

"***Today I am Covered. Not because I have a good husband, which I do, but because I know God loves me and has my best interest at heart.***

My Covering is not based on my husband's ability to love or protect me. My Covering is based on my faith believing my true Father God has imparted his love and protection into the Men in my life. This gives me hope and allows me to look for God's working presence in Men, rather than only see the places where they have failed me. This is so freeing, because I know my security is not dependent on a Man who may fall into to sin at any moment.

"My security is based on my faith that God will meet my needs in the areas my husband falls short. There is a verse in the Bible stating, **'Where sin increased, grace increased all the more.'**[4] I believe this means when a father or a husband falls short because he is in sin and acting like a 'boy,' God will give us the extra grace we need to endure any abuses or neglect we experience as women. Now I know I have to look to God for His love. So even when my husband is at his worst, I am still Covered. No Man or 'boy' has the ability to keep me from my Covering now that I know what God has done for me. It is absolutely true. God has given me His Covering, and I trust Him.

"I no longer resent God or avoid God like I used to, because I know He is truly there for me. I have seen God change my husband to the point where he puts my wellness, my everything, before himself. My husband's love for me makes me want to know God more.

"For the first time in my life, I am free to be who I am. If I want to pray for something, I pray. If I want to share my heart on something, I share it. This is totally different than how I was raised. In the past, I was always fearful to show the real me, because I was sure the real me would be rejected further by others.

"The whole time I was growing up, all the way through this last year, I always did things for a reason. The reason was to be loved or accepted in some way. The worst part was, even if people did show love for me, I was not presenting to them the real Sarah. So even their supposed acceptance, though rare, was fraudulent. Now, I do not need a reason to be myself. I am free to be Sarah. I am free to be loved.

"Recently, my husband Scott came home from work extremely frustrated and annoyed about his day. Usually, when he comes home, he is happy, and he will ask how my day went. This day I found him lying

---

4 Roman 5:20, NIV

down on our bedroom floor whining and complaining about life. He was wimping out and not in a good place.

"In years past, I would have been angry with him or fearful that everything in my life was coming unglued. I was surprised to see myself very peaceful. I thought, 'Shouldn't I be freaking out right now, because he is going sideways?' Then I remembered, I am Covered. Regardless of how or what he is doing, I am perfectly fine. I know my Covering is still in my husband, and God will ensure I am loved, protected and nurtured even if my husband is having a bad day. Actually, I know God will even give me a special dose of grace and love, because on this day I need the strength as his helpmate to overcome my husband's challenges.

"I said to Scott as he was still whining on the floor complaining about his life, 'What is going on with you?' Scott took a deep sigh and said, 'What should I do about my job?' I knew he was really asking me to do his job for him as a Man, and he also wanted me to make him feel better. I felt like he wanted me to be his Mom, and give him cookies and milk. Without even thinking, I blurted out, 'Hey! Don't even think about giving me your Keys. I do not want them!'

"As soon as I said this, both of us started laughing. Right away our relationship was put back in order. Scott realized what he was doing, and he then began to work on dealing with his own issues without putting his burden on me. In times past, a situation like this would have put a block in our relationship for a week or two until we moved on to the next crisis. It felt great to help our relationship, rather than add more grief to the drama. How awesome it is to be Covered. No matter what the problem is in our relationship, I know I have the strength and the backing to overcome.

Victim No More:

"I have been a Nanny for several families over the years. Lately, there have been situations bringing my security and my relationships with others to the forefront. I have found my growing self-esteem and identity as a queen and daughter of the King has caused me to overcome not only in my marriage and family life, but it has helped me to overcome in my relationships with everyone I interact with.

"At one home where I am a Nanny, I take care of a little girl named Nikki who is five years old. Nikki treated me like I was stupid, and she has totally discounted my authority as an adult. For the first two months on the job, I felt like she was the adult and I was the child. She was acting as a controlling adult, and I was letting her by acting like a little child.

"I struggled for decades with my identity as a loved daughter of God and more recently as a loved wife of my husband. Therefore, I did not feel worthy to be in authority over Nikki by parenting her. I allowed this little five year old girl to totally own me. I would come home to Scott and say, 'I do not know what to do. Nikki has got me on this one.' Here was this little five year old owning me bigger than life, and I knew I needed to win this battle.

"After Scott learned to be a Man, he would tell me I had authority in the Lord to take charge and bring Nikki in line. But at the time, I did not acknowledge that I was a daughter of God. How could I have authority, if I don't know whether God even cares for me? Scott told me I was able to walk in his authority as his wife and take charge in the very authority given to him, even if I did struggle with my relationship with God. A light bulb went on inside me. This was the first step to overcoming, because I knew Scott did have authority. I could now see it in him.

"After I learned God loves me unconditionally, everything was different. I was at work one day and Nikki was pulling the same old behavior. For the first time in my life something inside me said, 'I do not deserve to be treated like this anymore.' This was such an incredible revelation. I figured if I had so much value, and if God loved me enough that He was willing to even die for me, how could I allow Nikki to step on me?

"I began to tell Nikki 'No' with authority, and everything changed immediately. Even Nikki knew things were different from the moment I first walked in the house. I began to set down the law, and I made sure the law was enforced. It felt amazing to know I have value and that others were expected to honor me. I was not going to allow a sixty year old in the form of my Dad, or a five year old in the form of this little person step on me or my boundaries anymore.

"I now know who I am, and I know what I am supposed to do. The very moment I realized God loved me unconditionally was the very moment I stopped allowing people to push me around. I know I am a Queen, and you do not mess with a Queen. The idea I was royalty was powerful to me. Not because I am anything special in myself, but because

God says I am royalty and will defend his royal family no matter what. God owes us nothing at all, but He has given us everything. I felt in my heart that fear and the victim mentality were not going to be part of me ever again.

"When I was growing up, I was not aware I had Spiritual Enemies. I was clueless about the spirit realm or the fact my Spiritual Enemies had access to me, because of my Dad's inability to lead properly. At night I would think I saw very evil things that were trying to get me. Somehow I knew they were real. I now see this as a direct relation to my father not showering me in love or protecting me properly.

"These Spiritual Enemies continued to torment me all through my life until recently, when I grew to know my Father's love for me. Now, if ever I feel like I am being attacked, my husband and I sit down and talk about it in depth. Through prayer, understanding, and a few words, these intruders just leave.

"To the woman who has a husband working on walking as a Man, I have many things I would like to say to you. When I walked down the aisle to my husband, I felt like I was going to be with someone who cared about all the things I cared about. I knew Scott loved me, and I thought as much as I knew about love, I loved him too. And then I was married.

"We did not have a good relationship, because both of us were so untrained and messed up; but I always thought our marriage would get better. It did not get better, things got worse. Looking back, I can see it was actually good that things continued to be more difficult, because we desperately needed to get to the core of the problem and restructure our foundation.

"To the woman who has a 'boy' for a husband, have your husband read Man vs. 'boy.' I implore you to realize you are a daughter of the King, and not to stumble into the pitfall of thinking your father or your husband does not have God's impartation of love for you within him. It is there, whether you see it or not. They just haven't learned how to impart love.

"Scott always wanted to be a Man, and he tried as much as he knew how. It was frustrating for him because I would say many times; 'You are not being a Man.' He would then get mad and say, 'You are not being a woman.' Neither of us knew what was going on, and it was a mess. Now,

Scott never blames me for anything. Even when I make mistakes, he takes responsibility for helping me and supporting me in a way that helps me make better choices.

"When Scott first started changing this last year by removing his 'boyish' behaviors, I felt like he was disrupting my little world. He was going outside of my box, and I thought for sure he was going sideways. My life was manageable, even though there were major problems with the marriage. After he learned the principles of living as a Man and walking with his Keys, my heart started to tell me everything would be okay. Even when he was angry with me for not understanding him, there was always a soft spot where I could tell he wanted the best for me.

"I encourage all Men to rise up and be the Man they are called to be. My Dad was distant and lost in his own world. He was caring at times, but generally he was out to lunch. Gone fishing is a term coming to mind. I would say to myself, 'Are you in there Dad? Make eye contact, please.' Remember, the relationships you build with your wife and children will have a dramatic affect on them for either good or evil. My breakthrough came because a few good Men, my husband and his new friends, decided to stand up and love me the way God loves me, unconditionally.

"At times my husband seemed to be harsh and even insensitive. Looking back, I am glad he did all of the things he did to recapture the Keys back in his life. His actions were sometimes harsh, but necessary. This is because I had built up such a strong wall against the Truth. Now I know it was right for him to do whatever necessary to help me see clearly. I can attest that if you continue to love the women in your life, it will rebuild their trust in Men. This response may not happen overnight, but the results will eventually be totally worth it.

"Before Scott began to stand up and be a Man, I was living in fear. My health was seriously in question? I was upset and nervous all the time, because my life was based on my daily performance. I had little to no hope for future joy. Each day I would hold on to any comfort making me temporarily feel better, because I needed my marriage to fulfill my needs.

"Today, I feel totally loved and protected. I am physically healthier than I have ever been in my entire life. I have overwhelming victory, and I intend to pursue God's best for me as a loved daughter of the King. Food no longer owns me. I own food.

"I am looking forward now to having children and imparting to them the wonderful things I have learned. I know I am loved by God and my husband, and I have an incredible hope for a future filled with blessings. I did not write the script for my childhood and my life, but I definitely know I can choose how I will respond to this script and how the story is going to end. I have joy and peace in my heart, because I am truly Covered. I thank you God, for the gift of my Covering."

"For I know the thoughts and plans that I have for you, says the LORD, thoughts and plans for welfare and peace, and not for evil, to give you hope in the final outcome."[5]
Jeremiah – Book of Jeremiah

The Blessings of The Covered Women:

Once an "uncovered" woman becomes Covered through her understanding of the love and protection provided for in her Covering, a wonderful thing happens. The untrained male who carries her Covering, and doing a lousy job, is set free from the burden of attempting to do the impossible. He will no longer need to cater to the fears and insecurities of his wife and daughters, because the fears and insecurities will no longer be there to any degree.

At the core of every Man is his desire to please the women in his life whom he is Mandated to nurture and protect. By definition, this is what comes with the gift of the Covering. He will possess a deep longing to care for those he is entrusted to care for. It is built into his Mandate. Regarding a Man's wife, the Covering is imparted into him at the time he marries her. Regarding his daughter, the Covering is imparted at the time the daughter is conceived.

We must always remember a Covered woman is driven by her love for God, because she has faith that He will provide the protection and nurturing she longs for. Her greatest earthly desire is to love and respect her father and husband. When a women understands the blessings of her

5 Jeremiah 29:11, AB

Covering, she is then free to love, honor and respect her father and her husband, because she knows her Covering is a God-given gift resident with these males. It is not based on their performance and abilities. Her Covering is God's gift to her.

This is true even if the male is a "boy." Of course, it is much more difficult to love and honor a male who is a "boy." But when a woman understands the principle of the Covering, her real love and respect is for God, and the loving gift He has placed within the males in her life. When she loves and honors God, the males in her life will be more likely to feel love and respect carry over to them, because a part of God has been placed within them.

This is an extremely uplifting encouragement for her father and husband, even if they did not really deserve it. This is how good God is to us. When wives and daughters are open to their Covering, God will allow even irresponsible "boys" to experience a taste of his love, even if they have done nothing to earn it. This sense of love and respect the "boy" feels actually draws him towards God and becoming a Man. God desires us all to win in life by becoming closer to Him. When a woman is receptive and obedient to His ways, everyone close to her will experience a taste of His blessings.

When a male sees his wife (a Covered woman) respect and honor the gift of the Covering he is carrying within him, the pressure of performing tends to fall away, if he truly has the desire to be a Man. He will then find it easier to rest in the relationship, and he will be encouraged in a spiritual and emotional realm invisible to the natural eye. Although this encouragement is unseen, it is very real. Unseen encouragements are actually more important than seen encouragements. They speak the Truth of a person's heart, and they minister on a level that cannot be denied.

Let me be clear here. The responsibility of a male to be a Man falls fully on the shoulders of the Man, and the Man alone. His wife may not understand the Covering and be "uncovered," thereby making life much harder for him due to her behaviors. The husband still must stand up and be a Man. He must realize he is the one who chose his "uncovered" wife. He cannot blame her ever for discouraging his Manhood. If a woman believes her behavior is the responsible element in her husband becoming a Man, she has become matriarchal by becoming the initiator, rather than the responder.

Once again, women can promote the Manhood of the males in their lives, but they cannot dictate or impart it. A wife is not responsible for her husband to pick of the scepter and lead as a Man, but how wonderful it is when she encourages him to do so in a way that blesses them both. Ladies, I beg you; for yourself, and for the God who loves you, receive your Covering so you may promote peace in your lives and marriages.

Prayer For Women To Become "Covered"

Lord, I come before you as your daughter. I recognize Men have behaved as "boys" in my life, causing me to feel unprotected and unloved. I now forgive my father for any lack of love and protection he failed to provide for me, and I release any bitterness against all Men. Forgive me for times I have not trusted you. Thank you for imparting in my father your Covering for me, and for the times I have recognized the Covering working in and through him. I recognize your Covering in my father, and I receive the blessings you have for me. I forgive my mother for any part she took in keeping me from recognizing my Covering, and I release her fully.

Lord, I ask you to take away all the unhealthy and controlling behaviors I have embraced that have caused me to control or hurt myself and others. I forgive any male who has hurt me and caused me to resent you, or your Covering for me. Please bless and assist any Man who is called to help you in covering me.

In the name of Jesus, I declare from this day forward I am a daughter of the King. Nobody is allowed to interfere with my relationship with you. I shall love as I am loved, and I will leave a legacy of health, purity and victory for my family and friends. I receive you, and I receive your Covering, forever. Amen.

"He shall cover thee with his feathers, and under his wings shalt thou trust."
Book of Psalms[6]

6 Psalm 91:4, KJV

PART II: Kathy, Your Daddy Loves You!

Do you remember Mike from Chapter 3 and his "Total Victory?" After Mike retrieved back all of his Keys and shut the open Gates in his life, an incredible thing occurred. Mike was armed with an additional power to fulfill his Mandate and to walk as the Patriarch of his extended family.

Kathy is Mike's niece, and the following story occurred when Kathy phoned Mike with news about her recent engagement and her fiancé. Here is the true story of the incredible victory achieved by both Kathy and Mike. It all occurred because Mike had the courage and training to walk as a Patriarch.

Mike's Testimony:

Six months after I had learned to walk as a Patriarch, my niece Kathy called me with news about her upcoming marriage. Immediately upon hearing her voice, I could feel the great emotional turmoil in her life. Kathy was 23 years old at the time, and she is my sister's only daughter.

My whole extended family experienced shock and mourning when my sister suddenly passed away from cancer. Ever since her passing, it has been a long hard road for Kathy to come to terms with her mother's death. It was very difficult for her to talk about her mother without being bitter and upset in regard to the unfinished business between them. As we spoke on the phone, I was relieved Kathy did not bring her mother up in our conversation. I felt it would be unproductive for her to reenter the old wounds that have haunted her for years.

The passing of Kathy's mother was essentially the loss of her father as well. Right after her mother's funeral, Kathy's father totally checked out of Kathy's life. As soon as the last shovel full of dirt was poured on the coffin, Kathy's Dad had a huge garage sale and sold off nearly everything he owned. He then moved to Washington to be with his new wife-to-be. Kathy was devastated. My brother-in-law actually put a Realtors sign in the front yard saying "available soon" even before my sister passed away. It was not a good situation, and there was a real relational breakdown between Kathy and her Dad.

Adding to the pain, Kathy's Dad married a new wife within months after my sister's death, and he gave all of her mother's jewelry to his new wife. This was extremely traumatic for Kathy, because her parents were married for over 21 years, and Kathy longed to be very close to her Mother. Adding further insult to injury, one of the rings her Dad gave to his new wife was the wedding ring Kathy was promised by her mother when she planned to get married.

This leads us back to the phone call to me. Kathy and her fiancé had been shopping for rings, and their recent engagement brought up all of the pain and unfinished business in her relationship with her Dad. All the bad feelings were coming back to haunt her. And yes, there was still the issue with the ring.

Thank God I had been trained from "Man vs. boy" about my job as a Patriarch. I knew from the principles I learned in Chapter 3; these feelings Kathy was experiencing were actually there to help her, if she handled them properly. Immediately after her mother's death, Kathy went back to college, and the relationship with her father remained strained for years. They rarely spoke. On the rare occasion when they did speak, Kathy usually initiated it, and it never proved to be productive.

Kathy's Dad continued to be hands off concerning his relationship with Kathy. He did not help pay for her college education, and he seldom called to see how she was doing. Basically, Kathy's Dad was behaving like a selfish and irresponsible "boy." Over the years, the neglect and rejection Kathy experienced from her Dad hurt her heart to the point where she became extremely withdrawn and bitter towards him. She was "uncovered."

Thankfully, on this day Kathy called to tell me the good news about her new fiancé. She said the two of them had been ring shopping, and Kathy's fiancé was promised a large sum of money from his family. They were both very excited about getting married and purchasing a wedding ring for Kathy. Kathy called her Dad to share the good news, but she ended up speaking only to her step-mom.

This was a grave mistake, because her Dad's wife just blew Kathy out of the water with skepticism and coldness. She told Kathy she needed to take a "chill-pill" regarding getting married, and she felt Kathy was overly excited about her wedding. This totally leveled Kathy, and it caused her to be very angry. She was already not happy with her Dad's new wife, as the wife was still wearing the very ring Kathy was supposed to be given on her wedding day.

Kathy's Father Jack:

I have known Kathy's Dad for over 26 years. His name is Jack. Jack married my sister a year before I married my wife. He was the nicest guy outwardly. He had blond hair, blue eyes and a big smile. He was the kind of guy who would look you in the eye and greet you like a great host.

Jack was very self-centered, and he was definitely a "boy." He did not want to have children. He once said to my sister, "If you want a child, fine; but you are taking care of it." Jack also had two children from a previous marriage, and he had totally dropped the ball with them as well. For many years, Jack chose not to be in the lives of his first two children. On all fronts, the relationships Jack had with his children were strained.

Whenever I would go over to Jack's house, I found him working on his Jet Ski, or his forerunner, or his motorcycle, or whatever toy he happened to be into at the time. He was a total "boy" all the way. His whole life was about toys, and my sister served him faithfully despite his shortfalls. Looking back now, and understanding how the Man vs. "boy" principles were running course in his life, I have a great deal more empathy for the situation. Jack's father died when he was very young, and he never had a strong Man in his life to answer some of life's most begging questions. Consequently, he just never became a Man, and everyone around him suffered because of it.

As far as his relationship with God was concerned, Jack made an attempt to accept Christ outwardly, but it seemed it was only to get the heat off him. My sister was very involved in the compassion ministry in our church, and Jack would somehow tolerate any church activity she was involved in. I never saw any change in his life as a result. It appeared he was just going along with the flow. I never could identify the Spirit of God working through him in a noticeable way.

When my sister was in the hospital and her health was seriously failing, Jack's behavior upset me very much regarding how he handled the situation. I was totally disgusted when I learned he entered into a relationship with another woman even before my sister passed. The final straw came for me a week before my sister passed away. Jack put garage sale signs in the front yard and was already packing up to move away with his new fiancé, even though his wife was still clinging to life and asking for him. He behaved as a total "boy."

Kathy's Covering:

Due to Jack's selfish behaviors, Kathy's relationship with her Dad was very bad for many years. Since her father was very self-centered, she picked up a self-centered attitude as well. My sister used to serve them both hand and foot, and it seemed neither one could ever get enough attention from her. Kathy did eventually build a relationship with God, although she continued to battle the challenges of her family. Specifically, her Mom's death was a big blow to her. Although Kathy was never a "Daddy's girl," she still spent most of her life seeking her father's love in various subtle ways.

On Kathy's recent phone call, she was emphatic about not inviting her Dad to the wedding, but I could hear deep down that her heart clearly was saying she wanted things to be right with her Dad. Over the past four years, Kathy called me many times. I would encourage her to hang in there and attempt to build a relationship with her Dad. Even when I was untrained, I knew how important the father and daughter relationship is to a daughter's well being. Although I was the first person who wanted to punch Jack in the face because of his irresponsibility, I still encouraged her to engage her father in any healthy way she could.

As I was talking on the phone with Kathy, she elaborated on the forthcoming engagement and the financial wedding gift coming from her fiancé's family. My heart told me she was calling to get some fatherly direction, and I was the only available Man in the family who she felt had his act together. My sister and I were very close before she died, and I am the only uncle in which Kathy had a close relationship. I spent a lot of time at my sister's house, especially after she became sick.

After listening to Kathy for ten minutes, I said to her, "Kathy, the important thing in this situation is for you to understand God's principle regarding the Covering. I need to teach you about your Covering. Until recently, I never understood it myself. Once you understand the Covering, you will be set free of many of the hurt emotions and damage you have experienced at the hands of your father. Is it okay for me to share this with you?"

Kathy answered, "Of course Uncle Mike, I have always valued your insight."

I then said to Kathy, "Although your emotions are important, it would not be prudent for you to do what your emotions are saying. Your Dad has hurt you, but what is your Dad really saying to you in his heart?"

She replied, "He doesn't care about me. He doesn't care about anything except for money and things like that."

I said, "No. What is your father's heart ***really*** saying to you?" She was silent for a moment, and I said, "Your father loves you, doesn't he?"

Kathy remained very quiet for quite a while. I could sense she was replaying years of memories concerning her father. She then said, "I want to say, 'Yes,' but there has been so much he has done to me over the years that really hurt me. How could he love me and treat me so badly? That's a strange kind of love!"

I replied, "I believe that deep inside your heart, you know your father loves you, Kathy. If all of the other bad things had not happened, you know you would actually feel some of the love from your father."

Kathy gently responded, "Yes… maybe, but this is so confusing. I do not know what to do."

I then told her, "Let's start with the premise your father does love you. I do not discredit what your mind is saying; things like, 'He married another woman prematurely, or he gave your Mom's ring to his new wife.' But, all of those hurtful and selfish behaviors were your father's bad choices. The Truth is at the end of the day you are his daughter. He would tell you he loves you, if he was not so blinded by his own problems and bad choices."

Kathy said, "Yes, this is probably true."

I continued to say, "Knowing you love your father and that you would benefit from following Godly principles in your life, I would like to share an important principle with you. First, what is the only commandment with a promise? Obviously it is 'Honor your father and thy mother, so your days will be long in the land.' You need to know God desires you to honor your Dad, so you will live well and long and be blessed, and your stress will be less. Kathy, you know all about divorce and the problems and stresses of life, and you know God does not want strife and disappointment for you. In order to take advantage of this principle, your fiancé needs to go to your father and formally ask him in a respectable way for your hand in marriage."

She retorted back, "But Uncle Mike, I don't want him to do that, because I do not care what my father says about my marriage. He blew it with me years ago!"

I said, "Kathy, it does not matter that you feel like avoiding your father. What matters is honoring God's principle. This principle is for you, not against you."

Kathy said, "I don't know about that, Uncle Mike. If my Dad doesn't do his part, how can I honor that principle?"

I then said, "Let us talk about this. It is the father who walks the bride down the isle during a marriage ceremony and presents the bride to the groom before the altar. The Minister then says, 'Who gives this woman away to be married to this Man?' The father then says, 'I do.' It is the father who gives the bride away, and as he does this, he also gives the authority and the responsibility of caring for the bride away to this young Man. The daughter is then under the new Man's care, charge and protection. Do you understand? Your Dad needs to pass the Covering to your husband."

Kathy said, "Yes, I understand how it is supposed to happen. A lot of things are 'supposed to happen,' but my Dad is not acting like a Dad!"

I said, "Kathy, it doesn't matter if your Dad is behaving right or not. The commandment does not say your father must act Godly, or that he is a good Man who is protecting you, loving you and making you happy.

"This is your father. In honor of him, you are asked to follow God's principles. As his daughter, upon your very conception your father was given a Covering that is special for you. Although your father may be totally blowing it, you can be covered, protected, and cared for by your Father in heaven if you will simply honor the basic principle of the Covering.

"Your Covering was entrusted to your Dad regardless of whether he did a good job at fathering or not. For your sake and the sake of your marriage, you need to have it passed legally to your husband, in the spiritual realm. Your Covering must be handed over to your husband in order for him to legally do the job of taking care of you. Hopefully, your husband will do a much better job than your father at protecting and nurturing you. If you really want a life of peace and blessings, your fiancé must go with proper honor to your father and ask him to give his blessing."

Kathy said, "Uncle Mike, I can see that what you are saying might be true, but what if my father does not give his blessing? He doesn't believe in any of this stuff. How can he pass my supposed Covering, when he may just laugh at the whole principle?"

I then said, "In reality, it is God who passes the Covering. If you and your husband do your job and honor this principle, the Covering will be imparted regardless of you father's choices. Your obedience to this principle will ensure your success. God always blesses obedience, and my heart is saying that everything will work out well.

"If your fiancé goes to your father as a Man before God and asks your father for your hand in marriage with a right heart, your father will surely surrender his blessing. I hope that he will say, 'Yes, I will give the blessing to you.' Either way, I know that God will definitely pass the Covering to your husband, because you and your fiancé will have done the right thing. In your case, it is not enough for your fiancé to just ask for the blessing. He needs to ask your father to be at the wedding and walk you down the aisle. I believe in your heart, you really desire this to happen. Every woman deep down desires her father to give her away."

Kathy responded with, "No! I do not want him walking me down the aisle! I don't want him to ruin my wedding!"

I said, "You may be hurt right now over past grievances, but you really do want your father to walk you down the aisle and give you away. Even if your emotions say 'No' right now, trust me when I say you really do want and need your father to give you away. This is not just my idea, or what I am merely feeling; this is a timeless, biblical and cultural principle that will bless you. Kathy, this needs to happen."

I could sense that Kathy was really struggling with what I was saying, so I said, "In every culture and in every society, whether the families are

Christian or not, there is an innate need and desire for a bride to have her father give her away. I was extremely close to your mom. She was grateful I was with her in her last days, because your mother always loved me. I can tell you that even when your mother was on her deathbed, she still wanted her father next to her to comfort and take care of her.

"Even to the very end, your mother sought the love of her father, because she never felt like she was able to receive love from him freely and unconditionally. Your mother did not understand the principle of the Covering; therefore, she did not fully understand God is her true Covering. Her father was just a symbolic representation of the real love and protection that God had in store for her. Unfortunately, he failed to impart this love.

"Kathy, if you run from your father and the possibility of entering into a healthy relationship with him, you will always long for his blessing just as your mother did. This principle of the Covering is built into you, and it will always be there in you. You cannot continue the same chain of bondage that inflicted your mother. If you acknowledge God's principle by having your father pass the Covering to your future husband, you will be incredibly blessed. By honoring the Covering placed within your father, you will actually be honoring God and his perfect ways. Whether your father has done a good job or not, you will blessed because you will be honoring your Covering."

I could hear Kathy was quietly sobbing on the other end of the phone at the remembrance of all the pain her mother had suffered. I knew Kathy did not want to get caught in the same bondage that gripped her mother for most of her life.

After a short silence, Kathy said, "How am I going to do all this? The whole thing of including my Dad in my wedding feels overwhelming. What do I do?"

I said to Kathy, "Honoring God's principle here will allow you and your new husband to begin your marriage where it is built on a strong foundation in the blessings and favor of God. Kathy, these principles are not for God. They are for you, your fiancé and your father. God's principles always lead us to promote the restoration of relationships, and they will meet the needs of our hearts at the deepest level. When you and your fiancé request your father give you away, you will also give your father the opportunity to step up to the plate and begin to do his job as a father. He will have another opportunity to meet your needs as his daughter. If he does not participate, it will be his loss. Either way you will be blessed."

Kathy then said, "I do not think my Dad will do it. I don't think he will give me away, and I do not know whether I want him to or not. I need to talk to my fiancé about this."

Kathy's fiancé is a young 25 year-old Man, and he works as a counselor at a Christian College. I told Kathy, "I believe that with the counseling knowledge your fiancé has obtained, he will have the maturity and insight to know this is the right way to interact with your father. If you or your fiancé need any further understanding on the Covering principle, I would be happy to talk to both of you and share my heart on the matter."

Kathy said, "Okay Uncle Mike, but first tell me more about the Covering. I have never really understood how my relationship with my father is supposed to look."

Understanding Her Covering:

I further explained to Kathy about a principle that had been a mystery to me for most of my adult life. I repeated to her the words that I had just learned the year before. I said, "Kathy at the time you were conceived, there was an unseen Covering of love and protection placed within the heart of your father that is a gift from God. This Covering is a blessing and a sign of God's desire to nurture and protect you. Your Covering cannot be used to hurt you in any way. The love and power is resident in your father waiting to be poured out upon you.

"It cannot be used to control, neglect and abuse in any way. The power to nurture and protect with this Covering can only be utilized when your father wills in his heart that he is going to love you. The love displays itself in two ways. First it provides a tremendous protection for you. Next it provides love and nurturing for you. This is called your Covering, because it is there to cover you with protection and nurturing. Does this make sense to you?"

Kathy replied, "Yes, it sounds very beautiful. I wish father would just allow the love to come out of him."

I said, "Yes, this is why what I am telling you is so important. Your Dad has made a conscious choice not to allow love to come out to any of his children. This is why it is so important for you to marry a Man that understands and honors the principle of the Covering. This is why it is so important for your fiancé to do things right. Kathy, I want to see you blessed, and this is how it can happen.

"Your fiancé must ask for the blessing from your father, so that you can overcome the challenges that always plagued your mother. If your fiancé asks your father for your hand in marriage and your father says 'No,' I will call your father and explain God's principle of the Covering to him. I will ask your father to reconsider his actions. I assure you, after I explain to him the significance of the Covering, there is a good chance he will reconsider his reservations.

"Kathy, your obedience here will ensure your life will be blessed, regardless of whether your father desires for his life to be blessed or not. If he is unwilling to do his part again, I believe it is my responsibility as your uncle to approach your father on your behalf. I will tell him he is not following God's principles regarding his daughter. I may need to say to him, 'You need to do this so your daughter can be blessed!'"

Kathy replied, "I don't know, Uncle Mike. There has been so much "stuff" he has done."

I said to her, "Kathy, your father loves you. Your father has been selfish, unhelpful, and even conniving in his behavior with you and the family. Throughout his life, your father has chosen to satisfy his own selfishness by having the motorcycles, the sand rails, the jet skis and all of the toys a 'boy' will indulge in, at your expense. Understand this is every Man's battle. Every male has to overcome his tendency to behave like a 'boy' at the expense of his loved ones. This is an age-old conflict every male must contend with and overcome. I know it feels personal, but it is not. This is his problem.

"God desires for Men to die to their 'boyish' desires, and walk in a loving way being considerate to others. Any wrong behavior manifesting through a male is hurting him as well as his children. It is not the Spirit of God causing him to be a jerk. It is this 'boyish' spirit promoting the manifestation of selfish and hurtful behaviors. Your father is simply not a Man yet. He is a 'boy.' His parents died when he was very young, and there was no one else around to 'Bar Mitzvah' him into Manhood. A 'boy' cannot do the job of a Man.

"His job as a Man is to love you unconditionally and instill into you the value you have as a daughter. He did not acknowledge or impart value to you, as a father ought to, because he was and still is a 'boy' to this day. This is the hurt you have been feeling your entire life. This is the hurt your Mother was feeling her entire life. Her father was a 'boy,' and he had a similar difficulty in bestowing value and love into her. This is why she was crying out for her father's love even on her deathbed. Do you see it? Do you see you cannot allow your father to steal the blessings and joy God has for you?"

Kathy responded emotionally, "Yes, I see it. Our family has always struggled with being close and honest in relationships. I do not want to have the same problems in my marriage. I cannot live the rest of my life with this underlying pain always gnawing at me. I can't have my future children experience this same pain."

I replied, "Yes, you are right. You need to know the emotional pain and suffering you have been experiencing in your life is the manifestation of what is wrong with your Dad. This does not mean he cannot be fixed. Every Man was once a 'boy' who indulged in selfish behavior, many times at the expense of his daughters. Salvation is a 'boy' becoming a Man, a sinner becoming saved. If you cannot believe your Dad can get this right and turn from a 'boy' into a Man, then you do not believe Christ can save. Understanding this is actually a salvation principle. A 'boy' can become a Man.

"By becoming a Man, your father can redeem and restore the damage both he and his fathers before him have caused. When he does become a Man, he will be the father you have always needed. You will then get the love from your father you have always deserved. It will be the love God wants you to have, even though you have not really received it yet.

"Kathy, your father loves you. Even if he does not know how to show it, inside he desperately wants to be a Man. He has been behaving like a 'boy;' this means he has been beat down by his enemies for years. He may not see it clearly, because he has not been trained. I know somewhere inside him he wants to love you, and he wants to be the Man that God desires him to be. Right now he just does not know how to be that Man."

Kathy Forgives Her Dad:

I could tell Kathy was trying to absorb what I had just told her. Then she said, "Well, I guess my father is not all bad. He has done some very good things for me at times."

I said, "Kathy, your Dad loves you! He really does love you! And I love you."

When I said this to her one last time, Kathy just broke. After a heartfelt cry lasting a few minutes, she became quiet for a moment. I could hear her gently sobbing until she finally whispered, "My Daddy does love me. I know this. He just does not know how to be the Man that God intended him to be. Oh Daddy, why can't you just see what is going on?"

I could feel the healing presence of God blow through her heart. It reminded me of the verse in John where Jesus said, **"The wind blows where it pleases, and you hear the sound thereof, but you cannot tell where it comes from or where it is going, so is every one that is born of the Spirit."**[7]

As God was confirming and pouring out his love for Kathy as she was learning the Truth about her father and her Covering, Kathy began to feel my love for her. This greatly helped her to genuinely see that her father really did love her as well. I said to Kathy one more time, "Your father does love you very much, and if he does not respond to your fiancé in a right way, I will deal with him. You need to do what is right here. Sometimes you have to do the hard things in life so God can bless you."

Kathy responded calmly saying, "I don't think you will have to do that, Uncle Mike. My Dad will do the right thing."

I then said to Kathy, "I feel the same way. My heart is telling me if you follow God's lead here, your father will ultimately bow to God and honor what is right."

Mike's Reflections:

Kathy had made a 180-degree change in the short time we were on the phone, and I fully believed it would go well with her father. She

---

7 John 3:8, NIV

moved into a place where she believed that if her fiancé approached her Dad in a right way with good intentions in his heart, it would go well with her father's decision and the result would be positive.

Kathy and I were on the phone for about an hour and a half. I was amazed to see her both cheerful and optimistic about the future relationship with her father towards the end of the call. I had been Kathy's uncle for 23 years, and it was not until the phone call that I truly felt I was the loving Patriarch God called me to be for her.

As I hung up the phone, I knew I was right in the place God intended for me to be. I know Kathy called me because God knew I would handle it right, and I was so grateful I understood the Covering in such a way I could impart life to my niece Kathy. I knew without a shadow of a doubt what I imparted to her was absolutely true. I knew she was going to follow the directions I gave her, and everything would be fine because of it. I was walking as an ambassador for God and his loving principles, and my conversation with Kathy was a win on all accounts.

As I recall the words we exchanged, the sense of authority and power my words and counsel had on her was amazing. Our conversation not only blessed Kathy, but it was fulfilling for me personally. I experienced the feelings of accomplishment and honor I always longed for. I knew Kathy trusted and respected me, and I knew she was thankful I was in her life.

At the end of our conversation, I asked Kathy if she agreed with all of the things I shared with her. She responded by saying, "Yes, I do agree with you. And Uncle Mike, I love you! Thank you so much for sharing about my Covering. I always know that you are there for me." Words cannot express the fulfillment I felt in my heart. I can still hear her heart saying to me, "I am glad I called you. Even though you had to deal with me concerning my Dad, I am glad that you took the time and you are very special to me. I am thankful you are in my life."

In years past, if I received a phone call from Kathy, my counsel would start and end with something like; "God loves you. I love you. Your Dad is an idiot. Hopefully, at some point in your life you will get the love from your father you need and deserve. But if you don't, oh well." Then I would hang up the phone, apprehensive about what I just said. I would be left with little hope of victory, and I would pray things would not get worse. Usually, to my dismay, they did get worse.

I inherently knew her father's love for her was an essential need in her life; however, I was not able to identify or diagnose the reasons why Kathy's father was missing it so badly. In times past, I wasn't able to clearly identify the fact that Kathy's father was merely living as a "boy." Behaving like a "boy" was the primary reason he failed to impart love to his daughter.

I did not recognize the fact that her father's sinful and even demonic nature would manifest itself in an attempt to destroy every relationship in his life. This was sure to occur if he was not going to admit his problems and fight against them. It is important to note the relationships he was sabotaging were the same relationships he was supposed to nurture, support and protect. I was privy to all of the fallout evolving throughout her father's relationship with my sister. I can say, the spiritual or demonic powers were very successful in destroying every relationship in his life as he manifested his "boyish" behaviors.

Looking back, the main problem I was experiencing was that I had a limited ability to approach her father with any kind of fix or explanation about what was happening in their lives. It is sad I was not able to tell her father, "This is the spiritual fight you are fighting, and this is why you are doing the things you are doing. You are a 'boy,' and your Spiritual Enemies are using your ignorance to destroy you and your loved ones. You can be released today from your bondage, if you are willing to take responsibility for your Mandate, retrieve your Keys and take on the battle in a manner giving you victory."

Today, there are so many daughters who have fathers who have neglected their Mandate of caring for and nurturing them; but God will bring forth another Man to take on this delegated responsibility to fill the gap. It could be a Grandfather, an Uncle or even an older brother who will pick up the ball and carry it for the family. It is not hopeless. Most women are not trained to go to a delegated authority to get their needs met.

Kathy's father made it clear he really did not want children, and my sister would have to be the one to take care of them. The rejection Kathy experienced from her father's dereliction of duty left a huge hole God was using me to fill. Over the years, both Kathy's Dad and Mom delegated authority to me as a fatherly influence in her life. The good thing about walking as a Man and knowing God's principles of authority, is when somebody calls on you for help, you have something to give them.

I remember in times past when I was losing in my life, I would get the dreaded phone call from a friend who needed help in getting victory in his life. I would feel like I was being dragged into someone else's problems and conflicts to my own detriment. When you are walking as a "boy," you do not know what to do with the phone call. You are thinking inside yourself, "If I knew the answer to your problems, I would have the answer to my problems." Sometimes I would give okay advice, and sometimes I would give bad advice. This means half of the time I was imparting death to the poor victim who was on the other end of the line.

It is so good to know how to obtain victory, so I can impart life to whoever calls me and says, "I am hurting" or "I am losing." Diagnosing is so simple when you understand God's principles of Man vs. "boy." You just know what to do and how to overcome the challenge at hand. It is very refreshing and very reassuring to know I can walk as a Man, and I understand what is going on with others because of it. If you do not know these principles and someone calls you looking for answers, you are probably going to give a "boy" answer. You might get lucky, but you probably won't.

This is no way to live. Giving counseling responsibilities to an adult who is a "boy" is like giving a loaded gun to an untrained eight year old. They might not kill anyone, but then again they just might kill someone. Someone is probably going to get hurt. It may be the "boy," but usually it is other people around him. When you give the responsibility of a Man to an adult "boy," he usually will hurt everyone around him in his ignorance.

One of my favorite verses now is **"My people are destroyed for a lack of knowledge."**[8] Males are Mandated to walk in authority to heal relationships, and bring life to their families. Unfortunately, these are the same males who are bringing such devastation to our families and culture. They are doing this unwittingly, because they are simply duped by lies of the enemy and most of them do not see it. It is our job as the Patriarchs who do see the problem to come along side those who are deceived, and create an army of Men who will impart life, protection and love in a right way to their families.

About two years before Kathy's mother passed away, she wrote me a letter. The letter said to me she loved me and she felt I was walking in a way she respected. She was thankful for me being in her life. She said

---

8 Hosea 4:6, KJV

this in the letter because she trusted me, and she felt she could entrust the care of Kathy to me. At times I go back and read her letter. I am encouraged my sister actually understood the importance of her daughter having a healthy relationship with a Man in her life. In the letter, my sister reminded me of my God-given Mandate to watch out and take care of my extended family, particularly Kathy.

For several years after my sister passed away, I experienced the guilt of not being able to address the relational problems in Kathy's life constructively. This was especially true regarding her relationship with her father. I did my best to encourage Kathy with the relational skills I had, but I knew I was falling short of actually being there for Kathy the way she needed.

Since I am walking in victory in my own life as a Man, I can now really impart love and insight to Kathy. This was the fulfillment of one of my sister's last requests to me. I am so thankful I finally got it right. I know God has used me to take care of my niece in a healthy and Godly manner.

I am reminded of the book of John, when Jesus was dying on the cross. One of His dying wishes was to delegate the care and protection of His Mother to a dear friend and disciple, John. Jesus was the oldest male in His family and he was responsible for the Patriarchal care and protection of his Mother. Jesus knew after he was gone, a trusted Man needed to be appointed to provide the Covering for his Mother Mary. John received this responsibility and immediately took Mary home to be under his Covering and in his care. Even Jesus, walking as a Man, honored his own principles of the Covering.

"Come unto me, all you that labour and are heavy laden, and I will give you rest. Take my yoke upon you, and learn of me; for I am meek and lowly in heart: and you shall find rest unto your souls. For my yoke is easy, and my burden is light."[9]

Jesus of Nazareth,

---

9 Matthew 11:28-30, NKJV

The Power of a Loving Father Figure:

Regarding the conclusion in the story about Kathy and Mike, an unexpected turn of events occurred. Mike was successful as a surrogate Dad to Kathy by showing her the love of God and asking for forgiveness on behalf of Kathy's father. The result was her heart began to soften to the Truth and healing began in Kathy. The lie that "My father does not love me" would have eventually torn Kathy up, if Mike had not stepped in and diffused it.

Unfortunately for Kathy's Dad, he did not respond very well to his daughter's request that he walk her down the aisle and give her away at her marriage ceremony. Even after Mike dealt with him, Man to "boy," Kathy's Dad still did not warm up to the idea of being there for his daughter. Ultimately, he missed out on the blessing of giving his daughter away.

The good news is that Kathy was obedient to ask her father, and she was set free from the guilt she may have felt by not requesting her father's presence. Kathy faced her fears and entered into her marriage both Covered and loved by her new husband. Poetically, Mike was the Man who gave Kathy away. There was not a dry eye in the house as he lovingly ushered his niece down the aisle and gave her away to a deserving and responsible young Man. The wedding was very loving, fun and fantastic!

The most powerful point of the whole story is that Mike was able to be a surrogate father by literally imparting love into her, and this all occurred because he had chosen to walk as a Man. Even though Kathy's Dad dropped the ball, her needs were met because another Man was available and willing to fill the need.

Like Kathy, there are millions of women who need to embrace the Truth that their Daddy loves them, even though their Daddy may be unable or unwilling to show it. This same principle is true for our relationship with God. If we do not believe God loves us, we are not able to ask Him for forgiveness. Because we have no expectation that He will grant us His favor and goodness, we literally close off to the blessings of His forgiveness and His relationship with us.

Many people are living hellish lives thinking, "God does not love me because I have sinned, or been molested, or abused, or thrown around by family members. All of these horrible things have happened to me;

therefore, God does not love me." This creates a breach where people cannot accept forgiveness or receive the love of God.

Just like Mike, all Men have the opportunity to diffuse these types of relational problems and offenses by simply loving and empathizing with the brokenness of the people near them. When a person feels your love, the phrases "I am sorry" and "forgive me" have a much deeper impact on them. When a person knows that you feel their pain, the bitterness and the hurt feelings can begin to melt away in their heart.

It is no different than driving down the road and someone cuts you off. You may get fearful and angry because of the stress caused, but if that person waves to you, there is immediate reconciliation. When someone says they meant no offense, it is easier to forgive them and let it go.

In Christianity, many believers have walked away from church because they have not been taught a relational gospel of forgiveness and love from the Men in their lives. Ministering the love of God is the answer. Paul said in his letter to the Corinthians, we are to **"comfort them which are in any trouble, by the comfort wherewith we ourselves are comforted by God."**[10]

About 70% of Christians who go away to college fall away from their faith, because the males in their households have not ministered life and love properly. This is primarily due to the weak relationships with fathers, and a host of "boys" trying to lead families without knowing their true Father in heaven really loves them. Patriarchs are Mandated to minister life by ministering love. Mike is living proof that a Patriarch must first receive God's life and love before he can give it away. It goes back to the age-old principle that says, you cannot give what you do not have. Great job Mike!

"'I know my Daddy loves me' is the most important message a woman can ever believe."

10 2 Corinthians 1:4, KJV

PART III: Overcoming Abuse

One of the most difficult challenges for a woman is to overcome the damage caused when she has been seriously abused, violated or molested by her father or other significant males in her life. How can a woman be expected to receive the principle of the Covering as a gift from God, when the Covering was placed within a father who has perpetrated evil acts upon his own daughter?

First of all, I would like to point out both Sarah and Kathy, in the previous stories, received healing from the knowledge and Truth of their Covering without having any immediate communication with their fathers. This is of the utmost importance to understand, because I do not believe God desires women to subject themselves to emotional, physical or spiritual abuse of any kind from fathers who have proved to be very unsafe. Jesus said to his followers, "My yoke is easy, my burden is light." This book has been written to help set people free, not to ensnare them with additional bondage.

One of Satan's master plans is to entice fathers and husbands to behave as "boys" and commit a tragic sin; the molestation of the children of whom they are Mandated to protect and nurture. This is the ultimate crime of Satan, and it is intended as a big slap in the face to the God who created us. This crime takes all that is holy, good and pure, and attempts to destroy it with all that is unholy, bad and filthy. How can a woman be restored to purity, love and trust after such violations have occurred? I have only one comment to make, **"With God, all things are possible."**[11]

God has a plan for his daughters. He can deliver every girl and every woman from the effects and damages of molestation. He can and will bring you back into receiving your Covering. Every woman can be a living testimony that God really will make all things like new.

Maria:

I met Maria when she was in her mid twenties. She is a precious young woman who has spent her entire life battling the struggles of being surrounded by "boys." A close male family member repeatedly molested her for years when she was a little girl, and the wounds of her past haunt

11 Mark 10:27, KJV

every relationship in her life. Her heart is so damaged by the abuse and neglect she experienced at the hands of irresponsible "boys," she is hanging on for dear life to find her identity and her purpose as a daughter of the King.

Maria perfectly fits the definition of an "uncovered" woman. She calculates her way through life, frustrated with fear and a lack of trust in others as she attempts to find peace. She desperately seeks to grasp hold of her femininity and calling in her daily struggle to maintain. Her story is developing even now as a living script. Maria has looked her enemies straight in the face and declared war against them, but the battle is raging.

As I write this book, Maria is in the valley of decision pondering the most important choice in her adult life; whether to be Covered or "uncovered." Her entire life is hinged upon whether she can let go of familiar fixes and allow herself to trust again. Pray she finds the peace, love and protection of her Covering, and that the healing winds of God blow upon her broken heart.

Maria could be your daughter, your sister, or maybe even your future wife. She is one of millions of women crying out from the depth of her heart to be helped, healed and Covered. God willing, you will read about Maria's incredible victory in the next book, "Finally Covered!" The hope for the many Marias in this world is for Men to walk in their Mandates and repair the damage committed by other males before them. Are you that Man?

"I am the Lord that healeth thee."[12]
Book of Exodus - Moses

Finally Free and Covered:

For those women who desire to overcome the challenge of becoming and remaining Covered, join with a team of dedicated women across the nation and become one of the members of Finally Free. (www.Manvsboy.com) Each month members of Finally Free receive

12 Exodus 15:26, KJV

the best and latest resources, CD's and books bringing health, healing and success as they journey through life. Choose today to live your life nurtured, protected and Covered.

"Who shall separate us from the love of Christ? Shall tribulation, or distress, or persecution, or famine, or nakedness, or peril, or sword? As it is written: 'For Your sake we are killed all day long; We are accounted as sheep for the slaughter.' Yet in all these things we are more than conquerors through Him who loved us. For I am persuaded that neither death nor life, nor angels nor principalities nor powers, nor things present nor things to come, nor height nor depth, nor any other created thing, shall be able to separate us from the love of God which is in Christ Jesus our Lord."[13]

The Apostle Paul – Letter to the Romans

Does She Feel Beautiful?

Men like simple solutions; therefore, here is a simple golden nugget that can literally save your marriage. This advice alone is priceless; far out weighing the cost of this book.

Make your wife feel beautiful everyday, no matter what.

Women are made by God to feel beautiful. If they do not feel beautiful, they will emotionally, spiritually and physically wilt away like old, cut flowers. This is so important that I am going to repeat it. If women are not loved and made to feel beautiful, they will tend to emotionally and spiritually die.

13 Romans 8:35-39, NKJV

This is incredibly important for a Man to understand as it relates to the Covering. If the woman in your life feels beautiful inside and out, she will naturally allow herself to be Covered by the love of God. Truly feeling beautiful and appreciated is a sign that a woman is truly Covered.

For a woman to feel beautiful, it is all about trust. The beautiful feeling I am referring to is seen when a woman trusts the Man who is mandated to take care of her. This trust is established when she feels accepted, highly valued, protected, nurtured, appreciated and loved. Therefore, a Man must die to his selfish behaviors, and live to build trust with his wife.

Women long to be understood and listened to. If a Man can master the art of being attentive and giving, he will have won the heart of his bride. This will reveal itself in the radiance and glow of her countenance. This is a beauty that any woman, of any race, of any age, with any specific outward bodily features can possess, if the mandated males in her life have done their job.

It is common knowledge that many beauty queens and pageant winners do not feel truly beautiful inside. Many of these women fall into eating disorders and a host of dysfunctional behaviors, as we learned from Sarah's story earlier in this Chapter. This is a sign that the males in their lives have dropped the ball and failed them. Women feel ugly and undesirable because males have not made them feel beautiful by highly valuing them. Again, the Mandate for all Men is to make the women in their lives feel beautiful by treating them as priceless. A woman feels beautiful when she is loved and cherished.

God's Beautiful Women of the Bible:

I was always curious why God describes the various wives of the Patriarchs in the Bible as "beautiful." If God cares primarily about the heart of a person, why would He specifically mention that certain women in scripture are outwardly beautiful? Abraham's wife Sarah, Isaac's wife Rebecca, Jacob's wife Rachel and David's wife Abigail were all described as "fair" or "beautiful." Surely, there must be a poignant reason why there is this recurring theme of having a beautiful wife in Old Testament scripture.

The answer is indeed given in scripture. Abraham, Isaac, Jacob and David were all examples of Christ. Thus, their brides were destined to be beautiful, just as the bride and church of Christ is destined to be beautiful without spot or blemish.

By examining passages where the Lord shares His heart for His bride, we can further unlock the mystery about the beautiful women in the Bible. In the Song of Solomon, the potential bride of Solomon is intimately described as incredibly beautiful, passionate and enticing. Solomon says, **"Rise up, my love my fair (beautiful) one, and come away."**[14] And again he says, **"How beautiful you are, my darling! Oh, how beautiful! Your eyes behind your veil are doves."**[15]

Throughout the Bible, God gently teaches us about His loving nature towards His bride. Just as Solomon's bride responds to his loving advances towards her by returning his love, God's beloved people are created to respond to His advances.

The endearing and heartfelt passion found in the Song of Solomon paints a vivid picture of an intimate love scene that stirs the senses. When Solomon tells his beloved bride she is beautiful and that he desperately loves her, his bride responds as any women will respond when she is highly cherished by the Man in her life. She receives his love, and in return, she gives back her love to him.

Is this the way you speak on a daily basis to your wife, or your future wife? Learn from Solomon, the wisest Man of the Old Testament scriptures. Solomon is displaying to us the incredible value of intimacy, and the wonderful feeling of fulfillment a Man experiences by passionately making his wife feel loved and beautiful. Solomon is also showing us how a bride yearns to be adored and cherished as one of the king's finest possessions. To win their hearts, we must treat our brides as the princesses God created them to be.

"A Man's love makes his woman beautiful."

---

14 Songs of Solomon 2:10, KJV
15 Songs of Solomon 4:1, NIV

The Beautiful Wedding Ceremony:

In every culture on Earth, it is a known mystery that on the day of her wedding, a bride is supernaturally overcome with a beauty and glow that appears to come directly from heaven itself. On the special day when a bride is escorted down the aisle by her Father to the awaiting bridegroom, she will radiate both an inner brilliance and an outer beauty transcending all natural explanation. The glory of God indeed settles upon every true bride, because on this day she knows that her bridegroom loves her and thinks she is beautiful.

Adorned in a flowing white dress and a long, graceful train, the ceremonial procession appears as a symbolic replica of our eternal marriage with our Lord in heaven. It is a timeless sign portraying the cleansing and purity God has provided for us as we receive His Son's loving sacrifice, and His hand in marriage as the perfect Man. It is truly a remarkable event.

"And I John saw the holy city, New Jerusalem, coming down from God out of heaven, prepared as a bride adorned for her husband."[16]
The Apostle John – Book of Revelation

Throughout the scriptures, there is this incredible theme of the bridegroom being presented with a beautiful wife. In Revelation Chapter 21, the theme of the beautiful bride is described in great detail. The Lord's bride is adorned as a beautiful city, and she is presented as perfect and spotless (beautiful) before her bridegroom.

The bride is also mentioned by the Apostle Peter, as he describes her as a special people, without spot or wrinkle. This bride is the church of believers who enter into a holy and pure marriage covenant with the Lord, because He has made them beautiful. And why does she feel and look beautiful? Because the Lord of heaven and earth has made his bride feel accepted, highly valued, protected, nurtured, cherished and loved. It is true. God really loves you.

16 Revelation 21:2, KJV

It becomes clear as we learn about the fulfillment of Jesus' return for his bride in the New Testament, that Abraham, Isaac, Jacob and David of the Old Testament were all examples and types of the perfect Man and the perfect husband, Jesus of Nazareth. Today, Men are still called to be an example and emulate Christ. All Men have this incredible opportunity to model after our Lord by beautifying and loving their brides.

"Husbands, love your wives, even as Christ also loved the church, and gave himself for it. (her)" [17]
The Apostle Paul - Letter to the Ephesians

Many women have never experienced what it feels like to be honestly loved, and they have rarely been made to feel beautiful. When a woman is cherished and loved in such a way that she feels beautiful, she experiences a glimpse of how much God really loves her. A healthy woman responds so well to being loved and nurtured, that even a drop of heartfelt life and love given by her husband will melt her heart. She can then experience a deeper understanding of the incredible love of God, as He intimately reaches forth to make her beautiful.

Beauty is truly in the eye of the beholder, and as a bridegroom sees his bride walk down the aisle to marry him, he sees her true beauty. Throughout the marriage, when a Man fills his wife with love by making her feel beautiful, she will come to receive her Covering and she will find her peace. Blessings and love will then flow out of her and return to her husband, to her children, and to all who come in contact with her presence. Men! It is so simple. Be attentive and make her feel beautiful every day, and your love will return to you a hundredfold.

"How do you love and nurture a woman? You make her feel beautiful!"

---

17 Ephesians 5:25, KJV

The Ugly "uncovered" and "unloved" Woman:

As we learned earlier in this chapter regarding the "uncovered" woman, an unloved and resentful woman who does not feel beautiful will tend to become very cold, distant and busy, even to her own detriment. This resentment feeds a woman's determination to exclude Men from her life. Eventually, her resentment will cause her to shut down her emotional desires to be feminine, loving and soft, and she will be very hesitant to relinquish any power over her life. This is due primarily to her lack of trust in the males around her. The injured and distorted mentality of, "I can do it on my own" quickly leads to "Your not the boss of me."

As an "uncovered" woman figures out how to cope with life alone while continuing on her path to angry self-sufficiency, her "I do not need Men" attitude finally leaves her believing males have no positive value or purpose whatsoever. Her unhealthy independence will cause her to compensate for the hole in her heart with the duties and strains of stressful life, and she won't look back. Before you know it, you will be married to someone resembling Jezebel, the ultimate "unloved" and "uncovered" women of the Old Testament, and it will not be pretty. Divorce is looming right over the horizon.

Emotionally and spiritually starved women are everywhere, no thanks to the "boys" of this world who never seem to get around to doing their job. Daughters are begging their fathers and women are begging their husbands to fill them up with love, nurturing and life. All women desire Men to fulfill their wedding vows, "to love honor and cherish them."

Everyday, Men must compliment, adore and edify the women in their lives. It is Satan's job to make your woman feel ugly, worthless, unappreciated alone and taken for granted every day. If you participate in helping him, may God help you, because God will protect His daughters. Women are looking to the one person they are married to in life for love, encouragement and stability. If they do not get it, their hearts will slowly die away. When there is nothing left in their hearts, they will leave and find love elsewhere.

"Women do not give Keys away, they give their hearts away."

In this book you have learned that a defeated male has given away his Keys of authority. Women do not give Keys away, they give away their hearts. A defeated woman is a woman who has given her heart away to a "boy." She has made the mistake of depending on a "boy" to love, edify and nurture her heart in order to keep her emotionally sound. This is a tragedy, because a "boy" will never fill up a woman, or make her feel truly beautiful deep down in her heart. An unloved woman will spend all of her time looking for love, many times in all the wrong places.

A "boy" cannot make a woman feel beautiful, because it requires him to take responsibility for his Manhood. Remember Chapter 1, you cannot give what you do not have. As long as a male remains a "boy," he will not have either the ability or the desire to love his wife properly. Loving her and complimenting her seems like too much work for him, because he does not possess the love that she needs. Long beforehand, a "boy" has given away his Keys of authority, and lost with these Keys is the love and the ability to protect that she desperately longs for. Once again, a "boy's" selfishness will work to destroy the confidence of the women close to him.

Rather than becoming a Man and retrieving back his Keys, a "boy" will blame the females in his life for the problems that are clearly his fault. To make matters worse, often a "boy" will subtly sabotage a woman's self esteem and confidence, because he cannot handle the fact that he is intimidated and threatened by her strength. The stronger and more self-assured she is, the more he will feel the inadequacies and deficiencies of his character. A "boy" does not want to look at his own deficiencies, and he will usually mask it by his arrogance.

Deep inside, a "boy" knows that he does not have what it takes to love and protect his wife properly; therefore, he fears she is too good for him. This is actually true. She is too good for him, because no irresponsible "boy" is deserving of a healthy relationship with a woman. His own insecurities have disqualified him as a potential mate, and his self-fulfilling prophecies about his relationships will most assuredly come to pass.

The Bible says, **"Death and life are in the power of the tongue, and they that love it shall eat the fruit thereof."**[18] This means that

---

18 Proverbs 18:21, KJV

anyone who is careless with their mouth will suffer consequences. Daily, women are being slowly killed by the words of irresponsible "boys," and their damaged hearts are crying out for help.

Many times, a "boy" will insult and verbally abuse a woman for the purpose of "bringing her down to his level." By degrading a woman, a "boy" feels she will be less likely to leave him or see his inadequacies. The opposite is true, of course. The longer a "boy" fails to impart love and a sense of beauty into a woman, the more likely she will indeed leave, with no apologies. With a decimated heart and a soul full of remorse and sorrow, an unloved woman will eventually depart both emotionally and physically away from a "boy." This usually begins with indifference. After the pain of neglect becomes too unbearable, a woman will become indifferent by shutting down her emotions. The final result often leads to divorce, infidelity or long-term unhappiness.

A woman must be able to clearly identify a male as either a Man or a "boy." Her happiness and her true success in life depend on it. Fortunately, it is easy to do. She must be able to identify a Man who will take full responsibility for the relationship and make her feel loved and beautiful everyday. Again, a woman can identify a Man because he will impart life, love and security to her. He will make her feel beautiful.

A Woman's Love Account:

There is a timeless law in the universe. Whenever we invest our time and attention, this is where we will see the fruit of our harvest. It is the same principle with our bank accounts. If we do not deposit more into our bank accounts than we withdraw, we will show a negative balance.

We must make certain we deposit more than we withdraw from our wife's "love account." Otherwise, her love account will become overdrawn, and here comes those dreaded bank fees. With a wife, there is much more than a bounced check fee to worry about. A bounce fee would be getting off easy for most males who have not decided to love their wives unconditionally. Instead of a bounced check fee, we are going to experience the fruit of neglect. That ugly Jezebel is going to appear.

An unloved and neglected woman will manifest every form of "bounce fee" imaginable. She may become angry, bitter, bossy, rebellious, mean, nasty, belittling, resentful, demeaning, degrading, cruel, distant, unloving, and healthy intimacy is probably out of the question. And for those virile males, this means "No sex!" It probably is not going to happen tonight! Tonight's headache may be the least of your problem. It may be weeks, months or even years before the bedroom is back in order, all depending on how long and how much overdrawn her love account has fallen under her husband's watch.

Is this what your wife has become? Is her love account so negative that she resembles the depressed and "uncovered" witch named Jezebel, whom I previously described? Is the curse of Eve, the first neglected and "uncovered" woman, haunting your household? It may be time to realize that your wife is merely responding to your failure to make daily love deposits into her love account.

If you are bold, ask your wife how her love account is doing. The answer may surprise you, but this is a question you need to know the answer to. Using an account scale of negative one million to positive one million, ask her how much she feels is in her love account. If her account has a healthy supply of love, you have done a great job. If her account is very low or negative, it is time that you learn how to love her.

Men are made by God to be initiators in relationships, and women are made to respond to attentive and loving care. No matter how we slice, dice or justify our actions, our wives must be made to feel important and secure in our love for them. The universe and God's principles are not going to change for us, no matter how much we want them to. Just as gravity is always going to be a natural force on Earth, women are perfectly fashioned to ***always*** respond to the loving care they receive from the significant males in their lives.

Are we going to stand in our own righteousness and sacrifice our marriages and relationships because our arrogance won't allow us to humble ourselves and nurture our wives? At what point are we going to put our selfishness aside and just love them? When are we going to put our marriage first? When are we going to look at the beaten condition of the hearts of our wives?

There is a reason why women file for divorce in over 70% of the divorce cases in America. The primary reason given by women is emotional cruelty and/or neglect. This means that their love account has been severely negative for years. When a woman files for divorce, she usually is suffering from long-term love malnutrition.

If a Man decides that the condition of his wife's heart is his highest priority in life, he can be assured she will respond perfectly over time, and blossom into the loving princess she was created to be. Again, there is only one way to get her back after her love account balance has dropped to such an overdrawn status. You must make large deposits daily!

It took years for her to become so devastated and destitute of love, it may take a little time to bring her back into the fold. You must continually be committed to melt her heart and humble yourself by attentively caring for her every need, every day, just as the Lord does for you. This means your toys and your hobbies have to come second, after your beautiful bride. In ***every single*** area of your life, remember the old saying, "ladies first."

This leads us to the next few questions. Where are we spending our time and attention? Why do we not attend to our wives as well as we take care of our cars and our motorcycles? Why do our wives feel jealous and resentful about other possessions in our lives, possessions that have won our hearts? Do we really want our wives to feel they have to compete with the ESPN sports channels or video games? Do our wives really need to be jealous of our toys?

We spend hours polishing, waxing and delicately caring for our boats, our Harley Davidson motorcycles, our cars, our guns, our TV's and our electronic devices. Can we spend that same time and care on the most important and highly valued gift God has ever given to Mankind? Can we actually love our wives, and let them know they are incredibly important and beautiful to us? After all, this is what we promised on our wedding day.

Your side interests can never be allowed to usurp her position as your helpmate, your princess and the love of your life. She is not your "help-Maid!" Nor is she your "help-Matt" or your "help-Rug." She is your "helpmate." Your wife must know she is important, beautiful and cherished by the one person she has vowed to spend the rest of her life with. This is not something that should be taken lightly. The family structure in our country is disintegrating because males have failed to love their brides. Every woman is a beautiful and cherished gift of God in its purest form.

Grantley Morris stated in a recent article the following: ***"Any man not doing what he can to make his wife feel loved and secure and honored is not just a failure, he is doing the devil's work. I say that very deliberately. By his actions, or lack of them, such a man is in league with the Tempter, inciting his wife to go to someone who will honor her the way she deserves. If she yields to that temptation, she will be accountable before God for her sin. Regardless of her response, God holds her husband responsible for the temptation even existing. This is a grave responsibility. 'Temptations must come,' said Jesus, 'but woe to him who causes them. It would be better for him for a millstone to be placed around his neck and he be tossed into the sea' (Luke 17:1-2, paraphrase). Such a man might consider himself the model of faithfulness but in reality he has not only betrayed his wife, and his marriage vows, he is a disgrace to the name of Christ. You, however, were born to be a lover, and born again to receive divine empowering to soar way beyond what you could otherwise attain. Rise to your high calling and you will find fulfillment beyond your fondest dreams."***

Your wife is fashioned like fine silver, and she must be polished and nurtured daily to keep from tarnishing. Fine silver demands attention, you cannot let silver sit on the shelf. Keeping it beautiful takes time, tender commitment, and it takes elbow grease.

Men, think about this. How are you taking care of your wife sexually? The last thing I expected to do was write about sex and orgasms, but here goes. The important subject of sex is so relevant in life that it can make or break the success of a marriage. Is your wife sexually satisfied? If you do not know the answer to this question, you are a "boy."

A woman's ability to be pleased by her husband sexually is usually a direct response to the love, attention and protection she is receiving by her Man. It is a wonderful experience for a woman to be sexually satisfied. It is also overwhelmingly satisfying for a Man to know he can impart passion and pleasure, and to see and feel her receive this love so generously given. You are missing one of life's greatest God-given pleasures of feeling like a Man if you have not experienced this giving of love.

Showing love to your wife can occur in many ways. I suggest that you dote over your wife with a full body massage, and then expect ***nothing*** in return. This is a small thing you can do that will reap great rewards emotionally. Showing and telling your wife you love her 20 to 30 different ways throughout the day will bring you unbelievable responses. Be creative and keep open communication with your wife, because this is the pathway to her heart. A Man is committed to know and understand his wife's body as well as her heart.

Today is the day to make a conscious decision to share in this type of giving. It is never too late to learn of this special connection with your wife. A Man will give his wife that special time to sexually satisfy her needs before meeting his own… ***always!*** Let's look again at the phrase "ladies first?" In centuries past, this phrase was honored both in public and in the bedroom because selfless gallantry and honor used to be revered. Read the Song of Solomon if you desire to learn more on the subject. A Man will ask his wife if she feels satisfied. If you are a Man of courage, ask your wife who the bedroom is all about. Is it all about her, or is it all about you? If a male has selfishly made the bedroom all about him, he has failed his wife and he has failed one of the most important parts of his Mandate.

How many of us have spent hours and hours rubbing and polishing our cars, our boats and our toys in an effort to keep them beautiful? It is time to realize that our most precious silver is tarnishing right before our eyes, and we need to be spending much more time and put forth some serious commitment in order to get our silver shiny again. Our wives deserve our best! Will you choose to Man-up and give your wife your best? If you do, you may just find out that your wife will be in support of your hobbies, and you will find an inner peace in your relationship with her that goes beyond your wildest expectations.

In the Old Testament book of Genesis, Leah and Rachel were sisters who were both betrothed to the same Man, Jacob. Leah was described as not having an outer beauty, whereas her sister Rachel was described as beautiful. Christ has shown us that outer beauty means nothing to him without inner beauty. All of our outer beauty fades with time and age. Nevertheless, the Lord will still marry us, the seemingly uncomely Leah, because He sees the amazing inner beauty in each one of us as He fills us with His righteousness. Christ is also willing to wait for us, His future bride to be. This is symbolic to Jacob's love for Rachel, who is an example of the beautiful bride God longs for each woman to become.

God so desires a beautiful bride, he even named one of the heavenly gates in His perfect city with the name, "The Beautiful Gate."[19] This is one of the gates His glorious bride will enter through every day in order to worship at His royal throne. Do you make it your goal to see that your wife and your daughters feel beautiful everyday? If not, it is time to begin making them feel beautiful and loved. Inside of your wife and daughters are the hearts of Leah and Rachel, and they long to be nurtured, loved and reminded they are beautiful every single day.

"Forgive me, Lord, for I have not made my bride feel beautiful. Change me into the Man you created me to be. Please help me to be attentive, and to make my wife feel accepted, highly valued, protected, nurtured, cherished and loved."

Men have the incredible opportunity to invest daily into their marriages, thereby making the love of God tangible and real to women. As a Patriarch, this is part of your Mandate. Learning how to truly love your bride as the Lord loves you can be one of the most fulfilling blessings in a Man's life. Males are not entitled to have a wife. Having women in our lives is a gift from God, and we must continually invest in women with our love and attention if we have any expectation of a successful life and marriage. As the old saying goes, "Happy wife, happy life!"

Pam's Knight in Shining Armor:

The airplane landed abruptly onto a runway in Los Angeles International airport. Pam and Don both released a gasp of relief as the 747 taxied towards the gate after an arduous and bumpy three-hour flight.

"Are Sam and Mike picking us up at the terminal, or should we take a cab?" Pam inquired of Don as they unbuckled their seat belts.

Don replied, "I don't know. What did they say they were going to do?" Pam sighed as she gently rolled her eyes back and began to gather her belongings. Pam's continued frustrations with Don's lack of planning and

19 Acts 3:2

help had come to the forefront. She then sat back down, shook her head slowly and said, "Don! You know the stress I have been under concerning this trip. Are you telling me you do not even know how we are going to get to the hotel? I would think you could at least make one phone call before we got on the plane to find out what we were going to do? You know we are on a tight schedule!"

Don pulled down his luggage from the overhead and placated her with a slow reply, "Don't worry about it. I am sure it will all work out. I will call them when we get in the terminal."

Pam felt the continual gnawing in her stomach that was occurring more and more often due to Don's lack of consideration and help. She held her anger in as her jaw ground down tightly. She hastily grabbed her luggage and led the way ahead of Don to exit the plane. Don followed loosely behind only after holding up the departing line of people as he rearranged his luggage and checked his latest new cell phone program.

By the time Don found Pam, she had already called her business partners and procured a cab to meet them at the hotel. They were late. Don gallantly approached her, half grinning with delight over the book he had just purchased in the lobby bookstore. Pam pleaded for him to hurry up as they both exited the terminal into the cold night air.

After Pam helped the cab driver load their luggage into the trunk of the cab, Don made it a point to open the car door for Pam as she skirted her way across the seat. Pam waited for Don's instructions to the cab driver - to no avail. She then gave the cab driver directions where to take them.

Both Pam and Don were nervous about the upcoming meeting, as it was supposed to generate a profit of well over $50,000 for their real estate company. Pam was an excellent and thorough businesswoman, and she had succeeded in every venture she put her hand to. Due to Don's very poor credit and financial standing, they had to use Pam's corporation because her credit and reputation were in good standing. She was President and CEO to ensure control over her good name.

Pam began to feel unsettled as she entered the lobby of the plush hotel. As Don became preoccupied with the beauty and grandeur of the hotel, he made no move to inquire from the concierge where the meeting room was located. Finally, Pam asked the concierge where the meeting room was, and marched off to meet with Mike and Sam, with Don following. She knew Mike well, and she respected his knowledge and work ethic on previous deals. She had never met Sam in person, and had no idea what was in store for her.

Immediately after entering the meeting room, Sam took charge and began to go over the terms of the transaction, putting emphasis on the additional collateral that was needed to make all the partners "feel comfortable." Pam felt increasingly nervous and uncomfortable as the meeting progressed. Pam and Don represented the interests of major investors for this substantial real estate investment, and Pam felt particularly awkward with Sam as he directed all of his comments specifically to her.

As time progressed, it became obvious to Pam that the pressure of the whole deal was weighing on her shoulders. Sam continued to pound ahead for a solution regarding additional collateral for the real estate transaction. Finally, Sam looked straight at Pam and said, "You are going to have to personally put up your financial assets to back your share of this transaction, if this deal is going to proceed."

Pam became upset and her stomach dropped as a heavy and unsettled pit began to overwhelm her insides. She briefly looked at Don for help, but Don had a hand shadowing his eyes and cowardly looked down at a piece of paper on the table.

Pam looked back at Sam and said with an upset and trembling voice, "I will never consider putting my house and my stability on the line just to make this proposal go through!" She looked back at Don to see him still hiding his eyes and still looking down at the paper. She then said, "Don, do you think that I should do this? What do you think about this request?"

Don looked up and said, "It is your decision, Pam. You are the head of the company!"

Pam's countenance fell with disappointment as her boyfriend of 12 years stood by and allowed her to take the full brunt of the pressure from Sam. Don appeared to have no problem seeing Pam put up her personal assets in order for them both to make a healthy commission. Pam's whole body was shaking inside as she looked back to Sam and firmly stated, "Absolutely not! I will not put my house, my stability or my personal assets up to cover a business deal with risks attached to it. This is why I have a corporation! I am appalled and upset that you would ask me this.

I am sure no other investor is being asked to put up their personal assets for this deal!" Pam ended the meeting somewhat cordially. She then turned around and walked out, as she told Don they needed to go back to the airport.

Sam followed Pam and Don into the lobby where Sam continued to taunt Pam with subtle threats of a lawsuit. He then said, "You will never do business with us again in this town if you back out of this deal!"

Pam was on the verge of a meltdown as she stopped to confront Sam. She could feel her voice tremble with emotion as her heart cried out. "I don't give a damn, Sam! I'm leaving! Don, where are you? Let's go please!"

Sam immediately replied with harsh innuendos and personal accusations towards Pam just as Pam and Don's major investor and business partner, Harrison, entered the Lobby. Harrison was a short, stocky and balding Man who had a voice that was deep and resounding. Harrison quickly assessed the situation and said, "You are way out of line, Sam! You are never to speak to a woman that way! I know Pam. If she is upset, there is a good reason!"

Pam's boyfriend and business partner, Don, seemed to melt into the scenery as he looked on with bewilderment at the unfolding scene. He seemed quite embarrassed to have another Man defend Pam after he had failed to do so.

Sam backed up a few steps as Harrison got between Pam and him. Harrison put his hand upon Pam's shoulder gently. He then proceeded to inquire exactly what Sam was up to. When he heard the particulars from Pam, he became even more furious. His voice shook the hallways as he loudly shouted, "Sam! What in the hell are you attempting to pull here with Pam. This is unconscionable! I do not care how much money we may make on this deal, you call your people and tell them I am pulling out! There is no way I am going to let Pam put up further assets for these clowns. I am done! And if you know what is best for you…" Harrison pointed directly at Sam and demanded, "You!... You get back into that meeting room, RIGHT NOW!"

Sam mumbled a few expletives under his breath as he retreated back out of the lobby. Harrison turned to Pam and apologized that she was exposed to such manipulation, pressure and rudeness from one of the male species.

Pam's mouth dropped and her countenance began to soften as she peered right into Harrison's large round eyes. "Thank You, Harrison!" Without even thinking, Pam hugged Harrison tightly. She was feeling both relieved and surprised at what her business partner had done for her. She was blown away by the fact that Harrison had just given up potentially several hundred thousand dollars in profit by backing out of this transaction – for her.

Pam hugged Harrison again and quickly said goodbye. She then walked out of the lobby to the cab, Don following.

"I will call you later, Pam," Harrison called out. He then marched directly after Sam into the meeting room to "finish the business meeting."

On the ride to the airport, Pam was still and quiet as she looked out over the night-lights of the city. Don kept himself busy programming his new phone while attempting to order the cab driver where to take them. Pam kept reliving the incident over and over in her mind trying to make sense of Don's actions, or more specifically, his inactions.

Unexpectedly, Mike called on the cell phone to save the deal, and Don answered. Pam insisted that Don tell Mike that the deal was over, and that she did not want to discuss anything further. Don handed the phone to Pam and said, "It's your decision, you tell him."

Pam bitterly took the phone from Don and formally withdrew her company's participation from the transaction. She said, "Mike, I have always liked you, but I cannot be a part of a deal when I am being disrespected, manipulated and taken advantage of. Harrison has already pulled his funds from the deal."

It was obvious that Mike was devastated to lose investors at the eleventh hour. As she hung up the phone, she heard Don say under his breath, "Well, there goes twenty five thousand dollars."

Pam's entire being was stunned to see that Don was only worried about his half of the commission. Although Pam was a strong, successful and intelligent business woman, the reality was becoming clear. She was a woman first, with a woman's heart and a woman's emotional needs.

Pam looked over at the person she thought she loved, but inside she was empty and deeply saddened. She had just experienced a business colleague willingly give up hundreds of thousands of dollars for her sake, and her boyfriend and supposed love of her life was grieving over the loss of much less, at her expense. She was synthesizing in her mind how Harrison, a Man that was over a decade younger than Don, had just stood up for her and for what was right.

Pam then began to recall many times over the years when Don had embarrassed her, cowered at her expense or allowed her to be emotionally unprotected and hurt. She recalled the times when ***she*** was required to "save" a situation both in business and in their personal relationships. Pam was usually alone to endure the harsh realities of business and life without the support she needed from the main male in her life. Again, she sat alone in the back seat of the cab with no Knight in sight. Pam whispered to herself, "God, where did I go wrong? What am I going to do?"

Pam continued staring into the heavenly skyline of LA. Gentle tears streamed down her cold cheeks against the chilled glass of the cab window. The sharp coldness she felt from its smooth surface was a welcomed distraction to the incredible pain she was feeling in her heart. Inside, Pam's heart was crying out for her Knight in Shining Armor.

"Will he ever come for me?" she whispered. But no one seemed to hear.

Where are the Knights?

How do we even begin unraveling the perplexity of dynamics in the relationship between Pam and Don? It is easy to attack Don. It is obvious he pulled a major "boy" maneuver that day, and undoubtedly he has been a "boy" throughout his life. But there is not a Man alive that has not missed it. This story is not about Don. It is about Pam's broken heart and her choices, and how she is designed by God to long for her Knight.

Pam is one of the millions of women on this planet who are created to passionately search for their personal Knight in Shining Armor. Wouldn't it have been fantastic if Don had done his job as a Man that day? Yes, it was great that Harrison stepped in to rescue Pam. But Pam did not love Harrison, who was happily married with three lovely children. Pam loved Don, and she was finally realizing in grave disappointment that Don was not her Knight in Shining Armor.

Before Pam decided to get together with Don, she would have done herself a big favor by asking the following question before she selected Don as a potential husband: ***If I were walking down the street and someone assaulted me, do I feel that Don would save me, or would I have to save him?*** After reading this story, it is not hard to determine the answer.

Where did Don go wrong? Don had taken no time to understand just how women are created. Women are created to long for their Knight in Shining Armor to rescue them from a life of attacks and grief. Women may be intelligent and strong in business, but a healthy Man will understand a woman's deep down desire to be nurtured and protected. Don had not learned that life is full of opportunities for Men to be the Knight in Shining Armor. It is the job of a trained Man to look for these opportunities at every turn.

Every attack upon a woman is an opportunity for a Man to step up; to love, protect and be her Knight. These attacks come in many forms. An attack may be a bill collector calling for money. It may be a broken car, an uncooperative appliance such as a garbage disposal that needs immediate attention. The attack may be a sick child who needs to be picked up at school. The attack may come from an in-law who wants to control the family at holiday and family get-togethers. The attack may be the intimidating neighbor that has no emotional boundaries, or the controlling school board member that wants to order parents how to raise their child. In Pam's case, she needed her Knight to stand up and lead as a Man, by protecting her from emotional assaults and intimidations coming from Sam.

Let's look at just a few of the things Don could have done to be Pam's Man, her Knight in Shining Armor. A Knight would have put his life in order so that Pam did not have to be the head of their company with her name on the line. A Knight would not have dated and/or lived together with a woman for 12 years without the formal commitment of marriage. A Knight would have called ahead and made better plans for the business trip. A Knight would have been attentive to Pam, by getting her bags and escorting her out of the plane and treating her as the Princess he knows her to be. A Knight would not have selfishly played with his toys and bought new items thereby adding to Pam's pressure by leaving her alone in the airport. A Knight would have nurtured her in the cab by reassuring her he would love and protect her throughout the business meeting. A Knight would have sensed Pam's unsettled heart and the pressure she was feeling and been proactive towards comforting her. A Knight would have shielded all of Sam's attacks by intervening on multiple levels in the meeting room to assure the group that he was there to take the hits and protect the love of his life. A Knight would have been the one to deal with Sam in the hotel lobby. Don should have protected Pam and her assets and been the one to give up all prospect of financial profit, and show the world and all the powers that be that Pam was priceless, worth far more than a mere $25,000. A Knight would never have handed the phone to Pam making her be the strong one in the relationship by forcing her to give the bad news to Mike. A Knight would have been attentive, strong, loving and protecting on so many levels that a single book cannot contain them, and a Knight would have made Pam feel beautiful, appreciated, feminine and nurtured at all times whenever possible. Simply put, Don could have been Pam's Shining Knight, and he could have been her Man.

Instead, he lost it all. Now she's gone.

God and the Knights:

This entire book is dedicated to building Men, and building Knights. As we can see in the latest example in Pam's story, there are countless ways and opportunities to be a Knight. At times being a Knight may be as simple as believing your wife's gut instinct when she says there is a problem. Being a Knight may be staying home from the guy's Monday night football game to run a bath and have a candlelight dinner with your overwhelmed wife. Being a Knight may be honoring any of the Man points in the Man vs. "boy" list. Being a Knight is being a Man.

If you do not think that this is real, ask any woman in any country what her favorite movie is. There is a very good chance there is a Knight in a romantic movie that rescues some "fortunate" woman from the difficulties of life. Hollywood recognizes this timeless romantic principle. In the movie "Kate and Leopold," Hugh Jackman actually rode the fairytale white horse as he rescued Meg Ryan from the dangers of New York City. The scene and the movie worked, because every woman wants to be saved by her Knight.

Women long to be saved by Men who are built by God to be strong protectors and caretakers. I believe every woman is created to be a symbol of the bride of Christ, needing to be saved… and needing a Savior. God is the ultimate rescuer, and He has created His Men to display His rescuing nature. In Pam's story, Harrison saw the opportunity to be a Knight and display the nature of our Savior. And who can deny that his actions that night in the hotel lobby were noble, loving and God-like? His wife must glow.

There are traditionally three different roles that women desire to have fulfilled in their lives by Men: the father role, the brother role and the husband role. In a perfect world, every woman would have multiple Men in each of these roles that will step up to the plate and be that Shining Knight for them in the different areas of their life. Imagine how secure, loved and protected Pam would be if she had Men like Harrison supporting her in every close male relationship in her life; father figures, brothers and a husband that cared for her on every level by looking for ways to love and protect her.

Healthy male/female relationships ensure that a woman fulfills her womanhood. They build trust in God-ordained male/female relationships as a woman learns to allow Men in her life to love, protect and save her from most of life's overwhelming physical, spiritual and emotional attacks. In today's "advanced" societies, it is common for a woman to have never experienced even one reasonable facsimile of proper care from a truly loving and protective Man. Many women have no Harrisons to speak of.

When a woman loses faith in the Men in her life, she is actually losing faith in the God who created her. How can you trust a God who has set up a supposed Patriarchal system that degrades, abuses and fails to care for its women? It is very difficult for a broken woman to believe that God came as a Man to be the perfect Knight in Shining Armor riding on the white horse to save her, His damsel in distress. His damsel in distress is really all lost mankind made in the image of God.

A woman's femininity is directly related to her trust and hope for a Man to rescue her. As a woman loses her hopes and dreams for her Knight in Shining Armor, she will also begin to lose important aspects of her femininity. She will wrongly conclude that she is the problem, because she has futilely hoped and trusted in a male gender that cannot and will not ever meet any of her deep down emotional and spiritual needs.

She is then forced to "fix" herself by controlling every aspect of her environment. To the degree a woman loses this hope, to that degree, she will become painfully independent, and thus enter into the dreaded "uncovered" woman syndrome. As explained earlier in this Chapter in Sarah's story, an "uncovered" woman thinks she cannot be vulnerable to Men. In her mind she has already "fixed" herself by doing away with the ridiculous notion that a Man can have any part in helping her, let alone saving her. An "uncovered" woman has simply buried all hope that her Shining Knight will ever come.

Hope is a form of faith. One of my favorite verses is, **"Without faith it is impossible to please God, because anyone who comes to Him must believe that he exists and that he rewards those who earnestly seek him."**[20] When we lose our hope and our faith through the abuses of life experiences, we lose our ability to reach out to God and call upon His goodness. Our pride tells us that we are independent and strong, but in reality we are hurt and alone.

To the shame of all males, it is true that many women have been brutally abused both emotionally and spiritually by the "boys" in their lives. When a "boy" withholds his God-ordained protection and nurturing from a woman, he is actually withholding the love that God so desires to pour into her. Every time a "boy" has violated his conscience and acted out behaviors similar to the "boy" category on the Man vs. "boy" list, another piece of a woman's hope and trust is stolen away, and her heart is further hardened. You can only imagine the lack of trust Pam had developed in God after seeing Don's actions and believing they are supposedly representing the nature of God.

As a woman loses trust in Men, she will eventually lose all hope, and she will not allow herself to be saved, loved or protected by any Man, not even the perfect Man and Savior Jesus Christ. She may find herself alone in the back of a cab wondering what happened to the dreams and hopes in her life. Without God, she will be sentenced to the hard and impossible job of saving herself, and the deep needs of her heart will never be fulfilled. This is indeed the tragedy of our modern and secular progressive nation.

There is a solution. There is a Savior who has given us hope. Trusting that our Savior can and will work through Men is the answer. Our Savior came in the form of a flesh and blood Man, and Men are to learn of His ways. Although no Man can perfectly fill our Savior's shoes,

20 Hebrews 11:6, NIV

all Men are ordained and Mandated to display the characteristics of their Savior – who is the perfect Man.

For Pam, she received a glimpse of her Savior when Harrison stepped in and protected her from the attacks of Sam. Men may become living examples of their Savior, because they have been appointed to perform the role of the Knight in Shining Armor riding on the white horse. It is God our father who then gives Men the strength, courage and humility to perform this task. And it is His Son Jesus Christ who gets the complete glory, because He paved the way by dying for his bride on the cross at Calvary.

This is the ultimate plot in the ultimate romantic movie, or tragedy, depending on how or if the Men stand up and take on this great challenge and Mandate. It is more glorious than a Spielberg production, and more profound than Shakespeare's finest play, and we are its cast. Every one of us has a role to play, and every one of us has the opportunity to play the leading Man or the leading woman.

Women are asked to play the incredible role of the bride of Christ, as they long for the Men in their lives to exude characteristics of their Savior. Men are asked to attempt the amazing role of Jesus the Christ, the author and finisher of our faith and lover of the bride. Men are to die to their selfishness and become Men, and they are to become an example of the Knight in Shining Armor on the pure and perfect white horse.

In compliance with their role as the bride of Christ, every woman is given gifts and desires of the bride placed deep within the make-up of her heart. Every woman has within her a desire to be saved from the utter distresses and stresses of life and impossible circumstances of relationships gone wrong. Every woman wants the Men in her life to stand up and be Men, and display the characteristics of their loving and protecting Savior – the characteristics of the perfect Man.

Who can feasibly deny it is so? Books and movies successfully repeat this story endlessly with anticipation and longing for both roles to be fulfilled. These stories are all variations of the common eternal theme, which calls for a happy ending to come with the Knight rescuing his Princess in distress onto his white horse, and taking her away to safety into the sunset. Corny, you say? Maybe. Absolutely touching and profound? Yes! But only if the cast does its job diligently as it is played out over and over again in honor of our God in heaven who has not and will not deny us a Savior. No culture is exempt from the fulfillment of this plot, and no nation can plausibly deny its validity in the course of mankind. Woman desire to be rescued and saved, just as all mankind desires to be saved from its fallen condition.

In the movie "The Man from Snowy River," who could deny the power and emotion of young Jim Craig overcoming his "boyish" behaviors and riding to rescue horses from the herd of Brombies and the Black Stallion, and then to return for his girl awaiting the rescue from the Man she loves. If Jim Craig would have remained the "boy" from Snowy River, we would have never even heard of the movie or seen that great scene of him riding down that near vertical cliff on his incredible mountain bred horse. In the end, Kirk Douglas' character of Mr. Harrison calls young Jim a lad, (a "boy") even though everyone around knows that this lad is no longer a "boy." Mr. Harrison's brother Spur, also played by Douglas, shouts out from his coach in front of everyone to Mr. Harrison, "He is not a lad, brother, he's a Man! He's a Man!!" Yes, he indeed was the Man from Snowy River.

The theme is timeless. It resonates deep inside each one of us, because we are all created to act out this great romance; the romance of Christ coming to rescue His bride. Women are looking for a Man, the right Man, to take responsibility for the atrocities that have been perpetrated by his gender. If a woman can trust just one Man, it will be an essential stepping-stone that allows her to forgive. It was through the heroic actions of Harrison that Pam began to see and understand what she really desired in a husband. She desired a Knight and a Man. Through this revelation and forgiveness, any woman may become Covered and the healing process can begin from the core of her being.

Males cannot truly know the depths of a woman's desire to be rescued and saved. Men and women are different! It is not in the make-up of a male to desire to be saved as it is in the heart of women. The core make-up of a Man is to have an overwhelming need to save, love and protect the women in his life. If males do not understand this simple fact, they will miss their Mandate and unknowingly "train" women to ignore their femininity by squashing their hopes and emotions. Women are left having little or no hope for the Knight in Shining Armor riding on the beautiful white horse.

So let us be that Knight to our loved ones, and let us be amazing examples of the perfect Knight on the white horse who returns in all of his glory. Women are waiting for their Men to stand up and be the heroes they are called to be. Women are desperately looking for their faithful and true loves to rescue them from the trials and discouragements of life. Will you be that Man?

"And I saw heaven opened, and behold a white horse; and he that sat upon him was called Faithful and True, and in righteousness he doth judge and make war. His eyes were as a flame of fire, and on his head were many crowns; and he had a name written, that no man knew, but he himself. And he was clothed with a vesture dipped in blood: and his name is called The Word of God."

John – Book of Revelation[21]

The Loving Covering:

It is critical for Men to step up and do their jobs as loving Patriarchs if we are to save the American family. For our wives and children to receive God and the destiny planned for them, Men must do their jobs and become the embodiment of the loving Covering and protector they are called to be. As fathers and husbands, we are responsible to fashion the armor and self esteem of our wives, sons and daughters. We must love them unconditionally to fulfill this task. It all comes down to the Men.

I have interacted with father and daughter relationships for decades. I have seen first hand that the degree fathers have imparted love and protection to their daughters, is the degree in which the daughters will receive God's love and God's free Covering as they mature into women. This same principle is true in our relationships with our wives. Let us not handicap our daughters and the women in our lives any longer. Receive the Mantle of the Man, the Knight and the Patriarch and realize God places His Coverings in fathers and husbands, and lead your loved ones in strength, authority, and most of all, in love.

21 Revelation 19:11-13 KJV

In the next chapter, we will see first hand how a Man can overcome the challenges of life by learning to understand his wife and making her feel valuable and beautiful. Walking as a Man, a Patriarch and a Knight, we indeed can learn to love, protect and adorn the wife of our youth.

"Let us be glad and rejoice, and give honour to him: for the marriage of the Lamb is come, and his wife hath made herself ready. And to her was granted that she should be arrayed in fine linen, clean and white: for the fine linen is the righteousness of saints."[22]
John – Book of Revelation

22 Revelation 19:7-8, KJV

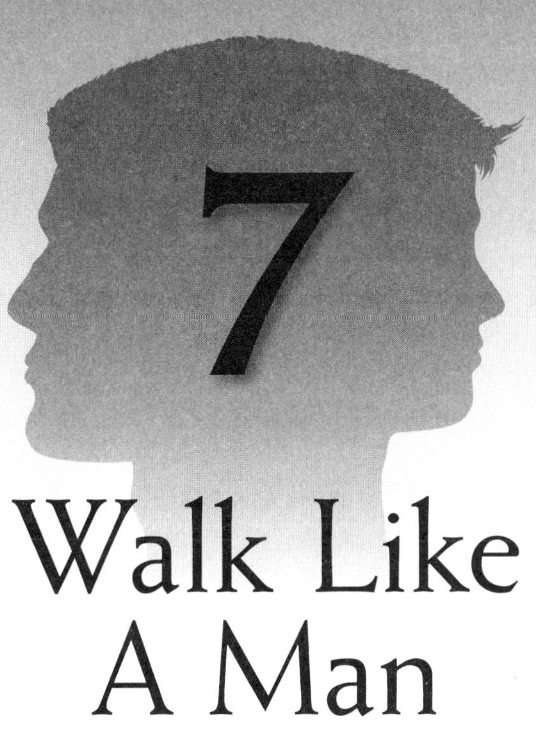

7 Walk Like A Man

The Patriarchal Man:

I suggest you truly prepare yourself for battle before you read this chapter, because it is going to test your Manhood. It is time to drop our toys and fight like Men. It is time to put down our video games and take a rest from the sports channels until we know we are fully winning in our Mandate.

Paul of Tarsus prayed the following prayer almost 2000 years ago. Men had the same needs back then. This short prayer simply asked God to build Men from the inside out, by the power of His Holy Spirit. Let it be our prayer for all Men today.

"That He would grant you, according to the riches of His glory, to be strengthened with might by his Spirit in the inner Man"
The Apostle Paul - Letter to the People in Ephesia

What does it mean to "Walk like a Man?" There is a word I like to use best describing what walking like a Man really means. The word is Patriarchal. One of the dictionary definitions for Patriarchal is "having the position and ***jurisdiction*** of a Patriarch." Understanding what it means to be Patriarchal is simplified by understanding jurisdiction. Jurisdiction is defined as, "the authority or legal power."

Throughout this book, you have learned about the legal power and authority given to Men. If you understand and honor this true and God-given authority, you are Patriarchal. If you choose not to understand and honor true and God-given authority, you are matriarchal. I will say it another way. Men are Patriarchal, "boys" are matriarchal.

Patriarchal Men will father their sons by encouraging and ushering them into Manhood. Matriarchal "boys" will attempt to mother their sons and encourage them to grow up to be sensitive "boys" who wet-nurse other "boys" (Point 10. on the Man vs. "boy" list). The real lie here is thinking that wet-nursing a "boy" is actually being sensitive. Teaching ours sons to be matriarchal is one of the most insensitive and abusive actions we can do, because it will steer them down a long and hard road of failure and insecurity as Men. This is a tough pill to swallow for many, especially if you have been trained to walk in the "boy" category, but it is better to hear it now and make changes while you still have a chance to get it right in your life.

Many females have been subconsciously trained by "boys" to fear the word "Patriarchal" because they have suffered at the hands of "boys." Every male on the planet has experienced the wrath of females who has been hurt or damaged by the "boys" in their lives. This in turn has caused them not to accept the God ordained "Patriarchal" authority in the males around them. A Man will not blame a woman for her lack of desire or ability to follow him. He will love, nurture and protect her still, because this is his job as a Man. If you are blaming females in any way for not accepting your authority or for not accepting the word "Patriarchal," I suggest you look at Man vs. "boy." Men are called to win over the hearts of women. Men are not allowed to blame.

Women have been wounded physically, emotionally and spiritually by fathers, brothers, boyfriends or other males in their lives who were supposed to walk as Patriarchs but did not. Males just like you and I have injured them greatly. To these wounded females, the word "Patriarchal" stirs up flashbacks of controlling, self-centered, and abusive "boys" who say they are Men, but they have wrongly used their supposed authority to stamp out and abuse the hearts of the females whom they were called to nurture and protect. A Man must look for ways to take responsibility for injustices done to females.

Just look at the Man vs. "boy" list again. There are 52 points on the list. If we choose to selfishly walk as "boys," each offense we commit will take another piece out of the hearts of the females in our lives. These women are precious and special gifts we are called to love. Each offense we commit against them destroys another degree of trust in Men and the Patriarchal system God has ordained. As Patriarchs, we must now go back and clean up the emotional and spiritual carnage and the relational fall-out caused by the "boyish" antics of our forefathers, our fathers and us. Are you up to the task?

Men, We Have Dropped The Ball!

Let us look at some of the more grievous offenses. Every time a little girl is molested, there is a male who has dropped the ball in protecting a precious and innocent little girl from becoming seriously damaged. Current data in America reveals a minimum of one out of every three little girls gets sexually molested before they are 18 years of age. This is only the reported instances of sexual abuse. The actual numbers are most definitely higher suggesting one out of every two little girls is getting violated.

Where are these little girl's Mandated "Coverings" (their fathers) when irresponsible and perverted "boys" are destroying their purity? Where are the Men who were assigned by God to love and protect these little ones? Do you realize how difficult it is for a female to accept God's Patriarchal authority after the Man assigned to be the Mandated Covering in her life has thrown her to the wolves and allowed her to be molested?

Without the help of God, it is impossible for a female to overcome such a traumatic childhood experience. Even with God's help, females often experience decades of pain, anguish and tears before they finally learn to love and trust the Men in their lives again. This is the consequence of males behaving as "boys." Can we as Men ask the females around us to forgive us for even being associated with a gender that would do such a thing? We can and we must, for we are those Men. As a Patriarch, this is your job.

You may be saying to yourself, "I tried to protect my daughter, but I didn't know etc…etc…etc." When it comes to protecting our daughters, there are no excuses. You have to do what is necessary to keep evil and selfish "boys" out of their space, period! Your job is to ***love and protect***. This means look ahead, pray, check things out and do not trust any male, even those in your own bloodline, unless absolute trust has been earned over time. Most molestation occurs by male family members, because they are the ones who have the "trusted" access.

If you are saying to yourself, "I did not have this information, therefore it's not my fault," you unfortunately are a "boy." If you are saying, "This seems kind of harsh," you are thinking like a "boy." If you are a Man, your heart is probably saying, "There is absolutely no excuse for allowing our daughters to get abused, molested, date raped, man handled or even ridiculed by other males. Forgive me God, for not having a stauncher stance regarding protecting the females in my life." Again, protecting women and children is your primary job as a Man.

Every time a female has an abortion, she experiences extreme trauma and damage to her body and soul, whether she is aware of it or not. Over one million women have abortions in America every year, and half of them are our daughters between the ages of 15 and 24. In every abortion, there are at least three males who have seriously dropped the ball in doing their job. First, there is the "boy" who got her pregnant and who was obviously irresponsible and selfish in some way. Second, there was the Mandated male who was supposed to love her, cover her, teach her, and protect her from selfish and irresponsible "boys." Third, there is usually a male doctor who participates in the murdering of her unborn child.

You will rarely find a Patriarch anywhere near an abortion unless he is stopping the abortion. Show me a female who has had an abortion, and I will show you at least three untrained and rebellious "boys" who neither know of their Mandate or their Calling. This is serious stuff. Are you Man enough to deal with this properly? As a Man you have to, or you cannot have the title.

If you are thinking, "I have never molested a girl! Or, I never killed a baby or got a girl pregnant." I suggest you think again. This is not

their problem. This is ***our*** problem! Look at Point 4. on the Man vs. "boy" list. Men look for ways to take responsibility and "boys" run from responsibility. We all suffer when a culture or a community has become reprobate, it does not matter who caused the problem.

Our Mandate as Men is to take responsibility for the destruction of our families and deal with it. Besides, do you expect the reprobate "boys" who have caused the worst damage to rise up and restore our families and our culture? We have all sat down on the job as the females in our lives are being hurt all around us. Usually it is because we have been selfish, lazy and rebellious, and we were not trained to understand the principles of being a Man. One look at the statistics in our culture, and it is obvious we have completely dropped the ball as Men. As Men, we are the ones who will bring about the restoration.

Traditional marriage and the family unit are the foundational building blocks of our once great nation. Over 60% of marriages end in divorce, with two-thirds of the divorce filings being initiated by women. The primary reasons given by women on filings are neglect, indifference, poor communication and emotional cruelty. America is seriously eroding away because males have not loved their wives properly. It is that simple. To love your wife, you must be a nurturing, protective and responsible Man. It is not that hard to make your wife feel beautiful, nurtured, loved and protected. Just make the right choices and do it!

"Pure religion and undefiled before God and the Father is this, To visit the fatherless and widows in their affliction, and to keep himself unspotted from the world."[1]

James, The Brother of Jesus – Book of James

Making Your Life a Fortress:

If you have embraced this book, you have received your Mandate to walk like a Man and to be Patriarchal. You understand the concept

1 James 1:27, KJV

and importance of having your "Man Diploma," and you have retrieved your Keys. You have secured the Gates in your life, both emotionally and spiritually. You also have an understanding of your Calling and you have made a declaration of victory towards fulfilling your Mandate by taking care of the women and children in your life. You are committed to providing a Covering for your loved ones and you have dedicated yourself to building up other Men in their Callings.

So let us all take the principles of our Mandate we have learned in this book, and build up our lives and our homes as a fortress that protects our loved ones. Each one of us can touch dozens of Men and share the principles of Man vs. "boy." One such Man who has received his Mandate and became a Patriarch while overcoming incredible odds, is a Man named Scott.

Scott:

Scott was 24 years old when I first shared the principles of the "Man vs. "boy" list with him. Here in his own words is his story. If you look closely, you can see how the principles expounded upon in this book were used by Scott to establish his Manhood and walk in his Mandate. His Keys, his Gates and his Calling were brought into order as he took charge of his life and walked as the Patriarch he is destined to be.

Scott's Testimony:

I first made the decision to become a Man when I was 11 years of age. I had decided to start a paper route. I thought at that young age, "I want to be a Man. I need to make my own money. I need to become independent." Over the following years as a teenager, I had many questions in my heart that can be summed up in one question, "How do I become a Man?"

When I asked my Dad general questions about the responsibilities of being a Man, it was common for him to give me a legalistic and religious answer that did not satisfy my heart. I quickly came to realize my Dad was missing some key elements to his Manliness and his Christian walk; the result being, he lacked the basic skills to impart Manhood to me.

My Dad responded to my questions with non-relational answers. Over the years, it became painfully apparent how confused and insecure he was regarding his masculinity. No matter how intimidated or confused he became by my questions, he would always come up with some Bible verse in an attempt to cover his deficiencies as a Man. My father knew he did not have solid answers for my questions, therefore giving me a Bible verse was the best he could do in his attempt to impart Manhood to me. Instead of imparting life, joy and encouragement, the brutal reality was I left his presence feeling confused, bitter and discouraged. The situation felt hopeless.

To make matters worse, my Pastor had the same problem of pacifying me with answers that did not satisfy my needs. Both my Dad and my Pastor (my Pastor had the Calling of Teacher) said they had the answers. Even at the ages of 12 to 17, I knew they did not have the answers for getting the victory in life, because on all fronts they were struggling. They were struggling financially. Their marriages were out of order, and their children were rebellious and confused about life.

They said they had the answers, but in my heart I was torn over whether to believe them, because I could see they were losing in their daily lives year after year. I worried if they had not figured things out at their age, how hopeless and disparaging it was for me? Ever since I was a child, I knew there was something incredibly wrong, but I couldn't quite put my finger on it.

Diagnosing The Problem:

I now know why. I thank God I can now laugh about it. My Dad had never been "Bar Mitzvahed." He did not have his so-called "Man Diploma." He simply was not a Man yet, and I knew this unfortunate fact deep down in my heart, even when I was a teenager.

Since my Dad displayed confusion regarding his Manhood, I became confused myself. I began to model his behavior by acting legalistic, non-relational and religious in an attempt to mask my lack of Manhood. At the same time, I also was bitter at my Dad because I could feel there was an extreme lack of love displayed towards me. What really upset and perplexed me was his serious lack of desire for me to mature as a Man.

In my Dad's attempt to go through the motions of making me a Man, he would press me to be financially successful and outwardly religious. I was asked to be presentable and socially acceptable as a "Christian nice guy," but he failed to show true concern for the condition of my heart. Basically, my Dad was training me to be a man-pleaser.

Ever since I was a child, I remember my Dad having a strong desire for me to do well in sports. When I was about eight years old, I played soccer in a community recreational league for a couple of months out of the year. I liked playing soccer; however, being only eight years old at the time, the concept of winning or losing was not overly important to me. I just liked to play soccer.

At times, my Dad would get very angry with me on the sidelines for not being aggressive enough in the game. Unexpectedly, he would vent his extreme frustration and anger leading me to feel stupid and rejected. Rather than connecting with me on a personal level, my Dad seemed more concerned with my outward performance on the soccer field and in my life.

This was a recurring theme throughout my involvement in High School sports. As a freshman, I ran varsity Cross Country leading our team to qualify for the State Cross Country Finals. My Cross Country coach was always quite pleased with my performances, and he chose me as the Most Valuable Runner one year.

Even though I excelled in sports, my Dad felt it necessary to criticize some area of my running in races without giving any positive encouragements. He seemed to impart his disappointment with my performance even when I won the race. My point in sharing this information is to say my Dad did not have the Manly security and confidence to establish and support me. Unwittingly, his actions were contributing to the breakdown of my strength and security as a male and as a Man.

I felt my Dad would subconsciously and consciously avoid promoting me to be successful, because inside he was intimidated by my achievements. Like the saying goes, "Misery loves company." This is further magnified in the father and son relationship. When a father is still a "boy," it is humiliating and shameful for him to admit he is failing at one of his primary duties of becoming a Man and building up his son to be a Man.

When I would ask my Dad for real answers about Manhood, unknowingly I was challenging his Manhood. My Dad would become subtly frustrated and angry with me. He would either dismiss me or shut me down. Again, I would leave the encounter feeling discouraged, and it would cause me to feel even more hopeless about my Manhood.

Today, I see that even if my Dad had fully wanted me to become a Man, he just did not have Manhood to impart. I now know you cannot teach 10th grade when you have only graduated from third grade. Looking back, I can also see "boys" do not want other "boys" to become Men. (Points 3., 8. and 9. on the Man vs. "boy" list reinforce this statement.) This means "boys" will usually resent Men, and they are envious of Men who walk in their God-given authority. True Men will promote, assist and even celebrate in the development and building of other Men.

Understanding these concepts set me free from bitterness and anger against my Dad. I now know this is normal behavior for a "boy." This is what "boys" do. As Point 39. from the Man vs. "boy" list states, "'boys' get angry when their Manhood is challenged." Until my Dad makes the decision to become a Man, it would be very unlikely for him to promote Manhood in me.

I also came to realize my Dad has the Calling of a Pastor/Manager, and I have the Calling of a CEO/Apostle. Before I understood the Callings, I was confused because I did not understand why my Dad was content with being a nine to five worker bee. I had big plans for the future, and I could not understand why he wasn't behind my plans, or why he did not have big plans for his own life.

As a CEO, building and making big plans was very important to me. My Dad was a Manager; therefore, he was content where he was working surrounded by familiar people. He held a solid job with a steady income, and this met his inner needs as a Manager. From the perspective of his Calling, I was taking on too much. I felt like he was constantly working against me and the big plans I had in my heart. Now I see it clearly. We were looking through different glasses, and I was expecting him to understand me and talk to me as a CEO. My Dad did not understand

Callings, thus he did not have the tools to understand my Calling or the motivations of a CEO.

The relationship with my Dad faltered because of a lack of training on many different levels. One of the primary reasons it faltered was he did not have his "Man Diploma." Secondly, we struggled because he was jealous of me potentially getting my Keys of authority before him. Thirdly, there were areas in my Dad's life and my life where our open Gates were affecting our relationship. As mentioned previously, in each case our ignorance regarding the Callings added even more misunderstanding to our relationship.

Understanding the principles about Manhood, Keys, Gates, and the Callings helped me greatly in diagnosing and solving the problems I had with my Dad. Learning all four of these concepts has enabled me to fully overcome and understand in a mighty way. These principles have made life easy for me. I will not give up what I know now for anything.

As I said before, I decided to become a Man when I was 11 years old. For 13 years until I was age 24, I angrily floundered around fighting a "boyish" system that did not give me the tools or the training to obtain victory as a Man. I wanted to get my Manhood, but I could not get it because there were no Men around me who could show me how to obtain my "Man Diploma." Since Men make Men, the cards were set against me because there were no Men in sight.

Finally when I was 24, I became good friends with some healthy Men at work, one being Ken Ventura, who exposed me to the principles from "Man vs. boy." For years, I was a "3" on the victory scale, and it was obvious to my new friends I was seriously losing in my life. They could see right through my fake smiles, and I knew it.

Within a short time, it was easy for me to see the Truth about the relationship between my Dad and me. Once I understood the dynamics of my Dad and his upbringing, I was able to forgive him for walking as a "boy" and not doing his job. This allowed me to rid myself of any bitterness or anger I had against my Dad, as well as any other males who had misled me. It became easy for me to see how they never acquired Manhood; therefore, they could not impart Manhood to me. I could not blame my Dad for doing what was impossible for him to do. It is a simple principle of life. You cannot give what you do not have. Unfortunately, for my Dad and for me, principles of "Man vs. boy" were never given to either of us.

The new Men I befriended had the strength, confidence and authority I desperately wanted. Entering into relationships with these Men made becoming a Man inevitable. I was able to ask my new Men friends the same questions I had asked my Dad when I was a teenager.

It was not long before the "Bar Mitzvah" I waited for since I was eleven, happened in one clean sweep. I was initiated, Mandated and celebrated all within half an hour. It was so easy to receive my Manhood, because I had already made the decision to become a Man years before. I am so thankful there were Men to impart to me the lessons of Manhood. Of course, being trained as a Man and behaving as a Man is a lifelong journey.

I felt an incredible victory and satisfaction knowing there was hope in my life, and a reason for all of my past despairs. All of the problems I battled in my life instantly changed from hopeless and unsurpassable expanses, to minor challenges I could easily overcome. It is eye-opening now to think I almost totally resigned myself to settling into a mode of accepting defeat, failure and having a right to be angry with God, when victory was just a revelation and a prayer away.

Here was my prayer to receive and become a Man:

Scott's Prayer:

"God, forgive me for not walking as a Man. Forgive me for not doing my job and using the authority You have given me. Forgive me for being bitter at You and for being righteous in my own eyes. Forgive me for judging my Dad and the males in my life for not being Men. Forgive me for the anger I have had towards You and toward my Dad, because of my lack of understanding. Forgive me for handing my Keys of authority to the religious and legalistic attitude that has controlled my Dad. Forgive me for allowing myself to lose hope, and believe the lie You and my Dad do not love me.

"Starting today, in the name of Jesus of Nazareth I choose to walk with the authority you have given me as a Man. I declare I am fully a Man, and I now take back any and all of my Keys from my Dad and every other male. I pray you show my Dad the same victory you have shown me, and you restore our relationship fully. I thank my Dad for everything he provided for me, and for the times he was loving and helpful to me. I thank You, God, for giving me the answers I have always yearned for. And I thank You for making it all so simple. Amen."

Getting My House In Order:

After I formally received my "Man Diploma," you can only imagine how excited I was about the new revelation concerning my Mandate and my Keys. I had just received the epiphany that becoming a Man is a simple choice and an act of one's will, but I was about to learn that walking daily as a Man is a lifelong process, and one of life's most difficult challenges. Walking as a Man is about honesty, integrity, and character, and it is about making things right in relationships.

Over the next few days, I started thinking about all the things I wanted to do that would set my house in order. Rather than look at my own selfish and "boyish" behaviors, I consistently thought about all the ways my wife Sarah needed to change; her nagging, her complaining, her controlling attitude, her failure to appreciate me, her making me feel like a little boy all the time, and most of all, her lack of respect for me as a Man. The more I thought about it, the more adamant and angry my attitude was becoming towards her. After reading Sarah's story in Chapter 6, you can truly understand just how insensitive, abusive and cruel my attitude was.

After years of treating Sarah in a way that endorsed and even created her behaviors, now I was going to chastise her for her actions, even though they were clearly a normal female response to my "boyish" irresponsibility. I attempted to appear gentle as I took her by the hand and proudly escorted her over to our bed. Self-righteousness must have just oozed out of me as I stated, "Things are going to be way different from now on."

Sarah and I then sat down facing one another as I held her hands in mine. I was on a mission to inform her about my newfound authority and do what I thought my job was as a Man. I said to her, "It is time for us to make some changes. As the Man of this house, I want to talk to you about your attitude."

Sarah peered at me with eyes that were distant, withdrawn and defensive. She was preparing for another male to pummel her with insensitive and abusive words telling her what she already knew, that she was worthless.

What happened next was extraordinary. Before I got a chance to say any of the things I wanted to talk to her about, my conscience was jolted. Looking at Sarah's battered and fearful eyes, I became overwhelmed and convicted right then and there about my own bad attitude. It seemed as if God Almighty had reached right into my heart and turned on a switch allowing the floodgates to open. An incredible flow of understanding and compassion for my wife began to fill my being for the first time in my life.

A flood of tears filled my eyes as I began to see some of the incredible hurt I had caused her over the years from my lack of sensitivity. I began to see many different areas where I was seriously missing it in my own personal life; the blaming, the irresponsible behavior, the pornography, the lack of nurturing, the neglect, and did I mention the blaming? A few of the points on the Man vs. "boy" list came to mind as I reminded myself that Men are never supposed to blame, ever!

For the first time in our marriage, I began to see my dereliction of duty as a Man. I suddenly realized I was both subtly, and not so subtly, abusing my wife. My actions were fully and totally my responsibility and they were causing her to lose all trust in me. I felt a great amount of shame. Even now, as I am recalling this event, I am ashamed at how I blamed her for problems she never would have had, if I had simply done my job. I had been behaving as a "boy," and a selfish one at that.

I looked at Sarah closely, as I began to remember various arguments and disagreements we had over the years. Years of frustration and pain were laid before me as clarity started to settle in my mind. Many times previously, I would argue with my wife and say to her, "I am just trying to do my job, and you do not respect me." Somehow I felt I deserved respect; even though in my heart I knew I was not acting right, and I was not deserving of her respect.

Looking back, I can see that both my belief system and my heart were off. I believed the lie that Sarah did not respect my authority, when actually she did not respect my "boyish" behavior of "trying." I was "trying" to do my job. I was "trying" to love her. I was "trying" to protect her and provide for her. I was "trying" to change and fix my wife. I was not "doing" my job. Sarah was not feeling either loved or protected, and worst of all, she did not feel beautiful. Now I know that if I really want my wife to change, I need to unconditionally love her.

The Truth was I didn't know the first thing about doing my job as a Man. I had given my Keys of authority away to my Dad and to my wife years before. Of course, Sarah was not going to respect me as a "boy," she shouldn't respect irresponsibility. My job was to become a Man, and then my job was to love her and protect her. My job was not to make her obey my control. I was totally missing my true responsibility. Was I loving and protecting her? The answer was "No."

I was acting like a "boy" every time I would argue with my wife. Rather than just doing my job as a Man, I was in the habit of fighting with her in an attempt to convince her she needed to obey me. I now know I do not have to make her obey. That is called control. She is going to either follow me as a Man, or she is ***not*** going to follow me as a Man. Either way, I do not have to worry. If I do my job, I know ultimately she will follow me.

I was not brought up to recognize the difference between submission and control. I thought to "obey" meant you were supposed to allow another person to control you. I learned this belief system as a child, and regrettably, I brought this dysfunction into my marriage.

In my ignorant zeal, I was trying to get my wife to obey in the wrong sense of the word, just like I did when I was a child in my parents' household. This was familiar territory for me, because this was exactly what I was trained to do by my role models. I was trained to give my Keys of authority away by blindly allowing others to control my life. This is what my Dad had done.

I knew I had lost my Keys of authority by my actions, and I knew I had to get them back at all cost. It was the worst "boyish" feeling I have ever experienced. I willingly had given away my Keys, and I had opened up the Gates of hell upon my wife. Unknowingly, I had given permission for evil to harm and ravage the one person I really loved. I then blamed and accused her of being the cause of her problems.

My plan of going to my wife and changing her behavior had failed miserably. My dictatorship was over, thank God. A deep pit settled in my gut, as I sensed how disappointed my wife was with me. My lecture quickly turned into a heartfelt apology as I sorrowfully pleaded to Sarah, "Will you please forgive me for my many shortcomings in our relationship over the years? I have not taken very good care of you. I have been an arrogant, insensitive little "boy," and I have not loved or protected you the way a real Man should. Sarah, you are so precious and beautiful to me. You will see that our relationship is going to be very different. It is going to be better."

Specifically, I asked Sarah to forgive me for the many times I argued with her in pride, and for the times I blamed her for failures that were clearly my fault. My voice cracked a little as I said to Sarah, "I have kept secrets from you regarding pornography and other things. I have not been honest with you. Over the past five years that we have been married, my 'boyish' approach to our marriage has caused both of us a lot of unnecessary grief and loss. Will you please forgive me?"

As these repentant words left my lips, I had a deep sense in my heart this is really what it meant to be a Man. For the first time in our marriage, I made myself totally vulnerable and honest before my wife about my shortcomings. It was as if a million pounds had lifted off me. Being a Man was nothing at all like I expected. I was quickly learning that authority, humility and truth are very close friends.

The room fell very silent. I could hear the gentle blow of the air conditioner as I watched my wife look at me in disbelief. I thought she would immediately come back at me with verbal attacks and "I told you so" comments, but she didn't.

Sarah sat there slightly perplexed, as she looked deep inside my soul with huge, surprised eyes. I could tell she knew something was different about me, and she was not sure whether it was good or bad. She then rose up and sternly said, "You have been lying to me! How could you keep things from me? I knew something was wrong!"

I thought, "Oh no, here we go again." But this time, I did not fall into the same old pattern. I knew today, I had to love Sarah no matter what the cost. I kept holding her hands as she dropped back down sitting across from me, and we continued to look directly into each other's eyes.

For about 20 minutes, I listened to every word she said, and I responded candidly and honestly when she asked me questions. Many things were spoken. Some were helpful, and some were not. But I kept reminding her that I loved her, and I was committed to our marriage until death do us part.

"If you think that there is no persecution in the United States, you have not heard the hearts of the women in America."

Sarah suddenly dropped her head and began to sob gently. She was quiet for a short time, and then she slowly began to reveal a glimpse of her heart to me. It was a Sarah I had never seen before. She looked up at me intently with a few small tears falling from her eyes as she said, "Do you know that I feel worthless and condemned when you try to correct me? I know you are unhappy with me. This is why I feel so ugly all of the time. When I see that you are mad at me, no amount of make-up I put on gets rid of the ugliness I feel inside. The main reason I don't share my heart with you is because you try to fix me all of the time, or you tell me that I am wrong in feeling a certain way. How can my heart be wrong? That is truly how I feel!"

My heart sank as Sarah's crushed heart cried out in despair over the years of neglect and intellectual abuse I had caused to her.

She then said, "I know you love me, but I do not feel your love for me. And some of that is probably my fault, because I am so messed up inside. But I know that you need to understand how lonely and depressed I feel in my heart when you do not validate me or my feelings. When I try to share with you what I am feeling, you discredit and devalue me by telling me that I should not feel that way. I simply shut down, because there is no point in subjecting myself to your condemnation or your reprimands. I can't handle it when you look down at me, because I love you too much. I want you to be happy with me."

With these words, my soul and my countenance fell to a depth so low and dark that I can only explain it as hell. I had done this to her. I had crushed her sweet, loving spirit for years without even the slightest knowledge of it. To think that even today, I was going to reprimand her again by telling her that she was the one with the bad attitude. I was devastated. I had to finally look at my pride, my selfishness and my insensitivity.

I knew there were no "I'm sorry" statements that could possibly atone for my incredibly "boyish" behaviors. Only the mercy of God could find anything redeeming or healing from this point on. My previous apology and crusade of asking for forgiveness, though sincere, seemed as a careless token compared to the destruction I now saw I had perpetrated against her. I was literally undone.

My mind reenacted scenes in our marriage where I saw myself yelling at Sarah and calling her brutal names in my fits of anger. I saw her crying in desperation, as I left her alone to drive around the neighborhood with no place to go. I saw myself punching the windshield of my truck in my frustration, and feeling angry at God for putting me in such a messed up marriage. I recalled seeing the cracks in the windshield every day thereafter reminding me of my failure as a Man and as a husband. It was I who needed to change. It was not Sarah, nor God, nor my parents that needed to change. It was me.

Without even saying a word, and with a strength I barely knew I had in myself, I leaned over and held my wife. I held her tighter and with more tenderness than I had ever held her before. We both wept in each other's arms for what seemed like 20 minutes, as the peace of God began to fill the room. A miracle was happening right before me, and I knew I could take absolutely no credit for any of it. I could sense Sarah's countenance warming up as a slight smile appeared on her face.

Suddenly, she held my face with both of her hands and looked me straight in the eyes. Then she calmly said, "I forgive you." Tears poured out of my eyes, because I knew I neither deserved nor expected forgiveness. I must have appeared incredibly shocked, because Sarah then left the room and began to clean the house as if nothing had ever happened. I remained in our room sitting on our bed in awe of the moment, not able to even move a muscle.

To my amazement, my wife began to overlook a thousand grievous offenses, because on that day I simply made an effort to melt her heart and make her ***feel*** loved. For a brief moment, I decided to die to myself and live for my wife. We shared the reward of a moment of emotional honesty together I will never forget, and we connected in a way like never before.

Over the following days, I sought the heart of God to help me understand the heart of my wife. Of course, I needed to retrieve all of my lost Keys I had given away in my selfishness, and God was gracious to me. I declared war against the fear and selfish pride keeping me from loving my wife over the years. I was quickly learning the best reason for having my Keys intact was to have my wife hold me like she did when she shared her heart with me on that day.

I have learned some extremely valuable tools for winning back the trust of my wife's heart. A respected friend challenged me by asking the following question; "How many times a day do you make it a point to show your wife she is loved and highly valued by giving her a loving comment or a tender display of affection?" I answered by saying, "I have to admit, the answer is usually 'zero.'" He then told me that he made it a point to say to his wife, "I love you" all throughout the day. He said that sometimes up to 20 plus times a day he purposely imparted some kind of tangible love to his wife. I thought to myself, "Wow! I am really missing it!"

My friend pointed out to me that I most likely never learned how to impart love to my wife, because my Dad rarely imparted or showed outward nurturing and affection to my mother. He nailed it! I cannot even remember one time that my Dad physically touched my mother in front of my brothers and sisters. The phrase "I love you" was a foreign term in our home. I had to face the tough fact that I was not imparting love to my wife, and I had created a marriage that was not built upon love or trust.

From that moment I made a promise to myself and to my wife that things were going to be different. Everyday, I now commit myself to do the following four things for her.

1. ***Make her feel Beautiful.***
2. ***Do something for her that melts her heart.***
3. ***Make sure she feels loved/nurtured.***
4. ***Be her Knight in Shining Armor. Make sure she feels safe and protected.***

My job is to continually make her feel beautiful, and to ask her if she feels validated, loved and protected every day. If she doesn't, I have some work to do. If I have not done something that melts her heart, I have some work to do. If Sarah does not feel loved and protected, I have to know why, and then I have to make it right. You would not believe the difference in the radiance and the attitude of Sarah after only a short time of me dying to myself and living for her. And you would not believe the difference it has made for me personally. I am a strong Man, and I am getting stronger every day.

Gradually, I am learning how to put on my new nature as a Man. What a huge breakthrough it was for me to commit myself to becoming sensitive to my wife. My relationship with Sarah is growing and healing at the same time. We had many ups and downs in the months following my breakthrough, but the miracles that I will share next are simply amazing.

Praying For Sarah & Setting Boundaries:

Over the next few months I put into my daily routine my goals to love Sarah better. I still continued to learn more about how the dynamics of my marriage were out of order, and how my wife was suffering because of it. As you may recall from Sarah's incredible story in Chapter 6, my wife was constantly battling the fear that arises when a women does not feel Covered. For over 10 years, she failed to have her monthly period, and daily she was distraught and overcome with worry.

I was challenged by the Men in my life to look at the problem as my problem. They asked me if I was taking responsibility for praying over my wife, and protecting her from anything that caused her grief. Immediately, I was reminded I had neither prayed for her as a Man, nor had I protected her in an acceptable way.

My wife and I lived near many of her family members. They would constantly come over unannounced, and they would usually bring unrest into our home. Interfering with our lives would cause division between Sarah and me. We both agreed her family had serious relational health and boundary problems, and they were causing a severe rift in our relationship. We knew we had to be free of these controlling and dysfunctional family dynamics. Something had to be done, and I knew I was the one to do it.

In the past, it was obvious that I had behaved like a "boy" by not addressing them directly. I had allowed other people to come between my wife and me, and I had not done my job of protecting Sarah. Simply put, I had cowered for years when my Manhood was challenged. I did not speak my mind to them when they broke my boundaries. As a result, I violated my conscience and gave more of my Keys away.

With my newfound Mandate, I knew this behavior had to stop. I first addressed these family members directly. I told each of them not to come over to our home uninvited. I specifically made a personal appearance to my mother-in-law. I had given away my Keys to her years before, and instinctively I knew that addressing her directly would be the avenue for me to get my Keys back.

One evening I drove to my mother-in-law's house and set a distinct and strong boundary regarding visitations to my home. To the family members that were there, I made it clear no one had authority to come to my house without my permission. As you can imagine, I could feel the knots forming in their stomachs as disgruntled family members began to interrogate me. They seemed to be uniting in an evil form of negative agreement reminding me somewhat of a lynch mob. I was soon accused of being controlling and overly protective of Sarah, and I am sure there were other unedifying comments said against me amongst them.

How ironic! They were accusing me of being controlling, after we had allowed them to control us for most of our adult lives. None of this bothered me anymore. I was doing my job as a Man, and I knew it. After some mildly heated discussions, I made it clear to them I did not need to further explain my decision. I strongly stated, "This is the way it is going to be."

The joy I experienced while driving home that night was a first time experience for me. It was a combination of joy, strength, self-confidence and peace that I still have today. I had more of my Keys back! For the first time in my marriage, I was setting boundaries with my in-laws and protecting my wife and myself from some of the family dysfunctions.

In addition to setting boundaries with her family, I soon began to pray over my wife regarding fear and other issues where she was struggling. Since this was all new to her, she wasn't overly enthused about me telling her I was the authority over the household. Sarah actually tried to subtly discourage me from praying by changing the subject and avoiding the topic of prayer altogether. However, I knew it was very important for me to follow my heart.

Instinctively, as a Man, I knew it was right for me to pray over her. I did not let her opposition persuade me. With her back to me as she was lying in bed, I put my hand on her shoulder and prayed blessings over my wife, Sarah. And for the first time in my life, I declared war against the fear and worry that was continually attacking her. I could feel it was powerful as Sarah began to relax her neck and shoulders. Deep inside, I also knew God was very pleased I was doing my job, finally. Something felt very different about the prayer I prayed that evening, and I could sense a great peace come over both of us as we fell asleep.

The next day, I was at work when I got the call from my wife. To both our amazement, she started her monthly cycle. After 10 years, she was healed! For years, we had tried all kinds of New Age herbs and diet techniques that did nothing, except drain the checkbook. When I started to operate and function in my Mandate, everything changed almost overnight. My wife was so overwhelmed by the event, she not only began to accept my authority as a Man, she now goes out of her way to make sure I pray for her when she feels down, fearful or defeated. It was so fulfilling to know she was beginning to trust me as a Man.

Finally, after years of frustration and loss, I obtained some of the necessary tools to break the generational chains handed to me by my forefathers. The Keys to my marriage were being restored to me, and I could see that the deep yearning of my heart to become a Patriarch was coming to pass.

Enforcing Your Boundaries:

Shortly after this great news from my wife, the unannounced visits from her family began. First, her older brother Abe came over without calling or asking permission beforehand. I met him at the door and looked him up and down for a moment. I then said, "What are you doing here?"

You could almost hear our heartbeats as I awaited his response. He then said with a sense of phony authority and a forced smile, "I just came over to say hello and see how you are doing. Do you want me to leave?" He pretended like I never even told him he needed to call first.

I then said to him, "Yes, you should respect my past requests and leave!"

Abe reached out to shake my hand and said, "Okay man, if that is how you want it to be." I was extremely agitated at this, as he was implying I was the one hurting the relationship. He was in the very act of breaking my boundaries, and he was trying to blame me for it.

I purposely did not shake his hand. I said, "You are full of *@%#." I pointed to his car and cordially made it clear he needed to leave. Abe walked away as he uttered a few comments under his breath denying any responsibility for coming to my house unannounced.

As I shut the door, I couldn't believe how great it felt to enforce my boundaries. For years, I ignorantly came under the control of this type of person, and I knew I was free of it. I sang "Victory in Jesus" for the next hour rejoicing over the encounter. I had retrieved more of my Keys back, but the real challenge was yet to come.

Boundaries Challenged:

A day later, my wife's brother-in-law and her oldest brother also came over unannounced in double power. I opened the door to find out why they were there, and they immediately asked if they could come in and talk. Against my better instinct, I let them in. I did not want them to think I was rude. Bad move. Looking back, I can see once again I gave away a Key or two because I violated my conscience by "boy" pleasing.

After they came in, I proceeded to debate with them to no avail for five hours. Yes, in my rebellion, I actually tolerated them breaking my boundaries for five hours. The whole time, I knew I was compromising by allowing them in my house. These two "boys" were knowingly going against every boundary I had set, and I was not dealing with the violation at hand. I violated my own conscience, and I was trying to make up for it by explaining my position to them. I figured I would save my reputation and myself by winning them over to my new way of thinking. Of course, this failed miserably.

After they left, I felt angry with myself because I folded to their control. I let them in my house against my better judgment. For hours, I walked around the house in defeat. I was confused and humiliated. At the time, I did not fully understand why my heart was feeling so down.

I sheepishly called a friend to get some feedback on the whole situation. He responded, "Scott, you got slaughtered! Those two guys stole it all from you, and they did it in your own home! Right now, as I am speaking to you on the phone, I can see you have nothing left. You gave your Keys away. What happened?" I knew my friend was right. I got slaughtered. Faithful are the wounds of a friend.

As I hung up the phone, I knew I had to get my Keys back right away. I did not like feeling like a "boy," and I was not about to stay in that condition. I repented for going against what I knew I was supposed to do, and for being disobedient to my conscience. I then retrieved my Keys back by making a proclamation to God and all the powers that be. I said, "Those Keys are mine! I am taking them back now, and I will never give them away again!" The victory came immediately. From that moment on, I decided and declared outwardly I would only allow people in my house if I truly desired them to enter.

"The wicked flee when no man pursues, but the righteous are as bold as a Lion."[2]
King Solomon – Book of Proverbs

I learned on that day you cannot violate your conscience when you set a healthy boundary, or you're going to lose some Keys. I also learned standing by your boundaries will always produce positive results in relationships. I must follow my heart and walk in the authority given to me. Debating with those two "boys" for five hours only produced frustration, because I did not want them in my house in the first place. My actions did nothing to build the relationship, because I compromised.

---

2 Proverbs 28:1, KJV

After two years, I have kept the promise of enforcing my boundaries. I have kept the peace in my house, and I have guarded my Keys. There were still a few skirmishes where I had to enforce my boundaries with family who still tried to come over unannounced. After a month or two, they all realized they were wasting their gas money and putting miles on their car only to get sent home.

Sarah and I are so pleased with the results of setting boundaries. We rarely experience the division that accompanied the past unexpected visits from family members. Some very incredible things occurred over the next few years. Gradually, the family has come to respect the wisdom of our decisions, and some have even begun to model our boundaries in their own households. Praise God, we have helped to eradicate the controlling and boundary breaking traditions plaguing our families for generations.

"Our life is like a fine piece of art where God is continually touching up the paint on the canvas. One day He will stand back and say with joy, 'It is finished.'"

Honest Abe Returns:

After a two year period since the time I told Abe to leave my house, he called me on the phone and asked if he and his wife could see my wife and me for the holidays. Abe seemed genuine, and he was honoring my boundaries since our last confrontation. For the first time in our 20 plus year relationship, Abe was actually reaching out to me in a way both honest and real.

As we spoke on the phone, I could sense he was genuinely interested in how I was doing. He noticed the difference in my attitude and demeanor, and he was very interested to know how I came to walk as a Man.

Abe said to me, "Scott, I really have missed your friendship these last few years. There was always something about you that made me want to hang with you. It has not been easy for me this last year. My wife and I have really had a rough time of it. I have really struggled with communicating with her properly." After hearing Abe's words, I was blown away because our talks were never so real in the past.

I felt compelled to share with him some of the principles changing my life. I said to him, "Abe, are you walking in victory in your life?"

Abe responded with a slow and unsure "Yes, but …" I knew in my heart the answer was a definite "No."

I said, "Abe, the reason we have not been very close these past few years is because I have had to minimize having close relationships with people who are not real with me. I have realized the family dynamics we both grew up with were very unhealthy in regards to building strong relationships. I totally restructured my life and became a Man. This has helped me to move on to the next level in my life. I realized I had given all of my Keys away, and getting them back was the only way I was going to be successful with my family. I have an important question for you. Do you realize your Dad has your Keys, and he has had them for years?"

Abe responded hesitantly by saying, "I know my Dad has made a lot of mistakes, but I have forgiven him."

I said, "I believe you have forgiven him, but I don't think you understand what is going on. Abe, your Dad still has your Keys! I can see it plain as day. How can you forgive your Dad, and still allow him to have your Keys? There is something wrong here. You will have to keep forgiving him moment by moment, because the offense of stealing your Keys is ongoing.

"Let me tell you something that changed my life. Forgiveness is a process that will totally revolutionize your life. Everything may not become perfect immediately just because we decide to forgive, but the restoration that forgiveness will deliver is incredible. I believe it would be very helpful for you to look at your relationship with your father closely and determine where you have offended one another.

"To be clear here, if you haven't really identified what the offense is, there really isn't true forgiveness. All the cards have to be laid on the table. The devil is a lawyer, and he is going to use every legal avenue to keep you down. If someone steals $100 from you, and you have not gone to him and demanded it back, you haven't taken the first step to reconcile the matter. It is like a convicted felon before a judge. All the crimes have to be acknowledged and brought forward before the judge can have mercy on the person who committed the crime.

"Both you and I were brought up in a very dysfunctional religious family system. The system pounded us with the belief that once we say 'I forgive you,' all would be restored. This is only half of the Truth, because there is still some work to do. We have to walk it out and start acting like Men. When we say 'Forgive me,' we really are only initiating the process of forgiveness.

"This is an awesome thing, because it is the first step in reconciliation and restoration of the relationship. But remember, God is totally relational. And what this means to me is He wants us to bring our relationships to the point where we walk as the Men we are called to be. In a healthy relationship, no one is ever allowed to have our Keys, ever! I need to tell you that your Dad still has your Keys, and he's always going to have them until you take them back. It is your duty to take them back. This is called, 'Being a Man.'"

Abe sounded a little troubled. He said, "Scott, what else can I do. I have forgiven my Dad. I do not know what you mean by saying he has my Keys. Can you give me a tangible example?" I felt I was the perfect person to share this information with Abe. I had made similar mistakes he had made, and I had grown up with the same family dynamics.

I said to him, "Abe, you know how many times you were angry with your Dad because he was manipulating you into doing the family church thing. Church is great when it is right, but something has always been wrong with the way your father has participated in church, and I think you know this. It was always about control. Everything about our lives had an underlying control attached to it by the supposed elders. This was so wrong. You were always angry at the fact you were expected to go along with every little thing your Dad was doing, even when you were well into you twenties.

"I remember the times you felt angry and just did nothing. You kept your mouth shut, and went along with the lies and manipulation, even though your conscience was telling you something was wrong. Behind your father's back, you would make little comments like some little 'boy' who was afraid to say the Truth to his face. By doing this, you violated your conscience and gave your God-given authority, your Keys, to your Dad.

"You are not a child. You are an adult. When you fail to act on your heart, you violate one of the basic principles of life. Stand up for what is right, and do not allow another person to control you. You gave your Keys to your Dad a thousand times over, and you are now paying the price because you do not have the authority God gave you."

Abe responded quickly and said, "I don't let my Dad do that anymore! I live in another State now. He can't do that anymore."

I could see Abe was getting a little edgy and defensive, so in a calm and steady voice I said, "It doesn't matter where you are. He still has your Keys! Let me say it this way. Let's say your Dad borrowed your truck without asking you, and you went outside and saw it was missing. You are floundering around on foot looking for your truck. Soon your Dad comes pealing up to you in your truck and says, 'Hello son, I hope you don't mind I took your truck.' In your heart, you are upset and you want to say, 'This is really wrong.' But instead of dealing with it, you say outwardly, 'That's okay, Dad. I don't mind.' Your Dad then nods his head and drives off… ***in your truck!***

"Now you have two problems. First, you wussed out by not having the balls to be honest with your Dad. Secondly, you aren't facing the obvious. He still has your truck! And he is using your gas. To make matters worse, he's not taking care of your truck. I can see him burning out around the corners running into things, taking out the fenders and reaming the engine.

"If you don't get it back soon, your truck is going to be totally thrashed. As for you, you are walking around trying to bum a ride off anyone who sees your thumb sticking up in the air. And heaven forbid that your Dad comes by, because half the time he is trying to run you over with your own truck. Do you get it now? Control is brutal. You have given away your Keys to a controlling person who is taking advantage of you.

"He still has your Keys, because you have not stood up like a Man and taken them back. A Man says, 'Get out of my truck and give me my Keys. Now! I am taking back my truck. And if you do not obey immediately, I am going to take this to the next level.' You said you have forgiven your Dad, but you really have not gone through the proper steps for forgiveness. You never confronted him with the actual offense;

therefore, the forgiveness couldn't fully occur. On top of this, what your Dad is really saying is, 'I don't want your forgiveness or a relationship with you. I just want your truck and your Keys.' Do you get it? Your Dad has been acting like a 'boy' ever since I can remember."

There was a long and painful silence on the end of the phone. I felt Abe was looking at his whole life from out of a vacuum. For the first time in his life, Abe was starting to see his father wasn't really looking for a close relationship with him, because he was sidetracked by his own deficiencies. I could see the dynamics in Abe's life so clearly. I knew it was time for Abe to get back his Keys. Actually I knew the time for this was long overdue. I then said, "Abe, do you see you have never stood up to your Dad and told him honestly how you feel? Can you see you have never addressed him for the offenses he has committed against you?

"After you realize you are lost and have gone down the wrong rabbit trail, you have to back up to where you got on the wrong trail in order to get back on the right path. This means you have to figure out where you first lost your Keys, and go back and get them. Unfortunately for you, you have to go all the way back to when you were a little kid, just like I did."

Abe breathed a deep sigh on the phone. I could tell he was seeing the problem, but the thought of confronting his Dad was just too big to look at. He said, 'Well, you have given me a lot to think about. I would like to get back to you after I mull some of this over."

I said to Abe, "Before you go, I need to talk about the time I told you to leave my home two years ago."

"I would like you to know I love you, and I was only enforcing boundaries I felt were important for my family. My actions were nothing against you personally. I set boundaries with everyone for the purpose of protecting my wife from all the control and weirdness occurring. I know it was the right thing for me to do. Do you see now what was going on?"

Abe then said, "Yes, I see I was missing it. I am really sorry for not listening to you." Of course, I explained to Abe the difference between "Sorry" and "Forgive me," so we could fully repair the foundations of our relationship. After a heartfelt discussion about our past conflicts, we both experienced some real healing in our relationship. I felt the phone call ended cordially and on a positive note. Even though Abe was not in a place to deal with his life head on yet, I had a peace that he was legitimately going to give the whole Keys principle an honest look. I needed to hear the Truth quite a few times before I really "got it" enough to make significant changes in my life.

A few weeks later, Abe called me. He was very happy. In his voice I could immediately hear there was something different about him, something stronger. He said excitedly, "Scott, you would not believe what happened! My Dad called me, and tried to manipulate me into coming to his house for Christmas. I could not believe it. It was so clear. He was almost ordering me to come spend Christmas Eve with him. For crying out loud, I am 30 years old.

"When I told him I could not make it, he started telling me how my Mom had already expected me to come. He said families should be together for Christmas, and it was God's will for everyone to be together. It was crazy. Something inside me snapped. I told him I was spending Christmas Eve with my wife's family, and I thought he was trying to manipulate me with his religious references to 'Honoring your parents.'

"I have stood up to him many times before, but usually I would angrily just be a jerk and not tell him what was really on my mind. When he heard me confront him with the manipulation thing, he totally changed his tune. He started to act like I had hurt him, and I was being unreasonable. I told him he was acting like a little kid, and I had already made plans months ago to spend Christmas Eve with my wife's parents.

"I then said to him something I had always wanted to say. I said, 'Dad, you have used this type of tactics to get your way my whole life, and it is over. I am going to do what I feel is best for April and me. I honor you as my Dad, but this does not mean I have to go along with all of your bull#*% #. I am taking back the Keys from you right now!

"Can you believe it? I told him I was taking my Keys back. I didn't even know if the Keys were real until I said this. Well, I know they are real now. My Dad was totally taken aback and he got angry. But I didn't care. I knew I was being honest with him. He then said to me that I obviously was not in a 'Godly' place, because I used profanity. I could not believe it. This is exactly what I thought about you when you told me to leave your house. Instead of seeing how I broke your boundaries, I only saw how you were dealing with me in a way I didn't like. I was seeing myself in my Dad. This was incredible!"

My heart was actually beating hard as Abe spoke. I then proceeded to tell Abe, "I call this thing 'The Machine!' It is like this huge steel machine trying to eat up people and spit them out like fodder."

Abe agreed wholeheartedly. I said to him, "So you got your Keys back!" He replied, "A few of them, but I know there are more to get. But yes, as you would say 'I got my truck back. And it is a little beat up.'"

We both laughed and then I recalled something. I said, "If I remember correctly, your Dad used to take your real truck all the time without asking you back in your younger days. I never even thought about this when we talked last week."

Abe was amazed as he said, "Yes, Yes! My Dad was notorious for just borrowing my stuff without asking. I felt like I had to let him because he was my Dad. This is too incredible. You know, even though my Dad was mad at me, he called me back the next day and was very nice. It was like he was showing me respect for the first time in my life."

I then said to Abe, "Wow, this is amazing. You can see why I am so adamant about keeping my Keys, can't you?" He responded he was now in total agreement with my actions. Abe and I talked for another hour, and I cannot ever remember feeling so close to him as a friend. I felt I had really helped him, even though he really did all the work.

Today Abe and I are both on the road to victory, and it is great. For years, we would talk about unimportant things as we were getting annihilated by family dysfunction. I know in the future, God has two more Patriarchs he can count on. I am excited to say my life is strong and intact, and I am now building my family in victory. I am looking forward to being able to impart this same victory to many other Men.

It feels right to be a Patriarch, and it is wonderful to see my wife be free, happy, loved and protected as she grows into the woman she is called to be. She is now living without fear, and on or near Mother's Day in 2009, my wife became pregnant with our first child, and we are so HAPPY!

"Life is about relationships, and healthy relationships are born through honesty."

Relational Circles:

In the previous section, we saw how Scott strengthened relationships in his life by setting some basic boundaries. Next, I would like to share with you how to categorize the relationships in your life using proper boundaries. This tool is called "Relational Circles," and it will greatly help you navigate through life as you strive to build strong and healthy relationships around you. One thing I have learned is this: if you desire to become more spiritual, you must become more relational. Being relational is being spiritual.

Many males fall into the same trap Scott fell into, where family and cultural systems train young males to unconditionally submit to older family members under the guise of being spiritual. This is especially prevalent regarding relationships we have with our fathers and mothers. After we are "Bar Mitzvaed" and become Men, we are all called to honor our parents.

The Bible promises in the 5th commandment, if we honor our parents, we shall live long in the land and things will go well for us. However, we are not called to obey them. Adults are not called by God to unconditionally obey other adults, ever. It is children, not adults, who are called to obey their parents. When a "boy" becomes a Man, he is no longer under the jurisdiction of his father. Of course it is always beneficial to get wise counsel. Hopefully, our parents are a primary resource for such wisdom and counsel.

Our responsibility as Men is to seek wise counsel and then make decisions based on our best judgment. Each one of us will receive the rewards and consequences of our decisions. If adult males were called to obey their parents until they passed away, an 80-year old Man would be expected to unconditionally obey the counsel and orders from his 100-year old father. This is a ridiculous concept, because it doesn't allow for a Man's sovereignty. This dysfunction keeps him in the state of being a "boy" indefinitely.

If you desire to be a Man and a successful Patriarch, you will put away the belief system that you have to be obedient to older family members or church leaders just because they say so. Submitting in this manner is dysfunctional and a killer to your Mandate. Patriarchs are never to give away their sovereignty.

As we have seen throughout this book, it is common for a "boy" to want to take orders unconditionally. This is because he will have someone to blame if things do not work out well. It is irresponsible for a Man to take counsel, and then blame the person who gave the counsel. This is a common way males give away their Keys of authority. As discussed in earlier chapters, we saw a Man should always allow his heart and his conscience to be his guide, once he is of age and has been "Bar Mitzvaed." A Patriarch is not to allow himself to be influenced by the ungodly traditions of men, or the controlling hierarchies of manmade systems.

It is all about relationships. Our number one goal and Mandate in life is to build close and intimate relationships with God and the people around us. Most people believe this is true, but very few know how to go about the task of building relationships productively. Many of us are untrained and unskilled in building relationships; therefore, our interaction with others actually hurts our relationships more than it helps.

I used to have the belief it was loving and relational to give people the benefit of the doubt, and always let them in very close until they proved themselves to be unworthy of this position. I would go for years giving people the benefit of the doubt in hope they would someday live up to my expectations. Of course this rarely ever occurred. I found myself consistently throwing good energy after bad in an attempt to justify my position, wishing someday the person would finally get it.

There is a word the old timers use for this type of belief system; it is called "stupidity." Counselors just call it codependency. Many of us have paid a dear price to learn this important lesson. It is a tough pill to swallow to learn you have spent years of your life and thousands of dollars supporting "unsafe" people. You may be working against God by hindering the growth and health of your loved ones.

Unrealistic Expectations:

Over the years, I have learned it is unfair and wrong to put a person in a position they have not earned. This will eventually hurt both of the people in the relationship, because it is based on unrealistic expectations. Unrealistic expectations are a distorted version of hope. Hope desires a person will obtain health and victory. Unrealistic expectations presume health and victory will come our way, and on our timetable. Hope is from

God, and it requires trust in Him. Unrealistic expectations are from our desire to control others, and from Satan's desire to deceive us.

We would never allow a four year old child to drive a car. This is because a four year old is untrained and unable to perform the task of driving both emotionally and physically. This would be abusive to both the child and to those who are in or around the car. It is equally abusive to put someone in your inner circle that does not have the maturity and the tools to be there.

I have a Pastor friend who says, "Life is difficult! And life is even more difficult when you are stupid." His message is really a simple one. He is saying if you are untrained as a Man, you are going to suffer and life is going to be frustrating and hard. Let us strive to be trained as good soldiers and use the tools available to us, so we can experience the joy of total victory.

"The General hopes and trusts, that every officer and Man, will endeavor so to live and act, as becomes a Christian Soldier defending the dearest Rights and Liberties of his country."

George Washington

(July 9, 1776 - Generals Orders to the troops 5 days after the Declaration of Independence was signed.)

Without further delay here is a very helpful tool that will assist in keeping relationships and boundaries in your life in order. This one tool has brought victory in the lives of many Men. I call it "Relational Circles."

Our Relational Circles:

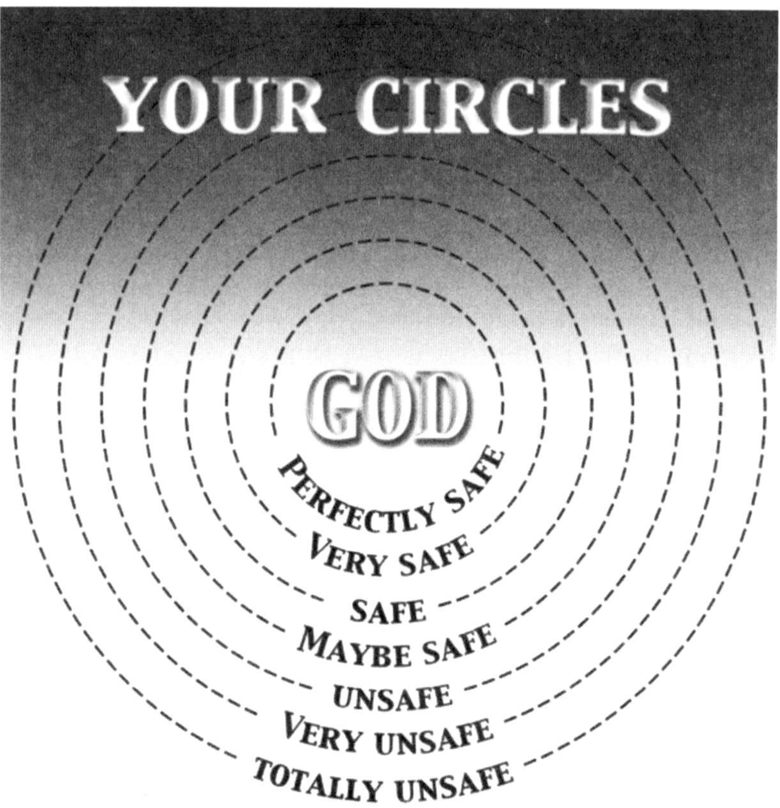

This diagram will help you decide where to categorize different relationships in your life. It is designed to protect both you and those in your sphere of influence from getting hurt in relationships. People in your life will have different levels of maturity and varying degrees of safeness with you. In this diagram, you will find the degree of safety listed in different concentric circles.

"The degree of intimacy you have in relationship with a person should be directly related to the degree of safety they have in relating with you."

Scott's family had developed a cultural belief system that promoted males to remain "boys." When a family member imposed on Scott, he was expected to violate his conscience by submitting to the family member as a "boy," regardless of what his heart was saying. Through training, honesty, and resolve, he quickly shattered the bondage of his family's age-old belief system. He obtained a great victory in his life by enforcing the boundaries of his heart. Family members who continued to show a blatant disregard for Scott's boundaries were moved into a place where they were categorized as "unSafe."

What does this mean? No, we are not trying to go back to the Old Testament treatment of leprosy by labeling people as "unclean." Acknowledging a person as "unSafe" is no different then acknowledging a person does not know how to drive a car. You may still let them ride in the car with you, but you are a fool to let them actually drive the car. This would be unwise and irresponsible.

Acknowledging someone is "unSafe," is only the realization this person does not have the maturity level to have access into your personal space at times. If you give an "unSafe" person access into your personal space, you will risk losing something precious. Eventually an "unSafe" person can be the demise of a marriage, a business, a friendship and even our children's safety. Due to certain people's propensity to abuse and control others, sometimes it is necessary to establish an emotional restraining order to keep them away from damaging a life. This is why it is so important to monitor how safe the people are that we allow close to us.

Please remember, just because a person is temporarily categorized as "unSafe," this does not mean they will always be categorized this way. Just as a person can be taught to drive a car, they can also be taught to be "Safe" in relationships. As people begin to relate properly in relationships and respect the boundaries of others, they will of course be invited to become closer in relationships. This process should occur at a slow rate, because it is very easy to fall into old patterns. Over time, it is encouraging to know anyone can learn to become a "Very Safe" person.

For those of you who feel this concept of categorizing people in circles feels a little too much like the "Circle of Trust" in the movie "Meet The Parents," we have already subconsciously set up degrees of closeness in the relationships in our lives. We all have enemies, acquaintances, friends, close friends and even very close friends. Most people acknowledge they already have an "Inner Circle" of friends. The question is; do you want to do the work it requires to become a "Very Safe" person for those "Inner Circle" of friends?

As a Patriarch, it is helpful to examine your relationships one step further and actually have a conscious plan of how to relate with people in your sphere of influence. Setting boundaries is not intended for the purpose of controlling the behaviors of those around us. Boundaries are made and enforced to stop others from controlling you. Boundaries are a way to take charge as a Man and Patriarch, and to put away the "boy" in you who has a tendency to be a victim of controlling powers.

Often, an "unSafe" person may have incredible feelings of love for you. Just because someone has love for you does not mean they are "Safe" for you, nor does it mean they will go to great lengths to display love for you. Life has clearly shown us people are capable of having intense feelings of love for one another without the maturity and training to act or behave lovingly.

In other words, if someone is prone to talk poorly about you and breach confidence with information you have given them, this person should not be confided in and this person is "unSafe" to a degree. If a person consistently lies to you, betrays you or steals from you, this person is definitely "Very unSafe" and should not be given any intimate access to you. Giving an "unSafe" person intimate access to your personal life is a foolish decision, because it caters to the person's weakness, and ultimately your relationship with them will be seriously compromised.

Called To Be "Safe":

Remember, everyone is called on a journey to learn how to become more relational, loving and "Safe." Categorizing someone as "unSafe" is merely expressing what our heart has already told us about a person. This practice is an exercise in Truth and honesty, and it is the best way to assist someone to work on becoming a "Safe" person in life. The most loving thing we can do for an "unSafe" person is to put them in a relational circle allowing us to best interact with their degree of maturity and honesty. Healthy relationships are born through honesty.

If you want to quickly figure out how safe a person is, just take a look at Man vs. "boy." Only God is "Perfectly Safe;" therefore, only God is allowed complete and unrestrained access to our heart, emotions and feelings. Men who have continually proven to operate in the Man category on the Man vs. "boy" list should be considered "Safe" or "Very Safe." Weaker Men who sometimes struggle with taking responsibility and who may be selfish are considered "Maybe Safe." A "boy" is either "unSafe" or "Very unSafe" depending on how irresponsible he is. Satan is an example of the ultimate "boy," and he is "Totally unSafe."

Important! The degree of safety has nothing to do with bloodline or family. It is normal and natural for family members to have a close place in your life. In today's society, there are many unhealthy people and family systems; therefore, it is a foolish decision to give family members a position of intimacy only because they are family.

If you have a family member who hurts you or who talks badly about you consistently, this person is "unSafe" or "Very unSafe." Family members are not to be given a free pass into intimacy in your life just because they are family. There are certain responsibilities we will always have with family. Allowing family members to control or abuse the relationship by taking on a position they do not have maturity for is not a luxury we can afford.

The degree of intimacy you have with a person should represent their level of safety. This is why Jesus of Nazareth said, **"For whosoever shall do the will of my Father which is in heaven, the same is My brother and sister, and Mother."**[3] If you are loving, considerate and obedient to God, you shall be awarded a closer relationship with Him, and will be treated like a family member.

Intimacy in relationships is the reward for behaving in a loving manner. This same principle goes for accountability. The degree of accountability we have with a person should mirror the degree of closeness we have in relationship to them. If you are highly accountable to someone you do not know very well relationally, it is time to restructure your Relational Circles.

King David understood this concept when he wrote the very first Psalm in the Old Testament. He wrote,

---

3 Matthew 12:50, KJV

"Blessed is the Man who does not walk in the counsel of the wicked or stand in the way of sinners or sin in the seat of mockers. But his delight is in the law of the LORD, and on His law he meditates day and night. He is like a tree planted by streams of water, which yields its fruit in season and whose leaf does not wither. Whatever he does shall prosper."
King David of Israel – Psalms 1

Understanding we need to set boundaries with the "unSafe" people in our lives is the beginning of prospering in all of our relationships. The good news is we can easily rectify past relational mistakes, and conduct an inventory on where people are positioned in our lives. Remember, the degree of intimacy you have in relationship with a person should be directly related to the degree of safeness you feel in relating with that person.

Look at the diagram and see where the close relationships fall in your life. Do you have confidants and close friends who are "unSafe?" If so, you are compromising your walk as a Man, and you are not protecting yourself or your loved ones. Remember, if you are bringing "unSafe people" into your inner circles, you are exposing your loved ones to the danger of "unSafe" people and the repercussion of your poor decisions.

Intimacy is something that must be earned, and it is earned through honesty, forgiveness and loving behaviors ***over time***. It may take years for a person to truly become "Very Safe." The worst part about having "unSafe people" in your inner circles is "Safe" people will have nothing to do with you. A "Safe" person has no choice but to put you in an "unSafe" circle, because you are allowing your Keys to be stolen by people who should not be close to you.

What does all of this mean? Here is where the rubber meets the road. "unSafe" people steal Keys! "unSafe" people will take advantage of you when they see an opening in your life. As a Patriarch, you cannot allow someone to babysit your children or take care of your family members unless they are "Very Safe." You do not go into a business partnership with a person who has not proven over time to be "Safe" or "Very Safe." It also means you do not allow family, siblings or parents to have significant input into your life unless they have proven to be Truthful and "Safe." This also means you will not hire an employee, or allow them to have close access to your financial or personal information, unless they are tried and proven worthy of this position. They must be "Safe!"

As we learned in Scott's story, no one should be allowed in your home unless you desire him or her to be there and they have proven to be generally "Safe" for you. This also means you will constantly monitor your "Safe Circles," and remove "unSafe" people from having close access into your life who could possibly compromise you, your family or your friends.

Getting your Relational Circles in order will greatly assist you to be the Patriarch you are called to be. I urge you to consider the people you have let into your life. How safe are they? Do you need to make adjustments in your life? Have you put people in a Relational Circle where they do not belong? It is easy to get your relationships in order. Just ask your heart about the people around you. If you are honest with yourself, you will have no trouble at all getting a healthy perspective on the relationships in your life. One of the most loving things we can do is relate with people in a way that allows us to best serve them.

"The most important single ingredient in the formula of success is knowing how to get along with people."
Theodore Roosevelt – 26th President of the United States

Our Relational Circles:

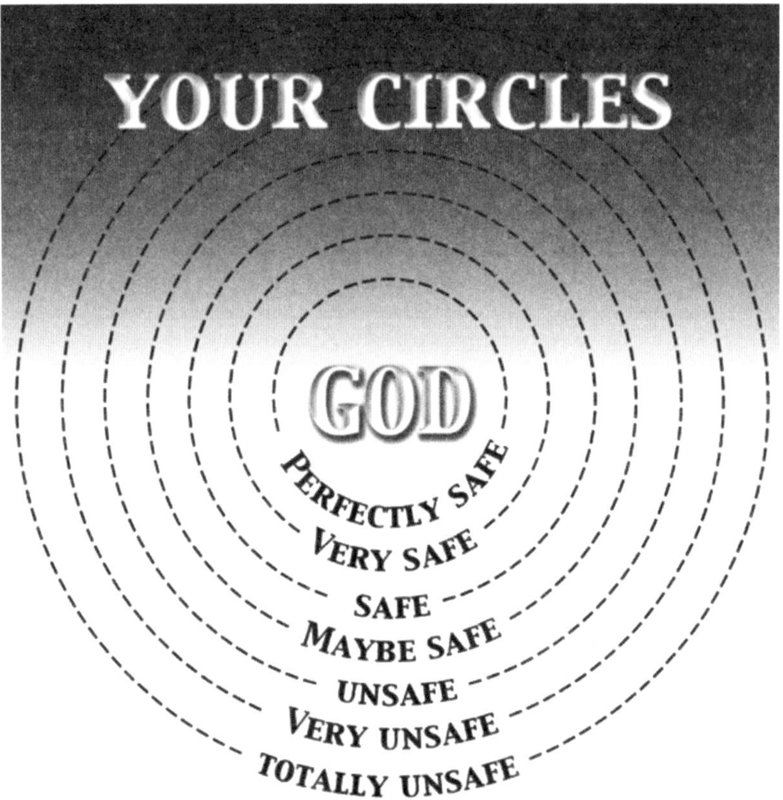

Using the "Relational Circles" diagram helps us to be free from setting up false or unreasonable expectations. If you are putting your wife or children in the "Perfectly Safe" category, you are doing them a disservice. No one can live up to the expectations they will be perfectly understanding, perfectly forgiving and perfectly loving. If you have put a stranger in the circle of "Very Safe," you are jeopardizing the peace of your family and your relationships by gambling on someone whom you have not checked out thoroughly. A Patriarch will not gamble with the relationships he is called to build and nurture. This means he will not gamble with his family.

Giving away your intimacy and your friendship to an "unSafe" person is like casting pearls before swine. Allowing healthy and "Safe" people to share and assist in your life, is like a sweet smelling incense bringing further joy and victory to you as a Patriarch. "Safe" people will assist you in acquiring and keeping your Keys of authority. "unSafe" people will consciously or subconsciously work to steal your Keys, and they will actively work to keep you from retrieving your Keys back when lost.

"unSafe" people will also hinder your walk with God. They will hinder your marriage, your business, your joy and your legacy as a Man, if they are allowed to enter into your intimate circles. On the other hand, "Safe" people will encourage your relationship with God, and they will have a deep desire for you to prosper in all areas of your life. Equally important, a "Safe" person will possess the tools and maturity to actually assist you in your quest to fulfill your Mandate as a Patriarch.

Many of us have allowed "unSafe" people close to us, because they supposedly professed to be "Christians." There are many stories of people who were abused, stolen from and molested, because an "unSafe' person was allowed by an untrained male to spend the night in the family home. In regards to our evaluation of the safeness of a person, missing it is not an option.

The price we pay for mistakes is much too high for us to go through life in a cavalier manner assuming everything will work out fine. We must understand the best way to love someone is to establish the relationship and intimacy upon the honesty, love and trust they have displayed towards us.

Even Jesus told us, if we are going to help someone and be like the "Good Samaritan," we should take the person in need to a hotel. We do not need to expose ourselves and our families to "unSafe" people in the name of the gospel, and then allow them to sleep in the bed next to our most prized possessions. Love is expressed when we build relationships upon the maturity of where a person actually is, not upon where we want them to be.

It is fraudulent, presumptuous and unloving to pretend someone is healthier then they actually are. Our error in judgment does everyone a disservice. We owe it to our loved ones and ourselves to take the time to examine if we truly are conducting our relationships in a healthy manner. Giving a person "the benefit of the doubt" should only be done when we are not sacrificing the relationships with the loved ones we are first Mandated to protect.

Jesus was the ultimate "Safe" person, because He was perfectly loving, perfectly honest and perfectly trustworthy. If you truly study His life, you will see He also modeled for us different degrees of intimacy in various relationships in His life. He displayed perfect love by establishing perfect boundaries. He only shared His full heart with His Father in heaven. He developed three "Very Safe" friends named Peter, John and James who were allowed a more intimate relationship with Him. He loved His other disciples equally, but He did not allow them the same intimacy for relational reasons He alone knew.

Jesus had numerous other relationships that were all given different degrees of access to Him personally. By modeling His life, we can see establishing healthy relationships is the job of a Patriarch. As a Patriarch, you will find setting boundaries and keeping healthy people close to you is essential as you walk on your road to victory.

"No Codependency" Clause:

Now that you know how to set relational boundaries with your Relational Circles, here is a fun parody on how we can keep from entering into unhealthy codependent relationships. Before you enter into any relationship, I offer you a special contractual clause you can use to help stay free from those nasty and undesirable codependent relationships and all the grief that comes with them. By adding this clause to your current relational contracts, you will ensure you will live a long and prosperous life, and your Relational Circles will always joyfully remain in perfect order. (Well maybe not, but we are going to have some fun with this.)

It is important to remember The "No Codependency" Clause is impossible to fulfill without knowing the loving principle of forgiveness. We will all make many mistakes as we function in relationships. If we have purposed in our hearts to do the right thing, we can become safe and helpful to those who we love. Remember, forgiveness is the answer to all relationship problems. As we read in Chapter 4, forgiveness is the antiseptic keeping the wounds of relational cuts from getting infected. You may want to read the "No Codependence" Clause as a prayer for how you would like to see the relationships in your life look like.

"No Codependency" Clause:

I hereby agree to not engage in a codependent relationship with________________. I will to do my utmost to keep my relational boundaries and circles in order, and I will love ________________ in such a manner that will encourage and assist him to fulfill his Mandate and live a long and healthy life. I will not drain or draw the life, energy or resources from ________________. I will obtain my own life and resources from the author of all life, God. I will do my best and fight in life to be a safe person, and I will strive to be a giver and not a taker. I will honor all relational boundaries set by __________________, and I will set healthy boundaries in my Relational Circles with all other people in my sphere of influence. I will be absolutely and painfully honest with _________________. When problems or challenges in the relationship arise, I will not argue, and I will settle any breach in the relationship with forgiveness, honesty, perseverance and steadfast love. I will not attempt to control or manipulate__________________, and I will not work against God's will for him in any way. I will read "Man vs. boy" once a year to remind me of the importance of his Mandate and the power of walking with his Keys of authority in hand. I will not steal Keys from_________________, and I will always look out for his best interests. I will carry around prayers of success and blessings in my heart for _________________ at all times, and I will communicate regularly with him as the Lord leads. I will learn to love _________________ in a way he receives according to how God has made him, and I will diligently make sure I love myself so I am able to give love to him in a healthy manner.

Signed:_____________________________(A True Friend.)

A Relational Gospel:

Relationships are everything. All great deeds have one thing in common. Love for people. Jesus of Nazareth said something that is seared into my heart. **"Inasmuch as you have done it to the least of these my brethren, you have done it to me."**[4] To some, setting up boundaries and Relational Circles may look like a mean or cruel thing to do; however, true love is about protecting the relationships in your life at all cost.

Life is not merely about doctrine or family traditions. Life is about relationships. Let us hear what our hearts are crying out for. Let us hear what the Spirit of God is saying. Jesus of Nazareth came that we might learn about the most important relationship of all, our relationship with our Maker.

The next and last chapter in this book will present to you the most perfect and relational Man who ever walked the earth. Gear up to learn and behold the most revered Man who ever touched the hearts of mankind.

"There is no limit to what you can accomplish if you don't care who gets the credit."
Ronald Reagan – 40th President of the United States

4 Matthew 25:40, KJV

8

Behold The Man

The Perfect Man!

Jesus of Nazareth is the only Man in history to fully ace the Man vs. "boy" list. He never once behaved as a "boy" in selfishness, pride or rebellion. Look at the Man vs. "boy" list again and see all of the behaviors plaguing males ever since Adam first lost his Keys of authority in the Garden of Eden. When Adam chose not to take responsibility for protecting his Mandate and his wife in the garden, he failed miserably and became the first "boy" to acquiesce his authority to God's enemy.

Consider Jesus never once failed to protect and love His family members and friends. He truly was and is the perfect Man, and He is the ultimate role model for all Men. This is why the original Jewish disciples written about in the New Testament sacrificially followed Jesus of Nazareth and traveled to the ends of the known world on a mission to spread the good news our Savior had come.

This is a Bible?

When I was only 9 years old, I recall sitting in my 4th grade classroom when my teacher Mrs. Caird (Yes, I still remember her name) asked each person in the class to bring a book to school to read during "free reading" time. She suggested each one of us choose a book portraying a role model for us to learn from.

I recall looking up and pondering whom I would choose as my role model, and my choice came to me clearly. I remembered my Dad was reading about an incredible Man named Jesus in a paperback book. He had told me Jesus was the only perfect Man who ever lived, and I believed him. The next day I brought the book "Good News For Modern Man" to school, and I could not wait to read about this revered and respected Man.

As I began reading the Gospel of John, my heart began to melt as I hung on every word flowing out of the mouth of Jesus. I wanted to be just like Him. I wanted to be bold, sensitive and insightful like Him as He walked the lands of Israel helping and healing His people. I wanted to be loved and honored like He is.

Of course, this was before I read the end of the Book of John and saw how everyone abandoned and even crucified Him on a cross. After seeing the price He paid from allowing his people to crucify Him, I knew there was something very special and compelling about this honest and forthright Man from Nazareth, whose name was Jesus.

The words emitting from the pages in those days seemed to permeate deep within my heart and soul like a gentle and refreshing stream. At one point, my teacher passed by me and noticed what I was reading and she said, "You brought a Bible to school to read!" I was surprised by what she had said. The term "Bible" seemed so religious and boring to me.

My image of the Bible was a large 40-pound book with dark, heavy bindings and cobwebs on it. This book was a light paperback saying, "Good News" on the cover, and it was exciting and fulfilling to read. I turned the book around in amazement and looked at the cover thinking, "This is a Bible?" I could tell by the tone of her voice what I had done was good, and I could feel it was a bold move. My teacher then nodded her head in affirmation and approval as she gently walked by.

What was the power I was sensing in the book I was holding? Little did I know at the time the words in that book were the cornerstone for America, and they were the foundation of many great leaders who helped establish this great country. How could I even imagine this same book I held in my hands packed such power, within a few decades there would be Supreme Court Justices who would decide whether it was even legal to read the Bible in school or in the public square. As I read the incredible words flowing off the pages, there was one thing I knew for sure in my heart. I knew Jesus of Nazareth was indeed the Man He said He was. I knew He would be my number one role model for the rest of my days.

I have continued to study and learn of my role model throughout my entire life. Many Men who have learned to overcome have said to me, "These principles are great! Where did you learn them?" My answer to them will always be: "The Bible is where I learned to be a Man."

I can testify both the Old Testament (Hebrew Bible) and the New Testament declare Jesus of Nazareth was and is the perfect Man. His sinless nature has ushered into mankind the ability to walk in full victory as Men. To fully grasp how to be a Man, I encourage you to look at the person and the life of Jesus of Nazareth as told in the Scriptures. He really is the perfect study on the perfect Man.

The Final Building Block:

The first seven chapters of this book have been a presentation focused on the practical applications of how to walk as a Man and utilize the Keys of authority reserved for you. This final chapter is the capstone and the final building block for you to receive as you continue on your mission to complete your Mandate.

Chapter 8 is dedicated to sharing with you some of the technical and theological aspects of these applications, which will be very important to you as you continue on to victory as a Man. Throughout this journey of discovery, you will have the opportunity to *Behold The Man,* and learn of the person whose name is Jesus of Nazareth. My prayer is you will clearly see the significance of Jesus being the perfect Son of Man, as well as the perfect Son of God. I will say it again. Jesus is a Man, and He is the fullness of God dwelling in a human body.

For those of you who may not appreciate, or who are bored by the historical Truths bringing many to understand the principles I have shared with you thus far, once again I challenge you to reach way down within and prepare yourselves for a deeper knowledge of the perfect Man. It is time to do your due diligence and study the most important and relevant subject in history. This is the study of God Himself. This Biblical history and foundation of our faith will be the most powerful building block for your development as a Man. So prepare yourself to be bold enough to undertake the task of looking deeper into the Man named Jesus, and the Mandate He chose to undertake.

What's Under the Hood?

The process of learning about our God and walking fully as a Man is similar to the process of buying and owning a new car. You may first be impressed by the color and sleek design of your new vehicle. You may be excited by how fast the car accelerates, or how amazing it feels when you drive it. But there comes a time when you have to lift up the hood and say, "What is the horsepower really powering this machine?" This is the time you examine the engine specifications, all of the high tech design, and the state of the art components intricately placed within the body of the vehicle.

As you read through the history and life of the one Man I believe to be the ultimate role model to all Men, I ask you to carefully consider the amazingly detailed account of who Jesus of Nazareth really is, and why He chose to dwell among us. Just as billions of people have done before you, I ask you to *Behold The Man!*

Jesus In History:

About 3,400 years ago, Moses brought down from Mt. Sinai the written law given to him directly by God. Ever since this momentous event, the Jewish sons of Abraham have been expecting the forthcoming appearance of their Messiah in the form of a Man descending from the tribe of Judah. Some knew this Man was not just a gift to the Jews, but He was a gift to all mankind. The Old Testament gives numerous references and prophecies declaring of this Man, who would fulfill a multitude of achievements as the King and Savior of the world.

God promised there would come an anointed Man who would dwell in the midst of Israel as the Savior. God also promised He Himself would dwell in the midst of Israel, and He would save us from our sinful nature.

As promised in Zechariah the Lord said, **"Sing and rejoice, O daughter of Zion: for lo, I come, and I will dwell in the midst of thee."**[1] Zechariah tells us we should be happy because God Himself will dwell in the midst of us as the Son of God and as the Son of Man.

How could a Man fulfill the role of the Messiah when God himself declared he would be the Messiah? The answer is given in the name and the person of Jesus of Nazareth. History and Scripture has revealed Jesus of Nazareth was the perfect Son of God, and as such only Jesus Himself could dwell in the midst of us in the form of a Man, and recapture the Keys of authority lost by Adam.

Some 1400 years after Moses, at around 4 B.C., the people of Israel began to hear rumors throughout Judea about a Kingly child who was born in a manger in Bethlehem. An Angel sent by God made an incredible announcement to country shepherds abiding in a field as they were watching over their flock by night. **"And, lo, the Angel of the lord came upon them, and the glory of the Lord shone round about them: and they were sore afraid. And the Angel said unto them, Fear not: for behold, I bring you good tidings of great joy, which shall be to all people. For unto you is born this day in the city of David a Savior, which is Christ the Lord."**[2]

This incredible event resounded strong enough throughout the land for King Herod to pronounce the judgment of death upon every child under two years of age in Bethlehem, and in all the surrounding coastal towns. This was a futile attempt by the enemies of God to stamp out the existence of the beholden child, who was said to be the forthcoming King of the Jews.

Why were God's enemies so intent on destroying the King of the Jews? You the reader are more a part of this story than you may realize. The enemy was really out to destroy you. You will find throughout this chapter, if Jesus had been destroyed as a child, your Keys of authority would be unattainable. Your chance to become an overcoming son of God who overcomes would have been lost forever. In other words, you would be done.

---

1 Zechariah 2:10, KJV
2 Luke 2:9-10, KJV

A Governor Beholds The Man!

Thirty-three years after the shepherds were a witness to the birth of the Son of Man, the Governor of Judea, Pontius Pilate, entered into the judgment hall and asked Jesus of Nazareth the ultimate question; **"Are you the King of the Jews?"**[3] The profoundness and impact of this question has continued to alter the course of history throughout the world. By asking Jesus whether He was indeed the King of the Jews, Pilate was actually asking a much deeper and compelling question which affects every descendant of Adam who has ever lived. Is Jesus truly the Son of God, sent by God Himself to deliver mankind from its fallen condition?

Indeed the Man from Nazareth named Jesus did enter into Pilate's hall of judgment nearly 2000 years ago. To the amazement of both Jew and Gentile alike, Jesus was preceded by whisperings of how He declared Himself to be both the Son of God and the Son of Man. When Pilate asked Jesus whether He was indeed the King of the Jews, Pilate was well aware of the seriousness and the repercussions of the true answer. With the dignity of a true King, Jesus stood before Pilate and confirmed Pilate's fear by proclaiming, **"You are right in saying that I am a King. In fact for this reason I was born, and for this reason I came into the world, to testify to the Truth."**[4]

What was Governor Pilate's reaction to this astounding declaration? The Apostle John wrote of Pilate's response; **"Then Pilate therefore took Jesus, and scourged him. And the soldiers platted a crown of thorns, and put it on his head, and they put on him a purple robe, and said, 'Hail, King of the Jews!' And they smote him with their hands. Pilate therefore went forth again, and said unto them, Behold, I bring him forth to you, that you may know that I find no fault in him. Then came Jesus forth, wearing the crown of thorns, and the purple robe. And Pilate said unto them, *Behold The Man!*"**[5]

How powerful is this declaration! We are not just beholding ***a*** Man. We are beholding ***The*** Man as prophesied throughout the ages! It is also no coincidence Pilate's wife told Pilate, **"Have you nothing to do with that just Man: for I have suffered many things this day in a dream because of Him."**[6] Truly, the wife of Pilate also beheld the Man who

---

3 Matthew 27:11, NKJV
4 John 18:37, NKJV
5 John 19:1-5, KJV
6 Matthew 27:19, NKJV

was called Jesus of Nazareth. Do you *Behold the Man*? I propose your future victory depends on it. Read on and see this theme has continued to resonate throughout the history of mankind.

Zechariah Beholds the Man!

Amazingly, Zechariah in the Old Testament (Hebrew Bible) also foretold this exact terminology and declaration over 500 years beforehand. Zechariah wrote, **"Thus speaks the LORD of hosts, saying, Behold The Man whose name is The BRANCH; and he shall grow up out of his place, and he shall build the temple of the LORD: Even he shall build the temple of the LORD; and he shall bear the glory, and shall sit and rule upon his throne; and he shall be a priest upon his throne: and the counsel of peace shall be between them both."**[7] It is no coincidence Zechariah's reference to "Behold The Man," and "The Branch" points directly to the name of Jesus of Nazareth. The Hebrew word for branch is "netzer," which many scholars have attributed as the root word in the name "Nazareth." Jesus of Nazareth is really Jesus the "BRANCH." He was foretold as the coming King who would bear the glory as He rules upon His throne as a Man.

It is nothing short of phenomenal that the Old Testament foretold the exact name of Joshua as being our Savior and High Priest. Zechariah states, **"Hear now, O Joshua the High Priest, ... behold, I will bring forth my servant the BRANCH. ..."**[8] The Hebrew name for Jesus is *Joshua*. In this passage the name of *Joshua* (Jesus) is given in direct relation to the term "Branch." *Joshua* actually means, "Jehovah God is our Savior." The name "Jesus" (*Joshua*) gives us clear insight into who our Savior is, and what He came to accomplish.

This is why it is so significant Pilate was resolute when he chose the exact terminology to be written on the cross of Jesus. The Gospel of John says: **"And Pilate wrote a title, and put it on the cross. And the writing was, Jesus of Nazareth (Joshua The Branch) – The King of the Jews."**[9] Here you have the tremendous fulfillment of Zechariah's written prophecy fulfilled through the directions of the Roman Governor Pilate. The title "Jesus of Nazareth – The King of the Jews," continues to resonate

---

7 Zechariah 6:12-13, KJV
8 Zechariah 3:8, KJV
9 John 19:19, KJV

throughout the ages as a proclamation to all those who consider the Man, Christ Jesus.

The name of "Joshua" (Jesus) is precisely the same name the Angel told Mary to call her future son when he said, **"Behold, you shall conceive in your womb, and bring forth a son, and shall call his name 'Jesus' (Joshua). He shall be great, and shall be called the Son of the Highest (Son of God): and the Lord God shall give unto him the throne of his father David (Son of Man): and he shall reign over the house of Jacob forever; and of his kingdom there shall be no end."**[10]

As most of us well know from the Christmas story, Jesus' Mother was a young virgin woman named Mary who providentially descended from the prophesied tribe of Judah. Mary of course was also a far-reaching descendant of the very first Man, Adam. Therefore, she was a legal heir to the authority given to Man. The Angel of the Lord told Mary that Jesus would be the Son of God and the Son of Man, who would take back all earthly authority and keep it forever. There are those Keys again! This is a direct reference to Zechariah's vision. It also refers to the heavenly and earthly positions Jesus came to fulfill as both the King and the High Priest of all mankind.

The Original Band of Brothers:

Do you recall Shakespeare's Band of Brothers from Chapter 2? Zechariah's words are some of the most profound words in the Bible, because they point to Jesus as both our King and our High Priest. Zechariah also reveals the close relationship Joshua had with His companions, the real Band of Brothers. Zechariah recounts just as Mary had testified an Angel of the Lord said to him, **"Hear now, O Joshua the High Priest, you, and *your companions* that sit before you: for they are Men wondered at: for, behold, I will bring forth my servant the BRANCH... and I will remove the iniquity of that land in one day."** [11]

Truly, it was Jesus who took away the iniquity of the land in one day, as He willingly stretched out His arms and allowed the powers of darkness to crucify Him. We are His companions (Band of Brothers) as we sit before Him and acknowledge Him for who He is. He is Jesus of Nazareth (Joshua the Branch), and He is the perfect Man.

---

10 Luke 1:31-33, NKJV
11 Zechariah 3: 8-9, NKJV

In the Old Testament, Moses taught that the High Priest was the only Man who could enter into the Holy of Holies in the tabernacle of God. This occurred once a year to provide the sacrifice for sin for all the people of Israel. Joshua (Jesus) is presented to Zechariah as the High Priest **"clothed with filthy garments"** whose filthy garments are taken away from him. The High Priest Joshua (Jesus) is then shown to be a servant of the Lord who **"will remove the iniquity of that land in one day."** This is an accurate description of Jesus, who ultimately went to the Roman cross and took on the sin of all mankind (He took on our filthy garments), and became a sacrifice for sin through His atoning death. By this one act, and in that **"one day,"** Jesus removed all the shame and sin plaguing mankind since Adam first became a "boy."

Here is where you and I come into the story. The **"companions"** are us, if we have received Jesus for who He really is. We are the Lord's companions, the Band of Brothers who are the followers of Jesus of Nazareth. We behold the High Priest, because we know He is the "King of the Jews." It takes both revelation and vision to see Joshua (Jesus) is coming as both the High Priest (suffering servant) and finally as the King of Kings.

This is why Herod and God's enemy tried so hard to take Jesus out when he was a child in Galilee. All the theologians and scholars of the day knew the Messiah was to be born in Bethlehem, and He would be the King of the Jews. As the reigning King, Jesus promised to make kings and priests of us all, as we behold and model after Him and our Father in heaven. This is very bad news for God's enemy, because he knows as Men reclaim authority (Keys) and walk as kings and priests, his reign and control over the earth are over.

Those who have this revelation become a testimony for the Son of Man as we reign with him. We truly know who the servant really is, and we have obtained the answer to life's most pressing spiritual questions, because we have learned of our Mandates, our Keys, our Gates and our Callings. These companions see the Lord as both the Son of Man and the Son of God, who has come to serve and to rule mankind. This is a wonder for those of us who follow Him, because our identity as Men is directly related to the revelation of who Jesus is.

The followers of Jesus of Nazareth have received the revelation to "*Behold The Man!*" This is a spiritual call to arms to Men much deeper and much more important than Shakespeare's Band of Brothers. This call is the ultimate and eternal call to victory and salvation for all mankind. Jesus said to His disciples, **"I no longer call you servants, because a servant does not know his master's business. Instead, I have called you friends (Band of Brothers), for everything that I learned from my Father I have made known to you."**[12] And again Jesus declared, **"For whosoever shall do the will of God, the same is my brother..."**[13]

The followers of Jesus Christ who rise up to know Him are lifted from the place of servants, to the place of "friends" and even "Brothers," in a Calling to fight against the enemy of God. What could be more exciting than overcoming in our personal lives as Men, as we team up with other Men to obtain a complete and total corporate victory for our Lord?

This Band of Brothers is to be a sign and wonder to the world, because they are walking in the victory as true conquering Men. If "boys" are going to become Men and fully overcome, ultimately their faith must be in God, who is the author of their Manhood. No one else but God is allowed to get the credit for our Manhood, because He is the author and finisher of it. Men who see the Son of God and behold the suffering servant, who paid the uttermost price for them, will be the Men who fulfill their main purpose in life. This is the message given by Zechariah to all mankind. Do you behold Him?

Isaiah Beholds The Man!

The prophet Isaiah also used a version of the term "*Behold The Man!*" He said, *"Behold My Servant!"* and he foretold of Jesus' coming over 700 years before Jesus of Nazareth walked the earth as a Man. Look at this powerful foretelling of the Man to come, who is a loving and "mighty Man" and a "Man of war" and one who will bring forth to all mankind "justice and Truth." The following passage from Isaiah describes the nature and character of the perfect Man and asks you to behold Him who brings us the Spirit of God.

---

12 Luke 2:49, NKJV
13 Mark 3:35, NKJV

"Behold My Servant, whom I uphold, My Elect One in whom My soul delights! I have put My Spirit upon Him; He will bring forth justice to the Gentiles. He will not cry out, nor raise His voice, nor cause His voice to be heard in the street. A bruised reed He will not break, and smoking flax He will not quench; He will bring forth justice for Truth. He will not fail nor be discouraged, till He has established justice in the earth; and the coastlands shall wait for His law." Thus says God the LORD, Who created the heavens and stretched them out, Who spread forth the earth and that which comes from it, Who gives breath to the people on it, and spirit to those who walk on it: 'I, the LORD, have called You in righteousness, and will hold Your hand; I will keep You and give You as a covenant to the people, as a light to the Gentiles, to open blind eyes, to bring out prisoners from the prison, those who sit in darkness from the prison house. ...Let them give glory to the LORD, and declare His praise in the coastlands. The LORD shall go forth like a mighty Man; He shall stir up His zeal like a Man of war. He shall cry out, yes, shout aloud; He shall prevail against His enemies."[14]
The Hebrew Prophet Isaiah

Isaiah saw it was a Man who would descend from the line of Adam, who would truly recapture the Keys of authority lost in the Garden of Eden. The Apostle Paul wrote to believers in Rome the following revelation, as he clearly saw Isaiah's prophecy fulfilled in Jesus of Nazareth. **"For if by one Man's offense death reigned by one; much more they which receive abundance of grace and of the gift of righteousness shall reign in life by one, Jesus Christ. Therefore as by the offense of one judgment came upon all men to condemnation; even so by the righteousness of one the free gift came upon all men unto justification of life."** [15] Simply stated, one Man, Adam, lost the Keys. Another Man, Jesus, rescued the Keys. Isaiah made it clear you can reign in life with your King, if only you receive the free gift of the Holy Spirit offered to you through Him.

14 Isaiah 42:1-7, 12-13, NKJV
15 Romans 5:17-18, KJV

Our Role Model and Hero:

Men were created with a deep down need to follow a role model. During America's foundation and early years, the role models for Men were Men like George Washington, Abraham Lincoln and Robert E. Lee. In the past century Men like Theodore Roosevelt, Winston Churchill, Martin Luther King Jr. and Ronald Reagan may have been our role models; however, over the past 2000 years the one Man who has been most modeled throughout the world has been Jesus of Nazareth.

"I am enthralled by the luminous figure of the Nazarene... No one can read the gospels without feeling the actual presence of Jesus. His personality pulsates in every word. No myth is filled with such life."
Albert Einstein – Scientist

It is so easy to lie on the couch and be lazy and say: "Nobody is perfect, and therefore I really do not have to try that hard to be perfect. It does not matter I am so messed up. Everyone is messed up." The Truth is there is someone who walked perfect as a Man, and His name is Jesus of Nazareth. God is so personal and so relational in His interaction with you. He knows the perfect way to inspire and communicate with you. After reading this book, you know Jesus had to become a Man to legally obtain the Keys lost by Adam, but His coming is so much more profound and personal.

Men need approachable and touchable role models and heroes whom they can strive to become. Men can identify with Jesus of Nazareth because they can behold and know Him on a personal level. God created Man to be in a close relationship with Him. He is a relational God, and we are made in His image to desire close and personal relationships with others. He knows Men will not be overly inspired to mimic a distant and untouchable divinity, where holiness is unattainable and unknowable.

Jesus of Nazareth came as a Man. He is real, approachable and even touchable. The companions foretold by Zechariah sit at the feet of Jesus, because He is approachable. We are allowed to sit before our brother and our King. There is no other place we want to be. Seeing Jesus walk as a Man is both encouraging and inspiring because we can relate to Him personally and strive to obtain His perfect character.

"Perfection is not attainable, but if we chase perfection we can catch excellence."
Vince Lombardi

Thank God we do have a perfect and true example of a Man to follow. The good news is Jesus is a complete, mature and perfect Man. All we have to do is *Behold The Man!,* and then surrender our lives to Him. Every Man must learn Jesus really is 100% Man and 100% God to fully appreciate what God has done for us. Even Jesus had to learn who He truly was as He grew into Manhood. Jesus' revelation of his identity occurred thru a process of learning and obeying throughout His life. History tells us He diligently searched the scriptures to learn about His Father, and to seek the depth of who He Himself was as the Son of Man and the Son of God.

The Physician Luke tells us in his account of the gospel how Jesus remained in Jerusalem alone after the Passover feast when He was twelve years old. Jesus then told His parents, **"Why were you searching for me? Did not you know I had to be in my Father's house?"**[16] Even at the young age of twelve, Jesus astonished the scholars and theologians of the day by closely listening to them, and asking them deep questions about God and the scriptures. This must have been shortly after Jesus of Nazareth was "Bar Mitzvaed." It appears He took on the responsibility of His Calling and Mandate by listening and learning from the most honored and taught Men of His day, without his earthly parent's direct consent.

The important revelations He learned as a young Man later developed in the heart and mind of Jesus the Man. He entered into the same temple 18 years later at the age of 30, and declared, **"Is it not written, My house shall be to all nations the house of prayer? But you have made it a den of thieves!"**[17] Jesus then proceeded to make whips and force out every

---

16 Luke 2:49, NKJV
17 Matthew 21:13, NKJV

ungodly male from the temple, making a statement He had the authority as the Son of God to cleanse and keep the temple.

Over the years, through obedience and studying, Jesus listened to and learned from His heavenly Father, as well as from the respected elders of His time. He searched the Scriptures, and communed with His Father as He learned His Father's house was His house, and it was His duty to oversee and build it up. Jesus knew the Keys to the house were His.

What a powerful Truth. Jesus had to learn through obedience just like every Man. I would expect nothing less of my role model. Paul of Tarsus clarified this further when he wrote to the Messianic Jews about Jesus of Nazareth. He said concerning Jesus, **"Although He was a Son, he learned obedience from what He suffered and, once made perfect, He became the source of eternal salvation for all who obey him..."**[18] Learning to walk as a Man is something we can identify with in Jesus. He had all the fleshly and earthly temptations all Men have to overcome, except He overcame fully and never sinned even once. This is our perfect role model!

Have you suffered in your life? Have the trials and tribulations of the effects of a sinful world taken its toll on you? We indeed have a role model who can identify with our hurts. In every way, He has experienced the pains and the grueling realities of an imperfect world. But just as He suffered and was made perfect as the Son of God, He is asking all Men to follow His path and endure their pains and tribulations for the purpose of becoming perfect and refined.

There is a wonderful purpose in our trials and our failures. We must allow God to use our experiences to refine our hearts with His understanding and His wisdom. Allow the words of Jesus to comfort your heart and your soul, as He gives you a promise of a better today.

"Come unto me, all you who labour and are heavy laden, and I will give you rest. Take my yoke upon you and learn of me, for I am meek and lowly in heart: and you shall find rest unto your souls. For my yoke is easy, and my burden is light."[19]
Jesus of Nazareth – Book of Matthew

---

18 Hebrews 5:8-9, NKJV
19 Matthew 11:28-29, NKJV

As we head toward the final stretch of our lives, let us all use our time well and allow God to refine and purify us as the silversmith refines silver. You will find as you are experiencing the fiery trials of life, the Son of Man will show up with you in the furnace to protect you, just as we see in the Book of Daniel. As you trust in Jesus, the strength and courage of the Son of God will come upon you. He will impart His relational health and guidance, enabling you to overcome and walk through every trial in life. Jesus proved this could be accomplished, and He did it as a Man. So can you.

"Follow Me, and I will make you fishers of Men."[20]
Jesus of Nazareth – Book of Matthew

The Real Man, Jesus:

In every respect, the Bible clearly shows Jesus was a Man's Man. The following situations are just a few of the numerous times Jesus of Nazareth displayed courage, faith, authority and strength, thus showing why He indeed is a worthy Man to be honored and followed. Jesus is a Man!

- Jesus boldly cleansed the holy temple in Jerusalem when it was filled with thousands of businessmen, soldiers and religious leaders, by brandishing whips. He displayed His true authority as He gave strong orders for all merchants and moneychangers to clear out declaring, **"My house shall be a house of prayer, and you have made it a den of thieves!"**[21]
- Jesus directly confronted the head religious authorities of Jerusalem, face to face, repeatedly exposing them as "hypocrites" even though the potential repercussions would be death on the cross.
- In the garden of Gethsemane, Jesus calmly faced many of the chief rulers of Jerusalem and a multitude of Roman soldiers who were carrying swords and staves. Jesus fearlessly challenged their motives

20 Matthew 4:19, NKJV
21 Matthew 21:13, NKJV

and Manhood as He asked them why they came at night to arrest Him when he preached openly and accessibly in the Synagogue in the daytime.

- Jesus protected the prostitute in strength and tenderness. He stood off a huge crowd of Scribes, Pharisees and Elders by stating to them **"He that is without sin among you, let him first cast a stone at her."** [22]
- At the cross, Jesus willingly and knowingly gave His life for those He loves by stretching out His arms and allowing the Roman soldiers to pierce His hands and feet, even unto death.

Do you *Behold The Man,* and see Jesus of Nazareth for who he is? Jesus of Nazareth truly is the Son of God, walking in an earthly body as the Son of Man. To our shame, our modern culture has often portrayed Jesus in various pictures, movies, TV and likenesses as a feminized, soft-spoken first century metro sexual with delicate features and silky white skin. In the outward and natural sense, the real Jesus of Nazareth was a tough and skilled Jewish carpenter who spent most of His first 30 years lifting stones and cutting wood in the rugged and hot terrain of Northern Israel.

Can you see Him walking up and down the steep, stone filled mountains of Galilee, muscling his way over the rocky slopes? I see Jesus as a strong and able-bodied craftsman, with calloused hands, tan skin and a healthy determination. Like most Men of his day, Jesus would have persevered through life. Life in Galilee consisted of working and sweating in the heat, while fighting wind and dust and the elements of weather, in a daily battle to care for and protect your loved ones. In a physical sense, the hard lands of Northern Israel forced "boys" to become Men.

From the records history gives us, Jesus of Nazareth was also a devout student of the Word of God, who studied the Holy Scriptures to the point where respected scholars and laymen alike called Him the honored and revered title of "Rabbi." When Jesus was a 30-year-old Man, He began to declare His purpose as Son of Man here on earth, as well as our purpose as sons of the Most High God.

Upon his return home to Nazareth, He went into the Jewish Synagogue on the Sabbath day and stood up to read from the Scriptures

---

22 John 8:7, NKJV

to the very people with whom He had grown up. The book of Isaiah was brought to Him, and He found the place where both His Mandate and the Mandate of every Man who accepts the call are written. Read the words carefully, because in them is a special Mandate for the Men of today.

Our Mandate – Isaiah 61:

"The Spirit of the Lord GOD is upon me; because the LORD hath anointed me to preach good tidings unto the meek; he hath sent me to bind up the brokenhearted, to proclaim liberty to the captives, and the opening of the prison to them that are bound;

To proclaim the acceptable year of the LORD, and the day of vengeance of our God; to comfort all that mourn;

To appoint unto them that mourn in Zion, to give unto them beauty for ashes, the oil of joy for mourning, the garment of praise for the spirit of heaviness; that they might be called trees of righteousness, the planting of the LORD, that he might be glorified.

And they shall build the old wastes, they shall raise up the former desolations, and they shall repair the waste cities, the desolations of many generations.

And strangers shall stand and feed your flocks, and the sons of the alien shall be your plowmen and your vinedressers.

But you shall be named the Priests of the LORD: Men shall call you the Ministers of our God: you shall eat the riches of the Gentiles, and in their glory shall you boast yourselves.

For your shame you shall have double; and for confusion they shall rejoice in their portion: therefore in their land they shall possess the double: everlasting joy shall be unto them."

Standing Orders For Our Mandate:

Did you catch your Mandate? This is the answer to the cry of every Man's heart, and the battle creed for the Band of Brothers. The word "they" in Isaiah 61 is directly talking about you and me. This Mandate calls us to have joy, to build, to conquer, to prosper, to nurture, to comfort, to heal, to save, to set free, to rescue, to have children, to lead, to bless, to be made whole and holy, and to take part in assuring righteousness and praises for God and His ways spring forth in all the nations.

These are our standing orders for our Mandate. They are the promises and blessings reserved for us if we choose to accept them. We are called by God to win. And win we will, if we will put away our "boyish" nature and take on the nature and Spirit of the Man, Jesus of Nazareth. He is the Man whom we are called to emulate. What Man does not want the losses, shame and confusion he has felt in his life to be replaced with a double portion of understanding, victory, lands, blessings and a deep down lasting joy? Each of us has a deep longing to rebuild the cities our victorious forefathers have built. We desire to repair the wasted desolations left by the males of previous generations, who have dropped the ball. Our role model did it as a Man, and so can you.

The Glorified Man:

"But we see Jesus, who was made a little lower than the angels for the suffering of death, crowned with glory and honor; that he by the grace of God should taste death for every Man. For it became him, for whom are all things, and by whom are all things, in bringing many sons unto glory, to make the captain of their salvation perfect through sufferings."[23]

Letter to the Hebrews

Catch what the writer to the Hebrews is saying here. Why would Jesus take on the nature of a Man and suffer such a brutal death on a cross? Why would the Son of God lower Himself to such an extent as to be shamed openly as a flesh and blood Man by His enemy when He did not have to?

The answer is: He did it for you and His fellow companions, His Band of Brothers. Now look at the beauty of this. He became the firstborn among many brothers, for the incredible purpose of tasting death for every Man, so we can be free from the fear of death. God's intention is to make

23 Hebrews 2:9-10, KJV

all of His sons perfect, so we all might take part in leading **"many sons to glory."**

You must understand there is now a Man in the glory. Jesus is the first glorified Man. This is absolutely profound. There is not just a spirit in the glory of heaven; there is an actual glorified Man in the glory. We have a flesh and blood Man who is both touchable and approachable.

Remember, He is the King of Kings. Through His suffering and subsequent resurrection Jesus of Nazareth became the first glorified Man, and He is asking all of us to follow Him into glory. In simple terms, this means he is asking each of us to walk as a righteous Man. The book of Hebrews then goes on to say, **"For both He that sanctifies, and they who are all sanctified, are all one: For which cause He is not ashamed to call them brothers."**[24] Jesus of Nazareth, our role model and the King of kings, is not ashamed to call us His brothers! He has received us because we beheld His glory and decided to follow Him into glory.

Your Father in heaven truly loves you and has an incredible plan for your life. God's ultimate intention is to bring **"many sons to glory."** This is why He has given to us Jesus of Nazareth as the firstborn and the **"Captain of our salvation."** Let us now look at several Men in Biblical history that beheld the glorified Man, and allowed Him to revolutionize their lives.

Thomas Beholds The Glorified Man:

After Jesus arose from the dead, He showed Himself to His followers. He specifically said to Thomas, **"Why are you troubled? And why do thoughts arise in your hearts? Behold my hands and my feet, that it is I Myself: handle me, and see: for a spirit has not flesh and bones, as you see me have.' And when He had thus spoken, He showed them His hands and His feet. And while they yet believed not for joy, and wondered, He said unto them, 'Have you here any meat?' And they gave Him a piece of a broiled fish, and of a honeycomb. And he took it, and did eat before them."**[25]

How amazing was this? Look how Jesus even ate food before His followers to show them He was not merely a spirit. He was an actual flesh and blood glorified Man. This is why Thomas no longer doubted

24 Hebrews 2:11, KJV
25 Luke 24:38-43, KJV

after Jesus revealed himself in His glorified state. Thomas was obviously awestruck and humbled, because he said to Jesus, **"My Lord and my God!"**

John Beholds the Glorified Man:

The Apostle John came to learn of the incredible revelation of Jesus as the glorified Man when he declared, **"And the Word was made flesh, and dwelt among us, (and we beheld His glory, the glory as of the only begotten of the Father,) full of grace and Truth."**[26] If you are wondering why John wrote he indeed beheld the glory of Jesus of Nazareth, I suggest you read the five books in the New Testament written by John. (John, 1 John, 2 John, 3 John & Revelation.) They are filled with John's first person account of the glory he saw in Jesus Christ. But to give you just a taste of what he experienced with Jesus, look at this account of his encounter with Jesus in the book of Revelation.

"His (The Son of Man, Jesus) head and His hairs were white like wool, as white as snow; and His eyes were as a flame of fire; And His feet like unto fine brass, as if they burned in a furnace; and He had in His right hand seven stars: and out of His mouth went a sharp two-edged sword: and his countenance was as the sun shines in his strength. And when I saw Him, I fell at His feet as dead. And he laid His right hand upon me, saying unto me, 'Fear not; I am the first and the last: I am He that lives, and was dead; and behold, I am alive for evermore, Amen; and have the Keys of hell and of death.'"[27]

The Apostle John – Revelation

Once again, you have the all-important Keys of authority mentioned by John. Understand, Jesus is telling us He has authority over death, because He totally conquered death by rising from the dead. This is why the resurrection is so important. Jesus was the first to overcome death;

26 John 1:14, NKJV
27 Revelation 1:14-18, NKJV

therefore, as a Man, He has the ability to give us those Keys of authority to overcome death.

Nathanael and Jacob Behold The Glorified Man:

> **"The day following Jesus would go forth into Galilee, and (He) finds Philip, and says unto him, 'Follow me.'**
>
> **Now Philip was of Bethsaida, the city of Andrew and Peter. Philip finds Nathanael and says unto him, 'We have found him, of whom Moses in the law, and the prophets, did write, Jesus of Nazareth, the son of Joseph.**
>
> **And Nathanael said unto him, 'Can there any good thing come out of Nazareth? Philip says unto him, 'Come and see.'**
>
> **Jesus saw Nathanael coming to Him, and says of him, 'Before that Philip called you, when you were under the fig tree, I saw you.'**
>
> **Nathanael answered and said unto Him, 'Rabbi, you are the Son of God; you are the King of Israel.**
>
> **Jesus answered and said unto him, 'Because I said unto you, I saw you under the fig tree, you believe? You will see greater things than these.**
>
> **And He said unto him; Verily, verily, I say unto you, Hereafter you shall see heaven open, and the Angels of God ascending and descending upon the Son of Man."[28]**

What was Jesus referring to when He makes such an interesting reply to Nathanael? Jesus was directly referring to Jacob, the grandson of the Patriarch Abraham, who was originally given the promise of a son. Jacob had a dream where he beheld a ladder set up on earth. The top of the ladder reached to heaven; and he beheld the Angels of God ascending and descending on it.

The ladder referred to in Jacob's dream is a revelation of the Son of Man breaking the wall of partition separating us from God. Jesus is the ladder who connects heaven to earth and earth to heaven. He is the glorified Man who has all the Keys of authority over heaven and earth. He now dwells in the glory of the throne of God. This means the blessings

---

28 John 1:43-51, NKJV

of God, and the **"Angels of God"** can freely ascend and descend upon the companions who have invited the Son of Man to dwell in their midst.

It is fascinating to see the son of promise was also Jacob's father, Isaac. No doubt a symbol for how our Son of promise, Jesus of Nazareth is also given the same likeness as our Father in heaven. Jesus affirmed this to his followers by saying, **"He that has seen me has seen the Father."** Jacob wrestled all night with this Man from the glory, and he would not let the Man go until the Man blessed him. He was then transformed into a Prince (son) of God and given the name of "Israel."

Who was this Man Jacob wrestled with and would not let go? This was indeed a vision of the glorified Man, Jesus of Nazareth. Jacob beheld the Man who was glorified, and he held on steadfast until he was blessed by Him. Jacob declared the next morning he had truly seen God face to face, and his life was saved.

So the story goes: "Jacob," which means "Deceiver," was transformed into "Israel," which means "Prince (son) of God." Jacob beheld the glorified Man, and he held on to Him until he was given the Keys to be saved as a Prince (son) of the Most High God. Can you see this is our template and model for overcoming in life? The Apostle Peter saw it, and he jumped at the opportunity to follow the Son of Man.

Peter Beholds The Glorified Man:

Jesus' disciple Peter, the fisherman and soon to be realized Apostle, was one of the first Men to be honored as one of the Band of Brothers, as he truly beheld the glorified Son of Man. After walking with Jesus of Nazareth for several years, Peter excitedly proclaimed to Jesus: **"You are the Christ, the Son of the living God!"** Jesus replied to Peter: **"Thou art Peter, and upon this rock (revelation) I will build my church; and the gates of hell shall not prevail against it. And I will give to you the Keys of the kingdom of heaven...**

Look at the profound relationship between the revelation proclaiming Jesus was indeed the glorified Man (Christ), and receiving our Keys of authority. Jesus of Nazareth is saying your victory as a Man is directly tied to seeing Him as both the Son of Man, and the Son of God. Indeed Peter did see who Jesus is. In doing so, he became one of the eternal

Band of Brothers who chose to walk as a Man with his Keys of authority in hand.

Giving Your All!

I can tell you from experience, when you truly *Behold The Man,* and walk in the revelation that you actually have a Mandate to fulfill the building of the house of God, no enemy can defeat you. You will storm the gates of hell with your Keys in hand as you build your family and the kingdom of God. This is what we are actually praying for when we say "**Thy kingdom come**" in the Lord's Prayer. The enemies of God and the gates of hell will be devastated by the power of God, when you have in your heart that revelation knowledge of your Mandate and Calling to model after the perfect Man.

Jesus Christ is looking for friends and brothers who are willing to give their all. God is seeking a few good Men who are willing to pay the ultimate price for their Mandate, and follow the only perfect Man who ever walked the earth. Death is always the price for freedom. Most Americans know the price of freedom has been our soldiers' willingness to put their lives on the line for our freedom. Are you willing to hold on all night to the Man Jesus of Nazareth, as Jacob did, until the Son of God and the Son of Man blesses you?

Just as Jesus of Nazareth had to die in order to deliver us our freedom from the wages of sin, we must die to our selfish ambitions and sinful nature in order to gain the freedom to overcome for our families. As we follow after the perfect glorified Man, we will be a sign and wonder to onlookers and a testimony to draw them into the knowledge of the Son of Man. This will be especially true when they see our love and our commitment for one another as the Band of Brothers!

Those who are willing to give God their all are going to reflect the image of who Jesus Christ really is. Let us remember, He truly gave us His all at the cross. Every one of us will become a sign and wonderment, if we reflect and reveal the glorified Man whose name is Jesus of Nazareth. To reveal who He is, we must see Him as He is, The Son of Man and the Son of God.

Reflecting Our Role Model:

We reflect the image of our role models. As we have seen throughout this chapter, the Bible is very clear about who the real Band of Brothers are. They are those who are beholding and reflecting the glory of the Lord. As Men take hold of their Manhood, the revelation of "Jesus the Man" becomes evident. Ultimately, it is not about becoming a Man for our own sakes. It is about reflecting the glory and image of the Lord who is the perfect Man.

First, we behold His glory. As we reflect His glory, we are transformed into the perfect Man He is. This is why the Apostle Paul said in his letter to the Corinthians; **"But we all, with open face beholding as in a glass the glory of the Lord, are changed into the same image from glory to glory, even as by the Spirit of the Lord."**[29] When you behold Jesus of Nazareth, you reflect the perfect and true image of the Man you are beholding. And how do we behold him? By acknowledging who He is as the Son of God and the Son of Man. Simply believe and have faith in Him.

Remember Jacob and how he beheld the glorified Man face to face? Jacob was first renamed "Israel" (Prince of God) because he saw the Son of Man, and the Son of God, and began to reflect the nature and character of God in his life. From this moment on, Jacob (Israel) began to face his problems head on, rather than manipulating and running in fear from the threats challenging him. Jacob (Israel) knew the Son of Man was the ladder who allowed God to bring His glory into our lives.

As we see the Son of Man in His glory, He shall alone be glorified. When He bears the glory in your life, He will bear the glory in your family and in the church. He will then build the temple, which is defined as His church and the 5 Callings. The counsel of peace between the state and the church, between the heavens and the earth, and between the Kingship and the Priesthood will all be established. It will be born by Him and Him alone, for He alone is the ladder who allows for the ascending and descending of the Spirit of God.

I encourage you to stand by the Lord your God, and be one of the Men and Band of Brothers who model after the perfect Man who was given to us and who laid down His life for us. As one of the Band of Brothers your true Father in heaven will refine and purify you into the

---

29 2 Corinthians 3:18, NKJV

Man you are "Called" to be. Next is a great story showing us how our God desires to make us into His very image.

The Silversmith Beholds:

"He will sit as a refiner and purifier of silver."
The Prophet Malachi (3:3)

A group of Men met at a Bible study and wondered about this verse from Malachi. They all pondered about what it was saying about the character and nature of God. One of the Men offered to the group he could find out the process of refining silver and get back to them at their next Bible Study. That week, the Man called a silversmith and made an appointment to watch him work. He didn't mention anything about the reason for his interest beyond his curiosity about the process of refining silver.

As he watched the silversmith, the silversmith held a piece of silver over the fire and let it heat up. He explained in refining silver, one needed to hold the silver in the middle of the fire where the flames were hottest as to burn away all the impurities.

The Man thought about God holding us in such a hot spot; then he thought again about the verse saying: ***"He sits as a refiner and purifier of silver."*** *He asked the silversmith if it was true he had to sit there in front of the fire the whole time the silver was being refined. The silversmith answered yes, he not only had to sit there holding the silver, but he had to keep his eyes on the silver the entire time it was in the fire. If the silver was left a moment too long in the flames, it would be destroyed.*

The Man was silent for a moment. He thought about how God promised to keep His eyes and His loving hand upon us all the days of our life. Then he asked the silversmith, "How do you know when the silver is fully refined?" The silversmith smiled at him and answered, "Oh, that's easy. The silver is perfectly purified and refined when I can clearly see my image in it."

If today you are feeling the heat of the fire, remember God has his eye on you and He will keep watching you until He sees His image in you.

Jesus and His Father:

Scripture is full of beautiful and personal interactions between Jesus and His Father. The words spoken between them are the words every son and father desire to say to one another, if they are healthy enough. If you want to see an example of how a loving relationship looks between a Father and a Son, look at the loving way Jesus and His Father spoke with one another. They truly honored The "No Codependency" Clause.

The proceeding is every documented word we have in the New Testament, displaying the intimate communication between Jesus and His Father. Note how real and honest Jesus is with His thoughts and feelings. As these words permeate into your heart and soul, may the last words of the Old Testament come to pass for you and your family: **"And he shall turn the heart of the fathers to the children, and the heart of the children to their fathers, lest I come and smite the earth with a curse."**[30]

Loving Words Between Jesus of Nazareth and His Father:

God the Father to His Son Jesus:

And the Holy Ghost descended in a bodily shape like a dove upon him, and a voice came from heaven, which said, **"You are my beloved Son; in you I am well pleased."**[31]

Jesus to His Father:

"I thank you, O Father, Lord of heaven and earth, because you have hid these things from the wise and the prudent, and have revealed them unto babes. Even so, Father; for so it seemed good in your sight."[32]

---

30 Malachi 4:6, KJV
31 Mark 1:11, NKJV
32 Luke 10:21, NKJV

God the Father to His Son Jesus:

Then came there a voice from heaven, saying, **"I have both glorified it, and will glorify it again."**[33]

Jesus to His Father:

"Our Father which art in heaven, Hallowed be Thy name. Thy kingdom come, Thy will be done in earth, as it is in heaven. Give us this day our daily bread. And forgive us our debts, as we forgive our debtors. And lead us not into temptation, but deliver us from evil: For Thine is the kingdom, and the power, and the glory forever. Amen."[34]

Jesus to His Father:

"Father, I thank you for you have heard me. And I know that you hear me always: but because of the people which stand by I said it, that they may believe that you have sent me."[35]

God the Father to His Son Jesus and to All Men:

While he yet spoke, behold, a bright cloud overshadowed them: and behold a voice out of the cloud, which said, **"This is my beloved Son, in whom I am well pleased; hear ye him. *(Behold Him)*"**[36]

Jesus to His Father:

These words spoke Jesus, and lifted up his eyes to heaven, and said, "**Father, the hour is come; glorify your Son, that your Son also may glorify you: As you have given him power over all flesh, that he should give eternal life to as many as you have given him.**

And this is life eternal, that they might know you the only true God, and Jesus Christ, whom you have sent. I have glorified thee on the earth: I have finished the work which you gave me to do.

And now, O Father, glorify thou me with your own self with the glory which I had with you before the world was. I have manifested thy name unto the men which thou gave me out of the world: yours they were, and you gave them me; and they have kept your word.

---

33 John 12:28, KJV
34 Matthew 6:9-13, KJV
35 John 11:41-42, KJV
36 Matthew 17:5, KJV

Now they have known that all things whatsoever you have given me are of you. For I have given unto them the words which thou gave me; and they have received them, and have known surely that I came out from you, and they have believed that you did send me.

I pray for them: I pray not for the world, but for them which you have given me; for they are yours. And all mine are yours, and yours are mine; and I am glorified in them. And now I am no more in the world, but these are in the world, and I come to you.

Holy Father, keep through your own name those whom you have given me, that they may be one, as we are. While I was with them in the world, I kept them in thy name: those that you gave me I have kept, and none of them is lost, but the son of perdition; that the scripture might be fulfilled.

And now come I to you; and these things I speak in the world, that they might have my joy fulfilled in themselves. I have given them your word; and the world hath hated them, because they are not of the world, even as I am not of the world. I pray not that you should take them out of the world, but that you should keep them from the evil. They are not of the world, even as I am not of the world. Sanctify them through your Truth: your word is Truth.

As you have sent me into the world, even so have I also sent them into the world. And for their sakes I sanctify myself, that they also might be sanctified through the Truth.

Neither pray I for these alone, but for them also which shall believe on me through their word; That they all may be one; as you, Father, art in me, and I in you, that they also may be one in us: that the world may believe that you have sent me. And the glory which you gave me I have given them; that they may be one, even as we are one: I in them, and you in me, that they may be made perfect in one; and that the world may know that you have sent me, and have loved them, as you have loved me.

Father, I will that they also, whom you have given me, be with me where I am; that they may behold my glory, which you have given me: for you loved me before the foundation of the world. O righteous Father, the world has not known you: but I have known you, and these have known that you have sent me. And I have declared unto them

your name, and will declare it: that the love wherewith you have loved me may be in them, and I in them."[37]

Jesus to His Father:

And he went a little farther, and fell on his face, and prayed, saying, **"O my Father, If it be possible, let this cup pass from me; nevertheless not as I will, but as you will."** ......He went away again the second time, and prayed, saying, **"O my Father, if this cup may not pass away from me, except I drink it, thy will be done."**

And he said, **"Abba, Father, all things are possible unto you: take away this cup from me; nevertheless not what I will, but what you will."**[38]

Jesus to His Father:

"Now is my soul troubled; and what shall I say? Father, save me from this hour: but for this cause came I unto this hour. Father, glorify your name."

God the Father to His Son Jesus:

Then came there a voice from heaven, saying, **"I have both glorified it, and will glorify it again."**[39]

Jesus to His Father:

"Father, forgive them; for they know not what they do."[40]

Jesus to His Father:

"Father, into your hands I commend my spirit."[41]

---

37 John Chapter 17, NKJV
38 Matthew 26:39, KJV; Luke 22:42, KJV; Mark 14:36, KJV
39 John 12:27-28, KJV
40 Luke 23:34, KJV
41 Luke 23:46, KJV

The words between Jesus and His Father are tender and powerful, and they reveal a relationship of the oneness in Spirit between them. There is complete trust and honesty. What a fantastic example we have to strive for in our relationships with our fathers and sons. Let each of us seek to communicate on a level of profound honesty and relational health, as we behold the relationship between Jesus and His Father. If you desire to learn how to be a perfect role model for your loved ones, continue to read the Scriptures and learn about God's nature. Follow in the steps of the Man Jesus, and be diligent to understand the interaction between the perfect Son and the perfect Father.

The Fatherly role of imparting and receiving Manhood is modeled throughout the Scriptures. Jesus is our perfect example of how we are to strive for perfection as a Man and learn from our Father in heaven. This is why Jesus said to all males, **"Every Man therefore that has heard, and has learned of the Father, comes unto me."** [42]

"All that the Father gives me shall come to me; and him that comes to me I will in no wise cast out. For I came down from heaven, not to do mine own will, but the will of him that sent me. And this is the Father's will which hath sent me, that of all which he hath given me I should lose nothing, but should raise it up again at the last day. And this is the will of him that sent me, that every one which sees (Beholds) the Son, and believes on him, may have everlasting life: and I will raise him up at the last day." [43]

Jesus of Nazareth, Book of John

Today's Battlefield:

The battle lines are being drawn today. They are between those who believe Jesus Christ is the Son of Man and the Son of God, and those who do not. From the time of the Gnostics to our modern day university scholars, there have always been those who denied Christ as coming in the flesh as the Son of Man, and they have continued to attempt to undermine

---

42 John 6:45, NKJV
43 John 6:37, NKJV

His Truth and His Word. As it says in the Word of God, **"Every spirit that confesses not that Jesus Christ is come in the flesh (as the Son of Man) is not of God: and this is the spirit of antichrist."**[44] Our challenge in our humanity as sons of God is to stress Jesus' divinity at all costs and overcome the ideals of those who deny Him.

This is the testimony of the battle we are wagering throughout the world today as the Band of Brothers. Understand this is really where the spiritual battle is taking place. It is in the minds of those who do not believe the Truth. Today we bear the testimony Jesus of Nazareth is the Savior promised throughout the Holy Scriptures. The price for this testimony may be the ultimate price. Everyone has to be willing to put it all on the line for something. The Band of Brothers has decided to put it all on the line for God, because He first put it all on the line for us.

"We love Him because He loved us first."[45]
The Apostle John

He Will Build It, and He Will Come:

The Son of Man promised he would build his Band of Brothers, and nothing would get in the way of His plan for us. We have seen throughout this book those who are bold enough to accept it are His chosen Band of Brothers. We are on a divine training mission, utilizing our God-given Keys of authority in an incredible partnership to build His kingdom while being transformed into His likeness. Ultimately, we are to meet Him when He comes again. Incredibly, we shall be presented as perfect in His sight on that day.

Are you prepared to meet the Son of Man? Near the end of his time on earth, Jesus of Nazareth said, **"At that time the sign of the Son of Man will appear in the sky, and all the nations of the earth will mourn. They will see the Son of Man coming on the clouds of the sky, with power and great glory."**[46] Why does Jesus come proclaiming the title

44 1 John 4:3, NKJV
45 1 John 4:19, NKJV
46 Matthew 24:30, NIV

"Son of Man" and not the title "Son of God?" This is because through the glorified Man the hosts of darkness are ultimately defeated. The demonic and satanic hosts who are **"gathered against the Lord and against His Messiah"** do not want to admit a glorified Man is their demise.

In the New Testament, the demonic hosts will acknowledge Jesus as the Son of God, but they will not dare acknowledge Him as the Son of Man, because they know exactly how they are going to be defeated. They know authority, and they know about the Keys. God's enemies know it must be a Man who defeats them, because the Keys of authority over the earth were given to the first Man, Adam. This is precisely why we as Men, His Band of Brothers, shall come riding with the Man Jesus of Nazareth as the **"armies of God"** to defeat God's enemies. Look it up in John's Revelation. It is a MAN who defeats God's enemies, and this Man's name is Jesus of Nazareth.

Human beings, on the other hand, have very little problem acknowledging Jesus as the Son of Man. Where we have difficulty, is in acknowledging Jesus as the Son of God. This is why Peter's confession was so powerful when he said, **"Thou art the Christ (Messiah), the Son of the Living God."**[47] Remember we learned from Jacob's dream about the ladder to heaven. We saw the Son of Man bringing heaven to earth, and earth to the heavens. As we acknowledge Jesus of Nazareth as the only true Son of God, we are actually fulfilling Jesus' accomplishment of bringing heaven to earth.

Our Coming Priest and King:

When Christ came the first time, He came as the humble and suffering servant who overcame death. Zechariah foretold this when he said, **"For behold, I am bringing forth My Servant the BRANCH."**[48] When He comes the second time, He will be the High Priest and King of all earthly authority, reigning as a Man just as He was when He left. Zechariah further proclaims this message saying, **"Behold the Man whose name is the BRANCH; From His place He shall branch out, and He shall build the temple of the LORD; Yes, He shall build the temple of the LORD...He shall bear the glory, and shall sit and rule on His throne;**

47 John 6:69, KJV
48 Zechariah 3:8, KJV

So He shall be a Priest on His Throne, and counsel of peace shall be between them both."[49]

Notice Jesus of Nazareth is to be head of both the office of the reigning King and the office of the High Priest who suffers and serves. In our natural "boyish" mentality, we desire to be a King before we desire the difficult work of a Priest. We want to claim all authority and "have it all" without the suffering and the serving. In God's economy the Priesthood comes before the Kingship. The Man, Jesus of Nazareth modeled how to overcome, first as a Man and a Priest who was willing to lay down his life, and then to reign as a King in righteous authority.

He first came as the Suffering Servant **"to give His life a ransom for many."**[50] When He comes the second time, He will come both as the glorified Priest and the reigning King. He will still be the humble Branch who serves, but when He returns, he will be wholly worthy to Judge all things in the world as our King, because He conquered as a flesh and blood Man. The Son of Man alone will bring peace between both the Priesthood and the Kingship, between the heavens and earth and between the Church and the State.

This was restated in the Book of Acts by two Men dressed in white apparel, seen just after Jesus ascended in the sight of His Band of Brothers. The Men said, **"This same Jesus, which is taken up from you into heaven, shall so come in like manner as you have seen him go into heaven."**[51] The one difference is Jesus will be coming as a King with sovereign reigning authority. The Man who now occupies the glory next to our Father in heaven will soon come in glory on the appointed day. He will come in power as a perfect and glorified Man, just as He was when he departed nearly 2000 years ago.

Are You Ready?

Do you remember the principle from Chapter 1 that says, "You cannot give what you do not have?" In Chapter 1, this principle refers to obtaining Manhood, and only a Man can impart Manhood to another male. This all-important principle is even more important when it comes

---

49 Zechariah 6:12-13, KJV
50 Matthew 20-28, KJV
51 Acts 1:11, KJV

to our eternal life. Do we know anyone who you can ask for the gift of eternal life?

When you decide to become a Man, another Man who desires your victory will joyfully give Manhood to you. To be a son of God is a similar process. Your Father in heaven will joyfully give you the perfection of His Son Jesus of Nazareth. The Apostle Paul said: **"If God is for us, who can be against us? He who did not spare His own Son, but delivered Him up for us all, how shall He not with Him also freely give us all things."**[52]

Men know instinctively they are not gods. Becoming whole as a Man and a son of God becomes attainable when we see Jesus of Nazareth lives and functions as a flesh and blood Man. In the same way the Holy Spirit was in Jesus, so God's Holy Spirit also operates in our spirit in our fleshly bodies. Jesus of Nazareth said, **"You must be born again."**[53] Being "born again" is not so different a process than getting "Bar Mitzvaed." Receiving the impartation of Manhood is similar to receiving the impartation of God's Holy Spirit into our lives. There is a tremendous parallel between becoming a Man and becoming a son of God. Both of these events are a once in a lifetime transformation given to us by an impartation from a Father.

Becoming "born again" and a true son of God is the ultimate achievement regarding our Calling and our Mandate. Jesus was so clear! Our primary purpose in life is to lay down our life, take of His nature and receive our Keys of authority. We are to see Him as He truly is; the Son of Man and the Son of God.

"Greater love hath no Man than this, that a Man lay down his life for his friends."[54]
Jesus of Nazareth – Book of John

52 Romans 8:32, NKJV
53 John 3:7, NKJV
54 John 15:13, KJV

The Ultimate Key!

I have good news for those of you who are unfamiliar with how to obtain the ultimate Key. The ultimate Key to eternal life is just a prayer away. The Man who can give you this Key, is Jesus of Nazareth, the glorified Man. This is why John wrote, **"Ask and it shall be given, seek and you shall find, knock and the door shall be opened."**[55] Your Keys to overcoming fear, loss and death are yours for the asking if you will simply and truthfully repent for your "boyish" behaviors and establish your intention to change. Jesus of Nazareth is the glorified Man who has the Key to open every door in your life. All you have to do is ask.

Your part is to purpose in your heart not to want to be a sinful "boy." God's part is to give you the power to overcome and make it a reality. It is time for us all to stop playing games. To follow the perfect Man Jesus of Nazareth, here is a simple prayer that will bring heaven into your life here on earth by completely cleansing you of your "boyish" past. If this is your heart, I welcome you as one of the Band of Brothers.

"Father in heaven, today I behold the Man Jesus Christ your perfect Son, and I confess Him as my personal Savior. Please forgive me for all the sins I have done against you. Jesus of Nazareth, today I receive Your life and Your Spirit. Lead me, and I will follow. Amen."

Men Called to Love:

My hope is you have seen the profound importance of how a father can pass love, encouragement and Manhood to his son. You have seen the loving interaction between Jesus and His Father as the Heavenly model for loving relationships. This is why it is so important for fathers to be Men, and to do their job by imparting love and Manhood to their sons.

This impartation is necessary for all of us, if we are to succeed and function in full victory. Generally, when "boys" without fathers or father figures grow up, they find it more difficult to grasp their Manhood and their Calling, because they have not seen what a Man looks like. This is why the Jewish tradition of Bar Mitzvah is so important as a model for our relationship with God.

---

55 Luke 11:9, NKJV

Every Man knows he is called to love; but as Men, we sometimes need more specific instructions. Many Men do not get overly excited when they read they are called to love. When we understand that we are called to be one of the Band of Brothers and do the things listed in Isaiah 61, we find it hard to stand still due to the great expectations of what is possible. Motivation can be everything for Men. God values people more than He values His principles. The highest principles are relational principles. Jesus did not die on the cross merely to honor principles. He died, conquered death, and rose again, because of His relational love for people.

Let us all capture our Great Mandate, and the Keys that have so long evaded us. Let us walk in the very Spirit Jesus walks in, and the very Spirit He promises will come upon us, as we *Behold The Man!* Make no mistake about exactly who Jesus of Nazareth is. He was and is a Man. And He is our God. He chose to walk in an earthly body and be the perfect example of the Loving Man we are called to be and the Man we will become, if you are willing and obedient to receive, and walk in the love of your Mandate.

"Love suffers long and is kind; love does not envy; love does not parade itself, is not puffed up; does not behave rudely, does not seek its own, is not provoked, thinks no evil; does not rejoice in iniquity, but rejoices in the Truth; bears all things, believes all things, hopes all things, endures all things. Love never fails."

The Apostle Paul – 1 Cor. 13:4-8

How exciting it is to know each one of us can attain both our earthly Calling as Men, and our heavenly Calling as a son of God. We have the duty and opportunity to walk in our Callings as Men. We can reign as Kings in our personal lives, because Jesus of Nazareth reigns as the King of Kings. Through the free gift we have in Christ Jesus, each one of us can be spiritually conformed into the perfect Man we seek to be.

Let God be God, and let us be the Men He designed us to be. Thinking and behaving like a "boy," is merely a disruption of our true heavenly call. This is more awesome than we could imagine. Jesus said, **"Whosoever is not with me is against me."[56]** We are all ministers. The question is, "What are you ministering?" Are we ministering life or are we ministering death? In our lives we will always be producing fruit. It will either be bad fruit as "boys," or good fruit as "Men."

"Likewise every good tree bears good fruit, but a bad tree bears bad fruit. A good tree cannot bear bad fruit, and a bad tree cannot bear good fruit. Every tree that does not bear good fruit is cut down and thrown into the fire. Thus, by their fruit you will recognize them."[57]
Jesus of Nazareth – Book of Matthew

Paul of Tarsus said it beautifully when he wrote to the Jews this famous encouragement, **"Wherefore seeing we also are compassed about with so great a cloud of witnesses (Band of Brothers), let us lay aside every weight, and the sin ("boyish" behaviors) which doth so easily beset us, and let us run with patience the race that is set before us, Looking unto Jesus (Behold The Man!) the author and finisher of our faith; who for the joy that was set before him endured the cross, despising the shame, and is set down at the right hand of the throne of God."[58]**

How can we stand still and ignore our Mandate once we behold Jesus of Nazareth, and see who He really is? How can we sit around and act like "boys," if we know the incredible benefit of receiving Him as the Son of God, and walking in His ways? The answer to all of these questions is: "We cannot." We must be the Men we are called to be. We have such a short time here on earth compared to the eternity when we shall live in His glory. Our wives, our children, our friends, and our Band of Brothers are counting on us.

I compel all Men; Get up! Run the race with all of your heart, and let none of you have a single regret about the sacrifices you are making for your families and your children. Once again, I say to each and every

56 Matthew 12:30, NKJV
57 Matthew 7:17-20, NIV
58 Hebrews 12:1-2, KJV

Man, "Get up, and take hold of your Keys!" It is time to build a legacy and a heritage for your family by loving them and giving them your lives.

Putting your life in the hands of God is very simple. Having a relationship with God is not complicated. If your heart is willing, just ask Him and He will help you walk in the Calling and Mandate freely given to you, and as you walk victoriously through life, always remember to "*Behold The Perfect Man!*" He will never let you down, and He will be your Best friend.

"For whosoever shall lose his life for My sake and the gospel's, the same shall save it."[59]
Jesus of Nazareth – Book of Mark

59 Mark 8:35, KJV

Now What? - Become a member in the Band of Brothers!

As one of the Band of Brothers, I invite you to become a member of a prestigious TEAM of Men who are determined to change the face of our culture using the principles described in this book. Join internationally with a host of successful Men who are dedicated to building their lives and the lives of other Men. Go to **www.Manvsboy.com** and become a member today, and receive the best tools and training to further your walk as the Man you are called to be. At our website, members will find the latest media, books, DVD's and resource materials all focused on the needs of the 21st century Man.

Referral Book Program!

"Man vs. boy" invites you to join our team! You now have the opportunity to be a Preferred Referral Partner and receive compensation for all book referrals. Preferred Referral Partners receive a special promotional code to be submitted when any person or organization orders the "Man vs. boy" book online through our website. Special rates are given to companies, churches or organizations that desire to participate in retail sales or bulk orders. Come join us at **www.Manvsboy.com**

Quotes From Men:

Famous Vince Lombardi Quotes:

Vince Lombardi was inducted into the Professional Football Hall of Fame in 1971, the same year the Super Bowl trophy was renamed in his honor. Considered the NFL's most prestigious award, the Vince Lombardi Trophy is coveted by every player and coach in the league. The honor assures Lombardi's name will never be forgotten, and his legacy as one of the greatest head coaches of all time will last an eternity. (www.vincelombardi.com)

"Confidence is contagious. So is lack of confidence."

"Fatigue makes cowards of us all."

"Football is like life. It requires perseverance, self-denial, hard work, sacrifice, dedication and respect for authority."

"If it doesn't matter who wins or loses, then why do they keep score?"

"Leaders aren't born, they are made. And they are made just like anything else, through hard work. And that's the price we'll have to pay to achieve that goal, or any goal."

"Once you agree upon the price you and your family must pay for success, it enables you to ignore the minor hurts, the opponent's pressure, and the temporary failures."

"Once you learn to quit, it becomes a habit."

"Practice does not make perfect. Only perfect practice makes perfect."

"Show me a good loser, and I'll show you a loser."

"The difference between a successful person and others is not a lack of strength, not a lack of knowledge, but rather a lack of will."

"The measure of who we are is what we do with what we have."

"The only place success comes before work is in the dictionary."

"The real glory is being knocked to your knees and then coming back. That's real glory. That's the essence of it."

"We would accomplish many more things if we did not think of them as impossible."

"Winners never quit and quitters never win."

"Winning is habit. Unfortunately, so is losing."

Famous Abraham Lincoln Quotes:

"If destruction be our lot, we must ourselves be its author and finisher. As a nation of freemen, we must live through all time, or die by suicide."

"You can not fail if you resolutely determine that you will not."

"Those who deny freedom to others, deserve it not for themselves; and under a just God, can not long retain it."

"As I would not be a slave, so I would not be a master."

"Whenever I hear anyone arguing for slavery I feel a strong impulse to see it tried on him personally."

"Don't interfere with anything in the Constitution. That must be maintained, for it is the only safeguard of our liberties."

"Give me six hours to chop down a tree and I will spend the first four sharpening the axe."

"I care not much for a man's religion whose dog and cat are not the better for it."

Famous Winston Churchhill Quotes:

"I like a man who grins when he fights."

"Never in the field of human conflict was so much owed by so many to so few."

"I have nothing to offer but blood, toil, tears and sweat."

"A fanatic is one who can't change his mind and won't change the subject."

"It is no use saying, 'We are doing our best.' You have got to succeed in doing what is necessary."

"The greatest lesson in life is to know that even fools are right sometimes."

"He has all the virtues I dislike and none of the vices I admire."

"The problems of victory are more agreeable than the problems of defeat, but they are no less difficult."

"History will be kind to me for I intend to write it."

"I like pigs. Dogs look up to us. Cats look down on us. Pigs treat us as equals."

"A pessimist sees the difficulty in every opportunity; an optimist sees the opportunity in every difficulty."

"Men occasionally stumble over the Truth, but most of them pick themselves up and hurry off as if nothing ever happened."

"Success is the ability to go from one failure to another with no loss of enthusiasm."

"The price of greatness is responsibility."

"We shall show mercy, but we shall not ask for it."

Famous Theodore Roosevelt Quotes:

"Keep your eyes on the stars, and your feet on the ground."

"Do what you can, with what you have, where you are."

"When they call the roll in the Senate, the Senators do not know whether to answer 'Present' or 'Not Guilty'."

"The things that will destroy America are prosperity at any price, peace at any price, safety first instead of duty first and love of soft living and the get-rich-quick theory of life."

"Rhetoric is a poor substitute for action, and we have trusted only to rhetoric. If we are really to be a great nation, we must not merely talk; we must act big."

"It is hard to fail, but it is worse never to have tried to succeed. In this life we get nothing save by effort."

"The only man who makes no mistakes is the man who never does anything."

"It is not the critic who counts; not the man who points out how the strong man stumbles, or where the doer of deeds could have done

them better. The credit belongs to the man who is actually in the arena, whose face is marred by dust and sweat and blood, who strives valiantly; who errs and comes short again and again; because there is not effort without error and shortcomings; but who does actually strive to do the deed; who knows the great enthusiasm, the great devotion, who spends himself in a worthy cause, who at the best knows in the end the triumph of high achievement and who at the worst, if he fails, at least he fails while daring greatly. So that his place shall never be with those cold and timid souls who know neither victory nor defeat."

"It behooves every man to remember that the work of the critic, is of altogether secondary importance, and that, in the end, progress is accomplished by the man who does things."

"Far better is it to dare mighty things, to win glorious triumphs, even though checked by failure...than to rank with those poor spirits who neither enjoy much nor suffer much, because they live in a gray twilight that knows not victory nor defeat."

"We can have no "50-50" allegiance in this country. Either a man is an American and nothing else, or he is not an American at all."

Famous Ronald Reagan Quotes:

"Abortion is advocated only by persons who have themselves been born."

"Politics is not a bad profession. If you succeed there are many rewards, if you disgrace yourself you can always write a book."

"Thomas Jefferson once said, 'We should never judge a president by his age, only by his works.' And ever since he told me that, I stopped worrying."

For more great quotes, information and training;
Go to www.Manvsboy.com

Notes

Notes

Notes